QUANTITATIVE METHODS

CFA® Program Curriculum
2025 • LEVEL I • VOLUME 1

WILEY

ISBN 9781953337986 (paper)
ISBN 9781961409101 (ebook)
May 2024

SKY9BB5403A-DDB4-4EB8-97D3-2CDCEAD9735E_032624

Please visit our website at
www.WileyGlobalFinance.com.

CONTENTS

Contents   v

How to Use the CFA Program Curriculum

The CFA* Program exams measure your mastery of the core knowledge, skills, and abilities required to succeed as an investment professional. These core competencies are the basis for the Candidate Body of Knowledge (CBOK™). The CBOK consists of four components:

> A broad outline that lists the major CFA Program topic areas (www .cfainstitute.org/programs/cfa/curriculum/cbok/cbok)

> Topic area weights that indicate the relative exam weightings of the top-level topic areas (www.cfainstitute.org/en/programs/cfa/curriculum)

> Learning outcome statements (LOS) that advise candidates about the specific knowledge, skills, and abilities they should acquire from curriculum content covering a topic area: LOS are provided at the beginning of each block of related content and the specific lesson that covers them. We encourage you to review the information about the LOS on our website (www.cfainstitute.org/programs/cfa/curriculum/study-sessions), including the descriptions of LOS "command words" on the candidate resources page at www.cfainstitute.org/-/media/documents/support/programs/cfa-and -cipm-los-command-words.ashx.

> The CFA Program curriculum that candidates receive access to upon exam registration

Therefore, the key to your success on the CFA exams is studying and understanding the CBOK. You can learn more about the CBOK on our website: www.cfainstitute .org/programs/cfa/curriculum/cbok.

The curriculum, including the practice questions, is the basis for all exam questions. The curriculum is selected or developed specifically to provide candidates with the knowledge, skills, and abilities reflected in the CBOK.

CFA INSTITUTE LEARNING ECOSYSTEM (LES)

Your exam registration fee includes access to the CFA Institute Learning Ecosystem (LES). This digital learning platform provides access, even offline, to all the curriculum content and practice questions. The LES is organized as a series of learning modules consisting of short online lessons and associated practice questions. This tool is your source for all study materials, including practice questions and mock exams. The LES is the primary method by which CFA Institute delivers your curriculum experience. Here, candidates will find additional practice questions to test their knowledge. Some questions in the LES provide a unique interactive experience.

DESIGNING YOUR PERSONAL STUDY PROGRAM

An orderly, systematic approach to exam preparation is critical. You should dedicate a consistent block of time every week to reading and studying. Review the LOS both before and after you study curriculum content to ensure you can demonstrate the knowledge, skills, and abilities described by the LOS and the assigned reading. Use the LOS as a self-check to track your progress and highlight areas of weakness for later review.

Successful candidates report an average of more than 300 hours preparing for each exam. Your preparation time will vary based on your prior education and experience, and you will likely spend more time on some topics than on others.

ERRATA

The curriculum development process is rigorous and involves multiple rounds of reviews by content experts. Despite our efforts to produce a curriculum that is free of errors, in some instances, we must make corrections. Curriculum errata are periodically updated and posted by exam level and test date on the Curriculum Errata webpage (www.cfainstitute.org/en/programs/submit-errata). If you believe you have found an error in the curriculum, you can submit your concerns through our curriculum errata reporting process found at the bottom of the Curriculum Errata webpage.

OTHER FEEDBACK

Please send any comments or suggestions to info@cfainstitute.org, and we will review your feedback thoughtfully.

Quantitative Methods

1

Rates and Returns

by Richard A. DeFusco, PhD, CFA, Dennis W. McLeavey, DBA, CFA, Jerald E. Pinto, PhD, CFA, David E. Runkle, PhD, CFA, and Vijay Singal, PhD, CFA.

Richard A. DeFusco, PhD, CFA, is at the University of Nebraska-Lincoln (USA). Dennis W. McLeavey, DBA, CFA, is at the University of Rhode Island (USA). Jerald E. Pinto, PhD, CFA, is at CFA Institute (USA). David E. Runkle, PhD, CFA, is at Jacobs Levy Equity Management (USA). Vijay Singal, PhD, CFA, is at Virginia Tech (USA).

LEARNING OUTCOMES

Mastery	The candidate should be able to:
☐	interpret interest rates as required rates of return, discount rates, or opportunity costs and explain an interest rate as the sum of a real risk-free rate and premiums that compensate investors for bearing distinct types of risk
☐	calculate and interpret different approaches to return measurement over time and describe their appropriate uses
☐	compare the money-weighted and time-weighted rates of return and evaluate the performance of portfolios based on these measures
☐	calculate and interpret annualized return measures and continuously compounded returns, and describe their appropriate uses
☐	calculate and interpret major return measures and describe their appropriate uses

INTRODUCTION

1

Interest rates are a critical concept in finance. In some cases, we assume a particular interest rate and in others, the interest rate remains the unknown quantity to determine. Although the pre-reads have covered the mechanics of time value of money problems, here we first illustrate the underlying economic concepts by explaining the meaning and interpretation of interest rates and then calculate, interpret, and compare different return measures.

LEARNING MODULE OVERVIEW

- An interest rate, r, can have three interpretations: (1) a required rate of return, (2) a discount rate, or (3) an opportunity cost. An interest rate reflects the relationship between differently dated cash flows.

- An interest rate can be viewed as the sum of the real risk-free interest rate and a set of premiums that compensate lenders for bearing distinct types of risk: an inflation premium, a default risk premium, a liquidity premium, and a maturity premium.

- The nominal risk-free interest rate is approximated as the sum of the real risk-free interest rate and the inflation premium.

- A financial asset's total return consists of two components: an income yield consisting of cash dividends or interest payments, and a return reflecting the capital gain or loss resulting from changes in the price of the financial asset.

- A holding period return, R, is the return that an investor earns for a single, specified period of time (e.g., one day, one month, five years).

- Multiperiod returns may be calculated across several holding periods using different return measures (e.g., arithmetic mean, geometric mean, harmonic mean, trimmed mean, winsorized mean). Each return computation has special applications for evaluating investments.

- The choice of which of the various alternative measurements of mean to use for a given dataset depends on considerations such as the presence of extreme outliers, outliers that we want to include, whether there is a symmetric distribution, and compounding.

- A money-weighted return reflects the actual return earned on an investment after accounting for the value and timing of cash flows relating to the investment.

- A time-weighted return measures the compound rate of growth of one unit of currency invested in a portfolio during a stated measurement period. Unlike a money-weighted return, a time-weighted return is not sensitive to the timing and amount of cashflows and is the preferred performance measure for evaluating portfolio managers because cash withdrawals or additions to the portfolio are generally outside of the control of the portfolio manager.

- Interest may be paid or received more frequently than annually. The periodic interest rate and the corresponding number of compounding periods (e.g., quarterly, monthly, daily) should be adjusted to compute present and future values.

- Annualizing periodic returns allows investors to compare different investments across different holding periods to better evaluate and compare their relative performance. With the number of compounding periods per year approaching infinity, the interest is compound continuously.

- Gross return, return prior to deduction of managerial and administrative expenses (those expenses not directly related to return generation), is an appropriate measure to evaluate the comparative performance of an asset manager.

- Net return, which is equal to the gross return less managerial and administrative expenses, is a better return measure of what an investor actually earned.

- The after-tax nominal return is computed as the total return minus any allowance for taxes on dividends, interest, and realized gains.

- Real returns are particularly useful in comparing returns across time periods because inflation rates may vary over time and are particularly useful for comparing investments across time periods and performance between different asset classes with different taxation.

- Leveraging a portfolio, via borrowing or futures, can amplify the portfolio's gains or losses.

INTEREST RATES AND TIME VALUE OF MONEY 2

☐ interpret interest rates as required rates of return, discount rates, or opportunity costs and explain an interest rate as the sum of a real risk-free rate and premiums that compensate investors for bearing distinct types of risk

The time value of money establishes the equivalence between cash flows occurring on different dates. As cash received today is preferred to cash promised in the future, we must establish a consistent basis for this trade-off to compare financial instruments in cases in which cash is paid or received at different times. An **interest rate (or yield)**, denoted r, is a rate of return that reflects the relationship between differently dated – timed – cash flows. If USD 9,500 today and USD 10,000 in one year are equivalent in value, then USD 10,000 – USD 9,500 = USD 500 is the required compensation for receiving USD 10,000 in one year rather than now. The interest rate (i.e., the required compensation stated as a rate of return) is USD 500/USD 9,500 = 0.0526 or 5.26 percent.

Interest rates can be thought of in three ways:

- First, they can be considered *required rates of return*—that is, the minimum rate of return an investor must receive to accept an investment.

- Second, interest rates can be considered *discount rates*. In the previous example, 5.26 percent is the discount rate at which USD 10,000 in one year is equivalent to USD 9,500 today. Thus, we use the terms "interest rate" and "discount rate" almost interchangeably.

- Third, interest rates can be considered *opportunity costs*. An **opportunity cost** is the value that investors forgo by choosing a course of action. In the example, if the party who supplied USD 9,500 had instead decided to spend it today, he would have forgone earning 5.26 percent by consuming rather than saving. So, we can view 5.26 percent as the opportunity cost of current consumption.

Determinants of Interest Rates

Economics tells us that interest rates are set by the forces of supply and demand, where investors supply funds and borrowers demand their use. Taking the perspective of investors in analyzing market-determined interest rates, we can view an interest rate r as being composed of a real risk-free interest rate plus a set of premiums that are required returns or compensation for bearing distinct types of risk:

r = Real risk-free interest rate + Inflation premium + Default risk premium + Liquidity premium + Maturity premium. (1)

- The **real risk-free interest rate** is the single-period interest rate for a completely risk-free security if no inflation were expected. In economic theory, the real risk-free rate reflects the time preferences of individuals for current versus future real consumption.

- The **inflation premium** compensates investors for expected inflation and reflects the average inflation rate expected over the maturity of the debt. Inflation reduces the purchasing power of a unit of currency—the amount of goods and services one can buy with it.

- The **default risk premium** compensates investors for the possibility that the borrower will fail to make a promised payment at the contracted time and in the contracted amount.

- The **liquidity premium** compensates investors for the risk of loss relative to an investment's fair value if the investment needs to be converted to cash quickly. US Treasury bills (T-bills), for example, do not bear a liquidity premium because large amounts of them can be bought and sold without affecting their market price. Many bonds of small issuers, by contrast, trade infrequently after they are issued; the interest rate on such bonds includes a liquidity premium reflecting the relatively high costs (including the impact on price) of selling a position.

- The **maturity premium** compensates investors for the increased sensitivity of the market value of debt to a change in market interest rates as maturity is extended, in general (holding all else equal). The difference between the interest rate on longer-maturity, liquid Treasury debt and that on short-term Treasury debt typically reflects a positive maturity premium for the longer-term debt (and possibly different inflation premiums as well).

The sum of the real risk-free interest rate and the inflation premium is the nominal risk-free interest rate:

The nominal risk-free interest rate reflects the combination of a real risk-free rate plus an inflation premium:

(1 + nominal risk-free rate) = (1 + real risk-free rate)(1 + inflation premium).

In practice, however, the nominal rate is often approximated as the sum of the real risk-free rate plus an inflation premium:

Nominal risk-free rate = Real risk-free rate + inflation premium.

Many countries have short-term government debt whose interest rate can be considered to represent the nominal risk-free interest rate over that time horizon in that country. The French government issues BTFs, or negotiable fixed-rate discount Treasury bills (Bons du Trésor à taux fixe et à intérêts précomptés), with maturities of up to one year. The Japanese government issues a short-term Treasury bill with maturities of 6 and 12 months. The interest rate on a 90-day US T-bill, for example, represents the nominal risk-free interest rate for the United States over the next three months. Typically, interest rates are quoted in annual terms, so the interest rate on a 90-day government debt security quoted at 3 percent is the annualized rate and not the actual interest rate earned over the 90-day period.

Whether the interest rate we use is a required rate of return, or a discount rate, or an opportunity cost, the rate encompasses the real risk-free rate and a set of risk premia that depend on the characteristics of the cash flows. The foundational set of premia consist of inflation, default risk, liquidity risk, and maturity risk. All these premia vary over time and continuously change, as does the real risk-free rate. Consequently, all interest rates fluctuate, but how much they change depends on various economic fundamentals—and on the expectation of how these various economic fundamentals can change in the future.

EXAMPLE 1

Determining Interest Rates

Exhibit 1 presents selected information for five debt securities. All five investments promise only a single payment at maturity. Assume that premiums relating to inflation, liquidity, and default risk are constant across all time horizons.

Exhibit 1: Investments Alternatives and Their Characteristics				
Investment	Maturity (in years)	Liquidity	Default Risk	Interest Rate (%)
1	2	High	Low	2.0
2	2	Low	Low	2.5
3	7	Low	Low	r_3
4	8	High	Low	4.0
5	8	Low	High	6.5

Based on the information in Exhibit 1, address the following:

1. Explain the difference between the interest rates offered by Investment 1 and Investment 2.

   Solution:

   Investment 2 is identical to Investment 1 except that Investment 2 has low liquidity. The difference between the interest rate on Investment 2 and Investment 1 is 0.5 percent. This difference in the two interest rates represents a liquidity premium, which represents compensation for the lower liquidity of Investment 2 (the risk of loss relative to an investment's fair value if the investment needs to be converted to cash quickly).

---

2. Estimate the default risk premium affecting all securities.

   Solution:

   To estimate the default risk premium, identify two investments that have the same maturity but different levels of default risk. Investments 4 and 5 both have a maturity of eight years but different levels of default risk. Investment 5, however, has low liquidity and thus bears a liquidity premium relative to Investment 4. From Part A, we know the liquidity premium is 0.5 percent. The difference between the interest rates offered by Investments 5 and 4 is 2.5 percent (6.5% – 4.0%), of which 0.5 percent is a liquidity premium. This implies that 2.0 percent (2.5% – 0.5%) must represent a default risk premium reflecting Investment 5's relatively higher default risk.

3. Calculate upper and lower limits for the unknown interest rate for Investment 3, r_3.

Solution:

Investment 3 has liquidity risk and default risk comparable to Investment 2, but with its longer time to maturity, Investment 3 should have a higher maturity premium and offer a higher interest rate than Investment 2. Therefore, the interest rate on Investment 3, r_3, should thus be above 2.5 percent (the interest rate on Investment 2).

If the liquidity of Investment 3 was high, Investment 3 would match Investment 4 except for Investment 3's shorter maturity. We would then conclude that Investment 3's interest rate should be less than the interest rate offered by Investment 4, which is 4 percent. In contrast to Investment 4, however, Investment 3 has low liquidity. It is possible that the interest rate on Investment 3 exceeds that of Investment 4 despite Investment 3's shorter maturity, depending on the relative size of the liquidity and maturity premiums. However, we would expect r_3 to be less than 4.5 percent, the expected interest rate on Investment 4 if it had low liquidity (4% + 0.5%, the liquidity premium). Thus, we should expect in the interest rate offered by Investment 3 to be between 2.5 percent and 4.5 percent.

3   RATES OF RETURN

☐   calculate and interpret different approaches to return measurement over time and describe their appropriate uses

Financial assets are frequently defined in terms of their return and risk characteristics. Comparison along these two dimensions simplifies the process of building a portfolio from among all available assets. In this lesson, we will compute, evaluate, and compare various measures of return.

Financial assets normally generate two types of return for investors. First, they may provide periodic income through cash dividends or interest payments. Second, the price of a financial asset can increase or decrease, leading to a capital gain or loss.

Some financial assets provide return through only one of these mechanisms. For example, investors in non-dividend-paying stocks obtain their return from price movement only. Other assets only generate periodic income. For example, defined benefit pension plans and retirement annuities make income payments over the life of a beneficiary.

Holding Period Return

Returns can be measured over a single period or over multiple periods. Single-period returns are straightforward because there is only one way to calculate them. Multiple-period returns, however, can be calculated in various ways and it is important to be aware of these differences to avoid confusion.

A **holding period return**, R, is the return earned from holding an asset for a single specified period of time. The period may be one day, one week, one month, five years, or any specified period. If the asset (e.g., bond, stock) is purchased today, time ($t = 0$), at a price of 100 and sold later, say at time ($t = 1$), at a price of 105 with no dividends or other income, then the holding period return is 5 percent [(105 – 100)/100)]. If the asset also pays income of two units at time ($t = 1$), then the total return is 7 percent. This return can be generalized and shown as a mathematical expression in which P is the price and I is the income, as follows:

$$R = \frac{(P_1 - P_0) + I_1}{P_0}, \tag{1}$$

where the subscript indicates the time of the price or income; ($t = 0$) is the beginning of the period; and ($t = 1$) is the end of the period. The following two observations are important.

- We computed a capital gain of 5 percent and an income yield of 2 percent in this example. For ease of illustration, we assumed that the income is paid at time $t = 1$. If the income was received before $t = 1$, our holding period return may have been higher if we had reinvested the income for the remainder of the period.
- Return can be expressed in decimals (0.07), fractions (7/100), or as a percent (7 percent). They are all equivalent.

A holding period return can be computed for a period longer than one year. For example, an analyst may need to compute a one-year holding period return from three annual returns. In that case, the one-year holding period return is computed by compounding the three annual returns:

$$R = [(1 + R_1) \times (1 + R_2) \times (1 + R_3)] - 1,$$

where R_1, R_2, and R_3 are the three annual returns.

Arithmetic or Mean Return

Most holding period returns are reported as daily, monthly, or annual returns. When assets have returns for multiple holding periods, it is necessary to normalize returns to a common period for ease of comparison and understanding. There are different methods for aggregating returns across several holding periods. The remainder of this section presents various ways of computing average returns and discusses their applicability.

The simplest way to compute a summary measure for returns across multiple periods is to take a simple arithmetic average of the holding period returns. Thus, three annual returns of –50 percent, 35 percent, and 27 percent will give us an average of 4 percent per year $= \left(\frac{-50\% + 35\% + 27\%}{3} \right)$. The arithmetic average return is easy to compute and has known statistical properties.

In general, the arithmetic or mean return is denoted by $\overline{R}_i$ and given by the following equation for asset i, where R_{it} is the return in period t and T is the total number of periods:

$$\overline{R}_i = \frac{R_{i1} + R_{i2} + \ldots + R_{i,T-1} + R_{iT}}{T} = \frac{1}{T} \sum_{t=1}^{T} R_{it}. \tag{2}$$

Geometric Mean Return

The arithmetic mean return assumes that the amount invested at the beginning of each period is the same. In an investment portfolio, however, even if there are no cash flows into or out of the portfolio the base amount changes each year. The previous year's earnings must be added to the beginning value of the subsequent year's investment—these earnings will be "compounded" by the returns earned in that subsequent year. We can use the geometric mean return to account for the compounding of returns.

A geometric mean return provides a more accurate representation of the growth in portfolio value over a given time period than the arithmetic mean return. In general, the geometric mean return is denoted by $\bar{R}_{Gi}$ and given by the following equation for asset i:

$$\bar{R}_{Gi} = \sqrt[T]{(1 + R_{i1}) \times (1 + R_{i2}) \times \ldots \times (1 + R_{i,T-1}) \times (1 + R_{iT})} - 1 \tag{3}$$

$$= \sqrt[T]{\prod_{t=1}^{T} (1 + R_t)} - 1 \, ,$$

where R_{it} is the return in period t and T is the total number of periods.

In the example in the previous section, we calculated the arithmetic mean to be 4.00 percent. Using Equation 4, we can calculate the geometric mean return from the same three annual returns:

$$\bar{R}_{Gi} = \sqrt[3]{(1 - 0.50) \times (1 + 0.35) \times (1 + 0.27)} - 1 = -0.0500.$$

Exhibit 2 shows the actual return for each year and the balance at the end of each year using actual returns.

Exhibit 2: Portfolio Value and Performance				
	Actual Return for the Year (%)	**Year-End Amount**	**Year-End Amount Using Arithmetic Return of 4%**	**Year-End Amount Using Geometric Return of −5%**
Year 0		EUR1.0000	EUR1.0000	EUR1.0000
Year 1	−50	0.5000	1.0400	0.9500
Year 2	35	0.6750	1.0816	0.9025
Year 3	27	0.8573	1.1249	0.8574

Beginning with an initial investment of EUR1.0000, we will have a balance of EUR0.8573 at the end of the three-year period as shown in the fourth column of Exhibit 2. Note that we compounded the returns because, unless otherwise stated, we earn a return on the balance as of the end of the prior year. That is, we will receive a return of 35 percent in the second year on the balance at the end of the first year, which is only EUR0.5000, not the initial balance of EUR1.0000. Let us compare the balance at the end of the three-year period computed using geometric returns with the balance we would calculate using the 4 percent annual arithmetic mean return from our earlier example. The ending value using the arithmetic mean return is EUR1.1249 (=1.0000 × 1.04³). This is much larger than the actual balance at the end of Year 3 of EUR0.8573.

In general, the arithmetic return is biased upward unless each of the underlying holding period returns are equal. The bias in arithmetic mean returns is particularly severe if holding period returns are a mix of both positive and negative returns, as in this example.

We will now look at three examples that calculate holding period returns over different time horizons.

EXAMPLE 2

Holding Period Return

1. An investor purchased 100 shares of a stock for USD34.50 per share at the beginning of the quarter. If the investor sold all of the shares for USD30.50 per share after receiving a USD51.55 dividend payment at the end of the quarter, the investor's holding period return is *closest* to:

   A. −13.0 percent.

   B. −11.6 percent.

   C. −10.1 percent.

   Solution:

   C is correct. Applying Equation 2, the holding period return is −10.1 percent, calculated as follows:

   $R = (3{,}050 − 3{,}450 + 51.55)/3{,}450 = −10.1\%.$

   The holding period return comprised of a dividend yield of 1.49 percent (= 51.55/3,450) and a capital loss of −11.59 percent (= −400/3,450).

EXAMPLE 3

Holding Period Return

1. An analyst obtains the following annual rates of return for a mutual fund, which are presented in Exhibit 3.

Exhibit 3: Mutual Fund Performance, 20X8–20X0	
Year	**Return (%)**
20X8	14
20X9	−10
20X0	−2

   The fund's holding period return over the three-year period is *closest* to:

   A. 0.18 percent.

   B. 0.55 percent.

   C. 0.67 percent.

   Solution:

   B is correct. The fund's three-year holding period return is 0.55 percent, calculated as follows:

   $R = [(1 + R_1) \times (1 + R_2) \times (1 + R_3)] − 1,$

   $R = [(1 + 0.14)(1 − 0.10)(1 − 0.02)] − 1 = 0.0055 = 0.55\%.$

EXAMPLE 4

Geometric Mean Return

1. An analyst observes the following annual rates of return for a hedge fund, which are presented in Exhibit 4.

Exhibit 4: Hedge Fund Performance, 20X8–20X0	
Year	**Return (%)**
20X8	22
20X9	−25
20X0	11

The fund's geometric mean return over the three-year period is *closest* to:

A. 0.52 percent.

B. 1.02 percent.

C. 2.67 percent.

Solution:

A is correct. Applying Equation 4, the fund's geometric mean return over the three-year period is 0.52 percent, calculated as follows:

$$\overline{R}_G = [(1 + 0.22)(1 - 0.25)(1 + 0.11)]^{(1/3)} - 1 = 1.0157^{(1/3)} - 1 = 0.0052$$
$$= 0.52\%.$$

EXAMPLE 5

Geometric and Arithmetic Mean Returns

1. Consider the annual return data for the group of countries in Exhibit 5.

Exhibit 5: Annual Returns for Years 1 to 3 for Selected Countries' Stock Indexes					
	52-Week Return (%)			**Average 3-Year Return**	
Index	**Year 1**	**Year 2**	**Year 3**	**Arithmetic**	**Geometric**
Country A	−15.6	−5.4	6.1	−4.97	−5.38
Country B	7.8	6.3	−1.5	4.20	4.12
Country C	5.3	1.2	3.5	3.33	3.32
Country D	−2.4	−3.1	6.2	0.23	0.15
Country E	−4.0	−3.0	3.0	−1.33	−1.38
Country F	5.4	5.2	−1.0	3.20	3.16
Country G	12.7	6.7	−1.2	6.07	5.91
Country H	3.5	4.3	3.4	3.73	3.73
Country I	6.2	7.8	3.2	5.73	5.72

Index	52-Week Return (%)			Average 3-Year Return	
	Year 1	Year 2	Year 3	Arithmetic	Geometric
Country J	8.1	4.1	−0.9	3.77	3.70
Country K	11.5	3.4	1.2	5.37	5.28

Calculate the arithmetic and geometric mean returns over the three years for the following three stock indexes: Country D, Country E, and Country F.

Solution:

The arithmetic mean returns are as follows:

Index	Annual Return (%)			Sum $\sum_{i=1}^{3} R_i$	Arithmetic Mean Return (%)
	Year 1	Year 2	Year 3		
Country D	−2.4	−3.1	6.2	0.7	0.233
Country E	−4.0	−3.0	3.0	−4.0	−1.333
Country F	5.4	5.2	−1.0	9.6	3.200

The geometric mean returns are as follows:

Index	1 + Return in Decimal Form $(1 + R_t)$			Product $\prod_{t}^{T}(1 + R_t)$	3rd root $\left[\prod_{t}^{T}(1 + R_t)\right]^{1/3}$	Geometric mean return (%)
	Year 1	Year 2	Year 3			
Country D	0.976	0.969	1.062	1.00438	1.00146	0.146
Country E	0.960	0.970	1.030	0.95914	0.98619	−1.381
Country F	1.054	1.052	0.990	1.09772	1.03157	3.157

In Example 5, the geometric mean return is less than the arithmetic mean return for each country's index returns. In fact, the geometric mean is always less than or equal to the arithmetic mean with one exception: the two means will be equal is when there is no variability in the observations—that is, when all the observations in the series are the same.

In general, the difference between the arithmetic and geometric means increases with the variability within the sample; the more disperse the observations, the greater the difference between the arithmetic and geometric means. Casual inspection of the returns in Exhibit 5 and the associated graph of means in Exhibit 6 suggests a greater variability for Country A's index relative to the other indexes, and this is confirmed with the greater deviation of the geometric mean return (−5.38 percent) from the arithmetic mean return (−4.97 percent). How should the analyst interpret these results?

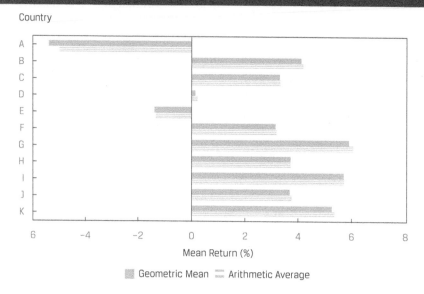

Exhibit 6: Arithmetic and Geometric Mean Returns for Country Stock Indexes, Years 1 to 3

The geometric mean return represents the growth rate or compound rate of return on an investment. One unit of currency invested in a fund tracking the Country B index at the beginning of Year 1 would have grown to (1.078)(1.063)(0.985) = 1.128725 units of currency, which is equal to 1 plus Country B's geometric mean return of 4.1189 percent compounded over three periods: $[1 + 0.041189]^3 = 1.128725$. This math confirms that the geometric mean is the compound rate of return. With its focus on the actual return of an investment over a multiple-period horizon, the geometric mean is of key interest to investors. The arithmetic mean return, focusing on average single-period performance, is also of interest. Both arithmetic and geometric means have a role to play in investment management, and both are often reported for return series.

For reporting historical returns, the geometric mean has considerable appeal because it is the rate of growth or return we would have to earn each year to match the actual, cumulative investment performance. Suppose we purchased a stock for EUR100 and two years later it was worth EUR100, with an intervening year at EUR200. The geometric mean of 0 percent is clearly the compound rate of growth during the two years, which we can confirm by compounding the returns: $[(1 + 1.00)(1 - 0.50)]^{1/2} - 1 = 0\%$. Specifically, the ending amount is the beginning amount times $(1 + R_G)^2$.

However, the arithmetic mean, which is [100% + –50%]/2 = 25% in the previous example, can distort our assessment of historical performance. As we noted, the arithmetic mean is always greater than or equal to the geometric mean. If we want to estimate the average return over a one-period horizon, we should use the arithmetic mean because the arithmetic mean is the average of one-period returns. If we want to estimate the average returns over more than one period, however, we should use the geometric mean of returns because the geometric mean captures how the total returns are linked over time.

The Harmonic Mean

The **harmonic mean**, $\overline{X}_H$, is another measure of central tendency. The harmonic mean is appropriate in cases in which the variable is a rate or a ratio. The terminology "harmonic" arises from its use of a type of series involving reciprocals known as a harmonic series.

Harmonic Mean Formula. The harmonic mean of a set of observations X_1, X_2, ..., X_n is:

$$\bar{X}_H = \frac{n}{\sum_{i=1}^{n}(1/X_i)},\qquad(4)$$

with $X_i > 0$ for $i = 1, 2, ..., n$.

The harmonic mean is the value obtained by summing the reciprocals of the observations,

$$\sum_{i=1}^{n}(1/X_i),$$

the terms of the form $1/X_i$, and then averaging their sum by dividing it by the number of observations, n, and, then finally, taking the reciprocal of that average,

$$\frac{n}{\sum_{i=1}^{n}(1/X_i)}.$$

The harmonic mean may be viewed as a special type of weighted mean in which an observation's weight is inversely proportional to its magnitude. For example, if there is a sample of observations of 1, 2, 3, 4, 5, 6, and 1,000, the harmonic mean is 2.8560. Compared to the arithmetic mean of 145.8571, we see the influence of the outlier (the 1,000) to be much less than in the case of the arithmetic mean. So, the harmonic mean is quite useful as a measure of central tendency in the presence of outliers.

The harmonic mean is used most often when the data consist of rates and ratios, such as P/Es. Suppose three peer companies have P/Es of 45, 15, and 15. The arithmetic mean is 25, but the harmonic mean, which gives less weight to the P/E of 45, is 19.3.

The harmonic mean is a relatively specialized concept of the mean that is appropriate for averaging ratios ("amount per unit") when the ratios are repeatedly applied to a fixed quantity to yield a variable number of units. The concept is best explained through an illustration. A well-known application arises in the investment strategy known as **cost averaging**, which involves the periodic investment of a fixed amount of money. In this application, the ratios we are averaging are prices per share at different purchase dates, and we are applying those prices to a constant amount of money to yield a variable number of shares. An illustration of the harmonic mean to cost averaging is provided in Example 6.

EXAMPLE 6

Cost Averaging and the Harmonic Mean

1. Suppose an investor invests EUR1,000 each month in a particular stock for $n = 2$ months. The share prices are EUR10 and EUR15 at the two purchase dates. What was the average price paid for the security?

   Solution:

   Purchase in the first month = EUR1,000/EUR10 = 100 shares.

   Purchase in the second month = EUR1,000/EUR15 = 66.67 shares.

   The investor purchased a total of 166.67 shares for EUR2,000, so the average price paid per share is EUR2,000/166.67 = EUR12.

   The average price paid is in fact the harmonic mean of the asset's prices at the purchase dates. Using Equation 5, the harmonic mean price is 2/[(1/10) + (1/15)] = EUR12. The value EUR12 is less than the arithmetic mean purchase price (EUR10 + EUR15)/2 = EUR12.5.

Because they use the same data but involve different progressions in their respective calculations, the arithmetic, geometric, and harmonic means are mathematically related to one another. We will not go into the proof of this relationship, but the basic result follows:

Arithmetic mean × Harmonic mean = (Geometric mean)^2.

Unless all the observations in a dataset are the same value, the harmonic mean is always less than the geometric mean, which, in turn, is always less than the arithmetic mean.

The harmonic mean only works for non-negative numbers, so when working with returns that are expressed as positive or negative percentages, we first convert the returns into a compounding format, assuming a reinvestment, as (1 + R), as was done in the geometric mean return calculation, and then calculate (1 + harmonic mean), and subtract 1 to arrive at the harmonic mean return.

EXAMPLE 7

Calculating the Arithmetic, Geometric, and Harmonic Means for P/Es

Each year in December, a securities analyst selects her 10 favorite stocks for the next year. Exhibit 7 presents the P/Es, the ratio of share price to projected earnings per share (EPS), for her top 10 stock picks for the next year.

Exhibit 7: Analyst's 10 Favorite Stocks for Next Year	
Stock	**P/E**
Stock 1	22.29
Stock 2	15.54
Stock 3	9.38
Stock 4	15.12
Stock 5	10.72
Stock 6	14.57
Stock 7	7.20
Stock 8	7.97
Stock 9	10.34
Stock 10	8.35

1. Calculate the arithmetic mean P/E for these 10 stocks.

   Solution:

   The arithmetic mean is calculated as:

   121.48/10 = 12.1480.

2. Calculate the geometric mean P/E for these 10 stocks.

   Solution:

   The geometric mean P/E is calculated as:

   $$\overline{\frac{P}{E}}_{Gi} = \sqrt[10]{\frac{P}{E_1} \times \frac{P}{E_2} \times \dots \times \frac{P}{E_9} \times \frac{P}{E_{10}}}$$

   $$= \sqrt[10]{22.29 \times 15.54 \dots \times 10.34 \times 8.35}$$

$$= \sqrt[10]{38,016,128,040} = 11.4287.$$

The geometric mean is 11.4287. This result can also be obtained as:

$$\frac{\overline{P}}{E}_{Gi} = e^{\frac{ln(22.29 \times 15.54 \dots \times 10.34 \times 8.35)}{10}} = e^{\frac{ln(38,016,128,040)}{10}} = e^{24.3613/10} = 11.4287.$$

3. Calculate the harmonic mean P/E for the 10 stocks.

Solution:

The harmonic mean is calculated as:

$$\overline{X}_H = \frac{n}{\sum_{i=1}^{n}(1/X_i)},$$

$$\overline{X}_H = \frac{10}{\left(\frac{1}{22.29}\right) + \left(\frac{1}{15.54}\right) + \dots + \left(\frac{1}{10.34}\right) + \left(\frac{1}{8.35}\right)},$$

$$\overline{X}_H = 10/0.9247 = 10.8142.$$

In finance, the weighted harmonic mean is used when averaging rates and other multiples, such as the P/E ratio, because the harmonic mean gives equal weight to each data point, and reduces the influence of outliers. These calculations can be performed using Excel:

- To calculate the arithmetic mean or average return, the =AVERAGE(return1, return2, ...) function can be used.

- To calculate the geometric mean return, the =GEOMEAN(return1, return2, ...) function can be used.

- To calculate the harmonic mean return, the =HARMEAN(return1, return2, ...) function can be used.

In addition to arithmetic, geometric, and harmonic means, two other types of means can be used. Both the trimmed and the winsorized means seek to minimize the impact of outliers in a dataset. Specifically, the **trimmed mean** removes a small defined percentage of the largest and smallest values from a dataset containing our observation before calculating the mean by averaging the remaining observations.

A winsorized mean replaces the extreme observations in a dataset to limit the effect of the outliers on the calculations. The **winsorized mean** is calculated after replacing extreme values at both ends with the values of their nearest observations, and then calculating the mean by averaging the remaining observations.

However, the key question is: Which mean to use in what circumstances? The choice of which mean to use depends on many factors, as we describe in Exhibit 8:

- Are there outliers that we want to include?
- Is the distribution symmetric?
- Is there compounding?
- Are there extreme outliers?

Exhibit 8: Deciding Which Measure to Use

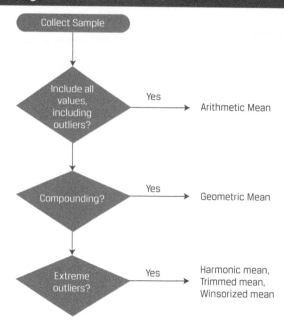

QUESTION SET

A fund had the following returns over the past 10 years:

Exhibit 9: 10-Year Returns

Year	Return
1	4.5%
2	6.0%
3	1.5%
4	−2.0%
5	0.0%
6	4.5%
7	3.5%
8	2.5%
9	5.5%
10	4.0%

1. The arithmetic mean return over the 10 years is *closest* to:

    A. 2.97 percent.

    B. 3.00 percent.

    C. 3.33 percent.

    Solution:

    B is correct. The arithmetic mean return is calculated as follows:

$\overline{R}$ = 30.0%/10 = 3.0%.

2. The geometric mean return over the 10 years is *closest* to:

    A. 2.94 percent.

    B. 2.97 percent.

    C. 3.00 percent.

    Solution:

    B is correct. The geometric mean return is calculated as follows:

    $$\overline{R}_G = \sqrt[10]{(1 + 0.045) \times (1 + 0.06) \times \ldots \times (1 + 0.055) \times (1 + 0.04)} - 1$$

    $$\overline{R}_G = \sqrt[10]{1.3402338} - 1 = 2.9717\%.$$

MONEY-WEIGHTED AND TIME-WEIGHTED RETURN

4

☐ | compare the money-weighted and time-weighted rates of return and evaluate the performance of portfolios based on these measures

The arithmetic and geometric return computations do not account for the timing of cash flows into and out of a portfolio. For example, suppose an investor experiences the returns shown in Exhibit 2. Instead of only investing EUR1.0 at the start (Year 0) as was the case in Exhibit 2, suppose the investor had invested EUR10,000 at the start, EUR1,000 in Year 1, and EUR1,000 in Year 2. In that case, the return of –50 percent in Year 1 significantly hurts her given the relatively large investment at the start. Conversely, if she had invested only EUR100 at the start, the absolute effect of the –50 percent return on the total return is drastically reduced.

Calculating the Money Weighted Return

The **money-weighted return** accounts for the money invested and provides the investor with information on the actual return she earns on her investment. The money-weighted return and its calculation are similar to the internal rate of return and a bond's yield to maturity. Amounts invested are cash outflows from the investor's perspective and amounts returned or withdrawn by the investor, or the money that remains at the end of an investment cycle, is a cash inflow for the investor.

For example, assume that an investor invests EUR100 in a mutual fund at the beginning of the first year, adds another EUR950 at the beginning of the second year, and withdraws EUR350 at the end of the second year. The cash flows are presented in Exhibit 10.

Exhibit 10: Portfolio Balances across Three Years

Year	1	2	3
Balance from previous year	EUR0	EUR50	EUR1,000
New investment by the investor (cash inflow for the mutual fund) at the start of the year	100	950	0
Net balance at the beginning of year	100	1,000	1,000
Investment return for the year	−50%	35%	27%
Investment gain (loss)	−50	350	270
Withdrawal by the investor (cash outflow for the mutual fund) at the end of the year	0	−350	0
Balance at the end of year	EUR50	EUR1,000	EUR1,270

The **internal rate of return** is the discount rate at which the sum of present values of cash flows will equal zero. In general, the equation may be expressed as follows:

$$\sum_{t=0}^{T} \frac{CF_t}{(1 + IRR)^t} = 0, \tag{5}$$

where T is the number of periods, CF_t is the cash flow at time t, and IRR is the internal rate of return or the money-weighted rate of return.

A cash flow can be positive or negative; a positive cash flow is an inflow where money flows to the investor, whereas a negative cash flow is an outflow where money flows away from the investor. The cash flows are expressed as follows, where each cash inflow or outflow occurs at the end of each year. Thus, CF_0 refers to the cash flow at the end of Year 0 or beginning of Year 1, and CF_3 refers to the cash flow at end of Year 3 or beginning of Year 4. Because cash flows are being discounted to the present—that is, end of Year 0 or beginning of Year 1—the period of discounting CF_0 is zero.

$$CF_0 = -100$$
$$CF_1 = -950$$
$$CF_2 = +350$$
$$CF_3 = +1,270$$
$$\frac{CF_0}{(1 + IRR)^0} + \frac{CF_1}{(1 + IRR)^1} + \frac{CF_2}{(1 + IRR)^2} + \frac{CF_3}{(1 + IRR)^3}$$
$$= \frac{-100}{1} + \frac{-950}{(1 + IRR)^1} + \frac{+350}{(1 + IRR)^2} + \frac{+1270}{(1 + IRR)^3} = 0$$
$$IRR = 26.11\%$$

The investor's internal rate of return, or the money-weighted rate of return, is 26.11 percent, which tells the investor what she earned on the actual euros invested for the entire period on an annualized basis. This return is much greater than the arithmetic and geometric mean returns because only a small amount was invested when the mutual fund's return was −50 percent.

All the above calculations can be performed using Excel using the =IRR(values) function, which results in an IRR of 26.11 percent.

Money-Weighted Return for a Dividend-Paying Stock

Next, we'll illustrate calculating the money-weighted return for a dividend paying stock. Consider an investment that covers a two-year horizon. At time $t = 0$, an investor buys one share at a price of USD200. At time $t = 1$, he purchases an additional share at a price of USD225. At the end of Year 2, $t = 2$, he sells both shares at a price of USD235. During both years, the stock pays a dividend of USD5 per share. The $t = 1$ dividend is not reinvested. Exhibit 11 outlines the total cash inflows and outflows for the investment.

Exhibit 11: Cash Flows for a Dividend-Paying Stock	
Time	**Outflows**
0	USD200 to purchase the first share
1	USD225 to purchase the second share

Time	**Inflows**
1	USD5 dividend received from first share (and not reinvested)
2	USD10 dividend (USD5 per share × 2 shares) received
2	USD470 received from selling two shares at USD235 per share

To solve for the money-weighted return, the first step is to group net cash flows by time. For this example, we have –USD200 for the $t = 0$ net cash flow, –USD220 = –USD225 + USD5 for the $t = 1$ net cash flow, and USD480 for the $t = 2$ net cash flow. After entering these cash flows, we use the spreadsheet's (such as Excel) or calculator's IRR function to find that the money-weighted rate of return is 9.39 percent.

$$CF_0 = -200$$
$$CF_1 = -220$$
$$CF_2 = +480$$
$$\frac{CF_0}{(1 + IRR)^0} + \frac{CF_1}{(1 + IRR)^1} + \frac{CF_2}{(1 + IRR)^2}$$
$$= \frac{-200}{1} + \frac{-220}{(1 + IRR)^1} + \frac{480}{(1 + IRR)^2} = 0$$
$$IRR = 9.39\%$$

All these calculations can be performed using Excel using the =IRR(values) function, which results in an IRR of 9.39 percent.

Now we take a closer look at what has happened to the portfolio during each of the two years.

In the first year, the portfolio generated a one-period holding period return of (USD5 + USD225 – USD200)/USD200 = 15%. At the beginning of the second year, the amount invested is USD450, calculated as USD225 (per share price of stock) × 2 shares, because the USD5 dividend was spent rather than reinvested.

At the end of the second year, the proceeds from the liquidation of the portfolio are USD470 plus USD10 in dividends (as outlined in Exhibit 11). So, in the second year the portfolio produced a holding period return of (USD10 + USD470 – USD450)/USD450 = 6.67%. The mean holding period return was (15% + 6.67%)/2 = 10.84%.

The money-weighted rate of return, which we calculated as 9.39 percent, puts a greater weight on the second year's relatively poor performance (6.67 percent) than the first year's relatively good performance (15 percent), as more money was invested in the second year than in the first. That is the sense in which returns in this method of calculating performance are "money weighted."

Although the money-weighted return is an accurate measure of what the investor earned on the money invested, it is limited in its applicability to other situations. For example, it does not allow for a return comparison between different individuals or different investment opportunities. Importantly, two investors in the *same* mutual fund or with the same portfolio of underlying investments may have different money-weighted returns because they invested different amounts in different years.

EXAMPLE 8

Computation of Returns

Ulli Lohrmann and his wife, Suzanne Lohrmann, are planning for retirement and want to compare the past performance of a few mutual funds they are considering for investment. They believe that a comparison over a five-year period would be appropriate. They gather information on a fund they are considering, the Rhein Valley Superior Fund, which is presented in Exhibit 12.

Exhibit 12: Rhein Valley Superior Fund Performance

Year	Assets under Management at the Beginning of Year (euros)	Annual Return (%)
1	30 million	15
2	45 million	−5
3	20 million	10
4	25 million	15
5	35 million	3

The Lohrmanns are interested in aggregating this information for ease of comparison with other funds.

Exhibit 13: Rhein Valley Superior Fund Annual Returns and Investments (euro millions)

Year	1	2	3	4	5
Balance from previous year	0	34.50	42.75	22.00	28.75
New investment by the investor (cash inflow for the Rhein fund)	30.00	10.50	0	3.00	6.25
Withdrawal by the investor (cash outflow for the Rhein fund)	0	0	−22.75	0	0
Net balance at the beginning of year	30.00	45.00	20.00	25.00	35.00
Investment return for the year	15%	−5%	10%	15%	3%
Investment gain (loss)	4.50	−2.25	2.00	3.75	1.05
Balance at the end of year	34.50	42.75	22.00	28.75	36.05

1. Compute the fund's holding period return for the five-year period.

   Solution:

   The five-year holding period return is calculated as:

   $$R = (1 + R_1)(1 + R_2)(1 + R_3)(1 + R_4)(1 + R_5) - 1$$

   $$R = (1.15)(0.95)(1.10)(1.15)(1.03) - 1 =$$

   $$R = 0.4235 = 42.35\%.$$

2. Compute the fund's arithmetic mean annual return.

   Solution:

   The arithmetic mean annual return is calculated as:

   $$\bar{R}_i = \frac{15\% - 5\% + 10\% + 15\% + 3\%}{5} = 7.60\%.$$

3. Compute the fund's geometric mean annual return. How does it compare with the arithmetic mean annual return?

   Solution:

   The geometric mean annual return can be computed as:

   $$\bar{R}_{Gi} = \sqrt[5]{1.15 \times 0.95 \times 1.10 \times 1.15 \times 1.03} - 1,$$

   $$\bar{R}_{Gi} = \sqrt[5]{1.4235} - 1 = 0.0732 = 7.32\%.$$

   Thus, the geometric mean annual return is 7.32 percent, which is slightly less than the arithmetic mean return of 7.60 percent.

4. The Lohrmanns want to earn a minimum annual return of 5 percent. The annual returns and investment amounts are presented in Exhibit 13. Is the money-weighted annual return greater than 5 percent?

   Solution:

   To calculate the money-weighted rate of return, tabulate the annual returns and investment amounts to determine the cash flows, as shown in Exhibit 13:

   $$CF_0 = -30.00,\ CF_1 = -10.50,\ CF_2 = +22.75,\ CF_3 = -3.00,\ CF_4 = -6.25,\ CF_5 = +36.05.$$

   We can use the given 5 percent return to see whether or not the present value of the net cash flows is positive. If it is positive, then the money-weighted rate of return is greater than 5 percent, because a 5 percent discount rate could not reduce the present value to zero.

   $$\frac{-30.00}{(1.05)^0} + \frac{-10.50}{(1.05)^1} + \frac{22.75}{(1.05)^2} + \frac{-3.00}{(1.05)^3} + \frac{-6.25}{(1.05)^4} + \frac{36.05}{(1.05)^5} = 1.1471.$$

   Because the value is positive, the money-weighted rate of return is greater than 5 percent. The exact money-weighted rate of return (found by setting the above equation equal to zero) is 5.86 percent.
   These calculations can be performed using Excel using the =IRR(cash flows) function, which results in an IRR of 5.86 percent.

Time-Weighted Returns

An investment measure that is not sensitive to the additions and withdrawals of funds is the time-weighted rate of return. The **time-weighted rate of return** measures the compound rate of growth of USD1 initially invested in the portfolio over a stated measurement period. For the evaluation of portfolios of publicly traded securities, the time-weighted rate of return is the preferred performance measure as it neutralizes the effect of cash withdrawals or additions to the portfolio, which are generally outside of the control of the portfolio manager.

Computing Time-Weighted Returns

To compute an exact time-weighted rate of return on a portfolio, take the following three steps:

1. Price the portfolio immediately prior to any significant addition or withdrawal of funds. Break the overall evaluation period into subperiods based on the dates of cash inflows and outflows.

2. Calculate the holding period return on the portfolio for each subperiod.

3. Link or compound holding period returns to obtain an annual rate of return for the year (the time-weighted rate of return for the year). If the investment is for more than one year, take the geometric mean of the annual returns to obtain the time-weighted rate of return over that measurement period.

Let us return to our dividend stock money-weighted example in the section, "Money-Weighted Return for a Dividend-Paying Stock" and calculate the time-weighted rate of return for that investor's portfolio based on the information included in Exhibit 11. In that example, we computed the holding period returns on the portfolio, Step 2 in the procedure for finding the time-weighted rate of return. Given that the portfolio earned returns of 15 percent during the first year and 6.67 percent during the second year, what is the portfolio's time-weighted rate of return over an evaluation period of two years?

We find this time-weighted return by taking the geometric mean of the two holding period returns, Step 3 in the previous procedure. The calculation of the geometric mean exactly mirrors the calculation of a compound growth rate. Here, we take the product of 1 plus the holding period return for each period to find the terminal value at $t = 2$ of USD1 invested at $t = 0$. We then take the square root of this product and subtract 1 to get the geometric mean return. We interpret the result as the annual compound growth rate of USD1 invested in the portfolio at $t = 0$. Thus, we have:

$$(1 + \text{Time-weighted return})^2 = (1.15)(1.0667)$$

$$\text{Time-weighted return} = \sqrt{(1.15)(1.0667)} - 1 = 10.76\%.$$

The time-weighted return on the portfolio was 10.76 percent, compared with the money-weighted return of 9.39 percent, which gave larger weight to the second year's return. We can see why investment managers find time-weighted returns more meaningful. If a client gives an investment manager more funds to invest at an unfavorable time, the manager's money-weighted rate of return will tend to be depressed. If a client adds funds at a favorable time, the money-weighted return will tend to be elevated. The time-weighted rate of return removes these effects.

In defining the steps to calculate an exact time-weighted rate of return, we said that the portfolio should be valued immediately prior to any significant addition or withdrawal of funds. With the amount of cash flow activity in many portfolios, this task can be costly. We can often obtain a reasonable approximation of the time-weighted rate of return by valuing the portfolio at frequent, regular intervals, particularly if additions and withdrawals are unrelated to market movements.

The more frequent the valuation, the more accurate the approximation. Daily valuation is commonplace. Suppose that a portfolio is valued daily over the course of a year. To compute the time-weighted return for the year, we first compute each day's holding period return. We compute 365 such daily returns, denoted R_1, R_2, ..., R_{365}. We obtain the annual return for the year by linking the daily holding period returns in the following way: $(1 + R_1) \times (1 + R_2) \times \ldots \times (1 + R_{365}) - 1$. If withdrawals and additions to the portfolio happen only at day's end, this annual return is a precise time-weighted rate of return for the year. Otherwise, it is an approximate time-weighted return for the year.

If we have several years of data, we can calculate a time-weighted return for each year individually, as above. If R_i is the time-weighted return for year i, we calculate an annualized time-weighted return as the geometric mean of N annual returns, as follows:

$$R_{TW} = \left[(1 + R_1) \times (1 + R_2) \times \dots \times (1 + R_N) \right]^{1/N} - 1. \tag{6}$$

Example 9 illustrates the calculation of the time-weighted rate of return.

EXAMPLE 9

Time-Weighted Rate of Return

Strubeck Corporation sponsors a pension plan for its employees. It manages part of the equity portfolio in-house and delegates management of the balance to Super Trust Company. As chief investment officer of Strubeck, you want to review the performance of the in-house and Super Trust portfolios over the last four quarters. You have arranged for outflows and inflows to the portfolios to be made at the very beginning of the quarter. Exhibit 14 summarizes the inflows and outflows as well as the two portfolios' valuations. In Exhibit 11, the ending value is the portfolio's value just prior to the cash inflow or outflow at the beginning of the quarter. The amount invested is the amount each portfolio manager is responsible for investing.

Exhibit 14: Cash Flows for the In-House Strubeck Account and the Super Trust Account (US dollars)

	Quarter			
	1	2	3	4
Panel A: In-House Account				
Beginning value	4,000,000	6,000,000	5,775,000	6,720,000
Beginning of period inflow (outflow)	1,000,000	(500,000)	225,000	(600,000)
Amount invested	5,000,000	5,500,000	6,000,000	6,120,000
Ending value	6,000,000	5,775,000	6,720,000	5,508,000
Panel B: Super Trust Account				
Beginning value	10,000,000	13,200,000	12,240,000	5,659,200
Beginning of period inflow (outflow)	2,000,000	(1,200,000)	(7,000,000)	(400,000)
Amount invested	12,000,000	12,000,000	5,240,000	5,259,200
Ending value	13,200,000	12,240,000	5,659,200	5,469,568

1. Calculate the time-weighted rate of return for the in-house account.

   Solution:

   To calculate the time-weighted rate of return for the in-house account, we compute the quarterly holding period returns for the account and link them into an annual return. The in-house account's time-weighted rate of return is 27.01 percent, calculated as follows:

1Q HPR: r_1 = (USD6,000,000 − USD5,000,000) / USD5,000,000 = 0.20
2Q HPR: r_2 = (USD5,775,000 − USD5,500,000) / USD5,500,000 = 0.05
3Q HPR: r_3 = (USD6,720,000 − USD6,000,000) / USD6,000,000 = 0.12
4Q HPR: r_4 = (USD5,508,000 − USD6,120,000) / USD6,120,000 = −0.10

$$R_{TW} = (1 + r_1)(1 + r_2)(1 + r_3)(1 + r_4) - 1,$$

$$R_{TW} = (1.20)(1.05)(1.12)(0.90) - 1 = 0.2701 \text{ or } 27.01\%.$$

2. Calculate the time-weighted rate of return for the Super Trust account.

    Solution:

    The account managed by Super Trust has a time-weighted rate of return of 26.02 percent, calculated as follows:

    1Q HPR: r_1 = (USD13,200,000 − USD12,000,000) / USD12,000,000 = 0.10
    2Q HPR: r_2 = (USD12,240,000 − USD12,000,000) / USD12,000,000 = 0.02
    3Q HPR: r_3 = (USD5,659,200 − USD5,240,000) / USD5,240,000 = 0.08
    4Q HPR: r_4 = (USD5,469,568 − USD5,259,200) / USD5,259,200 = 0.04

    $$R_{TW} = (1 + r_1)(1 + r_2)(1 + r_3)(1 + r_4) - 1,$$

    $$R_{TW} = (1.10)(1.02)(1.08)(1.04) - 1 = 0.2602 \text{ or } 26.02\%.$$

    The in-house portfolio's time-weighted rate of return is higher than the Super Trust portfolio's by 99 basis points. Note that 27.01 percent and 26.02 percent might be rounded to 27 percent and 26 percent, respectively. The impact of the rounding the performance difference (100 bp vs. 99 bp) may seem as trivial, yet it's impact on a large portfolio may be substantive.

Having worked through this exercise, we are ready to look at a more detailed case.

EXAMPLE 10

Time-Weighted and Money-Weighted Rates of Return Side by Side

Your task is to compute the investment performance of the Walbright Fund for the most recent year. The facts are as follows:

- On 1 January, the Walbright Fund had a market value of USD100 million.

- During the period 1 January to 30 April, the stocks in the fund generated a capital gain of USD10 million.

- On 1 May, the stocks in the fund paid a total dividend of USD2 million. All dividends were reinvested in additional shares.

- Because the fund's performance had been exceptional, institutions invested an additional USD20 million in Walbright on 1 May, raising assets under management to USD132 million (USD100 + USD10 + USD2 + USD20).

- On 31 December, Walbright received total dividends of USD2.64 million. The fund's market value on 31 December, not including the USD2.64 million in dividends, was USD140 million.

- The fund made no other interim cash payments during the year.

1. Compute the Walbright Fund's time-weighted rate of return.

   Solution:

   Because interim cash flows were made on 1 May, we must compute two interim total returns and then link them to obtain an annual return. Exhibit 15 lists the relevant market values on 1 January, 1 May, and 31 December, as well as the associated interim four-month (1 January to 1 May) and eight-month (1 May to 31 December) holding period returns.

Exhibit 15: Cash Flows for the Walbright Fund

1 January	Beginning portfolio value = USD100 million
1 May	Dividends received before additional investment = USD2 million
	Ending portfolio value = USD110 million
	Four-month holding period return:
	$R = \dfrac{USD2 + USD10}{USD100} = 12\%$
	New investment = USD20 million
	Beginning market value for last two-thirds of the year = USD132 million
31 December	Dividends received = USD2.64 million
	Ending portfolio value = USD140 million
	Eight-month holding period return:
	$R = \dfrac{USD2.64 + USD140 - USD132}{USD132} = 8.06\%$

   Now we must geometrically link the four- and eight-month holding period returns to compute an annual return. We compute the time-weighted return as follows:

   $$R_{TW} = 1.12 \times 1.0806 - 1 = 0.2103.$$

   In this instance, we compute a time-weighted rate of return of 21.03 percent for one year. The four-month and eight-month intervals combine to equal one year. (Note: Taking the square root of the product 1.12×1.0806 would be appropriate only if 1.12 and 1.0806 each applied to one full year.)

2. Compute the Walbright Fund's money-weighted rate of return.

   Solution:

   To calculate the money-weighted return, we need to find the discount rate that sets the sum of the present value of cash inflows and outflows equal to zero. The initial market value of the fund and all additions to it are treated as cash outflows. (Think of them as expenditures.) Withdrawals, receipts, and the ending market value of the fund are counted as inflows. (The ending market value is the amount investors receive on liquidating the fund.) Because interim cash flows have occurred at four-month intervals, we must solve for the four-month internal rate of return. Exhibit 15 details the cash flows and their timing.

   $CF_0 = -100$

   $CF_1 = -20$

   $CF_2 = 0$

$CF_3 = 142.64$

CF_0 refers to the initial investment of USD100 million made at the beginning of the first four-month interval on 1 January. CF_1 refers to the cash flows made at end of the first four-month interval or the beginning of the second four-month interval on 1 May. Those cash flows include a cash inflow of USD2 million for the dividend received and cash outflows of USD22 million for the dividend reinvested and additional investment, respectively. The second four-month interval had no cash flow so CF_2 is equal to zero. CF_3 refers to the cash inflows at the end of the third four-month interval. Those cash inflows include a USD2.64 million dividend received and the fund's terminal market value of USD140 million.

Using a spreadsheet or IRR-enabled calculator, we use −100, −20, 0, and USD142.64 for the $t = 0$, $t = 1$, $t = 2$, and $t = 3$ net cash flows, respectively. Using either tool, we get a four-month IRR of 6.28 percent.

$$\frac{CF_0}{(1 + IRR)^0} + \frac{CF_1}{(1 + IRR)^1} + \frac{CF_2}{(1 + IRR)^2} + \frac{CF_3}{(1 + IRR)^3} = 0$$

$$\frac{-100}{1} + \frac{-20}{(1 + IRR)^1} + \frac{0}{(1 + IRR)^2} + \frac{142.64}{(1 + IRR)^3} = 0 \quad .$$

$$IRR = 6.28\%$$

The quick way to annualize this four-month return is to multiply it by 3. A more accurate way is to compute it on a compounded basis as: $(1.0628)^3 - 1 = 0.2005$ or 20.05 percent.

These calculations can also be performed using Excel using the =IRR(cash flows) function, which results in an IRR of 6.28 percent.

3. Interpret the differences between the Fund's time-weighted and money-weighted rates of return.

Solution:

In this example, the time-weighted return (21.03 percent) is greater than the money-weighted return (20.05 percent). The Walbright Fund's performance was relatively poorer during the eight-month period, when the fund had more money invested, than the overall performance. This fact is reflected in a lower money-weighted rate of return compared with the time-weighted rate of return, as the money-weighted return is sensitive to the timing and amount of withdrawals and additions to the portfolio.

The accurate measurement of portfolio returns is important to the process of evaluating portfolio managers. In addition to considering returns, however, analysts must also weigh risk. When we worked through Example 9, we stopped short of suggesting that in-house management was superior to Super Trust because it earned a higher time-weighted rate of return. A judgment as to whether performance was "better" or "worse" must include the risk dimension, which will be covered later in your study materials.

5

ANNUALIZED RETURN

☐ | calculate and interpret annualized return measures and continuously compounded returns, and describe their appropriate uses

The period during which a return is earned or computed can vary and often we have to annualize a return that was calculated for a period that is shorter (or longer) than one year. You might buy a short-term treasury bill with a maturity of three months, or you might take a position in a futures contract that expires at the end of the next quarter. How can we compare these returns?

In many cases, it is most convenient to annualize all available returns to facilitate comparison. Thus, daily, weekly, monthly, and quarterly returns are converted to annualized returns. Many formulas used for calculating certain values or prices also require all returns and periods to be expressed as annualized rates of return. For example, the most common version of the Black–Scholes option-pricing model requires annualized returns and periods to be in years.

Non-annual Compounding

Recall that interest may be paid semiannually, quarterly, monthly, or even daily. To handle interest payments made more than once a year, we can modify the present value formula as follows. Here, R_s is the quoted interest rate and equals the periodic interest rate multiplied by the number of compounding periods in each year. In general, with more than one compounding period in a year, we can express the formula for present value as follows:

$$\text{PV} = \text{FV}_N \left(1 + \frac{R_s}{m}\right)^{-mN},$$ (7)

where

m = number of compounding periods per year,

R_s = quoted annual interest rate, and

N = number of years.

The formula in Equation 8 is quite similar to the simple present value formula. As we have already noted, present value and future value factors are reciprocals. Changing the frequency of compounding does not alter this result. The only difference is the use of the periodic interest rate and the corresponding number of compounding periods.

The following example presents an application of monthly compounding.

EXAMPLE 11

The Present Value of a Lump Sum with Monthly Compounding

The manager of a Canadian pension fund knows that the fund must make a lump-sum payment of CAD5 million 10 years from today. She wants to invest an amount today in a guaranteed investment contract (GIC) so that it will grow to the required amount. The current interest rate on GICs is 6 percent a year, compounded monthly.

---

1. How much should she invest today in the GIC?

Solution:

By applying Equation 8, the required present value is calculated as follow:

FV_N = CAD 5,000,000

R_s = 6% = 0.06

m = 12

R_s/m = 0.06/12 = 0.005

N = 10

mN = 12(10) = 120

$$PV = FV_N\left(1 + \frac{R_s}{m}\right)^{-mN}$$

= CAD 5,000,000(1.005)$^{-120}$

= CAD 5,000,000(0.549633)

= CAD 2,748,163.67

In applying Equation 8, we use the periodic rate (in this case, the monthly rate) and the appropriate number of periods with monthly compounding (in this case, 10 years of monthly compounding, or 120 months).

Annualizing Returns

To annualize any return for a period shorter than one year, the return for the period must be compounded by the number of periods in a year. A monthly return is compounded 12 times, a weekly return is compounded 52 times, and a quarterly return is compounded 4 times. Daily returns are normally compounded 365 times. For an uncommon number of days, we compound by the ratio of 365 to the number of days.

If the weekly return is 0.2 percent, then the compound annual return is 10.95 percent (there are 52 weeks in a year):

$$R_{annual} = \left(1 + R_{weekly}\right)^{52} - 1 = (1 + 0.2\%)^{52} - 1$$
$$= (1.002)^{52} - 1 = 0.1095 = 10.95\%$$

If the return for 15 days is 0.4 percent, then the annualized return is 10.20 percent, assuming 365 days in a year:

$$R_{annual} = \left(1 + R_{15}\right)^{365/15} - 1 = (1 + 0.4\%)^{365/15} - 1$$
$$= (1.004)^{365/15} - 1 = 0.1020 = 10.20\%$$

A general equation to annualize returns is given, where c is the number of periods in a year. For a quarter, c = 4 and for a month, c = 12:

$$R_{annual} = \left(1 + R_{period}\right)^c - 1. \tag{8}$$

How can we annualize a return when the holding period return is more than one year? For example, how do we annualize an 18-month holding period return? Because one year contains two-thirds of 18-month periods, c = 2/3 in the above equation. For example, an 18-month return of 20 percent can be annualized as follows:

$$R_{annual} = \left(1 + R_{18month}\right)^{2/3} - 1 = (1 + 0.20)^{2/3} - 1 = 0.1292 = 12.92\%.$$

Similar expressions can be constructed when quarterly or weekly returns are needed for comparison instead of annual returns. In such cases, c is equal to the number of holding periods in a quarter or in a week. For example, assume that you want to convert daily returns to weekly returns or annual returns to weekly returns for comparison between weekly returns. To convert daily returns to weekly returns, c = 5, assume that there are five trading days in a week. However, daily return calculations can be annualized differently. For example, five can be used for trading-day-based calculations, giving approximately 250 trading days a year; seven can be used on calendar-day-based calculations. Specific methods used conform to specific business practices, market conventions, and standards. To convert annual returns to weekly returns, $c = 1/52$. The expressions for annual returns can then be rewritten as expressions for weekly returns as follows:

$$R_{weekly} = \left(1 + R_{daily}\right)^5 - 1; \; R_{weekly} = \left(1 + R_{annual}\right)^{1/52} - 1. \tag{9}$$

One major limitation of annualizing returns is the implicit assumption that returns can be repeated precisely, that is, money can be reinvested repeatedly while earning a similar return. This type of return is not always possible. An investor may earn a return of 5 percent during a week because the market rose sharply that week, but it is highly unlikely that he will earn a return of 5 percent every week for the next 51 weeks, resulting in an annualized return of 1,164.3 percent ($= 1.05^{52} - 1$). Therefore, it is important to annualize short-term returns with this limitation in mind.

EXAMPLE 12

Annualized Returns

An analyst seeks to evaluate three securities she has held in her portfolio for different periods of time.

- Over the past 100 days, Security A has earned a return of 6.2 percent.
- Security B has earned 2 percent over the past four weeks.
- Security C has earned a return of 5 percent over the past three months.

1. Compare the relative performance of the three securities.

   Solution:

   To facilitate comparison, the three securities' returns need to be annualized:

   - Annualized return for Security A: $R_{SA} = (1 + 0.062)^{365/100} - 1 = 0.2455 = 24.55\%$
   - Annualized return for Security B: $R_{SB} = (1 + 0.02)^{52/4} - 1 = 0.2936 = 29.36\%$
   - Annualized return for Security C: $R_{SC} = (1 + 0.05)^4 - 1 = 0.2155 = 21.55\%$

   Security B generated the highest annualized return.

EXAMPLE 13

Exchange-Traded Fund Performance

An investor is evaluating the returns of three recently formed exchange-traded funds. Selected return information on the exchange-traded funds (ETFs) is presented in Exhibit 16.

Exhibit 16: ETF Performance Information

ETF	Time Since Inception	Return Since Inception (%)
1	146 days	4.61
2	5 weeks	1.10
3	15 months	14.35

---

1. Which ETF has the highest annualized rate of return?

   A. ETF 1

   B. ETF 2

   C. ETF 3

   Solution:

   B is correct. The annualized rate of return for the three ETFs are as follows:

   ETF 1 annualized return = $(1.0461^{365/146}) - 1 = 11.93\%$

   ETF 2 annualized return = $(1.0110^{52/5}) - 1 = 12.05\%$

   ETF 3 annualized return = $(1.1435^{12/15}) - 1 = 11.32\%$

   Despite having the lowest value for the periodic rate, ETF 2 has the highest annualized rate of return because of the reinvestment rate assumption and the compounding of the periodic rate.

Continuously Compounded Returns

An important concept is the continuously compounded return associated with a holding period return, such as R_1. The **continuously compounded return** associated with a holding period return is the natural logarithm of one plus that holding period return, or equivalently, the natural logarithm of the ending price over the beginning price (the price relative). Note that here we are using r to refer specifically to continuously compounded returns, but other textbooks and sources may use a different notation.

If we observe a one-week holding period return of 0.04, the equivalent continuously compounded return, called the one-week continuously compounded return, is ln(1.04) = 0.039221; EUR1.00 invested for one week at 0.039221 continuously compounded gives EUR1.04, equivalent to a 4 percent one-week holding period return.

The continuously compounded return from t to $t + 1$ is

$$r_{t,t+1} = \ln(P_{t+1}/P_t) = \ln(1 + R_{t,t+1}). \tag{10}$$

For our example, an asset purchased at time t for a P_0 of USD30 and the same asset one period later, $t + 1$, has a value of P_1 of USD34.50 has a continuously compounded return given by $r_{0,1} = \ln(P_1/P_0) = \ln(1 + R_{0,1}) = \ln(\text{USD34.50/USD30}) = \ln(1.15) = 0.139762$.

Thus, 13.98 percent is the continuously compounded return from $t = 0$ to $t = 1$. The continuously compounded return is smaller than the associated holding period return. If our investment horizon extends from $t = 0$ to $t = T$, then the continuously compounded return to T is

$$r_{0,T} = \ln(P_T/P_0). \tag{11}$$

Applying the exponential function to both sides of the equation, we have $\exp(r_{0,T}) = \exp[\ln(P_T/P_0)] = P_T/P_0$, so

$$P_T = P_0\exp(r_{0,T}).$$

We can also express P_T/P_0 as the product of price relatives:

$$P_T/P_0 = (P_T/P_{T-1})(P_{T-1}/P_{T-2}) \ldots (P_1/P_0). \tag{12}$$

Taking logs of both sides of this equation, we find that the continuously compounded return to time T is the sum of the one-period continuously compounded returns:

$$r_{0,T} = r_{T-1,T} + r_{T-2,T-1} + \ldots + r_{0,1}. \tag{13}$$

Using holding period returns to find the ending value of a USD1 investment involves the multiplication of quantities (1 + holding period return). Using continuously compounded returns involves addition (as shown in Equation 14), which is a desirable property of continuously compounded returns and which we will use throughout the curriculum.

OTHER MAJOR RETURN MEASURES AND THEIR APPLICATIONS

6

☐ | calculate and interpret major return measures and describe their appropriate uses

The statistical measures of return discussed in the previous section are generally applicable across a wide range of assets and time periods. Special assets, however, such as mutual funds, and other considerations, such as taxes or inflation, may require more specific return measures.

Although it is not possible to consider all types of special measures, we will discuss the effect of fees (gross versus net returns), taxes (pre-tax and after-tax returns), inflation (nominal and real returns), and the effect of **leverage**. Many investors use mutual funds or other external entities (i.e., investment vehicles) for investment. In those cases, funds charge management fees and expenses to the investors. Consequently, gross and net-of-fund-expense returns should also be considered. Of course, an investor may be interested in the net-of-expenses after-tax real return, which is in fact what an investor truly receives. We consider these additional return measures in the following sections.

Gross and Net Return

A gross return is the return earned by an asset manager prior to deductions for management expenses, custodial fees, taxes, or any other expenses that are not directly related to the generation of returns but rather related to the management and administration of an investment. These expenses are not deducted from the gross return because they may vary with the amount of assets under management or may vary because of the tax status of the investor. Trading expenses, however, such as commissions, *are* accounted for in (i.e., deducted from) the computation of gross return because trading expenses contribute directly to the return earned by the manager. Thus, gross return is an appropriate measure for evaluating and comparing the investment skill of asset managers because it does not include any fees related to the management and administration of an investment.

Net return is a measure of what the investment vehicle (e.g., mutual fund) has earned for the investor. Net return accounts for (i.e., deducts) all managerial and administrative expenses that reduce an investor's return. Because individual investors are most concerned about the net return (i.e., what they actually receive), small mutual funds with a limited amount of assets under management are at a disadvantage compared with the larger funds that can spread their largely fixed administrative expenses over a larger asset base. As a result, many small mutual funds waive part of the expenses to keep the funds competitive.

Pre-Tax and After-Tax Nominal Return

All return measures discussed up to this point are pre-tax nominal returns—that is, no adjustment has been made for taxes or inflation. In general, all returns are pre-tax nominal returns unless they are otherwise designated.

Many investors are concerned about the possible tax liability associated with their returns because taxes reduce the net return that they receive. Capital gains and income may be taxed differently, depending on the jurisdiction. Capital gains come in two forms: short-term capital gains and long-term capital gains. Long-term capital gains receive preferential tax treatment in a number of countries. Interest income is taxed as ordinary income in most countries. Dividend income may be taxed as ordinary income, may have a lower tax rate, or may be exempt from taxes depending on the country and the type of investor. The after-tax nominal return is computed as the total return minus any allowance for taxes on dividends, interest, and realized gains. Bonds issued at a discount to the par value may be taxed based on accrued gains instead of realized gains.

Because taxes are paid on realized capital gains and income, the investment manager can minimize the tax liability by selecting appropriate securities (e.g., those subject to more favorable taxation, all other investment considerations equal) and reducing trading turnover. Therefore, taxable investors evaluate investment managers based on the after-tax nominal return.

Real Returns

Previously this learning module approximated the relationship between the nominal rate and the real rate by the following relationship:

$$(1 + nominal\ risk\text{–}free\ rate) = (1 + real\ risk\text{–}free\ rate)(1 + inflation\ premium).$$

This relationship can be extended to link the relationship between nominal and real returns. Specifically, the nominal return consists of a real risk-free rate of return to compensate for postponed consumption; inflation as loss of purchasing power; and a risk premium for assuming risk. Frequently, the real risk-free return and the risk premium are combined to arrive at the real "risky" rate and is simply referred to as the real return, or:

$$(1 + real\ return) = \frac{(1 + real\ risk\text{–}free\ rate)(1 + risk\ premium)}{1 + inflation\ premium}. \tag{14}$$

Real returns are particularly useful in comparing returns across time periods because inflation rates may vary over time. Real returns are also useful in comparing returns among countries when returns are expressed in local currencies instead of a constant investor currency and when inflation rates vary between countries (which are usually the case).

Finally, the after-tax real return is what the investor receives as compensation for postponing consumption and assuming risk after paying taxes on investment returns. As a result, the after-tax real return becomes a reliable benchmark for making investment decisions. Although it is a measure of an investor's benchmark return, it is not commonly calculated by asset managers because it is difficult to estimate a general tax component applicable to all investors. For example, the tax component depends on an investor's specific taxation rate (marginal tax rate), how long the investor holds an investment (long-term versus short-term), and the type of account the asset is held in (tax-exempt, tax-deferred, or normal).

EXAMPLE 14

Computation of Special Returns

Let's return to Example 8. After reading this section, Mr. Lohrmann decided that he was not being fair to the fund manager by including the asset management fee and other expenses because the small size of the fund would put it at a competitive disadvantage. He learns that the fund spends a fixed amount of EUR500,000 every year on expenses that are unrelated to the manager's performance.

Mr. Lohrmann has become concerned that both taxes and inflation may reduce his return. Based on the current tax code, he expects to pay 20 percent tax on the return he earns from his investment. Historically, inflation has been around 2 percent and he expects the same rate of inflation to be maintained.

1. Estimate the annual gross return for the first year by adding back the fixed expenses.

   Solution:

   The gross return for the first year is higher by 1.67 percent (= EUR500,000/ EUR30,000,000) than the 15 percent% investor return reported by the fund. Thus, the gross return for the first year is 16.67 percent (= 15% + 1.67%).

2. What is the net return that investors in the Rhein Valley Superior Fund earned during the five-year period?

   Solution:

   The investor return reported by the mutual fund is the net return of the fund after accounting for all direct and indirect expenses. The net return is also the pre-tax nominal return because it has not been adjusted for taxes or inflation. From Example. 8, the net return for the five-year holding period was calculated as 42.35 percent.

3. What is the after-tax net return for the first year that investors earned from the Rhein Valley Superior Fund? Assume that all gains are realized at the end of the year and the taxes are paid immediately at that time.

   Solution:

   The net return earned by investors during the first year was 15 percent. Applying a 20 percent tax rate, the after-tax return that accrues to investors is 12 percent [= 15% – (0.20 × 15%)].

4. What is the after-tax real return that investors would have earned in the fifth year?

   Solution:

   The after-tax return earned by investors in the fifth year is 2.4 percent [= 3% – (0.20 × 3%)]. Inflation reduces the return by 2 percent so the after-tax real return earned by investors in the fifth year is 0.39 percent, as shown:

$$\frac{(1 + 2.40\%)}{(1 + 2.00\%)} - 1 = \frac{(1 + 0.0240)}{(1 + 0.0200)} - 1 = 1.0039 - 1 = 0.0039 = 0.39\%.$$

Note that taxes are paid before adjusting for inflation.

Leveraged Return

In the previous calculations, we have assumed that the investor's position in an asset is equal to the total investment made by an investor using his or her own money. This section differs in that the investor creates a leveraged position.

There are two ways of creating a claim on asset returns that are greater than the investment of one's own money. First, an investor may trade futures contracts in which the money required to take a position may be as little as 10 percent of the notional value of the asset. In this case, the leveraged return, the return on the investor's own money, is 10 times the actual return of the underlying security. Both the gains and losses are amplified by a factor of 10.

Investors can also invest more than their own money by borrowing money to purchase the asset. This approach is easily done in stocks and bonds, and very common when investing in real estate. If half (50 percent) of the money invested is borrowed, then the gross return to the investor is doubled, but the interest to be paid on borrowed money must be deducted to calculate the net return.

Using borrowed capital, debt, the size of the leveraged position increases by the additional, borrowed capital. If the total investment return earned on the leveraged portfolio, R_P, exceeds the borrowing cost on debt, r_D, taking on leverage increases the return on the portfolio. Denoting the return on a leveraged portfolio as R_L, then the return can be calculated as follows:

$$R_L = \frac{Portfolio\ return}{Portfolio\ equity} = \frac{[R_P \times (V_E + V_B) - (V_B \times r_D)]}{V_E} = R_p + \frac{V_B}{V_E}(R_p - r_D), \qquad (15)$$

where V_E is the equity of the portfolio and V_B is the debt or borrowed funds. If $R_P < r_D$ then leverage decreases R_L.

For example, for a EUR10 million equity portfolio that generates an 8 percent total investment return, R_P, over one year and is financed 30 percent with debt at 5 percent, then the leveraged return, R_L, is:

$$R_L = R_p + \frac{V_B}{V_E}(R_p - r_D) = 8\% + \frac{EUR3\ million}{EUR7\ million}(8\% - 5\%) = 8\% + 0.43 \times 3\%$$
$$= 9.29\%.$$

EXAMPLE 15

Return Calculations

An analyst observes the following historic asset class geometric returns:

Exhibit 17: Asset Class Geometric Return

Asset Class	Geometric Return (%)
Equities	8.0
Corporate Bonds	6.5
Treasury bills	2.5
Inflation	2.1

1. The real rate of return for equities is *closest* to:

   A. 5.4 percent.

   B. 5.8 percent.

   C. 5.9 percent.

   Solution:

   B is correct. The real rate of return for equities is calculated as follows:

   $(1 + 0.080)/(1 + 0.0210) - 1 = 5.8\%.$

2. The real rate of return for corporate bonds is *closest* to:

   A. 4.3 percent.

   B. 4.4 percent.

   C. 4.5 percent.

   Solution:

   A is correct. The real rate of return for corporate bonds is calculated as follows:

   $(1 + 0.065)/(1 + 0.0210) - 1 = 4.3\%.$

3. The risk premium for equities is closest to:

   A. 5.4 percent.

   B. 5.5 percent.

   C. 5.6 percent.

   Solution:

   A is correct. The risk premium for equities is calculated as follows:

   $(1 + 0.080)/(1 + 0.0250) - 1 = 5.4\%.$

4. The risk premium for corporate bonds is *closest* to:

   A. 3.5 percent.

   B. 3.9 percent.

   C. 4.0 percent.

   Solution:

   B is correct. The risk premium for corporate bonds is calculated as follows:

   $(1 + 0.0650)/(1 + 0.0250) - 1 = 3.9\%.$

PRACTICE PROBLEMS

1. The nominal risk-free rate is *best* described as the sum of the real risk-free rate and a premium for:

   A. maturity.

   B. liquidity.

   C. expected inflation.

2. Which of the following risk premiums is most relevant in explaining the difference in yields between 30-year bonds issued by the US Treasury and 30-year bonds issued by a small, private US corporate issuer?

   A. Inflation

   B. Maturity

   C. Liquidity

3. Consider the following annual return for Fund Y over the past five years:

Exhibit 1: Five-Year Annual Returns	
Year	Return (%)
Year 1	19.5
Year 2	−1.9
Year 3	19.7
Year 4	35.0
Year 5	5.7

   The geometric mean return for Fund Y is *closest* to:

   A. 14.9 percent.

   B. 15.6 percent.

   C. 19.5 percent.

4. A portfolio manager invests EUR5,000 annually in a security for four years at the following prices:

Exhibit 1: Five-Year Purchase Prices	
Year	Purchase Price (euros per unit)
Year 1	62.00
Year 2	76.00

Year	Purchase Price (euros per unit)
Year 3	84.00
Year 4	90.00

The average price is *best* represented as the:

A. harmonic mean of EUR76.48.

B. geometric mean of EUR77.26.

C. arithmetic average of EUR78.00.

5. Which of the following statements regarding arithmetic and geometric means is correct?

A. The geometric mean will exceed the arithmetic mean for a series with non-zero variance.

B. The geometric mean measures an investment's compound rate of growth over multiple periods.

C. The arithmetic mean measures an investment's terminal value over multiple periods.

6. A fund receives investments at the beginning of each year and generates returns for three years as follows:

Exhibit 1: Investments and Returns for Three Years

Year of Investment	Assets under Management at the Beginning of each year	Return during Year of Investment
1	USD1,000	15%
2	USD4,000	14%
3	USD45,000	–4%

Which return measure over the three-year period is negative?

A. Geometric mean return

B. Time-weighted rate of return

C. Money-weighted rate of return

7. At the beginning of Year 1, a fund has USD10 million under management; it earns a return of 14 percent for the year. The fund attracts another net USD100 million at the start of Year 2 and earns a return of 8 percent for that year. The money-weighted rate of return of the fund is *most likely* to be:

A. less than the time-weighted rate of return.

B. the same as the time-weighted rate of return.

C. greater than the time-weighted rate of return.

8. An investor is evaluating the returns of three recently formed ETFs. Selected

return information on the ETFs is presented in Exhibit 20:

Exhibit 1: Returns on ETFs

ETF	Time Since Inception	Return Since Inception (%)
1	125 days	4.25
2	8 weeks	1.95
3	16 months	17.18

Which ETF has the highest annualized rate of return?

A. ETF 1

B. ETF 2

C. ETF 3

9. The price of a stock at $t = 0$ is USD208.25 and at $t = 1$ is USD186.75. The continuously compounded rate of return, $r_{1,T}$ for the stock from $t = 0$ to $t = 1$ is *closest* to:

A. −10.90 percent.

B. −10.32 percent.

C. 11.51 percent.

10. A USD25 million equity portfolio is financed 20 percent with debt at a cost of 6 percent annual cost. If that equity portfolio generates a 10 percent annual total investment return, then the leveraged return is:

A. 11.0 percent.

B. 11.2 percent.

C. 13.2 percent

11. An investment manager's gross return is:

A. an after-tax nominal, risk-adjusted return.

B. the return earned by the manager prior to deduction of trading expenses.

C. an often used measure of an investment manager's skill because it does not include expenses related to management or administration.

12. The strategy of using leverage to enhance investment returns:

A. amplifies gains but not losses.

B. doubles the net return if half of the invested capital is borrowed.

C. increases total investment return only if the return earned exceeds the borrowing cost.

13. At the beginning of the year, an investor holds EUR10,000 in a hedge fund. The investor borrowed 25 percent of the purchase price, EUR2,500, at an annual interest rate of 6 percent and expects to pay a 30 percent tax on the return she

earns from his investment. At the end of the year, the hedge fund reported the information in Exhibit 22:

Exhibit 1: Hedge Fund Investment	
Gross return	8.46%
Trading expenses	1.10%
Managerial and administrative expenses	1.60%

The investor's after-tax return on the hedge fund investment is closest to:

A. 3.60 percent.

B. 3.98 percent.

C. 5.00 percent.

SOLUTIONS

1. C is correct. The nominal risk-free rate is approximated as the sum of the real risk-free interest rate and an inflation premium.

2. C is correct. US Treasury bonds are highly liquid, whereas the bonds of small issuers trade infrequently and the interest rate includes a liquidity premium. This liquidity premium reflects the relatively high costs (including the impact on price) of selling a position. As the two bond issues have the same 30-year maturity, the observed difference in yields would not be solely explained by maturity. Further, the inflation premium embedded in the yield of both bonds is likely to be similar given they are both US-based bonds with the same maturity.

3. A is correct. The geometric mean return for Fund Y is calculated as follows:

$$\overline{R}_G = [(1 + 0.195) \times (1 - 0.019) \times (1 + 0.197) \times (1 + 0.350) \times (1 + 0.057)]^{(1/5)} - 1$$
$$= 14.9\%.$$

4. A is correct. The harmonic mean is appropriate for determining the average price per unit as it gives equal weight to each data point and reduces the potential influence of outliers. It is calculated as follows:

$$\overline{X}_H = 4/[(1/62.00) + (1/76.00) + (1/84.00) + (1/90.00)] = EUR76.48.$$

5. B is correct. The geometric mean compounds the periodic returns of every period, giving the investor a more accurate measure of the terminal value of an investment.

6. C is correct. The money-weighted rate of return considers both the timing and amounts of investments into the fund. To calculate the money-weighted rate of return, tabulate the annual returns and investment amounts to determine the cash flows.

Year	1	2	3
Balance from previous year	0	USD1,150	USD4,560
New investment	USD1,000	USD2,850	USD40,440
Net balance at the beginning of year	USD1,000	USD4,000	USD45,000
Investment return for the year	15%	14%	-4%
Investment gain (loss)	USD150	USD560	-USD1,800
Balance at the end of year	USD1,150	USD4,560	USD43,200

$CF_0 = -USD1,000$, $CF_1 = -USD2,850$, $CF_2 = -USD40,440$, $CF_3 = +USD43,200$.

$$CF_0 = -1,000$$
$$CF_1 = -2,850$$
$$CF_2 = -40,440$$
$$CF_3 = +43,200$$

$$\frac{CF_0}{(1 + IRR)^0} + \frac{CF_1}{(1 + IRR)^1} + \frac{CF_2}{(1 + IRR)^2} + \frac{CF_3}{(1 + IRR)^3}$$
$$= \frac{-1,000}{1} + \frac{-2,850}{(1 + IRR)^1} + \frac{-40,440}{(1 + IRR)^2} + \frac{43,200}{(1 + IRR)^3} = 0$$

Solving for *IRR* results in a value of *IRR* = −2.22 percent.

Note that A and B are incorrect because the time-weighted rate of return (TWR) of the fund is the same as the geometric mean return of the fund and is positive:

$$R_{TW} = \sqrt[3]{(1.15)(1.14)(0.96)} - 1 = 7.97\%.$$

7. A is correct. Computation of the money-weighted return, r, requires finding the discount rate that sums the present value of cash flows to zero. Because most of the investment came during Year 2, the money-weighted return will be biased toward the performance of Year 2 when the return was lower. The cash flows are as follows:

$CF_0 = -10$

$CF_1 = -100$

$CF_2 = +120.31$

The terminal value is determined by summing the investment returns for each period $[(10 \times 1.14 \times 1.08) + (100 \times 1.08)]$.

$$\frac{CF_0}{(1 + IRR)^0} + \frac{CF_1}{(1 + IRR)^1} + \frac{CF_2}{(1 + IRR)^2}$$
$$\frac{-10}{1} + \frac{-100}{(1 + IRR)^1} + \frac{120.31}{(1 + IRR)^2} = 0$$

This results in a value of $IRR = 8.53$ percent.

The time-weighted return of the fund is calculated as follows:

$$R_{TW} = \sqrt[2]{(1.14)(1.08)} - 1 = 10.96\%.$$

8. B is correct. The annualized rate of return for

ETF 1 annualized return = $(1.0425^{365/125}) - 1 = 12.92\%$

ETF 2 annualized return = $(1.0195^{52/8}) - 1 = 13.37\%$

ETF 3 annualized return = $(1.1718^{12/16}) - 1 = 12.63\%$

Despite having the lowest value for the periodic rate, ETF 2 has the highest annualized rate of return because of the reinvestment rate assumption and the compounding of the periodic rate.

9. A is correct. The continuously compounded return from $t = 0$ to $t = 1$ is $r_{0,1} = \ln(S_1/S_0) = \ln(186.75/208.25) = -0.10897 = -10.90\%$.

10. A is correct.

$$R_L = R_p + \frac{V_B}{V_E}(R_p - r_D)$$

$$= 10\% + \frac{USD5\ million}{USD20\ million}(10\% - 6\%)$$

$$= 10\% + 0.25 \times 4\% = 11.0\%.$$

11. C is correct. Gross returns are calculated on a pre-tax basis; trading expenses *are* accounted for in the computation of gross returns as they contribute directly to the returns earned by the manager. A is incorrect because investment managers' gross returns are pre-tax and not adjusted for risk. B is incorrect because managers' gross returns do reflect the deduction of trading expenses since they contribute directly to the return earned by the manager.

12. C is correct. The use of leverage can increase an investor's return if the total investment return earned on the leveraged investment exceeds the borrowing cost on debt. A is incorrect because leverage amplifies both gains and losses. B is incorrect because, if half of the invested capital is borrowed, then the investor's gross (not net) return would double.

13. C is correct. The first step is to compute the investor's net return from the hedge fund investment. The net return is the fund's gross return less managerial and administrative expenses of 1.60 percent, or 8.46% − 1.60% = 6.86%. Note that trading expenses are already reflected in the gross return, so they are not subtracted.

The second step is to compute the investor's leveraged return (the investor borrowed EUR2,500 (25 percent) of the purchase), calculated as: follows

$$R_L = R_p + \frac{V_B}{V_E}(R_p - r_D)$$

$$R_L = 6.86\% + \frac{EUR2,500}{EUR7,500}(6.86\% - 6\%)$$

$$R_L = 6.86\% + 0.33 \times 0.86\% = 7.15\%.$$

The final step is to compute the after-tax return:
After-tax return = 7.15% (1 − 0.30) = 5.00%.

Time Value of Money in Finance

LEARNING OUTCOMES

Mastery	The candidate should be able to:
☐	calculate and interpret the present value (PV) of fixed-income and equity instruments based on expected future cash flows
☐	calculate and interpret the implied return of fixed-income instruments and required return and implied growth of equity instruments given the present value (PV) and cash flows
☐	explain the cash flow additivity principle, its importance for the no-arbitrage condition, and its use in calculating implied forward interest rates, forward exchange rates, and option values

INTRODUCTION

1

This learning module applies time value of money principles in valuing financial assets. The first lesson focuses on solving for the present value of expected future cash flows associated with bonds and stocks. In the second lesson, the focus shifts to solving for implied bond and stock returns given current prices. This includes solving for and interpreting implied growth rates associated with given stock prices. The final lesson introduces cash flow additivity, an important principle which ensures that financial asset prices do not allow investors to earn risk-free profits, illustrated with several examples. The material covered in this learning module provides an important foundation for candidates in understanding how financial assets are priced in markets.

LEARNING MODULE OVERVIEW

- The price of a bond is the sum of the present values of the bond's promised coupon payments and its par value. For discount bonds, the price reflects only the present value of the bond's par value.

- The value of a stock should reflect the sum of the present values of the stock's expected future dividends in perpetuity.

- Stock valuation models are classified by the expected growth pattern assumed for future dividends: (1) no growth, (2) constant growth, or (3) changing dividend growth.

> - If a bond's price is known, the bond's implied return can be computed using the bond's price and its promised future cash flows.
> - A stock's required return can be estimated given the stock's current price and assumptions about its expected future dividends and growth rates.
> - A stock's implied dividend growth rate can be estimated given the stock's current price and assumptions about its expected future dividends and required return.
> - If valuing two (or more) cash flow streams, the cash flow additivity principle allows for the cash flow streams to be compared (as long as the cash flows occur at the same point in time).
> - Application of cash flow additivity allows for confirmation that asset prices are the same for economically equivalent assets (even if the assets have differing cash flow streams).
> - Several real-world applications of cash flow additivity are used to illustrate no-arbitrage pricing.

2 TIME VALUE OF MONEY IN FIXED INCOME AND EQUITY

☐ | calculate and interpret the present value (PV) of fixed-income and equity instruments based on expected future cash flows

The timing of cash flows associated with financial instruments affects their value, with cash inflows valued more highly the sooner they are received. The time value of money represents the trade-off between cash flows received today versus those received on a future date, allowing the comparison of the current or present value of one or more cash flows to those received at different times in the future. This difference is based upon an appropriate discount rate r as shown in the prior learning module, which varies based upon the type of instrument and the timing and riskiness of expected cash flows.

In general, the relationship between a current or present value (PV) and future value (FV) of a cash flow, where r is the stated discount rate per period and t is the number of compounding periods, is as follows:

$$FV_t = PV(1 + r)^t. \tag{1}$$

If the number of compounding periods t is very large, that is, $t \rightarrow \infty$, we compound the initial cash flow on a continuous basis as follows:

$$FV_t = PVe^{r\,t}. \tag{2}$$

Conversely, present values can be expressed in future value terms, which requires recasting Equation 1 as follows:

$$FV_t = PV(1 + r)^t$$
$$PV = FV_t\left[\frac{1}{(1 + r)^t}\right]. \tag{3}$$
$$PV = FV_t(1 + r)^{-t}$$

The continuous time equivalent expression of Equation 3 is as follows:

$$PV_t = FVe^{-r\,t}. \tag{4}$$

Fixed-Income Instruments and the Time Value of Money

Fixed-income instruments are debt instruments, such as a bond or a loan, that represent contracts under which an issuer borrows money from an investor in exchange for a promise of future repayment. The discount rate for fixed-income instruments is an interest rate, and the rate of return on a bond or loan is often referred to as its yield-to-maturity (YTM).

Cash flows associated with fixed-income instruments usually follow one of three general patterns:

- Discount: An investor pays an initial price (PV) for a bond or loan and receives a single principal cash flow (FV) at maturity. The difference ($FV - PV$) represents the interest earned over the life of the instrument.

- Periodic Interest: An investor pays an initial price (PV) for a bond or loan and receives interest cash flows (PMT) at pre-determined intervals over the life of the instrument, with the final interest payment and the principal (FV) paid at maturity.

- Level Payments: An investor pays an initial price (PV) and receives uniform cash flows at pre-determined intervals (A) through maturity which represent both interest and principal repayment.

Discount Instruments

The discount cash flow pattern is shown in Exhibit 1:

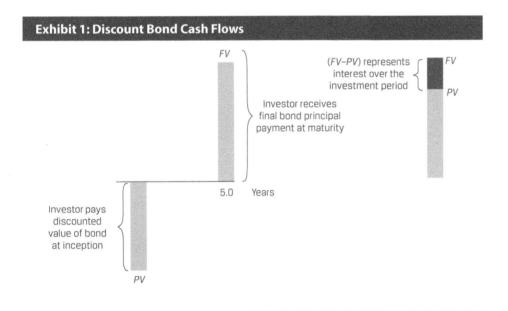

Exhibit 1: Discount Bond Cash Flows

FV

(FV–PV) represents interest over the investment period

FV

PV

Investor receives final bond principal payment at maturity

5.0   Years

Investor pays discounted value of bond at inception

PV

The present value (PV) calculation for a discount bond with principal (FV) paid at time t with a market discount rate of r per period is:

$$PV(\text{Discount Bond}) = FV_t \,/\, (1 + r)^t. \tag{5}$$

The investor's sole source of return is the difference between the price paid (*PV*) and full principal (*FV*) received at maturity. This type of bond is often referred to as a **zero-coupon bond** given the lack of intermediate interest cash flows, which for bonds are generally referred to as coupons.

EXAMPLE 1

Discount Bonds under Positive and Negative Interest Rates

While most governments issue fixed coupon bonds with principal paid at maturity, for many government issuers such as the United States, United Kingdom, or India, investors buy and sell individual interest or principal cash flows separated (or stripped) from these instruments as discount bonds. Consider a single principal cash flow payable in 20 years on a Republic of India government bond issued when the YTM is 6.70 percent. For purposes of this simplified example, we use annual compounding, that is, *t* in Equation 5 is equal to the number of years until the cash flow occurs.

---

1. What should an investor expect to pay for this discount bond per INR100 of principal?

   Solution:

   INR27.33

   We solve for *PV* given *r* of 6.70 percent, *t* = 20, and FV_{20} of INR100 using Equation 5:

   $$PV = INR100 \, / \, (1 + 0.067)^{20} = INR27.33.$$

   We may also use the Microsoft Excel or Google Sheets PV function:

   ```
   = PV (rate, nper, pmt, FV, type),
   ```

   where:

   rate = the market discount rate per period,

   nper = the number of periods,

   pmt = the periodic coupon payment (zero for a discount bond),

   FV = future or face value, and

   type = payments made at the end (0 as in this case) or beginning (1) of each period.

   As a cash outflow (or price paid), the Excel PV solution has a negative sign, so:

   $$PV = (27.33) = PV \ (0.067, 20, 0, 100, 0).$$

   While the principal (*FV*) is a constant INR100, the price (*PV*) changes as both time passes, and interest rates change.

---

2. If we assume that interest rates remain unchanged, what is the price (*PV*) of the bond in three years' time?

   Solution:

   INR33.21

Solve for *PV* by substituting $t = 17$ into the prior calculation using Equation 5:

$$PV = \text{INR}100 / (1 + 0.067)^{17} = \text{INR}33.21.$$

The INR5.88 price increase with a constant *r* represents implied interest earned over the three years. If the interest rate is positive, the *PV* generally rises (or accretes) over time to reach *FV* as time passes and *t* approaches zero.

3. Prices also change as interest rates change. Suppose after purchase at t = 0 we observe an immediate drop in the bond price to INR22.68224 per INR100 of principal. What is the implied interest rate on the discount bond?

   Solution:

   7.70 percent
   Here we may solve for *r* in Equation 5 as follows:

   $$\text{INR}22.68224 = \text{INR}100 / (1 + r)^{20}.$$

   Rearranging Equation 5, we get:

   $$r = 7.70 \text{ percent} = (100/22.68224)^{1/20} - 1.$$

   Alternatively, we may use the Microsoft Excel or Google Sheets RATE function:
   = RATE (nper, pmt, PV, FV, type, guess) using the same arguments as above, with *guess* as an optional estimate argument, which must be between 0 and 1 and defaults to 0.1, as follows:

   7.70 percent = RATE (20,0,-22.68224,100,0,0.1).

   This shows that a 100 basis point (1.00 percent) increase in *r* results in an INR4.65 price decrease, underscoring the inverse relationship between price and YTM.

4. Now consider a bond issued at negative interest rates. In July 2016, Germany became the first eurozone country to issue 10-year sovereign bonds at a negative yield. If the German government bond annual YTM was –0.05 percent when issued, calculate the present value (*PV*) of the bond per EUR100 of principal (*FV*) at the time of issuance.

   Solution:

   EUR100.50
   Solve for *PV* given *r* of –0.05 percent, $t = 10$, and FV_{10} of EUR100 using Equation 1:

   $$PV = \text{EUR}100.50 = \text{EUR}100 / (1 - 0.0005)^{10},$$

   or

   $$PV = (100.50) = \text{PV} (-0.0005,10,0,100,0).$$

   At issuance, this bond is priced at a **premium**, meaning that an investor purchasing the bond at issuance paid EUR0.50 above the future value expected at maturity, which is the principal.

5. Six years later, when German inflation reached highs not seen in decades and investors increased their required nominal rate of return, say we observed that the German government bond in question 4 is now trading at

a price (*PV*) of EUR95.72 per EUR100 principal. What is the YTM on this bond?

Solution:

1.10 percent

Use Equation 5 to solve for *r* given a *PV* of 95.72, *FV* of 100, and *t* = 4, we get:

EUR95.72 = EUR100 / $(1 + r)^4$; *r* = 1.10%,

or

1.10% = RATE (4,0,-95.72,100,0,0.1).

In the case of the Republic of India discount bond, a higher interest rate will reduce the bond's price. However, in contrast to the accreting price of a discount bond, the premium bond's price will decline (or amortize) over time to reach the EUR100 future value at maturity.

Coupon Instrument

A periodic cash flow pattern for fixed-income interest payments with principal repaid at maturity is shown in Exhibit 2. In this case, all the periodic cash flow payments are identical and occur on a semiannual basis.

Exhibit 2: Coupon Bond Cash Flows

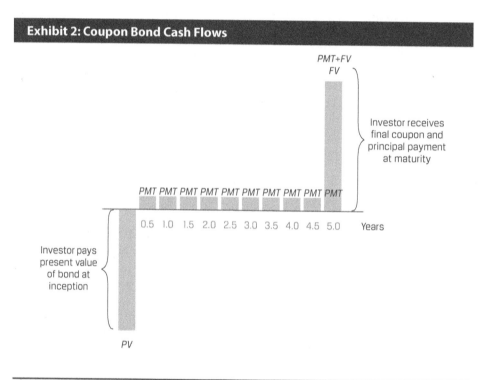

Pricing a coupon bond extends the single cash flow calculation for a discount bond to a general formula for calculating a bond's price (*PV*) given the market discount rate on a coupon date, as follows:

PV(Coupon Bond)

$$= PMT_1 / (1 + r)^1 + PMT_2 / (1 + r)^2 + \ldots + (PMT_N + FV_N) / (1 + r)^N. \tag{6}$$

EXAMPLE 2

Hellenic Republic of Greece Annual Coupon Bond

At the height of the COVID pandemic, the government of Greece issued a 2 percent annual coupon bond maturing in seven years.

1. If the observed YTM at issuance was 2.00 percent, what was the issuance price (PV) per EUR100 of principal?

   Solution:

   EUR100
   Solve for PV using Equation 6 with PMT_i = EUR2, r = 2.00%, and FV = EUR100:

   $$PV = \text{EUR}100$$

   $$= \frac{2}{1.02} + \frac{2}{1.02^2} + \frac{2}{1.02^3} + \frac{2}{1.02^4} + \frac{2}{1.02^5} + \frac{2}{1.02^6} + \frac{2}{1.02^7}.$$

   We may solve this using the Microsoft Excel or Google Sheets PV function introduced earlier (PV (0.02,7,2,100,0)). The issuance price equals the principal ($PV = FV$). This relationship holds on a coupon date for any bond where the fixed periodic coupon is equal to the discount rate.
   The present value of each cash flow may be solved using Equation 5. For example, the final EUR102 interest and principal cash flow in seven years is:

   $$PV = \text{EUR}88.80 = \text{EUR}102/(1.02)^7.$$

   The following table shows the present value of all bond cash flows:

Years/Periods	0	1	2	3	4	5	6	7
FV		2	2	2	2	2	2	102
PV	100.00	1.96	1.92	1.88	1.85	1.81	1.78	88.80

2. Next, let's assume that, exactly one year later, a sharp rise in Eurozone inflation drove the Greek bond's price lower to EUR93.091 (per EUR100 of principal). What would be the implied YTM expected by investors under these new market conditions?

   Solution:

   3.532 percent
   In this case, we must solve for r using Equation 6, with PV equal to 93.091, as follows:

   $$PV = 93.091 = 2/(1+r) + 2/(1+r)^2 + 2/(1+r)^3 + 2/(1+r)^4 + 102/(1+r)^5.$$

   Here we may use the Microsoft Excel or Google Sheets RATE function (RATE (5,2,93.091,100,0,0.1)) to solve for r of 3.532 percent. Investors in fixed coupon bonds face a capital loss when investors expect a higher YTM.

The interest rate r used to discount all cash flows in Equation 6 is the bond's YTM, which is typically quoted on an annual basis. However, many bonds issued by public or private borrowers pay interest on a semiannual basis. In Example 3, we revisit the Republic of India bond from which a single cash flow was stripped in an earlier simplified example.

EXAMPLE 3

Republic of India Semiannual Coupon Bond

Consider the 20-year Republic of India government bond from which the discount bond in Example 1 was separated (or stripped). The bond was issued at an annualized coupon rate of 6.70 percent and a YTM of 6.70 percent, and the coupon payments are semiannual.

---

1. Solve for the price of the bond at issuance.

   Solution:

   INR100

   As coupon periods are semiannual, for a principal of INR100, $PMT =$ INR3.35 (=6.70/2) and the periodic discount rate is 3.35 percent (=6.70 percent/2), as follows:

   $$PV = 3.35/(1.0335) + 3.35/(1.0335)^2 + \dots + 3.35/(1.0335)^{39} + 103.35/(1.0335)^{40}.$$

   As shown in Example 2, because *the coupon rate is equal to the YTM,* we expect this bond to have a *PV* of INR100 at issuance.

---

2. What is the bond's price if the YTM immediately rises to 7.70 percent?

   Solution:

   INR89.88

   We can solve for the *PV* as INR89.88 using Equation 6 with $r = 3.85\%$ (=7.70/2) or using the Microsoft Excel or Google Sheets PV function (PV (0.0385,40,3.35,100,0)). The first and final three cash flows are shown below:

	Years	0	0.5	1	1.5	19	19.5	20
r	Periods	0	1	2	3	38	39	40
	FV		3.35	3.35	3.35	3.35	3.35	103.35
6.70%	PV	100.00	3.24	3.14	3.03	0.96	0.93	27.66
7.70%	PV	89.88	3.23	3.11	2.99	0.80	0.77	22.81

---

3. Recalculate the discount bond price for the final principal payment in 20 years from Example 1 using a 6.70 percent semiannual discount rate.

   Solution:

   INR26.77

   Note that the PV calculation using the same annual discount rate for 40 semiannual periods will differ slightly using Equation 5, as follows:

   $$PV = \text{INR}27.66 = (PMT_{40} + FV_{40})/(1+r/2)^{40},$$

   $$PV(PMT_{40}) = \text{INR}0.90 = 3.35 / (1.0335)^{40},$$

   $$PV(FV_{40}) = \text{INR}26.77 = 100 / (1.0335)^{40}.$$

   Compounding on a semiannual basis for 40 periods, $PV(FV_{40})$ of 26.77 is less than the original PV of 27.33 using 20 annual periods from Example 1 (since $1/(1+r)^t > 1/(1+r/2)^{2t}$ when $r \geq 0$).

A **perpetual bond** is a less common type of coupon bond with no stated maturity date. Most perpetual bonds are issued by companies to obtain equity-like financing and often include redemption features. As $N \rightarrow \infty$ in Equation 6, we can simplify this to solve for the present value of a **perpetuity** (or perpetual fixed periodic cash flow without early redemption), where $r > 0$, as follows:

$$PV(\text{Perpetual Bond}) = PMT / r. \tag{7}$$

EXAMPLE 4

KB Financial Perpetual Bond

In 2020, KB Financial (the holding company for Kookmin Bank) issued KRW325 billion in perpetual bonds with a 3.30 percent quarterly coupon.

1. Calculate the bond's YTM if the market price was KRW97.03 (per KRW100).

   Solution:

   3.40 percent
   Solve for r in Equation 7 given a PV of KRW97.03 and a periodic quarterly coupon (PMT) of KRW0.825 (= (3.30% × KRW100)/4):

   KRW97.03 = KRW0.825 / r ;

   r = 0.85% per period, or 3.40% (=0.85% × 4) on an annualized basis.

Annuity Instruments

Examples of fixed-income instruments with level payments, which combine interest and principal cash flows through maturity, include fully amortizing loans such as mortgages and a fixed-income stream of periodic cash inflows over a finite period known as an annuity. Exhibit 3 illustrates an example of level monthly cash flows based upon a mortgage.

Exhibit 3: Mortgage Cash Flows

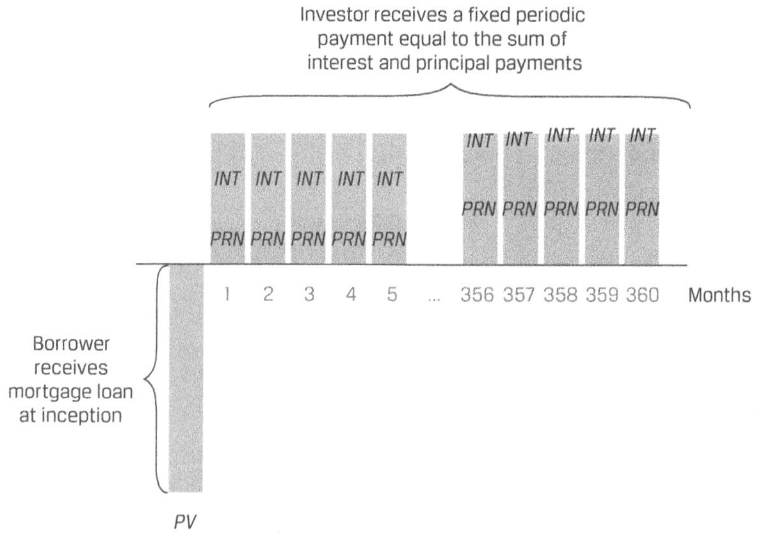

We may calculate the periodic annuity cash flow (A), which occurs at the end of each respective period, as follows:

$$A = \frac{r(PV)}{1 - (1 + r)^{-t}},$$ (8)

where:

     A = periodic cash flow,

     r = market interest rate per period,

   PV = present value or principal amount of loan or bond, and

     t = number of payment periods.

EXAMPLE 5

Mortgage Cash Flows

An investor seeks a fixed-rate 30-year mortgage loan to finance 80 percent of the purchase price of USD1,000,000 for a residential building.

1. Calculate the investor's monthly payment if the annual mortgage rate is 5.25 percent.

   Solution:

   Solve for A using Equation 8 with r = 0.4375% (= 5.25%/12), t of 360, and PV of USD800,000 (=80% × USD1,000,000):

   $$A = USD4,417.63 = \frac{0.4375\% \, (USD800,000)}{1 - (1 + 0.4375\%)^{-360}}.$$

   The 360 level monthly payments consist of both principal and interest.

2. What is the principal amortization and interest breakdown of the first two monthly cash flows?

   Solution:

   Month 1 interest is USD3,500 and principal is USD917.63
   Month 2 interest is USD3,495.99 and principal is USD921.64

       Month 1:

          Interest: USD3,500 = USD800,000 × 0.4375% (=$PV_0 \times r$)

          Principal Amortization: USD4,417.63 – USD3,500 = USD917.63

          Remaining Principal (PV_1): USD799,082.37 = USD800,000 – USD917.63

       Month 2:

          Interest: USD3,495.99 = USD799,082.37 × 0.4375% (=$PV_1 \times r$)

          Principal Amortization: USD4,417.63 – USD3,495.99 = USD921.64

          Remaining Principal (PV_2): USD798,160.73 = USD799,082.37 – USD921.64

   Although the periodic mortgage payment is constant, the proportion of interest per payment declines while the principal amortization rises over time. The following spreadsheet shows the first and final three monthly cash flows.

Month	Total Monthly Payment	Monthly Interest Payment	Monthly Principal Repayment	Remaining Principal
1	$ 4,417.63	$ 3,500.00	$ 917.63	$ 799,082.37
2	$ 4,417.63	$ 3,495.99	$ 921.64	$ 798,160.73
3	$ 4,417.63	$ 3,491.95	$ 925.68	$ 797,235.05
...				
358	$ 4,417.63	$ 57.48	$ 4,360.15	$ 8,777.61
359	$ 4,417.63	$ 38.40	$ 4,379.23	$ 4,398.39
360	$ 4,417.63	$ 19.24	$ 4,398.39	$ 0.00

Equity Instruments and the Time Value of Money

Equity investments, such as preferred or common stock, represent ownership shares in a company which entitle investors to receive any discretionary cash flows in the form of dividends. Unlike fixed-income instruments, equity investments have no maturity date and are assumed to remain outstanding indefinitely, or until a company is sold, restructured, or liquidated. One way to value a company's shares is by discounting expected future cash flows using an expected rate of return (r). These cash flows include any periodic dividends received plus the expected price received at the end of an investment horizon.

Common assumptions associated with valuing equity instruments based upon dividend cash flows often follow one of three general approaches:

- Constant Dividends: An investor pays an initial price (PV) for a preferred or common share of stock and receives a fixed periodic dividend (D).

- Constant Dividend Growth Rate: An investor pays an initial price (PV) for a share of stock and receives an initial dividend in one period (D_{t+1}), which is expected to grow over time at a constant rate of g.

- Changing Dividend Growth Rate: An investor pays an initial price (PV) for a share of stock and receives an initial dividend in one period (D_{t+1}). The dividend is expected to grow at a rate that changes over time as a company moves from an initial period of high growth to slower growth as it reaches maturity.

The simplest case of a stock that is assumed to pay constant dividends in perpetuity is shown in Exhibit 4.

Exhibit 4: Equity Cash Flows with Constant Dividends

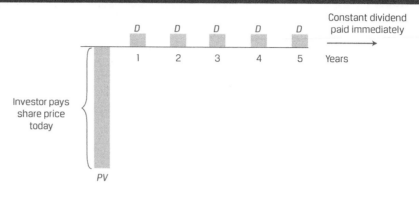

The price of a preferred or common share expected to pay a constant periodic dividend is an infinite series that simplifies to the formula for the present value of a perpetuity shown and is similar to the valuation of a perpetual bond that we encountered earlier. Specifically, the valuation in Equation 7:

$$PV_t = \sum_{i=1}^{\infty} \frac{D_t}{(1 + r)^i}, \text{ and} \tag{9}$$

$$PV_t = \frac{D_t}{r}. \tag{10}$$

EXAMPLE 6

Constant Dividend Cash Flows

Shipline PLC is a company that pays regular dividends of GBP1.50 per year, which are expected to continue indefinitely.

1. What is Shipline's expected stock price if shareholders' required rate of return is 15 percent?

   Solution:

   GBP10

   Solve for *PV* using Equation 10, where *D* is GBP1.50 and the rate of return per period *r* is 15 percent:

   $PV = $ GBP10.00 $=$ GBP1.50/0.15.

Alternatively, a common equity forecasting approach is to assume a constant dividend growth rate (*g*) into perpetuity, as illustrated in Exhibit 5.

Exhibit 5: Equity Cash Flows with Constant Dividend Growth

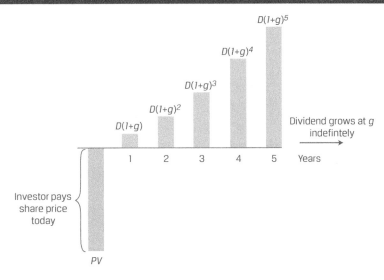

If dividends grow at a rate of g per period and are paid at the end of each period, the next dividend (at time $t + 1$) may be shown as follows:

$$D_{t+1} = D_t(1 + g),$$ (11)

or generally in i periods as:

$$D_{t+i} = D_t(1 + g)^i.$$ (12)

If dividend cash flows continue to grow at g indefinitely, then we may rewrite Equation 10 as follows:

$$PV_t = \sum_{i=1}^{\infty} \frac{D_t(1+g)^i}{(1+r)^i},$$ (13)

which simplifies to:

$$PV_t = \frac{D_t(1+g)}{r-g} = \frac{D_{t+1}}{r-g},$$ (14)

where $r - g > 0$.

An alternative to constant dividend growth is an assumption of changing growth. This is common for evaluating the share price of firms expected to experience an initial rapid rise in cash flow, followed by slower growth as a company matures. The simplest form of changing dividend growth is the two-stage model shown in Exhibit 6.

Exhibit 6: Equity Cash Flows with Two-Stage Dividend Growth

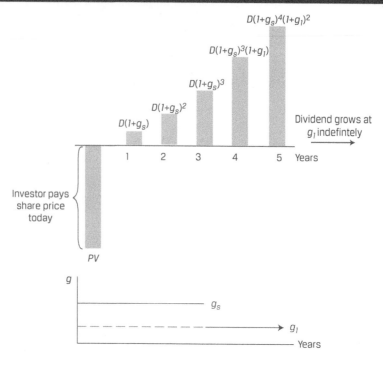

The example in Exhibit 6 shows a company with an initial higher short-term dividend growth of g_s for the first three years, followed by lower long-term growth (g_l, where $g_s > g_l$) indefinitely thereafter. If we generalize the initial growth phase to n periods followed by indefinite slower growth at g_l, we obtain a modified version of Equation 14 as follows:

$$PV_t = \sum_{i=1}^{n} \frac{D_t(1 + g_s)^i}{(1 + r)^i} + \sum_{j=n+1}^{\infty} \frac{D_{t+n}(1 + g_l)^j}{(1 + r)^j}. \tag{15}$$

Note that the second expression in Equation 15 involves constant growth starting in n periods, for which we can substitute the geometric series simplification:

$$PV_t = \sum_{i=1}^{n} \frac{D_t(1 + g_s)^i}{(1 + r)^i} + \frac{E(S_{t+n})}{(1 + r)^n}, \tag{16}$$

where the stock value of the stock in n periods ($E(S_{t+n})$ is referred to as the **terminal value**) and is equal to the following:

$$E(S_{t+n}) = \frac{D_{t+n+1}}{r - g_l}. \tag{17}$$

We revisit the Shipline PLC stock price example to evaluate the effects of constant dividend, constant dividend growth and changing dividend growth assumptions on a company's expected share price.

EXAMPLE 7

Constant and Changing Dividend Growth

Recall that based on a constant GBP1.50 annual dividend and required return of 15 percent, we showed Shipline PLC's expected stock price to be GBP10.00. Suppose instead that an investment analyst assumes that Shipline will grow its annual dividend by 6 percent per year indefinitely.

1. How does Shipline's expected share price change under the analyst's constant growth assumption?

   Solution:

   GBP17.67

   Using Equation 14, solve for PV using D_{t+1} of GBP1.59 (=GBP1.50 × (1 + 0.06)), r of 15%, and g of 6%:

   $$PV = \text{GBP}1.59 / (15\% - 6\%) = \text{GBP}17.67.$$

   Note that a higher growth rate g increases the PV by reducing the denominator $(r - g)$.

2. How does Shipline's expected share price change if we assume instead an initial dividend growth of 6 percent over a three-year period followed by constant 2 percent dividend growth thereafter?

   Solution:

   GBP13.05

   We may solve for Shipline's expected share price (PV) using Equations 15–17 and $D_t = 1.5$, $g_s = 6\%$, $n = 3$, r = 15%, and $g_l = 2\%$, as follows:

   $$PV_t = \sum_{i=1}^{3} \frac{1.50(1 + 0.06)^i}{(1 + 0.15)^i} + \sum_{j=4}^{\infty} \frac{D_{t+3}(1 + 0.02)^j}{(1 + 0.15)^j}.$$

   As a first step, we calculate the present value of dividends associated with the higher 6 percent growth rate over the first three years as shown in the first expression. As a second step, we calculate the present value of future dividends at a lower 2 percent growth rate for an indefinite period. The sum of these two steps is the expected share price.

   Step 1   Solve for the first step as GBP3.832 with dividend cash flows for the initial growth period as shown in the following spreadsheet:

t	D	PV(D) at r%
0	1.500	
1	1.590	1.383
2	1.685	1.274
3	1.787	1.175
PV(ST growth)		3.832

   Step 2   As shown in Equation 17, the second expression simplifies as follows:

   $$\frac{E(S_4)}{(1 + r)^3}; \text{ with } E(S_4) = \frac{D_4}{r - g_l}.$$

   We may solve for D_4 as GBP1.894 (=1.787 × 1.02 = $D_3(1 + g_l)$) and the second expression to be GBP9.22 as follows:

   $$\text{GBP}9.22 = \frac{1.894 \big/ (0.15 - 0.02)}{(1.15)^3}.$$

   Step 3   The sum of these two steps gives us an expected Shipline share price of GBP13.05 (=3.83 + 9.22).

   In the following table, we show the sensitivity of Shipline's expected share price (PV) to changes in the long-term growth rate (g_l) after three years of 6 percent dividend growth:

Share Price	LT Growth Rate
11.66	0%
13.05	2%
14.94	4%
17.67	6%

3   IMPLIED RETURN AND GROWTH

☐   calculate and interpret the implied return of fixed-income instruments and required return and implied growth of equity instruments given the present value (PV) and cash flows

Lesson 1 addressed the time value of money trade-off between cash flows occurring today versus those in the future for certain fixed income and equity instruments. Market participants often face a situation in which both the present and future values of instruments or cash flows may be known. In this case it becomes possible to solve for the implied return or growth rate implied by the current price and features of the future cash flows. In this sense, solving for the implied growth or return provides a view of the market expectations that are incorporated into the market price of the asset.

Implied Return for Fixed-Income Instruments

Fixed-income instruments are characterized by contractual interest and principal cash flows. If we observe the present value (or price) and assume that all future cash flows occur as promised, then the discount rate (r) or yield-to-maturity (YTM) is a measure of implied return under these assumptions for the cash flow pattern.

In the case of a discount bond or instrument, recall that an investor receives a single principal cash flow (FV) at maturity, with ($FV - PV$) representing the implied return, as shown in Exhibit 7.

Exhibit 7: Discount Bond Implied Return

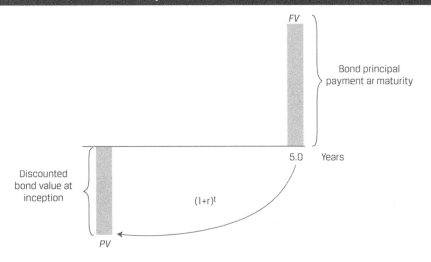

We may rearrange Equation 5 from to solve for the implied periodic return earned over the life of the instrument (t periods):

$$r = \sqrt[t]{\frac{FV_t}{PV}} - 1 = \left(\frac{FV_t}{PV}\right)^{\frac{1}{t}} - 1. \tag{18}$$

EXAMPLE 8

Discount Bond Implied Return

Recall from Example 1 that in 2016, German 10-year government bond investors faced a price of EUR100.50 per EUR100 principal and an annual YTM of −0.05 percent at issuance. That is, the German 10-year government bond was initially priced by the market to provide a negative return to the investor. Six years later, these bonds traded at a price (PV) of EUR95.72 per EUR100 principal.

1. What was the initial investor's implied return on this bond over the six-year holding period?

   Solution:

   −0.81 percent
   We can solve for an investor's annualized return (r) using Equation 18 and a PV of 100.5, FV of 95.72, and t of 6 as follows:

   $$r = -0.81\% = \left(\frac{95.72}{100.5}\right)^{\frac{1}{6}} - 1.$$

   Note that an investor who purchases the discount bond at issuance and receives EUR100 in 10 years expects an implied return equal to the issuance YTM of −0.05 percent. However, the EUR4.78 price decline for the first six years translates into an annualized return of −0.81 percent, which is below the initial YTM of −0.05 percent. This negative return is consistent with an expected decline in the price (PV) of a discount bond amid higher inflation.

2. What is the expected return of an investor who purchases the discount bond at EUR95.72 and holds it for the remaining four years?

   Solution:

   1.10 percent

   Here the current price of 95.72 in Equation 18 is now the PV, and the principal of 100 is FV, with $t = 4$:

   $$r = 1.10\% = \left(\frac{100}{95.72}\right)^{\frac{1}{4}} - 1.$$

   Note that r of 1.10 percent is equal to the YTM for the remaining four years we derived in Example 1. The cumulative returns across the two investors is equal to the initial –0.05 percent YTM, assuming no transaction costs as follows:

   $$-0.05\% = [(1 - 0.0081)^6 \times (1 + 0.011)^4]^{\frac{1}{10}} - 1.$$

   These relationships are summarized in the following diagram:

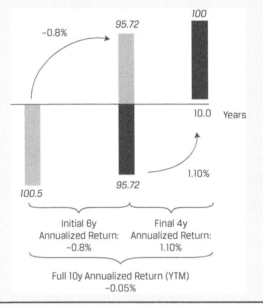

Unlike discount bonds, fixed-income instruments that pay periodic interest have cash flows throughout their life until maturity. The uniform discount rate (or internal rate of return) for all promised cash flows is the YTM, a single implied market discount rate for all cash flows regardless of timing as shown for a coupon bond in Exhibit 8.

Exhibit 8: Coupon Bond Implied Return

The YTM assumes an investor expects to receive all promised cash flows through maturity and reinvest any cash received at the same YTM. For coupon bonds, this involves periodic interest payments only, while for level payment instruments such as mortgages, the calculation assumes both interest and amortized principal may be invested at the same rate. Like other internal rates of return, the YTM cannot be solved using an equation, but it may be calculated using iteration with a spreadsheet or calculator, a process that solves for r in Equation 19, as follows:

$$PV(Coupon\ Bond)$$
$$= PMT_1 / (1 + r)^1 + PMT_2 / (1 + r)^2 + \ldots + (PMT_N + FV_N) / (1 + r)^N, \qquad (19)$$

where FV equals a bond's principal and N is the number of periods to maturity.

The Microsoft Excel or Google Sheets YIELD function can be used to calculate YTM for fixed-income instruments with periodic interest and full principal payment at maturity:

```
= YIELD (settlement, maturity, rate, pr, redemption,
frequency, [basis])
```

where:

settlement = settlement date entered using the DATE function;

maturity = maturity date entered using the DATE function;

rate = semi-annual (or periodic) coupon;

pr = price per 100 face value;

redemption = future value at maturity;

frequency = number of coupons per year; and

[basis] = day count convention, typically 0 for US bonds (30/360 day count).

Example 9 illustrates the implied return on fixed income instruments with periodic interest.

EXAMPLE 9

Greek Coupon Bond Implied Return

Recall from Example 2 that seven-year Greek government bonds issued in 2020 with a 2.00 percent annual coupon had a price of EUR93.091 per EUR100 principal two years later.

1. What is the implied two-year return for an investor able to reinvest periodic interest at the original YTM of 2.00 percent?

   Solution:

   −1.445 percent

   Using Equation 18 as for the discount bond, we must first calculate the future value (FV) after two years including the future price of 93.091 and all cash flows reinvested to that date:

   $$FV_2 = PMT_1(1 + r) + PMT_2 + PV_2$$

   $$FV_2 = 97.13 = 2 \times (1.02) + 2 + 93.091$$

   $$r = -1.445\% = \left(\frac{97.13}{100}\right)^{\frac{1}{2}} - 1.$$

   This negative annualized return was due to a EUR6.91 (=100 − 93.091) capital loss which exceeded the periodic interest plus reinvestment proceeds of EUR4.04 (=2 × (1.02) + 2). The fall in the price of the bond to EUR93.091 in 2022 was a result of a rise in Eurozone inflation over the period.

   For an investor purchasing the 2 percent coupon bond in 2022 at a price of EUR93.091, recall that we solved for an r (or YTM) of 3.532 percent. Note that this YTM calculation for the remaining five years assumes all cash flows can be reinvested at 3.532 percent through maturity. The rate(s) at which periodic interest can be reinvested is critical for the implied return calculation for coupon bonds as shown below. YTM is computed assuming that the bond is held to maturity.

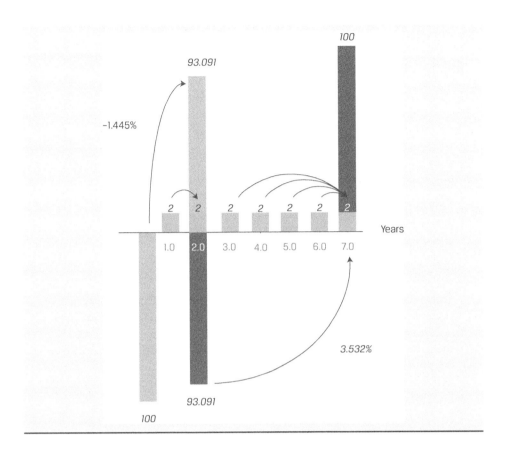

Equity Instruments, Implied Return, and Implied Growth

As noted in the discussion of calculating the present value of an equity investment, the price of a share of stock reflects not only the required return but also the growth of cash flows. If we begin with an assumption of constant growth of dividends from Equation 14, we can rearrange the formula as follows:

$$r - g = \frac{D_t(1 + g)}{PV_t} = \frac{D_{t+1}}{PV_t}. \tag{20}$$

The left-hand side of Equation 20 simply reflects the difference between the required return and the constant growth rate, and the right-hand side is the dividend yield of the stock based on expected dividends over the next period. Thus, the implied return on a stock given its expected dividend yield and growth is given by Equation 21, as follows:

$$r = \frac{D_t(1 + g)}{PV_t} + g = \frac{D_{t+1}}{PV_t} + g. \tag{21}$$

Simply put, if we assume that a stock's dividend grows at a constant rate in perpetuity, the stock's implied return is equal to its expected dividend yield plus the constant growth rate.

Alternatively, we may be interested in solving for a stock's implied growth rate, and this relation is given by Equation 22:

$$g = \frac{r * PV_t - D_t}{PV_t + D_t} = r - \frac{D_{t+1}}{PV_t}. \tag{22}$$

If a stock's next expected dividend is known, then we can calculate the implied growth by deducting its expected dividend yield from its required return.

EXAMPLE 10

Implied Return and Growth for a Stock

Coca-Cola Company stock trades at a share price of USD63.00 and its annualized expected dividend per share during the next year is USD1.76.

1. If an analyst expects Coca-Cola's dividend per share to increase at a constant 4 percent per year indefinitely, calculate the required return expected by investors.

   Solution:

   6.79 percent
   Using Equation 21,

   $$r = \frac{1.76}{63} + 0.04 = 0.0679.$$

   The required return expected for Coca-Cola stock is 6.79 percent given its current price, expected dividend, and expected dividend growth rate. Investor expectations of future stock returns are inferred by the combination of the current price, expected future cash flows and the cash flow growth rate. Suppose that, instead of attempting to estimate the required return, an investor wishes to determine an implied dividend growth rate. In this case, the investor must assume a future stock return, as in question 2.

2. If the analyst believes that Coca-Cola stock investors should expect a return of 7 percent, calculate the implied dividend growth rate for Coca-Cola.

   Solution:

   4.21 percent
   Using Equation 22,

   $$g = 0.07 - \frac{1.76}{63} = 0.0421.$$

   The implied dividend growth rate for Coca-Cola stock is 4.21 percent given its expected return, price, and expected dividend. Given that a higher expected return is assumed in this question compared to the case in question 1, the result is a higher implied dividend growth rate to justify Coca-Cola's stock price of USD63.00.

Rather than comparing equity share prices directly in currency terms, a common practice is to compare ratios of share price to earnings per share, or the **price-to-earnings ratio**.

PRICE-TO-EARNINGS RATIO

Price-to-earnings ratio is a relative valuation metric that improves comparability by controlling for a known driver of value (earnings per share) as well as currency. It is analogous to expressing the price of real estate using a price per square meter.

A stock trading at a price-to-earnings ratio of 20 implies that its share price is 20 times its earnings per share and investors are willing to pay 20 times earnings per share for each share traded, which is more expensive than a stock trading at a price to earnings ratio of 10.

Price-to-earnings ratios not only are used for individual stocks but also are a valuation metric for stock indexes, such S&P 500, FTSE 100, or Nikkei 225. Here, the stock index value is divided by a weighted sum of the index constituents' earnings per share. This will be explored in depth later in the curriculum, but we can relate the price-to-earnings ratio to our earlier discussion of relating a stock's price (PV) to expected future cash flows to make some useful observations. First, recall Equation 14:

$$PV_t = \frac{D_t(1+g)}{r-g}.$$

We can divide both sides by E_t, earnings per share for period t, to obtain:

$$\frac{PV_t}{E_t} = \frac{\frac{D_t}{E_t} \times (1+g)}{r-g}. \tag{23}$$

The left-hand side of Equation 23 is the price-to-earnings ratio, whereas the first term in the numerator on the right is the proportion of earnings distributed to shareholders as dividends known as the **dividend payout ratio**.

Given a price-to-earnings ratio and dividend payout ratio, we can solve for either required return or implied dividend growth rate (given an assumption about the other). The required return is useful in understanding investor return expectations on a forward-looking basis. The implied constant growth rate is useful to compare with the company's expected growth rate and historical growth rate. For example, if the implied constant growth rate is 10 percent yet the analyst estimates that the company can only grow by 5 percent, the analyst may judge the shares to be overvalued.

In practice, the **forward price-to-earnings ratio** or ratio of its share price to an estimate of its next period (t + 1) earnings per share is commonly used. With it, we can simplify the previous equation as follows:

$$\frac{PV_t}{E_{t+1}} = \frac{\frac{D_{t+1}}{E_{t+1}}}{r-g}. \tag{24}$$

From Equation 24, we can see that forward price-to-earnings ratio is positively related to higher expected dividend payout ratio and higher expected growth but is negatively related to the required return.

EXAMPLE 11

Implied Return and Growth from Price to Earnings Ratio

1. Suppose Coca-Cola stock trades at a forward price to earnings ratio of 28, its expected dividend payout ratio is 70 percent, and analysts believe that its dividend will grow at a constant rate of 4 percent per year. Calculate Coca-Cola's required return.

   Solution:

   6.50 percent
   Using Equation 24,

   $$28 = \frac{0.7}{r - 0.04}.$$

   Solving this equation for r, Coca-Cola's required return is 6.50 percent. Given the above result for Coca-Cola's required return, it should come as no surprise that if we instead assume that the required return on Coca-Cola stock is 6.50 percent, then we would find that Coca-Cola's implied growth rate is 4 percent, and this result is confirmed in question 2.

2. Suppose Coca-Cola stock trades at a forward price to earnings ratio of 28, its expected dividend payout ratio is 70 percent, and analysts believe that its required return is 6.50 percent. Calculate Coca-Cola's implied growth rate.

Solution:

4.00 percent
Using Equation 24,

$$28 = \frac{0.70}{0.065 - g}.$$

Solving this equation for g, Coca-Cola's implied growth rate is 4.00 percent. In particular, Coca-Cola's return is expected to be 2.5 percent greater than its dividend growth rate (i.e., 6.50% − 4.00%).

As discussed earlier, the same principles apply to understanding required returns and growth rates on stock indexes.

3. A stock index is trading at a forward price to earnings ratio of 19. If the expected dividend payout ratio on the index is 60 percent, and equity investors expect an index rate of return of 8 percent, calculate the implied constant growth rate for the index.

Solution:

4.84 percent
Using Equation 24:

$$19 = \frac{0.60}{0.08 - g}.$$

Solving for g, we find that investors expect the index's dividend growth rate to be 4.84 percent in the future. Alternatively, we could assume that investors expect a 4.84 percent growth rate and solve for r to calculate 8 percent as the required return. Thus, the index forward price-to-earnings ratio of 19 and an expected dividend payout ratio of 60 percent combine to reflect expectations of 8 percent return and 4.84 percent growth. Specifically, the required return exceeds the implied dividend growth rate by 3.16 percent (i.e., 8% − 4.84%).

An important point from the prior results is that equity prices, whether expressed simply as price or as a price-to-earnings ratio, reflect combined expectations about future returns and growth. Expectations of returns and growth are linked together by the difference between r and g. For example, the Coca-Cola example using a price-to-earnings ratio of 28 describes a situation in which investors must believe that the required return on Coca-Cola stock is 2.5 percent above its growth rate.

4. Suppose Coca-Cola stock trades at a forward price to earnings ratio of 28 and its expected dividend payout ratio is 70 percent. Analysts believe that Coca-Cola stock should earn a 9 percent return and that its dividends will grow by 4.50 percent per year indefinitely. Recommend a course of action for an investor interested in taking a position in Coca-Cola stock.

Solution:

Take a short position in Coca-Cola stock.
If we evaluate the above parameters using Equation 24, we can see that this results in an inequality.

$$28 > \frac{0.70}{0.09 - 0.045} = 15.56.$$

Coca-Cola's forward price-to-earnings ratio of 28 is much greater than 15.56, which is computed from the equation. Investor expectations of cash flow growth and return are inconsistent with Coca-Cola's forward price to earnings ratio. Specifically, an investor should consider a short position in Coca-Cola stock in the belief that its price should decline because its current price to earnings ratio is well above what its fundamentals imply. As shown in results for questions 1 and 2 in this example, expectations for the required return and growth rate must be such that $r - g = 2.50\%$ to justify a forward price-to-earnings ratio of 28 given the expected dividend payout ratio of 70 percent.

CASH FLOW ADDITIVITY

4

☐ explain the cash flow additivity principle, its importance for the no-arbitrage condition, and its use in calculating implied forward interest rates, forward exchange rates, and option values

The time value of money trade-off between cash flows occurring today versus those in the future may be extended beyond pricing future cash flows today or calculating the implied return on a single instrument using the **cash flow additivity principle**. Under cash flow additivity, the present value of any future cash flow stream indexed at the same point equals the sum of the present values of the cash flows. This principle is important in ensuring that market prices reflect the condition of no arbitrage, or that no possibility exists to earn a riskless profit in the absence of transaction costs.

Let's begin with a basic example to demonstrate the cash flow additivity principle.

EXAMPLE 12

Basic Cash Flow Additivity

Let's assume that you have GBP100 to invest, and have two strategies from which to choose with the following cash flow streams as shown in Exhibit 9.

Exhibit 9: Two Investment Strategies

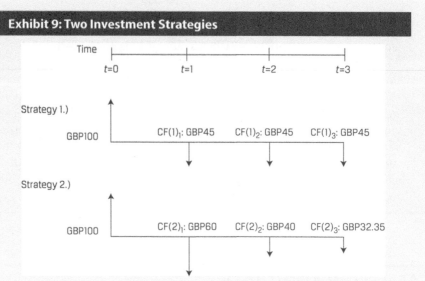

Your required return for both investment strategies is 10 percent per time period.

1. Recommend which investment strategy to choose.

   Solution:

   To make a recommendation between these two strategies, we need to establish which one has the higher present value as well as whether either has a positive present value. To accomplish these objectives, we can first compute the present values of both strategies and ensure that at least one has a positive present value in addition to comparing the present values of the two strategies. Alternatively, we can calculate the difference between the cash flows at each time period to effectively create a new set of cash flows. Both solution processes should yield an equivalent numeric result when comparing the two strategies, and this numeric equivalence represents the cash flow additivity principle. Let's first create the set of cash flows from the difference of the two strategies as shown in the diagram:

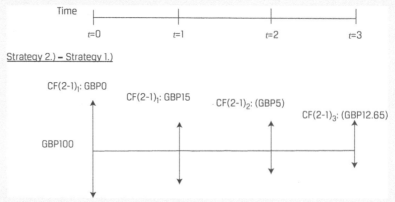

   The present value of these net cash flows is zero, indicating equivalence, as follows:

$$PV = 0 + \frac{15}{1.10} + \frac{-5}{(1.10)^2} + \frac{-12,65}{(1.10)^3} = 0.$$

   The conclusion from this analysis is that the two strategies are economically equivalent; therefore you should have no preference for one over the other. We must also determine whether these strategies are economically valuable. To do so, let's calculate the present value of each strategy individually.

For investment strategy 1, the present value is GBP11.91, as follows:

$$PV = -100 + \frac{45}{1.10} + \frac{45}{(1.10)^2} + \frac{45}{(1.10)^3} = 11.91.$$

For investment strategy 2, the present value is also GBP11.91, as follows:

$$PV = -100 + \frac{60}{1.10} + \frac{40}{(1.10)^2} + \frac{32.35}{(1.10)^3} = 11.91.$$

Both investment strategies are valuable in that the present value of the sums of their cash flows are positive. Since the present values are identical, subtracting the present value of strategy 1 from the present value of strategy 2 is zero (i.e., 11.91 − 11.91).

Either strategy is recommended as both are valuable and have equal present values.

In the following sections, we apply the cash flow additivity principle to three different economic situations and further illustrate the principle of no arbitrage by comparing two economically equivalent strategies in each situation.

Implied Forward Rates Using Cash Flow Additivity

Consider two risk-free discount bonds with different maturities as follows:

> One-year bond: $r_1 = 2.50\%$
>
> Two-year bond: $r_2 = 3.50\%$

A risk neutral investor seeking to earn a return on GBP100 over a two-year investment horizon has two possible strategies:

> *Investment strategy 1:* Invest today for two years at a known annualized yield of 3.50 percent. Using Equation 5, we may solve for the future value in two years (FV_2) as follows:

> GBP100 = $FV_2 / (1+r_2)^2$;
>
> FV_2 = GBP107.12.

> *Investment strategy 2:* Invest today for one year at a known yield of 2.50 percent and reinvest in one year's time for one year at a rate of $F_{1,1}$ (the one-year forward rate starting in one year).

These two strategies are summarized in Exhibit 10:

Exhibit 10: Implied Forward Rate Example

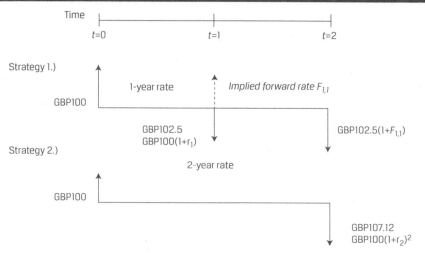

Under the cash flow additivity principle, a risk-neutral investor would be indifferent between strategies 1 and 2 under the following condition:

$$FV_2 = PV_0 \times (1+r_2)^2 = PV_0 \times (1+r_1)(1+F_{1,1}), \tag{25}$$

$$\text{GBP107.12} = \text{GBP100} \, (1.025)(1+F_{1,1}), \text{ and}$$

$$F_{1,1} = 4.51\%.$$

We can rearrange Equation 25 to solve for $F_{1,1}$ in general as follows:

$$F_{1,1} = (1+r_2)^2/(1+r_1) - 1.$$

To illustrate why the one-year forward interest rate must be 4.51 percent, let's assume an investor could lock in a one-year rate of 5 percent starting in one year. The following arbitrage strategy generates a riskless profit:

1. Borrow GBP100 for two years at 3.50 percent and agree to pay GBP107.12 in two years.

2. Invest GBP100 for the first year at 2.50 percent and in year two at 5 percent, so receive GBP107.63 in two years.

3. The combination of these two strategies above yields a riskless profit of GBP0.51 in two years with zero initial investment.

This set of strategies illustrates that forward rates should be set such that investors cannot earn riskless arbitrage profits in financial markets. This is demonstrated by comparing two economically equivalent strategies (i.e., borrowing for two years at a two-year rate versus borrowing for two one-year horizons at two different rates) The forward interest rate $F_{1,1}$ may be interpreted as the breakeven one-year reinvestment rate in one year's time.

EXAMPLE 13

Forward Interest Rate Changes

At its June 2022 meeting, the US Federal Reserve surprised markets by raising its target interest rate by a greater-than-expected 75 bps and suggested further increases in the future in response to sharply higher inflation. Exhibit 11 shows one-year and two-year US Treasury strip prices per USD100 at the end of May 2022 and after the Fed's decision in June:

Exhibit 11: One- and Two-Year US Treasury Strip Prices		
Date	**PV(1y)**	**PV(2y)**
31 May 2022	98.028	95.109
15 June 2022	97.402	93.937

1. Using the information in Exhibit 11, show the change in the breakeven one-year reinvestment in one year's time ($F_{1,1}$).

Solution:

62 bps or 0.62 percent

First, we use Equation 18 to solve for each market discount rate r. For example, in the case of the two-year discount bond on 15 June:

$$r = 3.177 \; percent \; = \; \left(\frac{100}{93.937}\right)^{\frac{1}{2}} - 1.$$

The following table summarizes the respective discount bond rates:

Date	r_1	r_2
31 May 2022	2.012%	2.539%
15 June 2022	2.667%	3.177%

Solve for the respective forward rates ($F_{1,1}$) by rearranging Equation 25:

$F_{1,1} = (1+r_2)^2/(1+r_1) - 1.$

$\underline{F_{1,1} \, (31 \, May):} F_{1,1} = 3.069\% = (1 + 2.539\%)^2/(1 + 2.012\%) - 1.$

$\underline{F_{1,1} (15 \, June):} \; F_{1,1} = 3.689\% = (1 + 3.177\%)^2/(1 + 2.667\%) - 1.$

While the higher r_1 and r_2 in mid-June shows that investors have factored the immediate 75 bp increase into their nominal discount rate, the 62 bp (0.62 percent) increase in $F_{1,1}$ is a measure of expected future rate increases given that the one-year nominal rate of return starts in one year's time. Note also that in a rising rate environment, $F_{1,1} > r_2$, as shown in the following diagram comparing r_1, r_2 and $F_{1,1}$ on 31 May (lower rates) to 15 June (higher rates).

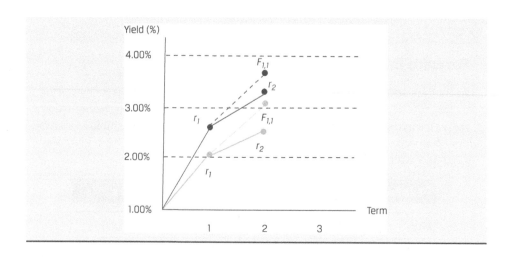

Forward Exchange Rates Using No Arbitrage

We now extend the principle of cash flow additivity to an economic scenario involving different currencies.

Assume that you have USD1,000 to invest for six months. You are considering a riskless investment in either US or Japanese six-month government debt. Let's assume that the current exchange rate between Japanese yen (JPY) and US dollars (USD) is 134.40 (i.e., JPY134.40 = USD1). The six-month Japanese yen risk-free rate is assumed to be 0.05 percent, and the six-month US dollar risk-free rate is 2.00 percent. This example assumes continuous compounding.

Investment strategy 1: Invest USD1,000 in a six-month US Treasury bill

At time $t = 0$: Invest USD1,000 at the 2.00 percent US-dollar risk-free rate for six months.

At time t = T in six months: Receive USD1,010.05 (= $1,000e^{(0.02 \times 0.5)}$).

Investment strategy 2: Convert the USD1,000 into Japanese yen at the current exchange rate of 134.40, invest in a six-month Japanese Treasury, and convert this known amount back into US dollars in six months at a six-month forward exchange rate set today of 133.096.

At time $t = 0$: Convert USD1,000 into JPY134,400. Lend the JPY134,400 at the 0.05 percent JPY risk-free rate for six months.

At time t = T in six months: Receive JPY loan proceeds of 134,433.60 (= $134,400e^{(0.0005 \times 0.5)}$). Exchange JPY loan proceeds for US dollars at the forward rate of 133.096 to receive USD1010.05 (=134,433.60/133.096).

These two strategies are economically equivalent in that both involve investing USD1000 at t = 0 and receiving USD1010.05 in six months. The element that links these two strategies is the six-month forward exchange rate of 133.096 JPY/USD. If this forward rate is set above or below 133.096, an arbitrage opportunity would exist for investors converting between Japanese yen and US dollars. Exhibit 12 provides a visual layout of the two strategies.

Exhibit 12: No-Arbitrage Condition in the Foreign Exchange Market

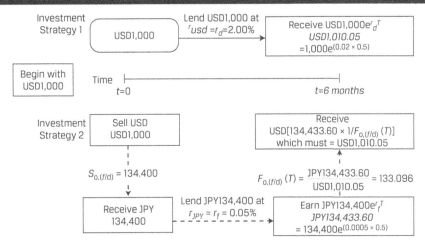

EXAMPLE 14

Foreign Exchange Forward Rates in a Changing Interest Rate Environment

Central banks responded differently to the sharp rise in inflation during 2022. For example, while the Fed raised rates by 75 bps to 1.75 percent in mid-June, the Bank of England opted for a more gradual approach, raising its benchmark rate by just 25 bps to 1.25 percent. Exhibit 13 compares one-year US Treasury strip rates (r_{USD}) from the prior example to UK gilt strip rates (r_{GBP}) over the same time frame:

Exhibit 13: Comparison of US Treasury Strip Rates

Date	r_{USD}	r_{GBP}
31 May 2022	2.012%	1.291%
15 June 2022	2.667%	1.562%

1. If we assume the USD/GBP spot price of 1.2602 (or USD1.2602 per GBP1.00) from 31 May remains constant, how does the change in risk-free US dollars versus British pounds rates affect the one-year USD/GBP forward rate?

   Solution:

   The no-arbitrage USD/GBP forward rate increases from 1.2693 to 1.2742. Assume an investor has GBP1,000 to invest for one year in a British-pound or US-dollar risk-free discount bond. The US dollars needed to purchase GBP1 in one year must have a spot price equal to the discounted future price.

   As of 31 May:

> Domestic Strategy: Invest GBP1,000 at the 1.291 percent one-year British-pound risk-free rate to receive GBP1,012.99 (= $1{,}000e^{(0.01291)}$) in one year.
>
> Foreign Strategy: Convert GBP1,000 at USD/GBP1.2602 to receive USD1,260.20, which invested at the one-year US-dollar risk-free rate of 2.012 percent generates a return of USD1,285.81 (=1,260.20 $e^{(0.02012)}$) in one year.

The no-arbitrage USD/GBP forward rate as of 31 May is therefore equal to 1.2693 (= USD1,285.81/GBP1,012.99).

As of 15 June:

> Domestic Strategy: Invest GBP1,000 at the 1.562 percent one-year British-pound risk-free rate to receive GBP1,015.74 (= $1{,}000e^{(0.01562)}$) in one year.
>
> Foreign Strategy: Convert GBP1,000 at 1.2602 to receive USD1,260.20, which invested at the one-year US-dollar risk-free rate of 2.667 percent returns USD1,294.27 (=1,260.20 $e^{(0.02667)}$) in one year.

The no-arbitrage USD/GBP forward rate as of 15 June is equal to 1.2742 (= USD1,294.26/GBP1,015.74).

As of mid-June, an investor agreeing to exchange US dollars for British pounds in one year must deliver more US dollars (1.2742 versus 1.2693) in exchange for GBP1 than if the same contract had been entered at the end of May. The greater increase in r_{USD} widens the interest rate differential ($r_{USD} - r_{GBP}$), causing US dollars to depreciate on a forward basis versus British pounds over the period. Differently put, the expectation for US-dollar depreciation on a forward basis versus British pounds would require a higher US-dollar interest rate to attract investors to US dollars versus British pounds.

Option Pricing Using Cash Flow Additivity

Let's assume an asset has a current price of 40 Chinese yuan (i.e., CNY40). The asset is risky in that its price may rise 40 percent to CNY56 during the next time period or its price may fall 20 percent to CNY32 during the next time period.

An investor wishes to sell a contract on the asset in which the buyer of the contract has the right, but not obligation, to buy the noted asset for CNY50 at the end of the next time period. We can apply the principle of cash flow additivity to establish no-arbitrage pricing for this contract.

The binomial tree in Exhibit 14 summarizes the two possible future outcomes of the asset:

Exhibit 14: One-Period Binomial Tree for the Asset's Price

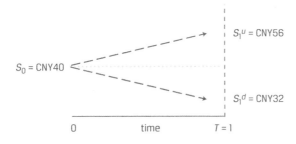

The contract value under the two scenarios is as follows (shown visually in Exhibit 15):

- Price Increase: The 40 percent increase results in a contract value of CNY 6 (=CNY56 – CNY50), as the contract owner will choose to buy the asset at CNY50 and is able to sell it at a market price of CNY56.

- Price Decrease: The 20 percent decrease results in a contract value of zero (CNY0), as the contract owner will choose not to buy the asset at CNY50 when the market price is only CNY32.

Exhibit 15: One-Period Binomial Tree for the Contract's Price

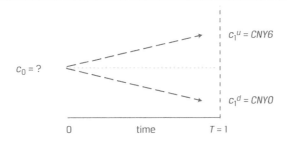

Consider the position of the contract seller as follows:

- At $t = 0$, the contract value is c_0.
- At $t = 1$, the contract value is either CNY6 (if the underlying asset rises to CNY56) or CNY0 (if the underlying stock falls to CNY32).

The initial contract value c_0 is unknown and may be determined using cash flow additivity and no-arbitrage pricing. That is, the value of the contract and the underlying asset in each future scenario may be used to construct a risk-free portfolio, or a portfolio where the value is the same in both scenarios. For example, assume at $t = 0$ an investor creates a portfolio in which the contract is sold at a price of c_0 and 0.25 units of the underlying asset are purchased. This portfolio is called a replicating portfolio in that it is designed specifically to create a matching future cash flow stream to that of a risk-free asset. Denoting the value of the portfolio as V at $t = 0$ and at $t = 1$ under both the price increase and price decrease scenarios, we have the following:

- $V_0 = 0.25 \times 40 - c_0$,
- $V_1^u = 0.25 \times 56 - 6 = 8$, and
- $V_1^d = 0.25 \times 32 - 0 = 8$.

As can be seen, the value of the replicating portfolio is equal to CNY8 regardless of whether the price of the asset increases or decreases. Because of this, the portfolio is risk-free and can be discounted as a risk-free asset. The payoffs for these two scenarios are shown in Exhibit 16.

Exhibit 16: Call Option Replication

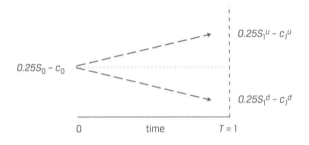

To solve for c_0, we set the present value of the replicating portfolio ($0.25 \times 40 - c_0$) equal to the discounted future value of the risk-free payoff of CNY8 under each outcome as in Equation 5. Assume r of 5 percent:

$$V_0 = 0.25S_0 - c_0,$$

$$V_0 = \frac{V_1^u}{1 + r} = \frac{V_1^d}{1 + r}, \text{ and}$$

$$0.25 \times 40 - c_0 = \frac{CNY8}{1.05}.$$

We solve for c_0 as CNY2.38. Thus, CNY2.38 is a fair price for the seller of the contract to receive from the buyer of the contract.

As part of the example above, we assumed that the investor buys 0.25 units of the asset as part of the portfolio. This proportion of the underlying asset is known as the **hedge ratio** in option pricing. In fact, the example just completed is a simplified process for solving for the value of a call option (this material will be covered in more detail later in the curriculum). As in our prior examples, we compare different strategies using cash flow additivity to help solve for a no-arbitrage price for a financial instrument.

EXAMPLE 15

Put Option

A put option grants the owner the right, but not the obligation to sell a stock at a predetermined exercise price X. If we assume $X = CNY50$, then the put option value in one period (p_1) is equal to $Max(0, CNY50 - S_1)$.

1. Using a one-period binomial tree model with the same prices in one year, initial stock price (S_0) of CNY40, and 5 percent discount rate, create a risk-free portfolio replicating the put option with 0.75 units of the underlying asset and solve for the put option price (p_0).

   Solution:

   The one-period binomial model is as follows:

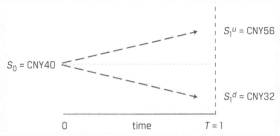

The put option value under the two scenarios is as follows:

- Price Increase ($p_1{}^u$): The 40 percent increase results in a put option value of CNY0, as the option owner will choose not to sell the stock at the exercise price.

- Price Decrease ($p_1{}^d$): The 20 percent decrease results in a put option value of CNY18 (CNY50 – CNY32), as the put option owner will choose to sell the stock with a market price of CNY32 at the exercise price of CNY50.

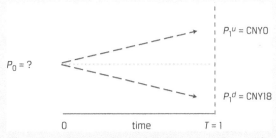

Unlike the call option, the put option increases in value as the stock price falls, so a risk-free portfolio combines a stock purchase with a purchased put option. Specifically, assume at $t = 0$, we sell a put option at a price of p_0 and purchase 0.75 units of the underlying stock. Portfolio values at t = 0 and t = 1 are as follows:

- $V_0 = 0.75S_0 + p_0$,
- $V_1{}^u = 0.75S_1{}^u + p_1{}^u$, and
- $V_1{}^d = 0.75S_1{}^d + p_1{}^d$,

where $V_1{}^u = V_1{}^d$.

The value of the risk-free portfolio in one period ($V_1 = 0.75S_1 + p_1$) under the two scenarios is:

- Price Increase ($V_1{}^u$): The portfolio value is CNY42 (=(0.75 × CNY56) + CNY 0)).

- Price Decrease ($V_1{}^d$): The portfolio value is CNY42 (=(0.75 × CNY32) + CNY18)).

Solve for p_0, by setting the present value of the replicating portfolio ($0.75S_0 + p_0$) equal to the discounted future value of the payoff, S_0 is CNY40 and r is 5 percent:

$$V_0 = 0.75S_0 + p_0,$$

$$V_0 = \frac{V_1^u}{1+r} = \frac{V_1^d}{1+r}, \text{ and}$$

$$p_0 = \frac{CNY42}{1.05} - 0.75(CNY40).$$

Solve for p_0 to be equal to CNY10. The higher put price is a result of the greater payoff of the put option versus the call option under the given parameters of the binomial model. The factors affecting option prices will be addressed in detail later in the curriculum.

PRACTICE PROBLEMS

1. Grupo Ignacia issued 10-year corporate bonds two years ago. The bonds pay an annualized coupon of 10.7 percent on a semiannual basis, and the current annualized YTM is 11.6 percent. The current price of Grupo Ignacia's bonds (per MXN100 of par value) is *closest* to:

   A. MXN95.47.

   B. MXN97.18.

   C. MXN95.39.

2. Grey Pebble Real Estate seeks a fully amortizing fixed-rate five-year mortgage loan to finance 75 percent of the purchase price of a residential building that costs NZD5 million. The annual mortgage rate is 4.8 percent. The monthly payment for this mortgage would be *closest* to:

   A. NZD70,424.

   B. NZD93,899.

   C. NZD71,781.

3. Mylandia Corporation pays an annual dividend to its shareholders, and its most recent payment was CAD2.40. Analysts following Mylandia expect the company's dividend to grow at a constant rate of 3 percent per year in perpetuity. Mylandia shareholders require a return of 8 percent per year. The expected share price of Mylandia is *closest* to:

   A. CAD48.00.

   B. CAD49.44.

   C. CAD51.84.

4. Suppose Mylandia announces that it expects significant cash flow growth over the next three years, and now plans to increase its recent CAD2.40 dividend by 10 percent in each of the next three years. Following the 10 percent growth period, Mylandia is expected to grow its annual dividend by a constant 3 percent indefinitely. Mylandia's required return is 8 percent. Based upon these revised expectations, The expected share price of Mylandia stock is:

   A. CAD49.98.

   B. CAD55.84.

   C. CAD59.71.

5. Consider a Swiss Confederation zero-coupon bond with a par value of CHF100, a remaining time to maturity of 12 years and a price of CHF89. In three years' time, the bond is expected to have a price of CHF95.25. If purchased today, the bond's expected annualized return is *closest* to:

   A. 0.58 percent.

   B. 1.64 percent.

C. 2.29 percent.

6. Grupo Ignacia issued 10-year corporate bonds four years ago. The bonds pay an annualized coupon of 10.7 percent on a semiannual basis, and the current price of the bonds is MXN97.50 per MXN100 of par value. The YTM of the bonds is *closest* to:

A. 11.28 percent.

B. 11.50 percent.

C. 11.71 percent.

7. Mylandia Corporation stock trades at CAD60.00. The company pays an annual dividend to its shareholders, and its most recent payment of CAD2.40 occurred yesterday. Analysts following Mylandia expect the company's dividend to grow at a constant rate of 3 percent per year. Mylandia's required return is:

A. 8.00 percent.

B. 7.00 percent.

C. 7.12 percent.

8. An analyst observes the benchmark Indian NIFTY 50 stock index trading at a forward price-to-earnings ratio of 15. The index's expected dividend payout ratio in the next year is 50 percent, and the index's required return is 7.50 percent. If the analyst believes that the NIFTY 50 index dividends will grow at a constant rate of 4.50 percent in the future, which of the following statements is correct?

A. The analyst should view the NIFTY 50 as overpriced.

B. The analyst should view the NIFTY 50 as underpriced.

C. The analyst should view the NIFTY 50 as fairly priced.

9. If you require an 8 percent return and must invest USD500,000, which of the investment opportunities in Exhibit 1 should you prefer?

Exhibit 1: Investment Opportunities				
Cash flows (in thousands)	t = 0	t = 1	t = 2	t = 3
Opportunity 1	−500	195	195	195
Opportunity 2	−500	225	195	160.008

A. Opportunity 1

B. Opportunity 2

C. Indifferent between the two opportunities.

10. Italian one-year government debt has an interest rate of 0.73 percent; Italian two-year government debt has an interest rate of 1.29 percent. The breakeven one-year reinvestment rate, one year from now is *closest* to:

A. 1.01 percent.

B. 1.11 percent.

C. 1.85 percent.

11. The current exchange rate between the euro and US dollar is USD/EUR1.025. Risk-free interest rates for one year are 0.75 percent for the euro and 3.25 percent for the US dollar. The one-year USD/EUR forward rate that *best* prevents arbitrage opportunities is:

A. USD/EUR1.051.

B. USD/EUR1.025.

C. USD/EUR0.975.

12. A stock currently trades at USD25. In one year, it will either increase in value to USD35 or decrease to USD15. An investor sells a call option on the stock, granting the buyer the right, but not the obligation, to buy the stock at USD25 in one year. At the same time, the investor buys 0.5 units of the stock. Which of the following statements about the value of the investor's portfolio at the end of one year is correct?

A. The portfolio has a value of USD7.50 in both scenarios.

B. The portfolio has a value of USD25 in both scenarios.

C. The portfolio has a value of USD17.50 if the stock goes up and USD7.50 if the stock goes down.

SOLUTIONS

1. C is correct. The coupon payments are 5.35 (=10.7/2), the discount rate is 5.8 percent (=11.6%/2) per period, and the number of periods is 16 (=8×2). Using Equation 6, the calculation is as follows:

$$95.39 = \frac{5.35}{1.058} + \frac{5.35}{1.058^2} + \frac{5.35}{1.058^3} + \frac{5.35}{1.058^4} + \dots + \frac{5.35}{1.058^{14}} + \frac{5.35}{1.058^{15}} + \frac{105.35}{1.058^{16}}.$$

Alternatively, using the Microsoft Excel or Google Sheets PV function (PV (0.058,16,5.35,100,0)) also yields a result of MXN95.39.

A is incorrect. MXN95.47 is the result when incorrectly using coupon payments of 10.7, a discount rate of 11.6 percent, and 8 as the number of periods.

B is incorrect. MXN97.18 is the result when using the correct semiannual coupons and discount rate, but incorrectly using 8 as the number of periods.

2. A is correct. The present value of the mortgage is NZD3.75 million (=0.75×5,000,000), the periodic discount rate is 0.004 (=0.048/12), and the number of periods is 60 (=5×12). Using Equation 8,

$$A = \$70,424 = \frac{0.4\% \, (NZD3,750,000)}{1 - (1 + 0.4\%)^{-60}}.$$

Alternatively, the spreadsheet PMT function may be used with the inputs stated earlier.

B is incorrect. NZD93,899 is the result if NZD5 million is incorrectly used as the present value term.

C is incorrect. NZD71,781 is the result if the calculation is made using 4.8 percent as the rate and 5 as the number of periods, then the answer is divided by 12.

3. B is correct. Mylandia's next expected dividend is CAD2.472 (=2.40×1.03), and using Equation 14,

$$PV_t = \frac{2.40(1 + 0.03)}{0.08 - 0.03} = \frac{2.472}{0.05} = 49.44.$$

4. C is correct. Following the first step, we observe the following expected dividends for Mylandia for the next three years:

> In 1 year: D_1 = CAD2.64 (=2.40×1.10)
> In 2 years: D_2 = CAD2.90 (=2.40×1.10^2)
> In 3 years: D_3 = CAD3.19 (=2.40×1.10^3)

The second step involves a lower 3 percent growth rate. At the end of year four, Mylandia's dividend (D_4) is expected to be CAD3.29 (=2.40×1.10^3×1.03). At this time, Mylandia's expected terminal value at the end of three years is CAD65.80 using Equation 17, as follows:

$$E(S_{t+n}) = \frac{3.29}{0.08 - 0.03} = 65.80.$$

Third, we calculate the sum of the present values of these expected dividends using Equation 16:

$$PV_t = \frac{2.64}{1.08} + \frac{2.90}{1.08^2} + \frac{3.19}{1.08^3} + \frac{65.80}{1.08^3} = 59.71.$$

5. C is correct. The FV of the bond is CHF95.25, the PV is CHF89, and the number of annual periods (t) is 3. Using Equation 18,

2.29 percent = $(92.25/89)^{(1/3)} - 1$.

A is incorrect as the result is derived using t of 12. B is incorrect as this result is derived using a PV of CHF95.25 and an FV of 100.

6. A is correct. The YTM is calculated by solving for the RATE spreadsheet function with the following inputs: number of periods of 12 (=6 × 2), coupon payments of 5.35 (=10.7/2), PV of –97.50, and FV of 100. The resulting solution for RATE of 5.64 percent is in semiannual terms, so multiply by 2 to calculate annualized YTM of 11.28 percent.

   B is incorrect, as 11.50 percent is the result if number of periods used is eight, instead of 12. C is incorrect, as 11.71 percent is the result if the number of periods used is 6, instead of 12.

7. C is correct. We may solve for required return based upon the assumption of constant dividend growth using Equation 21:

   $$r = \frac{2.40(1.03)}{60} + 0.03 = 0.0712.$$

   B is incorrect as 7.00 percent is the result if we use the previous dividend of CAD2.40 instead of the next expected dividend. A is incorrect as 8.00 percent is simply the required return assumed from one of the Mylandia examples in Question Set 1 in which the price is solved to be a lower value.

8. B is correct. Using Equation 24, the previous input results in the following inequality:

   $$15 < \frac{0.50}{0.075 - 0.045} = 16.67.$$

   The above inequality implies that the analyst should view the NIFTY 50 as priced too low. The fundamental inputs into the equation imply a forward price to earnings ratio of 16.67 rather than 15. An alternative approach to answering the question would be to solve for implied growth using the observed forward price to earnings ratio of 15 and compare this to the analyst's growth expectations:

   $$15 = \frac{0.50}{0.075 - g}.$$

   Solving for g yields a result of 4.1667 percent. Since the analyst expects higher NIFTY 50 dividend growth of 4.50 percent, the index is viewed as underpriced.

9. Using cash flow additivity, compare the two opportunities by subtracting Opportunity 2 from Opportunity 1 yielding the following cash flows:

Opportunity 1 – Opportunity 2	0	–30	0	34.992

   Finding the present value of the above cash flows at 8 percent discount rate shows that both investment opportunities have the same present value. Thus, the two opportunities are economically identical, and there is no clear preference for one over the other.

10. C is correct. The one-year forward rate reflects the breakeven one-year reinvestment rate in one year, computed as follows:

    $$F_{1,1} = (1+r_2)^2/(1+r_1) - 1,$$

    $$F_{1,1} = (1.0129)^2/(1.0073) - 1 = 0.0185.$$

11. A is correct. To avoid arbitrage opportunities in exchanging euros and US dollars, investors must be able to lock in a one-year forward exchange rate of USD/

EUR1.051 today. The solution methodology is shown below.

In one year, a single unit of euro invested risk-free is worth EUR1.0075 (=$e^{0.0075}$).

In one year, a single unit of euro converted to US dollars and then invested risk-free is worth USD1.0589 (=$1.025*e^{0.0325}$).

To convert USD1.0589 into EUR1.0075 requires a forward exchange rate of USD/EUR1.051 (=1.0589/1.0075).

12. A is correct. Regardless of whether the stock increases or decreases in price, the investor's portfolio has a value of USD7.50 as follows:

If stock price goes to USD35, value = 0.5×35 − 10 = 7.50.

If stock price goes to USD15, value = 0.5×15 − 0 = 7.50.

If the stock price rises to USD35, the sold call option at USD25 has a value to the buyer of USD10, offsetting the rise in the stock price.

3

Statistical Measures of Asset Returns

by Pamela Peterson Drake, PhD, CFA, and Wu Jian, PhD.

Pamela Peterson Drake, PhD, CFA, is at James Madison University (USA). Jian Wu, PhD, is at State Street (USA).

LEARNING OUTCOMES	
Mastery	*The candidate should be able to:*
☐	calculate, interpret, and evaluate measures of central tendency and location to address an investment problem
☐	calculate, interpret, and evaluate measures of dispersion to address an investment problem
☐	interpret and evaluate measures of skewness and kurtosis to address an investment problem
☐	interpret correlation between two variables to address an investment problem

INTRODUCTION

1

Data have always been a key input for securities analysis and investment management, allowing investors to explore and exploit an abundance of information for their investment strategies. While this data-rich environment offers potentially tremendous opportunities for investors, turning data into useful information is not so straightforward.

This module provides a foundation for understanding important concepts that are an indispensable part of the analytical tool kit needed by investment practitioners, from junior analysts to senior portfolio managers. These basic concepts pave the way for more sophisticated tools that will be developed as the quantitative methods topic unfolds, which are integral to gaining competencies in the investment management techniques and asset classes that are presented later in the CFA curriculum.

This learning module focuses on how to summarize and analyze important aspects of financial returns, including key measures of central tendency, dispersion, and the shape of return distributions—specifically, skewness and kurtosis. The learning module finishes with a graphical introduction to covariance and correlation between two variables, a key concept in constructing investment portfolios to achieve diversification across assets within a portfolio.

LEARNING MODULE OVERVIEW

- Sample statistics—such as measures of central tendency, dispersion, skewness, and kurtosis—help with investment analysis, particularly in making probabilistic statements about returns.

- Measures of central tendency include the mean, the median and the mode, and specify where data are centered.

- The arithmetic mean is the sum of the observations divided by the number of observations. It is the most frequently used measure of central tendency.

- The median is the value of the middle item of observations, or the mean of the values of the two middle items, when the items in a set are sorted into ascending or descending order. Since the median is not influenced by extreme values, it is most useful in the case of skewed distributions.

- The mode is the most frequently observed value and is the only measure of central tendency that can be used with nominal or categorical data. A distribution may be unimodal (one mode), bimodal (two modes), trimodal (three modes), or have even more modes.

- Quantiles, as the median, quartiles, quintiles, deciles, and percentiles, are location parameters that divide a distribution into halves, quarters, fifths, tenths, and hundredths, respectively.

- A box and whiskers plot illustrates the distribution of a set of observations. The "box" depicts the interquartile range, the difference between the first and the third quartile. The "whiskers" outside of the "box" indicate the others measures of dispersion.

- Dispersion measures, such as the range, mean absolute deviation (MAD), variance, standard deviation, target downside deviation, and coefficient of variation, describe the variability of outcomes around the arithmetic mean.

- The range is the difference between the maximum value and the minimum value of the dataset. The range has only a limited usefulness because it uses information from only two observations.

- The MAD for a sample is the average of the absolute deviations of observations from the mean.

- The variance is the average of the squared deviations around the mean, and the standard deviation is the positive square root of variance. In computing sample variance, s^2, and sample standard deviation, s, the average squared deviation is computed using a divisor equal to the sample size minus 1.

- The target downside deviation, or target semideviation, is a measure of the risk of being below a given target.

- The coefficient of variation (CV) is the ratio of the standard deviation of a set of observations to their mean value. By expressing the magnitude of variation among observations relative to their average size, the CV allows for the direct comparisons of dispersion across different datasets. Reflecting the correction for scale, the CV is a scale-free measure, that is, it has no units of measurement.

- Skewness describes the degree to which a distribution is asymmetric about its mean. An asset return distribution with positive skewness has frequent small losses and a few extreme gains compared to a normal distribution. An asset return distribution with negative skewness has frequent small gains and a few extreme losses compared to a normal distribution. Zero skewness indicates a symmetric distribution of returns.

- Kurtosis measures the combined weight of the tails of a distribution relative to the rest of the distribution. A distribution with fatter tails than the normal distribution is referred to as fat-tailed (leptokurtic); a distribution with thinner tails than the normal distribution is referred to as thin-tailed (platykurtic). The kurtosis of a normal distribution is 3.

- The correlation coefficient measures the association between two variables. It is the ratio of covariance to the product of the two variables' standard deviations. A positive correlation coefficient indicates that the two variables tend to move together, whereas a negative coefficient indicates that the two variables tend to move in opposite directions. Correlation does not imply causation, simply association. Issues that arise in evaluating correlation include the presence of outliers and spurious correlation.

MEASURES OF CENTRAL TENDENCY AND LOCATION   2

☐ | calculate, interpret, and evaluate measures of central tendency and location to address an investment problem

In this lesson, our focus is on measures of central tendency and other measures of location. A **measure of central tendency** specifies where the data are centered. For a return series, a measure of central tendency shows where the empirical distribution of returns is centered, essentially a measure of the "expected" return based on the observed sample. **Measures of location**, mean, the **median**, and the **mode** include not only measures of central tendency but also other measures that illustrate other aspects of the location or distribution of the data.

Frequency distributions, histograms, and contingency tables provide a convenient way to summarize a series of observations on an asset's returns as a first step toward describing the data. For example, a histogram for the frequency distribution of the daily returns for the fictitious EAA Equity Index over the past five years is shown in Exhibit 1.

Exhibit 1: Histogram of Daily Returns on the EAA Equity Index

Number of Observations

Measures of Central Tendency

The Arithmetic Mean

Analysts and portfolio managers often want one number that describes a representative possible outcome of an investment decision. The arithmetic mean is one of the most frequently used measures of central tendency.

> **Arithmetic Mean.** The **arithmetic mean** is the sum of the values of the observations in a dataset divided by the number of observations.

The Sample Mean

The sample mean is the arithmetic mean, or arithmetic average, computed for a sample.

> **Sample Mean Formula.** The **sample mean** or average, $\bar{X}$ (read "X-bar"), is the arithmetic mean value of a sample:

$$\bar{X} = \frac{\sum_{i=1}^{n} X_i}{n}, \tag{1}$$

> where n is the number of observations in the sample.

A property and potential drawback of the arithmetic mean is its sensitivity to extreme values, or outliers. Because all observations are used to compute the mean and are given equal weight (i.e., importance), the arithmetic mean can be pulled sharply upward or downward by extremely large or small observations, respectively. The most common approach in this situation is to report the median, or middle value, in place of or in addition to the mean.

The Median

A second important measure of central tendency is the median.

> **Definition of Median.** The median is the value of the middle item of a dataset that has been sorted into ascending or descending order. In an odd-numbered sample of n observations, the median is the value of the

observation that occupies the $(n + 1)/2$ position. In an even-numbered sample, we define the median as the mean of the values of the observations occupying the $n/2$ and $(n + 2)/2$ positions (the two middle observations).

Whether we use the calculation for an even- or odd-numbered sample, an equal number of observations lie above and below the median. A distribution has only one median. A potential advantage of the median is that, unlike the mean, outliers do not affect it.

The median, however, does not use all the information about the size of the observations; it focuses only on the relative position of the ranked observations. Calculating the median may also be more complex. Mathematicians express this disadvantage by saying that the median is less mathematically tractable than the mean.

The Mode

A third important measure of central tendency is the mode.

> **Definition of Mode.** The mode is the most frequently occurring value in a dataset. A dataset can have more than one mode, or even no mode. When a dataset has a single value that is observed most frequently, its distribution is said to be **unimodal**. If a dataset has two most frequently occurring values, then it has two modes and its distribution is referred to as **bimodal**. When all the values in a dataset are different, the distribution has no mode because no value occurs more frequently than any other value.

Stock return data and other data from continuous distributions may not have a modal outcome. Exhibit 2 presents the frequency distribution of the daily returns for the EAA Equity Index over the past five years.

Exhibit 2: Frequency Distribution for Daily Returns of EAA Equity Index

Return Bin (%)	Absolute Frequency	Relative Frequency (%)	Cumulative Absolute Frequency	Cumulative Relative Frequency (%)
−5.0 to −4.0	1	0.08	1	0.08
−4.0 to −3.0	7	0.56	8	0.64
−3.0 to −2.0	23	1.83	31	2.46
−2.0 to −1.0	77	6.12	108	8.59
−1.0 to 0.0	470	37.36	578	45.95
0.0 to 1.0	555	44.12	1,133	90.06
1.0 to 2.0	110	8.74	1,243	98.81
2.0 to 3.0	13	1.03	1,256	99.84
3.0 to 4.0	1	0.08	1,257	99.92
4.0 to 5.0	1	0.08	1,258	100.00

A histogram for the frequency distribution of these daily returns was shown in Exhibit 1. The modal interval always has the highest bar in the histogram; in this case, the modal interval is 0.0 to 0.9 percent, and this interval has 493 observations out of a total of 1,258 observations.

Dealing with Outliers

In practice, although an extreme value or outlier in a financial dataset may represent a rare value in the population, it may also reflect an error in recording the value of an observation or an observation generated from a different population. After having checked and eliminated errors, we can address what to do with extreme values in the sample.

When dealing with a sample that has extreme values, there may be a possibility of transforming the variable (e.g., a log transformation) or of selecting another variable that achieves the same purpose. If, however, alternative model specifications or variable transformations are not possible, then three options exist for dealing with extreme values:

Option 1   Do nothing; use the data without any adjustment.

Option 2   Delete all the outliers.

Option 3   Replace the outliers with another value.

The first option is appropriate if the values are legitimate, correct observations, and it is important to reflect the whole of the sample distribution. Because outliers may contain meaningful information, excluding or altering these values may reduce valuable information. Further, because identifying a data point as extreme leaves it up to the judgment of the analyst, leaving in all observations eliminates that need to judge a value as extreme.

The second option excludes the extreme observations. One measure of central tendency in this case is the **trimmed mean**, which is computing an arithmetic mean after excluding a stated small percentage of the lowest and highest values. For example, a 5 percent trimmed mean discards the lowest 2.5 percent and the highest 2.5 percent of values and computes the mean of the remaining 95 percent of values. A trimmed mean is used in sports competitions when judges' lowest and highest scores are discarded in computing a contestant's score.

The third option involves substituting values for the extreme values. A measure of central tendency in this case is the **winsorized mean**. It is calculated after assigning one specified low value to a stated percentage of the lowest values in the dataset and one specified high value to a stated percentage of the highest values in the dataset. For example, a 95 percent winsorized mean sets the bottom 2.5 percent of values in the dataset equal to the value at or below which 2.5 percent of all the values lie (as will be seen shortly, this is called the "2.5th percentile" value) and the top 2.5 percent of values in the dataset equal to the value at or below which 97.5 percent of all the values lie (the "97.5th percentile" value).

Often comparing the statistical measures of datasets with outliers included and with outliers excluded can reveal important insights about the dataset. Such comparison can be particularly helpful when investors analyze the behavior of asset returns and rate, price, spread and volume changes.

In Example 1, we show the differences among these options for handling outliers using daily returns for the fictitious Euro-Asia-Africa (EAA) Equity Index in Exhibit 2.

EXAMPLE 1

Handling Outliers: Daily Returns to an Index

Using daily returns on the EAA Equity Index for the past five years, consisting of 1,258 trading days, we can see the effect of trimming and winsorizing the data:

	Arithmetic Mean	Trimmed Mean (Trimmed 5%)	Winsorized Mean (95%)
Exhibit 3: Effect of Trimming and Winsorizing			
Mean	0.035%	0.048%	0.038%
Number of Observations	1,258	1,194	1,258

The trimmed mean eliminates the lowest 2.5 percent of returns, which in this sample is any daily return less than −1.934 percent, and it eliminates the highest 2.5 percent, which in this sample is any daily return greater than 1.671 percent. The result of this trimming is that the mean is calculated using 1,194 observations instead of the original sample's 1,258 observations.

The winsorized mean substitutes a return of −1.934 percent (the 2.5 percentile value) for any observation below −1.934 and substitutes a return of 1.671 percent (the 97.5 percentile value) for any observation above 1.671. The result in this case is that the trimmed and winsorized means are higher than the arithmetic mean, suggesting the potential evidence of significant negative returns in the observed daily return distribution.

Measures of Location

Having discussed measures of central tendency, we now examine an approach to describing the location of data that involves identifying values at or below which specified proportions of the data lie. For example, establishing that 25 percent, 50 percent, and 75 percent of the annual returns on a portfolio provides concise information about the distribution of portfolio returns. Statisticians use the word **quantile** as the most general term for a value at or below which a stated fraction of the data lies. In the following section, we describe the most commonly used quantiles—quartiles, quintiles, deciles, and percentiles—and their application in investments.

Quartiles, Quintiles, Deciles, and Percentiles

We know that the median divides a distribution of data in half. We can define other dividing lines that split the distribution into smaller sizes. **Quartiles** divide the distribution into quarters, **quintiles** into fifths, **deciles** into tenths, and **percentiles** into hundredths. The **interquartile range** (IQR) is the difference between the third quartile and the first quartile, or IQR = $Q_3 - Q_1$.

Example 2 illustrates the calculation of various quantiles for the daily return on the EAA Equity Index.

EXAMPLE 2

Percentiles, Quintiles, and Quartiles for the EAA Equity Index

Using the daily returns on the EAA Equity Index over the past five years and ranking them from lowest to highest daily return, we show the return bins from 1 (the lowest 5 percent) to 20 (the highest 5 percent) as follows:

Exhibit 4: EAA Equity Index Daily Returns Grouped by Size of Return

Bin	Cumulative Percentage of Sample Trading Days (%)	Daily Return (%) between Lower Bound	Daily Return (%) between Upper Bound	Number of Observations
1	5	−4.108	−1.416	63
2	10	−1.416	−0.876	63
3	15	−0.876	−0.629	63
4	20	−0.629	−0.432	63
5	25	−0.432	−0.293	63
6	30	−0.293	−0.193	63
7	35	−0.193	−0.124	62
8	40	−0.124	−0.070	63
9	45	−0.070	−0.007	63
10	50	−0.007	0.044	63
11	55	0.044	0.108	63
12	60	0.108	0.173	63
13	65	0.173	0.247	63
14	70	0.247	0.343	62
15	75	0.343	0.460	63
16	80	0.460	0.575	63
17	85	0.575	0.738	63
18	90	0.738	0.991	63
19	95	0.991	1.304	63
20	100	1.304	5.001	63

Because of the continuous nature of returns, it is not likely for a return to fall on the boundary for any bin other than the minimum (Bin = 1) and maximum (Bin = 20).

Using the data in Exhibit 4, complete the following tasks:

1. Identify the 10th and 90th percentiles.

Solution:

The 10th and 90th percentiles correspond to the bins or ranked returns that include 10 percent and 90 percent of the daily returns, respectively. The 10th percentile corresponds to the return of −0.876 percent (and includes returns of that much and lower), and the 90th percentile corresponds to the return of 0.991 percent (and lower).

2. Identify the first, second, and third quintiles.

Solution:

The first quintile corresponds to the lowest 20 percent of the ranked data, or −0.432 percent (and lower).

The second quintile corresponds to the lowest 40 percent of the ranked data, or −0.070 percent (and lower).

The third quintile corresponds to the lowest 60 percent of the ranked data, or 0.173 percent (and lower).

3. Identify the first and third quartiles.

Solution:

The first quartile corresponds to the lowest 25 percent of the ranked data, or −0.293 percent (and lower).
The third quartile corresponds to the lowest 75 percent of the ranked data, or 0.460 percent (and lower).

4. Identify the median.

Solution:

The median is the return for which 50 percent of the data lies on either side, which is 0.044 percent, the highest daily return in the 10th bin out of 20.

5. Calculate the interquartile range.

Solution:

The interquartile range is the difference between the third and first quartiles, 0.460 percent and −0.293 percent, or 0.753 percent.

One way to visualize the dispersion of data across quartiles is to use a diagram, such as a box and whisker chart. A **box and whisker plot** is shown in Exhibit 5. The "box" represents the lower bound of the second quartile and the upper bound of the third quartile, with the median or arithmetic average noted as a measure of central tendency of the entire distribution. The whiskers are the lines that run from the box and are bounded by the "fences," which represent the lowest and highest values of the distribution.

Exhibit 5: Box and Whisker Plot

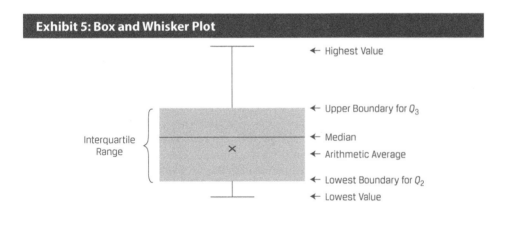

There are several variations for box and whisker displays. For example, for ease in detecting potential outliers, the fences of the whiskers may be a function of the interquartile range instead of the highest and lowest values like that in Exhibit 5.

In Exhibit 5, visually, the interquartile range is the height of the box and the fences are set at extremes. But another form of box and whisker plot typically uses 1.5 times the interquartile range for the fences. Thus, the upper fence is 1.5 times the interquartile range added to the upper bound of Q_3, and the lower fence is 1.5 times the interquartile range subtracted from the lower bound of Q_2. Observations beyond the fences (i.e., outliers) may also be displayed.

We can see the role of outliers in such a box and whisker plot using the EAA Equity Index daily returns, as shown in Exhibit 6.

Exhibit 6: Box and Whisker Chart for EAA Equity Index Daily Returns

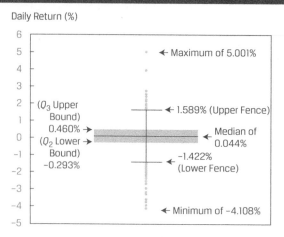

Exhibit 6 reveals the following:

- The maximum and minimum values of the distribution are 5.001 and −4.108, respectively, while the median (50th percentile) value is 0.044.

- The interquartile range is 0.753 [= 0.460 − (−0.293)], and when multiplied by 1.5 and added to the Q_3 upper bound of 0.460 gives an upper fence of 1.589 [= (1.5 × 0.753) + 0.460].

- The lower fence is determined in a similar manner, using the Q_2 lower bound, to be −1.422 [= −(1.5 × 0.753) + (−0.293)].

As noted, any observation above (below) the upper (lower) fence is deemed to be an outlier.

Quantiles in Investment Practice

Quantiles are used in portfolio performance evaluation as well as in investment strategy development and research.

Investment analysts use quantiles to rank performance, such as the performance of assets, indexes, and portfolios. The performance of investment managers is often characterized in terms of the percentile in which their performance falls relative to the performance of their peer group of managers. The widely used Morningstar investment fund star rankings, for example, associate the number of stars with percentiles of performance metrics relative to similar-style investment funds.

Another key use of quantiles is in investment research. Dividing data into quantiles based on a specific objectively quantifiable characteristic, such as sales, market capitalization, or asset size allows analysts to evaluate the impact of that specific characteristic on a quantity of interest, such as asset returns, sales, growth, or valuation metrics. For instance, quantitatively driven investors often rank companies based on the market value of their equity, or their market capitalization, before sorting them into deciles. The first decile contains the portfolio of those companies with the smallest market values, usually called small capitalization companies. The tenth decile contains those companies with the largest market values, usually called large capitalization companies. Ranking companies by decile allows analysts to compare the absolute and relative performance of small market capitalization companies with large ones.

QUESTION SET

The histogram in Exhibit 7 shows a distribution of the annual returns for the S&P 500 Index for a 50-year period.

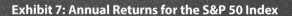

Exhibit 7: Annual Returns for the S&P 50 Index

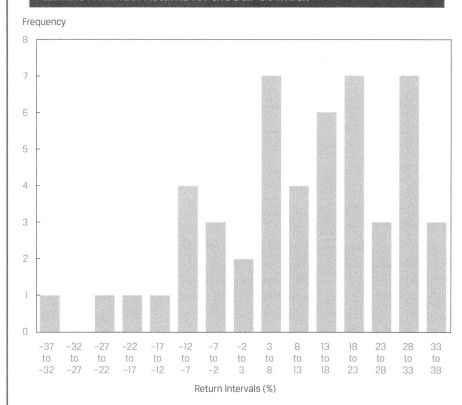

1. The bin containing the median return is:

   A. 3 percent to 8 percent.

   B. 8 percent to 13 percent.

   C. 13 percent to 18 percent.

   Solution:

   C is correct. Because 50 data points are in the histogram, the median return would be the mean of the 50/2 = 25th and (50 + 2)/2 = 26th positions. The sum of the return bin frequencies to the left of the 13 percent to 18 percent interval is 24. As a result, the 25th and 26th returns will fall in the 13 percent to 18 percent interval.

2. Based on Exhibit 7, the distribution would be *best* described as being:

   A. unimodal.

   B. bimodal.

   C. trimodal.

   Solution:

   C is correct. The mode of a distribution with data grouped in intervals is the interval with the highest frequency. The three intervals of 3 percent to 8 percent, 18 percent to 23 percent, and 28 percent to 33 percent all have the highest frequency of 7.

Consider the annual returns in Exhibit 8 for three portfolios for Portfolios P, Q and R. Portfolios P and R were created in Year 1, Portfolio Q was created in Year 2.

Exhibit 8: Annual Portfolio Returns

	Year 1 (%)	Year 2 (%)	Year 3 (%)	Year 4 (%)	Year 5 (%)
Portfolio P	−3.0	4.0	5.0	3.0	7.0
Portfolio Q	NA	−3.0	6.0	4.0	8.0
Portfolio R	1.0	−1.0	4.0	4.0	3.0

3. The median annual return for:

   A. Portfolio P is 4.5 percent.

   B. Portfolio Q is 4.0 percent.

   C. Portfolio R is higher than its arithmetic mean annual return.

   Solution:

   C is correct. The median of Portfolio R is 0.8 percent higher than the mean for Portfolio R. A is incorrect because the median annual return for Portfolio P is 4.0 percent. B is incorrect because the median annual return for Portfolio Q is 5.0 percent (midpoint of 4 percent and 6 percent).

4. The mode for Portfolio R is:

   A. 1.0 percent.

   B. 3.0 percent.

   C. 4.0 percent.

   Solution:

   C is correct. The mode is the most frequently occurring value in a dataset, which for Portfolio R is 4.0 percent.

A fund had the following returns over the past 10 years:

Exhibit 9: Fund Returns for 10 Years

Year	Return
1	4.5%
2	6.0%
3	1.5%
4	−2.0%
5	0.0%
6	4.5%
7	3.5%
8	2.5%

Year	Return
9	5.5%
10	4.0%

5. The fund's arithmetic mean return over the 10 years is *closest* to:

   A. 2.97 percent.

   B. 3.00 percent.

   C. 3.33 percent.

   Solution:

   B is correct. The sum of the returns is 30.0 percent, so the arithmetic mean is 30.0%/10 = 3.0%.

6. The fund's geometric mean return over the 10 years is *closest* to:

   A. 2.94 percent.

   B. 2.97 percent.

   C. 3.00 percent.

   Solution:

   B is correct. The geometric mean return is calculated as follows:

   $$\overline{R}_G = \sqrt[10]{(1 + 0.045) \times (1 + 0.06) \times \ldots \times (1 + 0.055) \times (1 + 0.04)} - 1,$$

   $$\overline{R}_G = \sqrt[10]{1.3402338} - 1 = 2.9717\%.$$

7. The harmonic mean return over the 10 years is *closest* to:

   A. 2.94 percent.

   B. 2.97 percent.

   C. 3.00 percent.

   Solution:

   A is correct. The harmonic mean is calculated as follows:

   $$\overline{X}_H = \frac{n}{\sum_{i=1}^{n}(1/(1 + r_i))} - 1,$$

   $$\overline{X}_H = \frac{10}{\left(\frac{1}{1.045}\right) + \left(\frac{1}{1.06}\right) + \ldots + \left(\frac{1}{1.055}\right) + \left(\frac{1}{1.04}\right)} - 1,$$

   $$\overline{X}_H = \left(\frac{10}{9.714}\right) - 1 = 2.9442\%.$$

Consider the box and whisker plot in Exhibit 10:

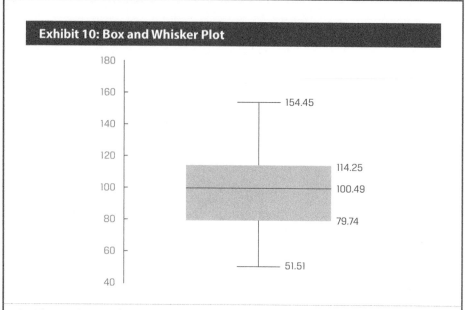

Exhibit 10: Box and Whisker Plot

8. The median is *closest* to:

   A. 34.51.

   B. 100.49.

   C. 102.98.

   Solution:

   B is correct. In a box and whisker plot, the "box" represents the lower bound of the second quartile and the upper bound of the third quartile, with the median or arithmetic average noted as a measure of central tendency of the entire distribution. The median is indicated within the box, which is 100.49.

9. The interquartile range is *closest* to:

   A. 13.76.

   B. 25.74.

   C. 34.51.

   Solution:

   C is correct. The interquartile range is the height of the box, which is the difference between 114.25 and 79.74, equal to 34.51.

3

MEASURES OF DISPERSION

☐ | calculate, interpret, and evaluate measures of dispersion to address an investment problem

Few would disagree with the importance of expected return or mean return in investments: To understand an investment more completely, however, we also need to know how returns are dispersed around the mean. **Dispersion** is the variability around the central tendency. If mean return addresses reward, then dispersion addresses risk and uncertainty.

In this lesson, we examine the most common measures of dispersion: range, mean absolute deviation, variance, and standard deviation. These are all measures of **absolute dispersion**. Absolute dispersion is the amount of variability present without comparison to any reference point or benchmark.

The Range

We encountered range earlier when we discussed the construction of frequency distributions. It is the simplest of all the measures of dispersion.

> **Definition of Range.** The **range** is the difference between the maximum and minimum values in a dataset:

Range = Maximum value − Minimum value.   (2)

An alternative way to report the range is to specify both the maximum and minimum values. This alternative definition provides more information as the range is reported as "from Maximum Value to Minimum Value."

One advantage of the range is ease of computation. A disadvantage is that the range uses only two pieces of information from the distribution. It cannot tell us how the data are distributed (i.e., the shape of the distribution). Because the range is the difference between the maximum and minimum values in the dataset, it is also sensitive to extremely large or small observations ("outliers") that may not be representative of the distribution.

Mean Absolute Deviations

Measures of dispersion can be computed using all the observations in the distribution rather than just the highest and lowest. We could compute measures of dispersion as the arithmetic average of the deviations around the mean, but the problem is that deviations around the mean always sum to 0. Therefore, we need to find a way to address the problem of negative deviations canceling out positive deviations.

One solution is to examine the absolute deviations around the mean as in the **mean absolute deviation** (MAD).

> **MAD Formula.** The MAD for a sample is:

$$\text{MAD} = \frac{\sum_{i=1}^{n} |X_i - \bar{X}|}{n},$$ (3)

> where $\bar{X}$ is the sample mean, n is the number of observations in the sample, and the | | indicate the absolute value of what is contained within these bars.

The MAD uses all of the observations in the sample and is thus superior to the range as a measure of dispersion. One technical drawback of MAD is that it is difficult to manipulate mathematically compared with the next measure we will introduce, sample variance.

Sample Variance and Sample Standard Deviation

A second approach to the problem of positive and negative deviations canceling out is to square them. Variance and standard deviation, which are based on squared deviations, are the two most widely used measures of dispersion. **Variance** is defined as the average of the squared deviations around the mean. **Standard deviation** is the square root of the variance.

Sample Variance

In investments, we often do not know the mean of a population of interest, so we estimate it using the mean from a sample drawn from the population. The corresponding measure of dispersion is the sample variance or standard deviation.

Sample Variance Formula. The **sample variance**, s^2, is:

$$s^2 = \frac{\sum_{i=1}^{n}(X_i - \overline{X})^2}{n - 1}, \tag{4}$$

where $\overline{X}$ is the sample mean and n is the number of observations in the sample.

The variance calculation takes care of the problem of negative deviations from the mean canceling out positive deviations by squaring those deviations.

For the sample variance, by dividing by the sample size minus 1 (or $n - 1$) rather than n, we improve the statistical properties of the sample variance. The quantity $n - 1$ is also known as the number of degrees of freedom in estimating the population variance. To estimate the population variance with s^2, we must first calculate the sample mean, which itself is an estimated parameter. Therefore, once we have computed the sample mean, there are only $n - 1$ independent pieces of information from the sample; that is, if you know the sample mean and $n - 1$ of the observations, you could calculate the missing sample observation.

Sample Standard Deviation

Variance is measured in squared units associated with the mean, and we need a way to return to those original units. Standard deviation, the square root of the variance, solves this problem and is more easily interpreted than the variance.

A useful property of the sample standard deviation is that, unlike sample variance, it is expressed in the same unit as the data itself. If the dataset is percentage of daily returns for an index, then both the average and the standard deviation of the dataset is in percentage terms, while the variance is in squared percentage of daily returns.

Sample Standard Deviation Formula. The **sample standard deviation**, s, is:

$$s = \sqrt{\frac{\sum_{i=1}^{n}(X_i - \overline{X})^2}{n - 1}}, \tag{5}$$

where $\overline{X}$ is the sample mean and n is the number of observations in the sample.

Because the standard deviation is a measure of dispersion about the arithmetic mean, we usually present the arithmetic mean and standard deviation together when summarizing data. When we are dealing with data that represent a time series of percentage changes, presenting the geometric mean (i.e., representing the compound rate of growth) is also very helpful.

Downside Deviation and Coefficient of Variation

An asset's variance or standard deviation of returns is often interpreted as a measure of the asset's risk. Variance and standard deviation of returns take account of returns above and below the mean, or upside and downside risks, respectively. However, investors are typically concerned only with **downside risk**—for example, returns below the mean or below some specified minimum target return. As a result, analysts have developed measures of downside risk.

Downside Deviation

In practice, we may be concerned with values of return (or another variable) below some level other than the mean. For example, if our return objective is 6.0 percent annually (our minimum acceptable return), then we may be concerned particularly with returns below 6.0 percent a year. The target downside deviation, also referred to as the **target semideviation**, is a measure of dispersion of the observations (here, returns) below a target—for example 6.0 percent. To calculate a sample target semideviation, we first specify the target. After identifying observations below the target, we find the sum of those squared negative deviations from the target, divide that sum by the total number of observations in the sample minus 1, and, finally, take the square root.

> **Sample Target Semideviation Formula.** The target semideviation, s_{Target}, is:

$$s_{Target} = \sqrt{\sum_{\text{for all} X_i \leq B}^{n} \frac{(X_i - B)^2}{n - 1}},$$ (6)

> where B is the target and n is the total number of sample observations. We illustrate this in Example 3.

EXAMPLE 3

Calculating Target Downside Deviation

Consider the monthly returns on a portfolio as shown in Exhibit 11:

Exhibit 11: Monthly Portfolio Returns

Month	Return (%)
January	5
February	3
March	−1
April	−4
May	4
June	2
July	0
August	4
September	3
October	0
November	6
December	5

1. Calculate the target downside deviation when the target return is 3 percent.

   Solution:

Month	Observation	Deviation from the 3% Target	Deviations below the Target	Squared Deviations below the Target
January	5	2	—	—
February	3	0	—	—
March	−1	−4	−4	16
April	−4	−7	−7	49
May	4	1	—	—
June	2	−1	−1	1
July	0	−3	−3	9
August	4	1	—	—
September	3	0	—	—
October	0	−3	−3	9
November	6	3	—	—
December	5	2	—	—
Sum				84

$$\text{Target semideviation} = \sqrt{\frac{84}{(12-1)}} = 2.7634\%.$$

2. If the target return were 4 percent, would your answer be different from that for question 1? Without using calculations, explain how would it be different?

Solution:

If the target return is higher, then the existing deviations would be larger and there would be several more values in the deviations and squared deviations below the target; so, the target semideviation would be larger.

How does the target downside deviation relate to the sample standard deviation? We illustrate the differences between the target downside deviation and the standard deviation in Example 4, using the data in Example 3.

EXAMPLE 4

Comparing the Target Downside Deviation with the Standard Deviation

1. Given the data in Example 3, calculate the sample standard deviation.

   Solution:

Month	Observation	Deviation from the Mean	Squared Deviation
January	5	2.75	7.5625
February	3	0.75	0.5625
March	−1	−3.25	10.5625
April	−4	−6.25	39.0625
May	4	1.75	3.0625
June	2	−0.25	0.0625

Month	Observation	Deviation from the Mean	Squared Deviation
July	0	−2.25	5.0625
August	4	1.75	3.0625
September	3	0.75	0.5625
October	0	−2.25	5.0625
November	6	3.75	14.0625
December	5	2.75	7.5625
Sum	27		96.2500

The sample standard deviation is $\sqrt{\frac{96.2500}{11}} = 2.958\%$.

2. Given the data in Example 3, calculate the target downside deviation if the target is 2 percent.

   Solution:

Month	Observation	Deviation from the 2% Target	Deviations below the Target	Squared Deviations below the Target
January	5	3	—	—
February	3	1	—	—
March	−1	−3	−3	9
April	−4	−6	−6	36
May	4	2	—	—
June	2	0	—	—
July	0	−2	−2	4
August	4	2	—	—
September	3	1	—	—
October	0	−2	−2	4
November	6	4	—	—
December	5	3	—	—
Sum				53

The target semideviation with 2 percent target $= \sqrt{\frac{53}{11}} = 2.195$ percent.

3. Compare the standard deviation, the target downside deviation if the target is 2 percent, and the target downside deviation if the target is 3 percent.

   Solution:

   The standard deviation is based on the deviation from the mean, or 27% / 12 = 2.25%. The standard deviation includes all deviations from the mean, not just those below it. This results in a sample standard deviation of 2.958 percent.

   Considering just the four observations below the 2 percent target, the target semideviation is 2.195 percent. It is less than the sample standard deviation since target semideviation captures only the downside risk (i.e., deviations below the target). Considering target semideviation with a 3 percent target, there are now five observations below 3 percent, so the target semideviation is higher, at 2.763 percent.

Coefficient of Variation

We noted earlier that the standard deviation is more easily interpreted than variance because standard deviation uses the same units of measurement as the observations. We may sometimes find it difficult to interpret what standard deviation means in terms of the relative degree of variability of different sets of data, however, either because the datasets have markedly different means or because the datasets have different units of measurement. In this section, we explain a measure of relative dispersion, the coefficient of variation that can be useful in such situations. **Relative dispersion** is the amount of dispersion relative to a reference value or benchmark.

The coefficient of variation is helpful in such situations as that just described (i.e., datasets with markedly different means or different units of measurement).

> **Coefficient of Variation Formula.** The **coefficient of variation** (CV) is the ratio of the standard deviation of a set of observations to their mean value:

$$CV = \frac{s}{\overline{X}},$$

(7)

> where s is the sample standard deviation and $\overline{X}$ is the sample mean.

When the observations are returns, for example, the CV measures the amount of risk (standard deviation) per unit of reward (mean return). An issue that may arise, especially when dealing with returns, is that if $\overline{X}$ is negative, the statistic is meaningless.

The CV may be stated as a multiple (e.g., two times) or as a percentage (e.g., 200 percent). Expressing the magnitude of variation among observations relative to their average size, the CV permits direct comparisons of dispersion across different datasets. Reflecting the correction for scale, the CV is a scale-free measure (i.e., , it has no units of measurement).

We illustrate the usefulness of CV for comparing datasets with markedly different standard deviations using two hypothetical samples of companies in Example 5.

EXAMPLE 5

Coefficient of Variation of Returns on Assets

Suppose an analyst collects the return on assets (ROA), in percentage terms, for 10 companies for each of two industries:

Exhibit 12: Returns on Assets for Two Industries		
Company	Industry A	Industry B
1	−5	−10
2	−3	−9
3	−1	−7
4	2	−3
5	4	1
6	6	3
7	7	5
8	9	18

Company	Industry A	Industry B
9	10	20
10	11	22

These data can be represented graphically as shown in Exhibit 13:

Exhibit 13: Returns on Assets Depicted Graphically

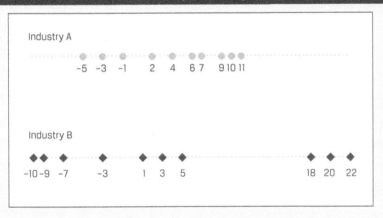

1. Calculate the average ROA for each industry.

   Solution:

   The arithmetic mean ROA for both industries is the sum of the 10 observations, which in both cases is 40, divided by the 10 observations, or 40/10 = 4%.

2. Calculate the standard deviation of ROA for each industry.

   Solution:

   Using Equation 5, the standard deviation for Industry A is 5.60 and 12.12 for Industry B.

3. Calculate the coefficient of variation (CV) of the ROA for each industry.

   Solution:

   Using Equation 7, the CV for Industry A = 5.60/4 = 1.40 and the CV for Industry B = 12.12/4 = 3.03.

   Though the two industries have the same arithmetic mean ROA, the dispersion is quite different—with Industry B's returns on assets being much more disperse than those of Industry A. The CV for these two industries reflects this, with Industry B having a larger CV. The interpretation is that the risk per unit of mean return is more than two times (2.16 = 3.03/1.40) greater for Industry B than Industry A.

QUESTION SET

Consider the annual MSCI World Index total returns for a 10-year period, as shown in Exhibit 14:

Exhibit 14: MSCI World Index Total Returns

Year		Year	
Year 1	15.25%	Year 6	30.79%
Year 2	10.02%	Year 7	12.34%
Year 3	20.65%	Year 8	−5.02%
Year 4	9.57%	Year 9	16.54%
Year 5	−40.33%	Year 10	27.37%

1. For Years 6 through 10, the mean absolute deviation (MAD) of the MSCI World Index total returns is *closest* to:

   A. 10.20 percent.

   B. 12.74 percent.

   C. 16.40 percent.

   Solution:

   A is correct. The MAD is calculated as follows:

   Step 1   Sum annual returns and divide by n to find the arithmetic mean ($\bar{X}$) of 16.40 percent.

   Step 2   Calculate the absolute value of the difference between each year's return and the mean from Step 1. Sum the results and divide by n to find the MAD:

   $$\text{MAD} = \frac{\sum_{i=1}^{n} |X_i - \bar{X}|}{n},$$

   $$\text{MAD} = \frac{50.98\%}{5} = 10.20\%.$$

   These calculations are shown in the following table:

	Step 1	Step 2
Year	**Return**	$|X_i - \bar{X}|$
Year 6	30.79%	14.39%
Year 7	12.34%	4.06%
Year 8	−5.02%	21.42%
Year 9	16.54%	0.14%
Year 10	27.37%	10.97%
Sum:	82.02%	50.98%
n:	5	5
$\bar{X}$:	16.40%	10.20%

   Annual returns and summary statistics for three funds are listed as follows:

	Annual Returns (%)		
Year	**Fund ABC**	**Fund XYZ**	**Fund PQR**
Year 1	−20.0	−33.0	−14.0
Year 2	23.0	−12.0	−18.0

	Annual Returns (%)		
Year	Fund ABC	Fund XYZ	Fund PQR
Year 3	−14.0	−12.0	6.0
Year 4	5.0	−8.0	−2.0
Year 5	−14.0	11.0	3.0
Mean	−4.0	−10.8	−5.0
Standard deviation	17.8	15.6	10.5

2. The fund with the mean absolute deviation (MAD) is Fund:

   A. ABC.

   B. XYZ.

   C. PQR.

   Solution:

   A is correct. The MAD of Fund ABC's returns is the highest among the three funds. Using Equation 3, the MAD for each fund is calculated as follows:

   MAD for Fund ABC =

   $$\frac{|-20-(-4)|+|23-(-4)|+|-14-(-4)|+|5-(-4)|+|-14-(-4)|}{5} = 14.4\%.$$

   MAD for Fund XYZ =

   $$\frac{|-33-(-10.8)|+|-12-(-10.8)|+|-12-(-10.8)|+|-8-(-10.8)|+|11-(-10.8)|}{5}$$

   $$= 9.8\%.$$

   MAD for Fund PQR =

   $$\frac{|-14-(-5)|+|-18-(-5)|+|6-(-5)|+|-2-(-5)|+|3-(-5)|}{5} = 8.8\%.$$

3. Consider the statistics in Exhibit 15 for Portfolio A and Portfolio B over the past 12 months:

Exhibit 15: Portfolio A and Portfolio B Statistics

	Portfolio A	Portfolio B
Average Return	3%	3%
Geometric Return	2.85%	?
Standard Deviation	4%	6%

4. The geometric mean return of Portfolio B is *most likely* to be:

   A. less than 2.85 percent.

   B. equal to 2.85 percent.

C.   greater than 2.85 percent.

Solution:

A is correct. The higher the dispersion of a distribution, the greater the difference between the arithmetic mean and the geometric mean.

4   MEASURES OF SHAPE OF A DISTRIBUTION

☐ interpret and evaluate measures of skewness and kurtosis to address an investment problem

Mean and variance may not adequately describe an investment's distribution of returns. In calculations of variance, for example, the deviations around the mean are squared, so we do not know whether large deviations are likely to be positive or negative. We need to go beyond measures of central tendency, location, and dispersion to reveal other important characteristics of the distribution. One important characteristic of interest to analysts is the degree of symmetry in return distributions.

If a return distribution is symmetrical about its mean, each side of the distribution is a mirror image of the other. Thus, equal loss and gain intervals exhibit the same frequencies.

One of the most important distributions is the normal distribution, depicted in Exhibit 16. This symmetrical, bell-shaped distribution plays a central role in the mean–variance model of portfolio selection; it is also used extensively in financial risk management. The normal distribution has the following characteristics:

- Its mean, median, and mode are equal.

- It is completely described by two parameters—its mean and variance (or standard deviation).

Exhibit 16: The Normal Distribution

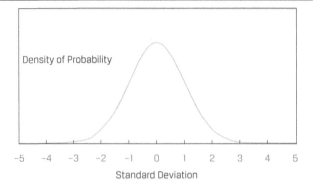

Other distributions may require more information than just the mean and variance to characterize their shape.

Skewness

A distribution that is not symmetrical is termed **skewed**. A return distribution with positive skew has frequent small losses and a few extreme gains. A return distribution with negative skew has frequent small gains and a few extreme losses. Panel A of Exhibit 17 illustrates a continuous positively skewed distribution, which has a long tail on its right side; Panel B illustrates a continuous negatively skewed distribution, which has a long tail on its left side.

Exhibit 17: Properties of Skewed Distributions

A. Positively Skewed

B. Negatively Skewed

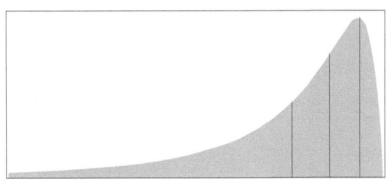

For a continuous positively skewed unimodal distribution, the mode is less than the median, which is less than the mean. For the continuous negatively skewed unimodal distribution, the mean is less than the median, which is less than the mode. For a given expected return and standard deviation, investors should be attracted by a positive skew because the mean return lies above the median. Relative to the mean return, positive skew amounts to limited, though frequent, downside returns compared with somewhat unlimited, but less frequent, upside returns.

Skewness is the name given to a statistical measure of skew. (The word "skewness" is also sometimes used interchangeably for "skew.") Like variance, skewness is computed using each observation's deviation from its mean. **Skewness** (sometimes referred to as relative skewness) is computed as the average cubed deviation from the mean, standardized by dividing by the standard deviation cubed to make the measure free of scale.

Cubing, unlike squaring, preserves the sign of the deviations from the mean. If a distribution is positively skewed with a mean greater than its median, then more than half of the deviations from the mean are negative and less than half are positive. However, for the sum of the cubed deviations to be positive, the losses must be small and likely and the gains less likely but more extreme. Therefore, if skewness is positive, the average magnitude of positive deviations is larger than the average magnitude of negative deviations.

The approximation for computing **sample skewness** when n is large (100 or more) is:

$$\text{Skewness} \approx \left(\frac{1}{n}\right) \frac{\sum_{i=1}^{n}(X_i - \overline{X})^3}{s^3}. \tag{8}$$

As you will learn later in the curriculum, different investment strategies may introduce different types and amounts of skewness into returns.

Kurtosis

Another way in which a return distribution might differ from a normal distribution is its relative tendency to generate large deviations from the mean. Most investors would perceive a greater chance of extremely large deviations from the mean as higher risk.

Kurtosis is a measure of the combined weight of the tails of a distribution relative to the rest of the distribution—that is, the proportion of the total probability that is outside of, say, 2.5 standard deviations of the mean. A distribution that has fatter tails than the normal distribution is referred to as **leptokurtic** or **fat-tailed**; a distribution that has thinner tails than the normal distribution is referred to as being **platykurtic** or **thin-tailed**; and a distribution similar to the normal distribution as it concerns relative weight in the tails is called **mesokurtic**. A fat-tailed (thin-tailed) distribution tends to generate more frequent (less frequent) extremely large deviations from the mean than the normal distribution.

Exhibit 18 illustrates a distribution with fatter tails than the normal distribution. By construction, the fat-tailed and normal distributions in Exhibit 18 have the same mean, standard deviation, and skewness. Note that this fat-tailed distribution is more likely than the normal distribution to generate observations in the tail regions defined by the intersection of the distribution lines near a standard deviation of about ±2.5. This fat-tailed distribution is also more likely to generate observations that are near the mean, defined here as the region ±1 standard deviation around the mean. However, to ensure probabilities sum to 1, this distribution generates fewer observations in the regions between the central region and the two tail regions.

Exhibit 18: Fat-Tailed Distribution Compared to the Normal Distribution

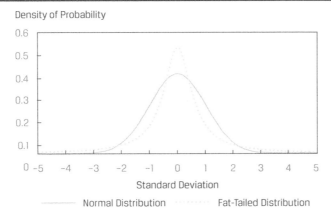

The calculation for kurtosis involves finding the average of deviations from the mean raised to the fourth power and then standardizing that average by dividing by the standard deviation raised to the fourth power. A normal distribution has kurtosis of 3.0, so a fat-tailed distribution has a kurtosis above 3.0 and a thin-tailed distribution has a kurtosis below 3.0.

Excess kurtosis is the kurtosis relative to the normal distribution. For a large sample size ($n = 100$ or more), **sample excess kurtosis** (K_E) is approximately as follows:

$$K_E \approx \left[\left(\frac{1}{n} \right) \frac{\sum_{i=1}^{n} (X_i - \overline{X})^4}{s^4} \right] - 3. \tag{9}$$

As with skewness, this measure is free of scale. Many statistical packages report estimates of sample excess kurtosis, labeling this as simply "kurtosis."

Excess kurtosis thus characterizes kurtosis relative to the normal distribution. A normal distribution has excess kurtosis equal to 0. A fat-tailed distribution has excess kurtosis greater than 0, and a thin-tailed distribution has excess kurtosis less than 0. A return distribution with positive excess kurtosis—a fat-tailed return distribution—has more frequent extremely large deviations from the mean than a normal distribution.

Exhibit 19: Summary of Kurtosis

If kurtosis is ...	then excess kurtosis is ...	Therefore, the distribution is ...	And we refer to the distribution as being ...
above 3.0	above 0	fatter-tailed than the normal distribution.	fat-tailed (leptokurtic)
equal to 3.0	equal to 0	similar in tails to the normal distribution.	mesokurtic
less than 3.0	less than 0	thinner-tailed than the normal distribution.	thin-tailed (platykurtic)

Most equity return series have been found to be fat-tailed. If a return distribution is fat-tailed and we use statistical models that do not account for that distribution, then we will underestimate the likelihood of very bad or very good outcomes. Example 6 revisits the EAA Equity Index from the earlier Example 1 and quantifies the shape of it return distribution.

EXAMPLE 6

Skewness and Kurtosis of EAA Equity Index Daily Returns

Consider the statistics in Exhibit 20 for the EAA Equity Index:

Exhibit 20: Properties of Skewed Distributions

	Daily Return (%)
Arithmetic mean	0.0347
Standard deviation	0.8341
Measure of Symmetry	
Skewness	−0.4260
Excess kurtosis	3.7962

The returns reflect negative skewness, which is illustrated in Exhibit 21 by comparing the distribution of the daily returns with a normal distribution with the same mean and standard deviation.

Exhibit 21: Negative Skewness

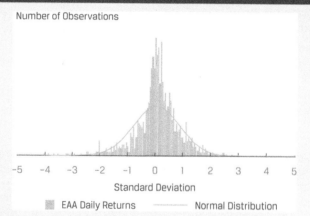

Number of Observations

Standard Deviation

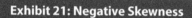
■ EAA Daily Returns   —— Normal Distribution

Using both the statistics and the graph, we see the following:

- The distribution is negatively skewed, as indicated by the negative calculated skewness of −0.4260 and the influence of observations below the mean of 0.0347 percent.

- The highest frequency of returns occurs within the 0.0 to 0.5 standard deviations from the mean (i.e., the mode is greater than the mean as the positive returns are offset by extreme negative deviations).

- The distribution is fat-tailed, as indicated by the positive excess kurtosis of 3.7962. In Exhibit 21, we can see fat tails, a concentration of returns around the mean, and fewer observations in the regions between the central region and the two-tail regions.

To understand the trading liquidity of a stock, investors often look at the distribution of the daily trading volume for a stock. Analyzing the daily volume can provide insights about the interest in the stock, what factors may drive interest in the stock as well as whether the market can absorb a large trade in the stock. The latter may be of interest to investors interested in either establishing or exiting a large position in the particular stock.

INTERPRETING SKEWNESS AND KURTOSIS

Consider the daily trading volume for a stock for one year, as shown in Exhibit 22. In addition to the count of observations within each bin or interval, the number of observations anticipated based on a normal distribution (given the sample arithmetic average and standard deviation) is provided as well. The average trading volume per day for the stock during the year was 8.6 million shares, and the standard deviation was 4.9 million shares.

Exhibit 22: Histogram of Daily Trading Volume for a Stock for One Year

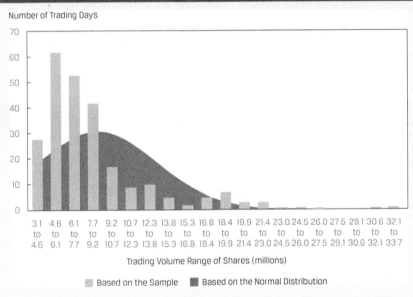

1. Would the distribution be characterized as being skewed? If so, what could account for this situation?

   Solution:

   The distribution appears to be skewed to the right, or positively skewed. This is likely due to: (1) no possible negative trading volume on a given trading day, so the distribution is truncated at zero; and (2) greater-than-typical trading occurring relatively infrequently, such as when there are company-specific announcements.
   The actual skewness for this distribution is 2.1090, which supports this interpretation.

2. Does the distribution displays kurtosis? Explain.

   Solution:

   The distribution appears to have excess kurtosis, with a right-side fat tail and with maximum shares traded in the 4.6 to 6.1 million range, exceeding what is expected if the distribution was normally distributed. There are also fewer observations than expected between the central region and the tail.

The actual excess kurtosis for this distribution is 5.2151, which supports this interpretation.

QUESTION SET

1. An analyst calculates the excess kurtosis of a stock's returns as −0.75. From this information, the analyst should conclude that the distribution of returns is:

   A. normally distributed.

   B. fat-tailed compared to the normal distribution.

   C. thin-tailed compared to the normal distribution.

   Solution:

   C is correct. The distribution is thin-tailed relative to the normal distribution because the excess kurtosis is less than zero.

Use Exhibit 23 to answer questions 2–4.

An analyst examined a cross-section of annual returns for 252 stocks and calculated the following statistics:

Exhibit 23: Cross-Section of Annual Returns

Arithmetic Average	9.986%
Geometric Mean	9.909%
Variance	0.001723
Skewness	0.704
Excess Kurtosis	0.503

2. The coefficient of variation (CV) is closest to:

   A. 0.02.

   B. 0.42.

   C. 2.41.

   Solution:

   B is correct. The CV is the ratio of the standard deviation to the arithmetic average, or $\sqrt{0.001723}/0.09986 = 0.416$.

3. This distribution is best described as:

   A. negatively skewed.

   B. having no skewness.

   C. positively skewed.

   Solution:

   C is correct. The skewness is positive, so it is right-skewed (positively skewed).

4. Compared to the normal distribution, this sample's distribution is best described as having tails of the distribution with:

   A. less probability than the normal distribution.

   B. the same probability as the normal distribution.

   C. more probability than the normal distribution.

   Solution:

   C is correct. The excess kurtosis is positive, indicating that the distribution is "fat-tailed"; therefore, there is more probability in the tails of the distribution relative to the normal distribution.

CORRELATION BETWEEN TWO VARIABLES

5

☐ | interpret correlation between two variables to address an investment problem

Scatter Plot

A **scatter plot** is a useful tool for displaying and understanding potential relationships between two variables. Suppose an analyst is interested in the relative performance of two sectors, information technology (IT) and utilities, compared to the market index over a specific five-year period. The analyst has obtained the sector and market index returns for each month over the five years under investigation. Exhibit 24 presents a scatterplot of returns for the IT sector index versus the S&P 500, and Exhibit 25 presents a scatterplot of returns for the utilities sector index versus the S&P 500.

Tight (loose) clustering signals a potentially stronger (weaker) relationship between the two variables.

Exhibit 24: Scatter Plot of Information Technology Sector Index Return versus S&P 500 Index Return

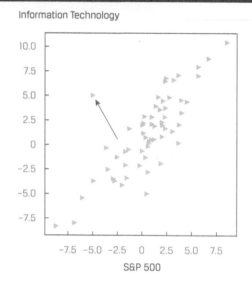

Exhibit 25: Scatter Plot of Utilities Sector Index Return versus S&P 500 Index Return

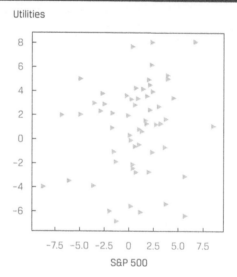

Despite their relatively straightforward construction, scatter plots convey valuable information. First, it is important to inspect for any potential association between the two variables. The pattern of the scatter plot may indicate no apparent relationship, a linear association, or a non-linear relationship. Furthermore, the strength of the association can be determined by how closely the data points are clustered around a line drawn across the observations.

Examining Exhibit 24 we can see the returns of the IT sector are highly positively associated with S&P 500 Index returns because the data points are tightly clustered along a positively sloped line. In contrast, Exhibit 25 tells a different story for relative performance of the utilities sector and S&P 500 index returns: The data points appear to be distributed in no discernable pattern, indicating no clear relationship among these variables.

Second, observing the data points located toward the ends of each axis, which represent the maximum or minimum values, provides a quick sense of the data range. Third, if a relationship among the variables is apparent, inspecting the scatter plot can help to spot extreme values (i.e., outliers). For example, an outlier data point is readily detected in Exhibit 24 as indicated by the arrow. Finding these extreme values and handling them with appropriate measures is an important part of the financial modeling process.

Scatter plots are a powerful tool for finding patterns between two variables, for assessing data range, and for spotting extreme values. In some situations, however, we need to inspect for pairwise associations among many variables—for example, when conducting feature selection from dozens of variables to build a predictive model.

Now that we have some understanding of sample variance and standard deviation, we can more formally consider the concept of correlation between two random variables that we previously explored visually in the scatter plots.

Covariance and Correlation

Correlation is a measure of the linear relationship between two random variables. The first step in considering how two variables vary together, however, is constructing their covariance.

> **Definition of Sample Covariance.** The **sample covariance** (s_{XY}) is a measure of how two variables in a sample move together:

$$s_{XY} = \frac{\sum_{i=1}^{n}(X_i - \bar{X})(Y_i - \bar{Y})}{n-1}. \tag{10}$$

Equation 10 indicates that the sample covariance is the average value of the product of the deviations of observations on two random variables (X_i and Y_i) from their sample means. If the random variables are returns, the units would be returns squared. Also, note the use of $n-1$ in the denominator, which ensures that the sample covariance is an unbiased estimate of population covariance.

Stated simply, covariance is a measure of the joint variability of two random variables. If the random variables vary in the same direction—for example, X tends to be above its mean when Y is above its mean, and X tends to be below its mean when Y is below its mean—then their covariance is positive. If the variables vary in the opposite direction relative to their respective means, then their covariance is negative.

The size of the covariance measure alone is difficult to interpret as it involves squared units of measure and so depends on the magnitude of the variables. This brings us to the normalized version of covariance, which is the correlation coefficient.

> **Definition of Sample Correlation Coefficient.** The **sample correlation coefficient** is a standardized measure of how two variables in a sample move together. The sample correlation coefficient (r_{XY}) is the ratio of the sample covariance to the product of the two variables' standard deviations:

$$r_{XY} = \frac{s_{XY}}{s_X s_Y}. \tag{11}$$

Importantly, the correlation coefficient expresses the strength of the linear relationship between the two random variables.

Properties of Correlation

We now discuss the correlation coefficient, or simply correlation, and its properties in more detail:

1. Correlation ranges from −1 and +1 for two random variables, X and Y:

$-1 \leq r_{XY} \leq +1$.

2. A correlation of 0, termed uncorrelated, indicates an absence of any linear relationship between the variables.

3. A positive correlation close to +1 indicates a strong positive linear relationship. A correlation of 1 indicates a perfect linear relationship.

4. A negative correlation close to −1 indicates a strong negative (i.e., inverse) linear relationship. A correlation of −1 indicates a perfect inverse linear relationship.

We return to scatter plots to illustrate correlation visually. In contrast to the correlation coefficient, which expresses the relationship between two data series using a single number, a scatter plot depicts the relationship graphically. Therefore, scatter plots are a very useful tool for the sensible interpretation of a correlation coefficient.

Exhibit 26 shows examples of scatter plots. Panel A shows the scatter plot of two variables with a correlation of +1. Note that all the points on the scatter plot in Panel A lie on a straight line with a positive slope. Whenever variable X increases by one unit, variable Y increases by two units. Because all of the points in the graph lie on a straight line, an increase of one unit in X is associated with an exact two-unit increase in Y, regardless of the level of X. Even if the slope of the line were different (but positive), the correlation between the two variables would still be +1 as long as all the points lie on that straight line. Panel B shows a scatter plot for two variables with a correlation coefficient of −1. Once again, the plotted observations all fall on a straight line. In this graph, however, the line has a negative slope. As X increases by one unit, Y decreases by two units, regardless of the initial value of X.

Exhibit 26: Scatter Plots Showing Various Degrees of Correlation

A. Variables With a Correlation of +1

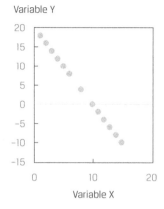

B. Variables With a Correlation of –1

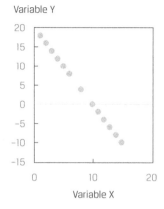

C. Variables With a Correlation of 0

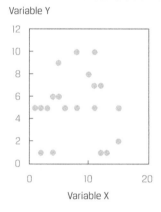

D. Variables With a Strong Nonlinear Association

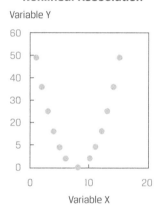

Panel C shows a scatter plot of two variables with a correlation of 0; they have no linear relation. This graph shows that the value of variable X tells us nothing about the value of variable Y. Panel D shows a scatter plot of two variables that have a non-linear relationship. Because the correlation coefficient is a measure of the linear association between two variables, it would not be appropriate to use the correlation coefficient in this case.

Limitations of Correlation Analysis

Exhibit 26 illustrates that correlation measures the linear association between two variables, but it may not always be reliable. Two variables can have a strong *nonlinear* relation and still have a very low correlation. A nonlinear relation between variables X and Y is shown in Panel D. Even though these two variables are perfectly associated, there is no linear association between them and hence no meaningful correlation.

Correlation may also be an unreliable measure when outliers are present in one or both variables. As we have seen, outliers are small numbers of observations at either extreme (small or large) of a sample. Correlation may be quite sensitive to outliers. In such a situation, we should consider whether it makes sense to exclude those outlier observations and whether they are noise or true information. We use judgment to determine whether those outliers contain information about the two variables' relationship, and should be included in the correlation analysis, or contain no information, and should be excluded. If they are to be excluded from the correlation analysis, as we have seen previously, outlier observations can be handled by trimming or winsorizing the dataset.

Importantly, keep in mind that correlation does not imply causation. Even if two variables are highly correlated, one does not necessarily cause the other in the sense that certain values of one variable bring about the occurrence of certain values of the other.

Moreover, with visualizations too, including scatter plots, we must be on guard against unconsciously making judgments about causal relationships that may or may not be supported by the data.

The term **spurious correlation** has been used to refer to:

- correlation between two variables that reflects chance relationships in a particular dataset;

- correlation induced by a calculation that mixes each of two variables with a third variable; and

- correlation between two variables arising not from a direct relation between them but from their relation to a third variable.

As an example of the chance relationship, consider the monthly US retail sales of beer, wine, and liquor and the atmospheric carbon dioxide levels from 2000 to 2018. The correlation is 0.824, indicating that a positive relation exists between the two. However, there is no reason to suspect that the levels of atmospheric carbon dioxide are related to the retail sales of beer, wine, and liquor.

As an example of the second type of spurious correlation, two variables that are uncorrelated may be correlated if divided by a third variable. For example, consider a cross-sectional sample of companies' dividends and total assets. While there may be a low correlation between these two variables, dividing each by market capitalization may increase the correlation.

As an example of the third type of spurious correlation, height may be positively correlated with the extent of a person's vocabulary, but the underlying relationships are between age and height and between age and vocabulary.

Investment professionals must be cautious in basing investment strategies on high correlations. Spurious correlations may suggest investment strategies that appear profitable but would not be, if implemented.

A further issue is that correlation does not tell the whole story about the data. Consider Anscombe's Quartet, discussed in Example 7, for which dissimilar graphs can be developed with variables that have the same mean, same standard deviation, and same correlation.

EXAMPLE 7

Anscombe's Quartet

Francis Anscombe, a British statistician, developed datasets that illustrate why just looking at summary statistics (i.e., mean, standard deviation, and correlation) does not fully describe the data. He created four datasets (designated I, II, III, and IV), each with two variables, X and Y, such that:

- The Xs in each dataset have the same mean and standard deviation, 9.00 and 3.32, respectively.

- The Ys in each dataset have the same mean and standard deviation, 7.50 and 2.03, respectively.

- The Xs and Ys in each dataset have the same correlation of 0.82.

Exhibit 27: Summary Statistics

Observation	I		II		III		IV	
	X	Y	X	Y	X	Y	X	Y
1	10	8.04	10	9.14	10	7.46	8	6.6
2	8	6.95	8	8.14	8	6.77	8	5.8
3	13	7.58	13	8.74	13	12.74	8	7.7
4	9	8.81	9	8.77	9	7.11	8	8.8
5	11	8.33	11	9.26	11	7.81	8	8.5
6	14	9.96	14	8.1	14	8.84	8	7
7	6	7.24	6	6.13	6	6.08	8	5.3
8	4	4.26	4	3.1	4	5.39	19	13
9	12	10.8	12	9.13	12	8.15	8	5.6
10	7	4.82	7	7.26	7	6.42	8	7.9
11	5	5.68	5	4.74	5	5.73	8	6.9
N	11	11	11	11	11	11	11	11
Mean	9.00	7.50	9.00	7.50	9.00	7.50	9.00	7.50
Standard deviation	3.32	2.03	3.32	2.03	3.32	2.03	3.32	2.03
Correlation	0.82		0.82		0.82		0.82	

While the X variable has the same values for I, II, and III in the quartet of datasets, the Y variables are quite different, creating different relationships. The four datasets are:

I An approximate linear relationship between X and Y.

II A curvilinear relationship between X and Y.

III A linear relationship except for one outlier.

IV A constant X with the exception of one outlier.

Depicting the quartet visually,

Exhibit 28: Visual Depiction

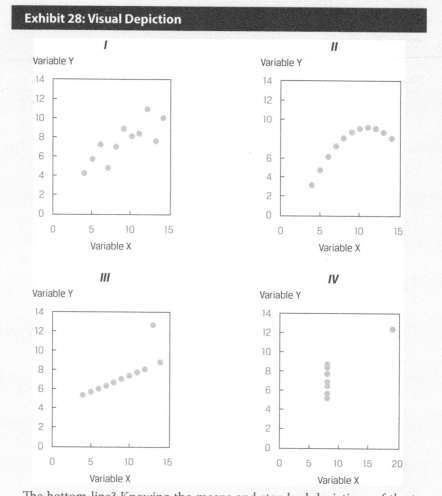

The bottom line? Knowing the means and standard deviations of the two variables, as well as the correlation between them, does not tell the entire story.

Source: Francis John Anscombe, "Graphs in Statistical Analysis," *American Statistician* 27 (February 1973): 17–21.

QUESTION SET

1. A correlation of 0.34 between two variables, X and Y, is *best* described as:

   A. changes in X causing changes in Y.

   B. a positive association between X and Y.

   C. a curvilinear relationship between X and Y.

   Solution:

   B is correct. The correlation coefficient is positive, indicating that the two series move together.

2. Which of the following is a potential problem with interpreting a correlation coefficient?

   A. Outliers

   B. Spurious correlation

C. Both outliers and spurious correlation

Solution:

C is correct. Both outliers and spurious correlation are potential problems with interpreting correlation coefficients.

Use the information in Exhibit 29 to answer questions 3 and 4.

An analyst is evaluating the tendency of returns on the portfolio of stocks she manages to move along with bond and real estate indexes. She gathered monthly data on returns and the indexes:

Exhibit 29: Monthly Data on Returns and Indexes

	Returns (%)		
	Portfolio Returns	Bond Index Returns	Real Estate Index Returns
Arithmetic average	5.5	3.2	7.8
Standard deviation	8.2	3.4	10.3
	Portfolio Returns and Bond Index Returns	Portfolio Returns and Real Estate Index Returns	
Covariance	18.9	−55.9	

3. Without calculating the correlation coefficient, the correlation of the portfolio returns and the bond index returns is *most likely* to be:

   A. negative.

   B. zero.

   C. positive.

   Solution:

   C is correct. The correlation coefficient is positive because the covariance is positive.

4. Without calculating the correlation coefficient, the correlation of the portfolio returns and the real estate index returns is:

   A. negative.

   B. zero.

   C. positive.

   Solution:

   A is correct. The correlation coefficient is negative because the covariance is negative.

5. Consider two variables, A and B. If variable A has a mean of −0.56, variable B has a mean of 0.23, and the covariance between the two variables is positive, the correlation between these two variables is:

   A. negative.

   B. zero.

C. positive.

Solution:

C is correct. The correlation coefficient must be positive because the covariance is positive. The fact that one or both variables have a negative mean does not affect the sign of the correlation coefficient.

PRACTICE PROBLEMS

The following information relates to questions 1-5

Consider the results of an analysis focusing on the market capitalizations of a sample of 100 firms:

Exhibit 1: Market Capitalization of a Sample of 100 Firms

Bin	Cumulative Percentage of Sample (%)	Market Capitalization (euro billions)		Number of Observations
		Lower Bound	Upper Bound	
1	5	0.28	15.45	5
2	10	15.45	21.22	5
3	15	21.22	29.37	5
4	20	29.37	32.57	5
5	25	32.57	34.72	5
6	30	34.72	37.58	5
7	35	37.58	39.90	5
8	40	39.90	41.57	5
9	45	41.57	44.86	5
10	50	44.86	46.88	5
11	55	46.88	49.40	5
12	60	49.40	51.27	5
13	65	51.27	53.58	5
14	70	53.58	56.66	5
15	75	56.66	58.34	5
16	80	58.34	63.10	5
17	85	63.10	67.06	5
18	90	67.06	73.00	5
19	95	73.00	81.62	5
20	100	81.62	96.85	5

1. The tenth percentile corresponds to observations in bin(s):

   A. 2.

   B. 1 and 2.

   C. 19 and 20.

2. The second quintile corresponds to observations in bin(s):

   A. 8.

B. 5, 6, 7, and 8.

C. 6, 7, 8, 9, and 10.

3. The fourth quartile corresponds to observations in bin(s):

A. 17.

B. 17, 18, 19, and 20.

C. 16, 17, 18, 19, and 20.

4. The median is *closest* to:

A. 44.86.

B. 46.88.

C. 49.40.

5. The interquartile range is *closest* to:

A. 20.76.

B. 23.62.

C. 25.52.

---

6. Exhibit 12 shows the annual MSCI World Index total returns for a 10-year period.

Exhibit 1: MSCI World Index Returns			
Year 1	15.25%	Year 6	30.79%
Year 2	10.02%	Year 7	12.34%
Year 3	20.65%	Year 8	−5.02%
Year 4	9.57%	Year 9	16.54%
Year 5	−40.33%	Year 10	27.37%

The fourth quintile return for the MSCI World Index is *closest* to:

A. 20.65 percent.

B. 26.03 percent.

C. 27.37 percent.

The following information relates to questions 7-9

A fund had the following experience over the past 10 years:

Exhibit 1: Performance over 10 Years	
Year	**Return**
1	4.5%
2	6.0%
3	1.5%
4	−2.0%
5	0.0%
6	4.5%
7	3.5%
8	2.5%
9	5.5%
10	4.0%

7. The fund's standard deviation of returns over the 10 years is *closest* to:

   A. 2.40 percent.

   B. 2.53 percent.

   C. 7.58 percent.

8. The target semideviation of the returns over the 10 years, if the target is 2 percent, is *closest* to:

   A. 1.42 percent.

   B. 1.50 percent.

   C. 2.01 percent.

9. Consider the mean monthly return and the standard deviation for three industry sectors, as shown in Exhibit 2:

Exhibit 2: Mean Monthly Return and Standard Deviations		
Sector	**Mean Monthly Return (%)**	**Standard Deviation of Return (%)**
Utilities (UTIL)	2.10	1.23
Materials (MATR)	1.25	1.35
Industrials (INDU)	3.01	1.52

   Based on the coefficient of variation (CV), the riskiest sector is:

   A. utilities.

   B. materials.

   C. industrials.

SOLUTIONS

1. B is correct. The tenth percentile corresponds to the lowest 10 percent of the observations in the sample, which are in bins 1 and 2.

2. B is correct. The second quintile corresponds to the second 20 percent of observations. The first 20 percent consists of bins 1 through 4. The second 20 percent of observations consists of bins 5 through 8.

3. C is correct. A quartile consists of 25 percent of the data, and the last 25 percent of the 20 bins are 16 through 20.

4. B is correct. The center of the 20 bins is represented by the market capitalization of the highest value of the 10th bin and the lowest value of the 11th bin, which is 46.88.

5. B is correct. The interquartile range is the difference between the lowest value in the second quartile and the highest value in the third quartile. The lowest value of the second quartile is 34.72, and the highest value of the third quartile is 58.34. Therefore, the interquartile range is 58.34 − 34.72 = 23.62.

6. B is correct. Quintiles divide a distribution into fifths, with the fourth quintile occurring at the point at which 80 percent of the observations lie below it. The fourth quintile is equivalent to the 80th percentile. To find the yth percentile (P_y), we first must determine its location. The formula for the location (L_y) of a yth percentile in an array with n entries sorted in ascending order is $L_y = (n + 1) \times (y/100)$. In this case, $n = 10$ and $y = 80\%$, so

$$L_{80} = (10 + 1) \times (80/100) = 11 \times 0.8 = 8.8.$$

With the data arranged in ascending order (−40.33 percent, −5.02 percent, 9.57 percent, 10.02 percent, 12.34 percent, 15.25 percent, 16.54 percent, 20.65 percent, 27.37 percent, and 30.79 percent), the 8.8th position would be between the eighth and ninth entries, 20.65 percent and 27.37 percent, respectively. Using linear interpolation, $P_{80} = X_8 + (L_y − 8) \times (X_9 − X_8)$,

$$P_{80} = 20.65 + (8.8 − 8) \times (27.37 − 20.65)$$

$$= 20.65 + (0.8 \times 6.72) = 20.65 + 5.38$$

$$= 26.03 \text{ percent.}$$

7. B is correct. The fund's standard deviation of returns is calculated as follows:

Year	Return	Deviation from Mean	Deviation Squared
1	4.5%	0.0150	0.000225
2	6.0%	0.0300	0.000900
3	1.5%	−0.0150	0.000225
4	−2.0%	−0.0500	0.002500
5	0.0%	−0.0300	0.000900
6	4.5%	0.0150	0.000225
7	3.5%	0.0050	0.000025
8	2.5%	−0.0050	0.000025
9	5.5%	0.0250	0.000625

Year	Return	Deviation from Mean	Deviation Squared
10	4.0%	0.0100	0.000100
Mean	3.0%		
Sum			**0.005750**

The standard deviation is the square root of the sum of the squared deviations, divided by $n - 1$:

$$s = \sqrt{\frac{0.005750}{(10 - 1)}} = 2.5276\%.$$

8. B is correct. The target semideviation of the returns over the 10 years with a target of 2 percent is calculated as follows:

Year	Return	Deviation Squared below Target of 2%
1	4.5%	
2	6.0%	
3	1.5%	0.000025
4	−2.0%	0.001600
5	0.0%	0.000400
6	4.5%	
7	3.5%	
8	2.5%	
9	5.5%	
10	4.0%	
Sum		0.002025

The target semideviation is the square root of the sum of the squared deviations from the target, divided by $n - 1$:

$$s_{\text{Target}} = \sqrt{\frac{0.002025}{(10 - 1)}} = 1.5\%.$$

9. B is correct. The CV is the ratio of the standard deviation to the mean, where a higher CV implies greater risk per unit of return.

$$CV_{UTIL} = \frac{s}{\bar{X}} = \frac{1.23\%}{2.10\%} = 0.59,$$

$$CV_{MATR} = \frac{s}{\bar{X}} = \frac{1.35\%}{1.25\%} = 1.08,$$

$$CV_{INDU} = \frac{s}{\bar{X}} = \frac{1.52\%}{3.01\%} = 0.51.$$

Probability Trees and Conditional Expectations

by Richard A. DeFusco, PhD, CFA, Dennis W. McLeavey, DBA, CFA, Jerald
E. Pinto, PhD, CFA, and David E. Runkle, PhD, CFA.

*Richard A. DeFusco, PhD, CFA, is at the University of Nebraska-Lincoln (USA). Dennis W.
McLeavey, DBA, CFA, is at the University of Rhode Island (USA). Jerald E. Pinto, PhD,
CFA, is at CFA Institute (USA). David E. Runkle, PhD, CFA, is at Jacobs Levy Equity
Management (USA).*

LEARNING OUTCOMES	
Mastery	*The candidate should be able to:*
☐	calculate expected values, variances, and standard deviations and demonstrate their application to investment problems
☐	formulate an investment problem as a probability tree and explain the use of conditional expectations in investment application
☐	calculate and interpret an updated probability in an investment setting using Bayes' formula

INTRODUCTION

Investment decisions are made under uncertainty about the future direction of the economy, issuers, companies, and prices. This learning module presents probability tools that address many real-world problems involving uncertainty and applies to a variety of investment management applications.

Lesson 1 introduces the calculation of the expected value, variance, and standard deviation for a random variable. These are essential quantitative concepts in investment management. Lesson 2 introduces probability trees that help in visualizing the conditional expectations and the total probabilities for expected value.

When making investment decisions, analysts often rely on perspectives, which may be influenced by subsequent observations. Lesson 3 introduces Bayes' formula, a rational method to adjust probabilities with the arrival of new information. This method has wide business and investment applications.

LEARNING MODULE OVERVIEW

- The expected value of a random variable is a probability-weighted average of the possible outcomes of the random variable. For a random variable X, the expected value of X is denoted $E(X)$.

- The variance of a random variable is the expected value (the probability-weighted average) of squared deviations from the random variable's expected value $E(X)$: $\sigma^2(X) = E\{[X - E(X)]^2\}$, where $\sigma^2(X)$ stands for the variance of X.

- Standard deviation is the positive square root of variance. Standard deviation measures dispersion (as does variance), but it is measured in the same units as the variable.

- A probability tree is a means of illustrating the results of two or more independent events.

- A probability of an event given (conditioned on) another event is a conditional probability. The probability of an event A given an event B is denoted $P(A \mid B)$, and $P(A \mid B) = P(AB)/P(B)$, $P(B) \neq 0$.

- According to the total probability rule, if $S1$, $S2$, ..., Sn are mutually exclusive and exhaustive scenarios or events, then $P(A) = P(A \mid S1)$ $P(S1) + P(A \mid S2)P(S2) + ... + P(A \mid Sn)P(Sn)$.

- Conditional expected value is $E(X \mid S) = P(X_1 \mid S)X_1 + P(X_2 \mid S)X_2 + ...$ $+ P(X_n \mid S)X_n$ and has an associated conditional variance and conditional standard deviation.

- Bayes' formula is a method used to update probabilities based on new information.

- Bayes' formula is expressed as follows: Updated probability of event given the new information = [(Probability of the new information given event)/(Unconditional probability of the new information)] × Prior probability of event.

2

EXPECTED VALUE AND VARIANCE

☐ | calculate expected values, variances, and standard deviations and demonstrate their application to investment problems

The expected value of a random variable is an essential quantitative concept in investments. Investors continually make use of expected values—in estimating the rewards of alternative investments, in forecasting earnings per share (EPS) and other corporate financial variables and ratios, and in assessing any other factor that may affect their financial position. The **expected value of a random variable** is the probability-weighted average of the possible outcomes of the random variable. For a random variable X, the expected value of X is denoted $E(X)$.

Expected value (e.g., expected stock return) looks either to the future, as a forecast, or to the "true" value of the mean (the population mean). We should distinguish expected value from the concepts of historical or sample mean. The sample mean also summarizes in a single number a central value. However, the sample mean presents a central value for a particular set of observations as an equally weighted average of those observations. In sum, the contrast is forecast versus historical, or population versus sample.

An equation that summarizes the calculation of the expected value for a discrete random variable X is as follows:

$$E(X) = P(X_1)X_1 + P(X_2)X_2 + \ldots + P(X_n)X_n = \sum_{i=1}^{n} P(X_i)X_i, \tag{1}$$

where X_i is one of n possible outcomes of the discrete random variable X.

The expected value is our forecast. Because we are discussing random quantities, we cannot count on an individual forecast being realized (although we hope that, on average, forecasts will be accurate). It is important, as a result, to measure the risk we face. Variance and standard deviation measure the dispersion of outcomes around the expected value or forecast.

The **variance of a random variable** is the expected value (the probability-weighted average) of squared deviations from the random variable's expected value:

$$\sigma^2(X) = E[X - E(X)]^2. \tag{2}$$

The two notations for variance are $\sigma^2(X)$ and $\mathrm{Var}(X)$.

Variance is a number greater than or equal to 0 because it is the sum of squared terms. If variance is 0, there is no dispersion or risk. The outcome is certain, and the quantity X is not random at all. Variance greater than 0 indicates dispersion of outcomes. Increasing variance indicates increasing dispersion, all else being equal.

The following equation summarizes the calculation of variance:

$$\sigma^2(X) = P(X_1)[X_1 - E(X)]^2 + P(X_2)[X_2 - E(X)]^2$$
$$+ \ldots + P(X_n)[X_n - E(X)]^2 = \sum_{i=1}^{n} P(X_i)[X_i - E(X)]^2, \tag{3}$$

where X_i is one of n possible outcomes of the discrete random variable X.

Variance of X is a quantity in the squared units of X. For example, if the random variable is return in percent, variance of return is in units of percent squared. Standard deviation is easier to interpret than variance because it is in the same units as the random variable. **Standard deviation** is the square root of variance. If the random variable is return in percent, standard deviation of return is also in units of percent. In the following examples, when the variance of returns is stated as a percent or amount of money, to conserve space, we may suppress showing the unit squared.

The best way to become familiar with these concepts is to work examples.

EXAMPLE 1

BankCorp's Earnings per Share, Part 1

As part of your work as a banking industry analyst, you build models for forecasting earnings per share of the banks you cover. Today you are studying BankCorp. In Exhibit 1, you have recorded a probability distribution for BankCorp's EPS for the current fiscal year.

Exhibit 1: Probability Distribution for BankCorp's EPS	
Probability	**EPS (USD)**
0.15	2.60
0.45	2.45
0.24	2.20

Probability	EPS (USD)
0.16	2.00
1.00	

1. What is the expected value of BankCorp's EPS for the current fiscal year?

   Solution:

   Following the definition of expected value, list each outcome, weight it by its probability, and sum the terms.

   $E(\text{EPS}) = 0.15(\text{USD}2.60) + 0.45(\text{USD } 2.45) + 0.24(\text{USD } 2.20) + 0.16(\text{USD } 2.00)$

   $= \text{USD}2.3405$

   The expected value of EPS is USD2.34.

2. Using the probability distribution of EPS from Exhibit 1, you want to measure the dispersion around your forecast. What are the variance and standard deviation of BankCorp's EPS for the current fiscal year?

   Solution:

   The order of calculation is always expected value, then variance, and then standard deviation. Expected value has already been calculated. Following the previous definition of variance, calculate the deviation of each outcome from the mean or expected value, square each deviation, weight (multiply) each squared deviation by its probability of occurrence, and then sum these terms.

   $\sigma^2(\text{EPS}) = P(2.60)[2.60 - E(\text{EPS})]^2 + P(2.45)[2.45 - E(\text{EPS})]^2$
   $+ P(2.20)[2.20 - E(\text{EPS})]^2 + P(2.00)[2.00 - E(\text{EPS})]^2$
   $= 0.15(2.60 - 2.34)^2 + 0.45(2.45 - 2.34)^2$
   $+ 0.24(2.20 - 2.34)^2 + 0.16(2.00 - 2.34)^2$
   $= 0.01014 + 0.005445 + 0.004704 + 0.018496 = 0.038785$

   Standard deviation is the positive square root of 0.038785:

   $\sigma(\text{EPS}) = 0.038785^{1/2} = 0.196939$, or approximately 0.20.

3

PROBABILITY TREES AND CONDITIONAL EXPECTATIONS

☐ formulate an investment problem as a probability tree and explain the use of conditional expectations in investment application

In investments, we make use of any relevant information available in making our forecasts. When we refine our expectations or forecasts, we are typically updating them based on new information or events; in these cases, we are using **conditional expected values**. The expected value of a random variable X given an event or scenario S is denoted $E(X \mid S)$. Suppose the random variable X can take on any one of n distinct outcomes $X_1, X_2, ..., X_n$ (these outcomes form a set of mutually exclusive and exhaustive events). The expected value of X conditional on S is the first outcome, X_1, times the probability of the first outcome given S, $P(X_1 \mid S)$, plus the second outcome, X_2, times the probability of the second outcome given S, $P(X_2 \mid S)$, and so forth, as follows:

$$E(X \mid S) = P(X_1 \mid S)X_1 + P(X_2 \mid S)X_2 + ... + P(X_n \mid S)X_n. \tag{4}$$

We will illustrate this equation shortly.

Parallel to the total probability rule for stating unconditional probabilities in terms of conditional probabilities, there is a principle for stating (unconditional) expected values in terms of conditional expected values. This principle is the **total probability rule for expected value**.

Total Probability Rule for Expected Value

The formula follows:

$$E(X) = E(X \mid S)P(S) + E(X \mid S^C)P(S^C), \tag{5}$$

where S^C is the "complement of S," which means event or scenario "S" does not occur.

$$E(X) = E(X \mid S_1)P(S_1) + E(X \mid S_2)P(S_2) + ... + E(X \mid S_n)P(S_n), \tag{6}$$

where $S_1, S_2, ..., S_n$ are mutually exclusive and exhaustive scenarios or events.

The general case, Equation 6, states that the expected value of X equals the expected value of X given Scenario 1, $E(X \mid S_1)$, times the probability of Scenario 1, $P(S_1)$, plus the expected value of X given Scenario 2, $E(X \mid S_2)$, times the probability of Scenario 2, $P(S_2)$, and so forth.

To use this principle, we formulate mutually exclusive and exhaustive scenarios that are useful for understanding the outcomes of the random variable. This approach was employed in developing the probability distribution of BankCorp's EPS in Example 1, as we now discuss.

EXAMPLE 2

BankCorp's Earnings per Share, Part 2

The earnings of BankCorp are interest rate sensitive, benefiting from a declining interest rate environment. Suppose there is a 0.60 probability that BankCorp will operate in a *declining interest rate environment* in the current fiscal year and a 0.40 probability that it will operate in a *stable interest rate environment* (assessing the chance of an increasing interest rate environment as negligible). If a *declining interest rate environment* occurs, the probability that EPS will be USD2.60 is estimated at 0.25, and the probability that EPS will be USD2.45 is estimated at 0.75. Note that 0.60, the probability of *declining interest rate environment*, times 0.25, the probability of USD2.60 EPS given a *declining interest rate environment*, equals 0.15, the (unconditional) probability of USD2.60 given in the table in Exhibit 1. The probabilities are consistent. Also, 0.60(0.75) = 0.45, the probability of USD2.45 EPS given in Exhibit 1. The **probability tree diagram** in Exhibit 2 shows the rest of the analysis.

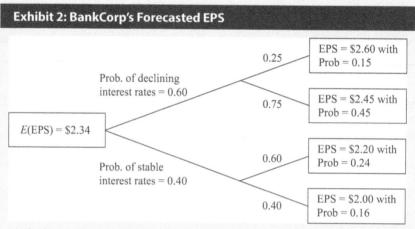

Exhibit 2: BankCorp's Forecasted EPS

A declining interest rate environment points us to the **node** of the tree that branches off into outcomes of USD2.60 and USD2.45. We can find expected EPS given a declining interest rate environment as follows, using Equation 6:

E(EPS | *declining interest rate environment*)

= 0.25(USD2.60) + 0.75(USD2.45)

= USD2.4875

If interest rates are stable,

E(EPS | *stable interest rate environment*) = 0.60(USD2.20) + 0.40(USD2.00)

= USD2.12

Once we have the new piece of information that interest rates are stable, for example, we revise our original expectation of EPS from USD2.34 downward to USD2.12. Now using the total probability rule for expected value,

E(EPS)
= E(EPS | declining interest rate environment)P(declining interest rate environment)
+ E(EPS | stable interest rate environment)P(stable interest rate environment)

So, E(EPS) = USD2.4875(0.60) + USD2.12(0.40) = USD2.3405 or about USD2.34.

This amount is identical to the estimate of the expected value of EPS calculated directly from the probability distribution in Example 1. Just as our probabilities must be consistent, so too must our expected values, unconditional and conditional, be consistent; otherwise, our investment actions may create profit opportunities for other investors at our expense.

To review, we first developed the factors or scenarios that influence the outcome of the event of interest. After assigning probabilities to these scenarios, we formed expectations conditioned on the different scenarios. Then we worked backward to formulate an expected value as of today. In the problem just worked, EPS was the event of interest, and the interest rate environment was the factor influencing EPS.

We can also calculate the variance of EPS given each scenario:

σ^2(EPS|*declining interest rate environment*)

= P(USD2.60|*declining interest rate environment*)

× [USD2.60 − E(EPS|*declining interest rate environment*)]^2

+ P(USD2.45|*declining interest rate environment*)

$\times$ [USD2.45 − E(EPS|*declining interest rate environment*)]^2

= 0.25(USD2.60 − USD2.4875)^2 + 0.75(USD2.45 − USD2.4875)^2 = 0.004219

Similarly, σ^2(EPS | *stable interest rate environment*) is found to be equal to

= 0.60(USD2.20 − USD2.12)^2 + 0.40(USD2.00 − USD2.12)^2 = 0.0096

These are **conditional variances**, the variance of EPS given a *declining interest rate environment* and the variance of EPS given a *stable interest rate environment*. The relationship between unconditional variance and conditional variance is a relatively advanced topic. The main points are that (1) variance, like expected value, has a conditional counterpart to the unconditional concept; and (2) we can use conditional variance to assess risk given a particular scenario.

EXAMPLE 3

BankCorp's Earnings per Share, Part 3

Continuing with the BankCorp example, you focus now on BankCorp's cost structure. One model, a simple linear regression model, you are researching for BankCorp's operating costs is

$\hat{Y} = a + bX$,

where $\hat{Y}$ is a forecast of operating costs in millions of US dollars and X is the number of branch offices; and $\hat{Y}$ represents the expected value of Y given X, or $E(Y \mid X)$. You interpret the intercept a as fixed costs and b as variable costs. You estimate the equation as follows:

$\hat{Y} = 12.5 + 0.65X$.

BankCorp currently has 66 branch offices, and the equation estimates operating costs as 12.5 + 0.65(66) = USD55.4 million. You have two scenarios for growth, pictured in the tree diagram in Exhibit 3.

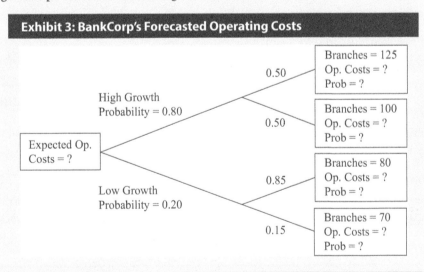

Exhibit 3: BankCorp's Forecasted Operating Costs

1. Compute the forecasted operating costs given the different levels of operating costs, using $\hat{Y} = 12.5 + 0.65X$. State the probability of each level of the number of branch offices. These are the answers to the questions in the terminal boxes of the tree diagram.

Solution:

Using $\hat{Y} = 12.5 + 0.65X$, from top to bottom, we have

Operating Costs	Probability
$\hat{Y}$ = 12.5 + 0.65(125) = USD93.75 million	0.80(0.50) = 0.40
$\hat{Y}$ = 12.5 + 0.65(100) = USD77.50 million	0.80(0.50) = 0.40
$\hat{Y}$ = 12.5 + 0.65(80) = USD64.50 million	0.20(0.85) = 0.17
$\hat{Y}$ = 12.5 + 0.65(70) = USD58.00 million	0.20(0.15) = 0.03
	Sum = 1.00

2. Compute the expected value of operating costs under the high growth scenario. Also calculate the expected value of operating costs under the low growth scenario.

Solution:

US dollar amounts are in millions.

E(operating costs|*high growth*) = 0.50(USD93.75) + 0.50(USD77.50)

= USD85.625

E(operating costs|*low growth*) = 0.85(USD64.50) + 0.15(USD58.00)

= USD63.525

3. Refer to the question in the initial box of the tree: What are BankCorp's expected operating costs?

Solution:

US dollar amounts are in millions.

E(operating costs) = *E*(operating costs|*high growth*)P(*high growth*)

+ *E*(operatingcosts|*low growth*)P(*low growth*)

= 85.625(0.80) + 63.525(0.20) = 81.205

BankCorp's expected operating costs are USD81.205 million.

In this section, we have treated random variables, such as EPS, as standalone quantities. We have not explored how descriptors, such as expected value and variance of EPS, may be functions of other random variables. Portfolio return is one random variable that is clearly a function of other random variables, the random returns on the individual securities in the portfolio. To analyze a portfolio's expected return and variance of return, we must understand that these quantities are a function of characteristics of the individual securities' returns. Looking at the variance of portfolio return, we see that the way individual security returns move together or covary is key. We cover portfolio expected return, variance of return, and importantly, covariance and correlation in a separate learning module.

QUESTION SET

1. Suppose the prospects for recovering principal for a defaulted bond issue depend on which of two economic scenarios prevails. Scenario 1 has probability 0.75 and will result in recovery of USD0.90 per USD1 principal value with probability 0.45, or in recovery of USD0.80 per USD1 principal

value with probability 0.55. Scenario 2 has probability 0.25 and will result in recovery of USD0.50 per USD1 principal value with probability 0.85, or in recovery of USD0.40 per USD1 principal value with probability 0.15.

Using the data for Scenario 1 and Scenario 2, calculate the following:

A. Compute the expected recovery, given the first scenario.

B. Compute the expected recovery, given the second scenario.

C. Compute the expected recovery.

D. Graph the information in a probability tree diagram.

E. Compute the probability of each of the four possible recovery amounts: USD0.90, USD0.80, USD0.50, and USD0.40.

Solution:

A. *Outcomes associated with Scenario 1:* With a 0.45 probability of a USD0.90 recovery per USD1 principal value, given Scenario 1, and with the probability of Scenario 1 equal to 0.75, the probability of recovering USD0.90 is 0.45 (0.75) = 0.3375. By a similar calculation, the probability of recovering USD0.80 is 0.55(0.75) = 0.4125.

Outcomes associated with Scenario 2: With a 0.85 probability of a USD0.50 recovery per USD1 principal value, given Scenario 2, and with the probability of Scenario 2 equal to 0.25, the probability of recovering USD0.50 is 0.85(0.25) = 0.2125. By a similar calculation, the probability of recovering USD0.40 is 0.15(0.25) = 0.0375.

B. *E(recovery | Scenario 1)* = 0.45(USD0.90) + 0.55(USD0.80) = USD0.845

C. *E(recovery | Scenario 2)* = 0.85(USD0.50) + 0.15(USD0.40) = USD0.485

D. *E(recovery)* = 0.75(USD0.845) + 0.25(USD0.485) = USD0.755

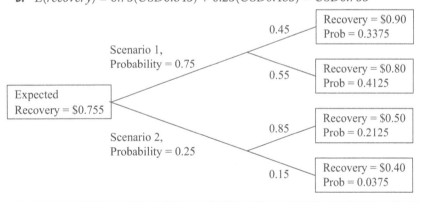

BAYES' FORMULA AND UPDATING PROBABILITY ESTIMATES

4

☐ | calculate and interpret an updated probability in an investment setting using Bayes' formula

A topic that is often useful in solving investment problems is Bayes' formula: what probability theory has to say about learning from experience.

Bayes' Formula

When we make decisions involving investments, we often start with viewpoints based on our experience and knowledge. These viewpoints may be changed or confirmed by new knowledge and observations. **Bayes' formula** is a rational method for adjusting our viewpoints as we confront new information. Bayes' formula and related concepts are used in many business and investment decision-making contexts.

Bayes' formula makes use of the total probability rule:

$$P(A) = \sum_n P(A \cap B_n). \tag{7}$$

To review, that rule expresses the probability of an event as a weighted average of the probabilities of the event, given a set of scenarios. Bayes' formula works in reverse; more precisely, it reverses the "given that" information. Bayes' formula uses the occurrence of the event to infer the probability of the scenario generating it. For that reason, Bayes' formula is sometimes called an inverse probability. In many applications, including those illustrating its use in this section, an individual is updating his/her beliefs concerning the causes that may have produced a new observation.

Bayes' Formula. Given a set of prior probabilities for an event of interest, if you receive new information, the rule for updating your probability of the event is as follows:

Updated probability of event given the new information

$$= \frac{\text{Probability of the new information given event}}{\text{Unconditional probability of the new information}} \times \text{ Prior probability of event.}$$

In probability notation, this formula can be written concisely as follows:

$$P(\text{Event} \mid \text{Information}) = \frac{P(\text{Information} \mid \text{Event})}{P(\text{Information})} P(\text{Event}). \tag{8}$$

Consider the following example using frequencies—which may be more straightforward initially than probabilities—for illustrating and understanding Bayes' formula. Assume a hypothetical large-cap stock index has 500 member firms, of which 100 are technology firms, and 60 of these had returns of >10 percent, and 40 had returns of ≤10 percent. Of the 400 non-technology firms in the index, 100 had returns of >10 percent, and 300 had returns of ≤10 percent. The tree map in Exhibit 4 is useful for visualizing this example, which is summarized in the table in Exhibit 5.

Exhibit 4: Tree Map for Visualizing Bayes' Formula Using Frequencies

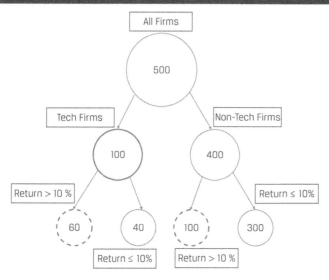

$P (Tech \mid R > 10\%) = 60/(60+100)$

Exhibit 5: Summary of Returns for Tech and Non-Tech Firms in Hypothetical Large-Cap Equity Index

Rate of Return (R)	Type of Firm in Stock Index		
	Non-Tech	Tech	Total
R >10%	100	60	160
R ≤10%	300	40	340
Total	400	100	500

What is the probability a firm is a tech firm given that it has a return of >10 percent or $P(tech \mid R > 10\%)$? Looking at the frequencies in the tree map and in the table, we can see many empirical probabilities, such as the following:

- $P(tech) = 100 / 500 = 0.20$,
- $P(non\text{-}tech) = 400 / 500 = 0.80$,
- $P(R > 10\% \mid tech) = 60 / 100 = 0.60$,
- $P(R > 10\% \mid non\text{-}tech) = 100 / 400 = 0.25$,
- $P(R > 10\%) = 160 / 500 = 0.32$, and, finally,
- $P(tech \mid R > 10\%) = 60/ 160 = 0.375$.

This probability is the answer to our initial question.

Without looking at frequencies, let us use Bayes' formula to find the probability that a firm has a return of >10 percent and then the probability that a firm with a return of >10 percent is a tech firm, $P(tech \mid R > 10\%)$. First,

$P(R > 10\%)$

$= P(R > 10\% \mid tech) \times P(tech) + P(R > 10\% \mid non\text{-}tech) \times P(non\text{-}tech)$

$$= 0.60 \times 0.20 + 0.25 \times 0.80 = 0.32.$$

Now we can implement the Bayes' formula answer to our question:

$$P(tech|R > 10\%) = \frac{P(R > 10\%|tech) \times P(tech)}{P(R > 10\%)} = \frac{0.60 \times 0.20}{0.32} = 0.375.$$

The probability that a firm with a return of >10 percent is a tech firm is 0.375, which is impressive because the probability that a firm is a tech firm (from the whole sample) is only 0.20. In sum, it can be readily seen from the tree map and the underlying frequency data (Exhibit 4 and 5, respectively) or from the probabilities in Bayes' formula that 160 firms have R >10 percent, and 60 of them are tech firms, so

$$P(tech \mid R > 10\%) = 60/160 = 0.375.$$

Users of Bayesian statistics do not consider probabilities (or likelihoods) to be known with certainty but believe that these should be subject to modification whenever new information becomes available. Our beliefs or probabilities are continually updated as new information arrives over time.

To further illustrate Bayes' formula, we work through an investment example that can be adapted to any actual problem. Suppose you are an investor in the stock of DriveMed, Inc. Positive earnings surprises relative to consensus EPS estimates often result in positive stock returns, and negative surprises often have the opposite effect. DriveMed is preparing to release last quarter's EPS result, and you are interested in which of these three events happened: *last quarter's EPS exceeded the consensus EPS estimate, last quarter's EPS exactly met the consensus EPS estimate,* or *last quarter's EPS fell short of the consensus EPS estimate.* This list of the alternatives is mutually exclusive and exhaustive.

On the basis of your own research, you write down the following **prior probabilities** (or priors, for short) concerning these three events:

- *P(EPS exceeded consensus)* = 0.45
- *P(EPS met consensus)* = 0.30
- *P(EPS fell short of consensus)* = 0.25

These probabilities are "prior" in the sense that they reflect only what you know now, before the arrival of any new information.

The next day, DriveMed announces that it is expanding factory capacity in Singapore and Ireland to meet increased sales demand. You assess this new information. The decision to expand capacity relates not only to current demand but probably also to the prior quarter's sales demand. You know that sales demand is positively related to EPS. So now it appears more likely that last quarter's EPS will exceed the consensus.

The question you have is, "In light of the new information, what is the updated probability that the prior quarter's EPS exceeded the consensus estimate?"

Bayes' formula provides a rational method for accomplishing this updating. We can abbreviate the new information as *DriveMed expands*. The first step in applying Bayes' formula is to calculate the probability of the new information (here: *DriveMed expands*), given a list of events or scenarios that may have generated it. The list of events should cover all possibilities, as it does here. Formulating these conditional probabilities is the key step in the updating process. Suppose your view, based on research of DriveMed and its industry, is

P(DriveMed expands | EPS exceeded consensus) = 0.75

P(DriveMed expands | EPS met consensus) = 0.20

P(DriveMed expands | EPS fell short of consensus) = 0.05

Conditional probabilities of an observation (here: *DriveMed expands*) are sometimes referred to as **likelihoods**. Again, likelihoods are required for updating the probability.

Next, you combine these conditional probabilities or likelihoods with your prior probabilities to get the unconditional probability for DriveMed expanding, *P(DriveMed expands)*, as follows:

P(DriveMed expands)

= *P(DriveMed expands|EPS exceeded consensus)* × *P(EPS exceeded consensus)*

+ *P(DriveMed expands|EPS met consensus)* × *P(EPS met consensus)*

+*P(DriveMed expands|EPS fell short of consensus)* × *P(EPS fell short of consensus)*

= 0.75(0.45) + 0.20(0.30) + 0.05(0.25) = 0.41, *or* 41%.

This is the total probability rule in action. Now you can answer your question by applying Bayes' formula, Equation 8:

P(EPS" " exceeded" " consensus $\mid$ DriveMed" " expands)

$$= \frac{P(DriveMed\ expands|EPS\ exceeded\ consensus)}{P(DriveMed\ expands)} P(EPS\ exceeded\ consensus)$$

=(0.75/0.41)(0.45)=1.829268(0.45)

=0.823171

Before DriveMed's announcement, you thought the probability that DriveMed would beat consensus expectations was 45 percent. On the basis of your interpretation of the announcement, you update that probability to 82.3 percent. This updated probability is called your **posterior probability** because it reflects or comes after the new information.

The Bayes' calculation takes the prior probability, which was 45 percent, and multiplies it by a ratio—the first term on the right-hand side of the equal sign. The denominator of the ratio is the probability that DriveMed expands, as you view it without considering (conditioning on) anything else. Therefore, this probability is unconditional. The numerator is the probability that DriveMed expands, if last quarter's EPS actually exceeded the consensus estimate. This last probability is larger than unconditional probability in the denominator, so the ratio (1.83 roughly) is greater than 1. As a result, your updated or posterior probability is larger than your prior probability. Thus, the ratio reflects the impact of the new information on your prior beliefs.

EXAMPLE 4

Inferring Whether DriveMed's EPS Met Consensus EPS

You are still an investor in DriveMed stock. To review the givens, your prior probabilities are *P(EPS exceeded consensus)* = 0.45, *P(EPS met consensus)* = 0.30, and *P(EPS fell short of consensus)* = 0.25. You also have the following conditional probabilities:

P(DriveMed expands | EPS exceeded consensus) = 0.75

P(DriveMed expands | EPS met consensus) = 0.20

P(DriveMed expands | EPS fell short of consensus) = 0.05

1. What is your estimate of the probability P(EPS exceeded consensus | DriveMed expands)?

    Recall that you updated your probability that last quarter's EPS exceeded the consensus estimate from 45 percent to 82.3 percent after DriveMed announced it would expand. Now you want to update your other priors.

    Update your prior probability that DriveMed's EPS met consensus.
    Solution:
    The probability is P(EPS met consensus | DriveMed expands) =

    $$\frac{P(DriveMed\ expands|EPS\ met\ consensus)}{P(DriveMed\ expands)} P(EPS\ met\ consensus)$$

    The probability P(DriveMed expands) is found by taking each of the three conditional probabilities in the statement of the problem, such as P(DriveMed expands | EPS exceeded consensus); multiplying each one by the prior probability of the conditioning event, such as P(EPS exceeded consensus); and then adding the three products. The calculation is unchanged from the problem in the text above: P(DriveMed expands) = 0.75(0.45) + 0.20(0.30) + 0.05(0.25) = 0.41, or 41 percent. The other probabilities needed, P(DriveMed expands | EPS met consensus) = 0.20 and P(EPS met consensus) = 0.30, are givens. So

    P(EPS met consensus | DriveMed expands)

    = [P(DriveMed expands | EPS met consensus)/P(DriveMed expands)]P(EPS met consensus)

    = (0.20/0.41)(0.30) = 0.487805(0.30) = 0.146341

    After taking account of the announcement on expansion, your updated probability that last quarter's EPS for DriveMed just met consensus is 14.6 percent compared with your prior probability of 30 percent.

2. Update your prior probability that DriveMed's EPS fell short of consensus.
    Solution:
    P(DriveMed expands) was already calculated as 41 percent. Recall that P(DriveMed expands | EPS fell short of consensus) = 0.05 and P(EPS fell short of consensus) = 0.25 are givens.

    P(EPS fell short of consensus | DriveMed expands)

    = [P(DriveMed expands | EPS fell short of consensus)/

    P(DriveMed expands)]P(EPS fell short of consensus)

    = (0.05/0.41)(0.25) = 0.121951(0.25) = 0.030488

    As a result of the announcement, you have revised your probability that DriveMed's EPS fell short of consensus from 25 percent (your prior probability) to 3 percent.

3. Show that the three updated probabilities sum to 1. (Carry each probability to four decimal places.)

Solution:

The sum of the three updated probabilities is

P(EPS exceeded consensus|DriveMed expands) + P(EPS met consensus|DriveMed expands) + P(EPS fell short of consensus|DriveMed expands)

$= 0.8232 + 0.1463 + 0.0305 = 1.000$

The three events (*EPS exceeded consensus, EPS met consensus*, and *EPS fell short of consensus*) are mutually exclusive and exhaustive: One of these events or statements must be true, so the conditional probabilities must sum to 1. Whether we are talking about conditional or unconditional probabilities, whenever we have a complete set of distinct possible events or outcomes, the probabilities must sum to 1. This calculation serves to check your work.

4. Suppose, because of lack of prior beliefs about whether DriveMed would meet consensus, you updated on the basis of prior probabilities that all three possibilities were equally likely: *P(EPS exceeded consensus) = P(EPS met consensus) = P(EPS fell short of consensus) = 1/3.*

Solution:

Using the probabilities given in the question,

P(DriveMed expands)

= P(DriveMed expands|EPS exceeded consensus)P(EPS exceeded consensus) + P(DriveMed expands|EPS met consensus)P(EPS met consensus) + P(DriveMed expands|EPS fell short of consensus)P(EPS fell short of consensus)

$= 0.75(1/3) + 0.20(1/3) + 0.05(1/3) = 1/3$

Not surprisingly, the probability of DriveMed expanding is one-third (1/3) because the decision maker has no prior beliefs or views regarding how well EPS performed relative to the consensus estimate.

Now we can use Bayes' formula to find *P(EPS exceeded consensus | DriveMed expands) = [P(DriveMed expands | EPS exceeded consensus)/P(DriveMed expands)] P(EPS exceeded consensus) = [(0.75/(1/3)]* (1/3) = 0.75, or 75 percent. This probability is identical to your estimate of *P(DriveMed expands | EPS exceeded consensus).*

When the prior probabilities are equal, the probability of information given an event equals the probability of the event given the information. When a decision maker has equal prior probabilities (called **diffuse priors**), the probability of an event is determined by the information.

QUESTION SET

The following example shows how Bayes' formula is used in credit granting in cases in which the probability of payment given credit information is higher than the probability of payment without the information.

1. Jake Bronson is predicting the probability that consumer finance applicants granted credit will repay in a timely manner (i.e., their accounts will not

become "past due"). Using Bayes' formula, he has structured the problem as follows:

$$P(\text{Event} \mid \text{Information}) = \frac{P(\text{Information} \mid \text{Event})}{P(\text{Information})} P(\text{Event}),$$

where the event (A) is "timely repayment" and the information (B) is having a "good credit report."

Bronson estimates that the unconditional probability of receiving timely payment, *P(A)*, is 0.90 and that the unconditional probability of having a good credit report, *P(B)*, is 0.80. The probability of having a good credit report given that borrowers paid on time, *P(B | A)*, is 0.85.

What is the probability that applicants with good credit reports will repay in a timely manner?

A. 0.720

B. 0.944

C. 0.956

Solution:

The correct answer is C. The probability of timely repayment given a good credit report, *P(A | B)*, is

$$P(A|B) = \frac{P(B|A)}{P(B)} P(A) = \frac{0.85}{0.80} \times 0.90 = 0.956$$

2. You have developed a set of criteria for evaluating distressed credits. Companies that do not receive a passing score are classed as likely to go bankrupt within 12 months. You gathered the following information when validating the criteria:

- Forty percent of the companies to which the test is administered will go bankrupt within 12 months: P(*non-survivor*) = 0.40.

- Fifty-five percent of the companies to which the test is administered pass it: P(*pass test*) = 0.55.

- The probability that a company will pass the test given that it will subsequently survive 12 months, is 0.85: P(*pass test | survivor*) = 0.85.

Using the information validating your criteria, calculate the following:

A. What is P(*pass test | non-survivor*)?

B. Using Bayes' formula, calculate the probability that a company is a survivor, given that it passes the test; that is, calculate P(*survivor | pass test*).

C. What is the probability that a company is a *non-survivor*, given that it fails the test?

D. Is the test effective?

Solution:

A. We can set up the equation using the total probability rule:

P(*pass test*) = P(*pass test|survivor*)P(*survivor*)

$+ P$ (*pass test*|*non-survivor*)P(*non-survivor*)

We know that P(*survivor*) = $1 - P$(*non-survivor*) = $1 - 0.40 = 0.60$. Therefore, P(*pass test*) = $0.55 = 0.85(0.60) + P$(*pass test* | *non-survivor*)(0.40). Thus, P(*pass test* | *non-survivor*) = $[0.55 - 0.85(0.60)]/0.40 = 0.10$.
B. We can calculate the probability that a company is a survivor as follows:

P(*survivor*|*pass test*) $= [P$(*pass test*|*survivor*)$/P$(*pass test*)$]P$(*survivor*)

$= (0.85/0.55)0.60 = 0.927273$

The information that a company passes the test causes you to update your probability that it is a survivor from 0.60 to approximately 0.927.
C. According to Bayes' formula, P(*non-survivor* | *fail test*) = $[P$(-*fail test* | *non-survivor*)$/ P$(*fail test*)$]P$(*non-survivor*) = $[P$(*fail test* | *non-survivor*)$/0.45]0.40$.
We can set up the following equation to obtain P(*fail test* | *non-survivor*):

P(*fail test*) $= P$(*fail test*|*non* − *survivor*)P(*non* − *survivor*)

$+ P$(*fail test*|*survivor*)P(*survivor*)

$0.45 = P$(*fail test*|*non* − *survivor*)$0.40 + 0.15(0.60)$

where P(*fail test* | *survivor*) = $1 - P$(*pass test* | *survivor*) = $1 - 0.85 = 0.15$. So, P(*fail test* | *non-survivor*) = $[0.45 - 0.15(0.60)]/0.40 = 0.90$.
Using this result with the previous formula, we find P(*non-survivor* | *fail test*) = $[0.90/0.45]0.40 = 0.80$. Seeing that a company fails the test causes us to update the probability that it is a non-survivor from 0.40 to 0.80.
D. A company passing the test greatly increases our confidence that it is a survivor. A company failing the test doubles the probability that it is a non-survivor. Therefore, the test appears to be useful.

---

3. An analyst estimates that 20 percent of high-risk bonds will fail (go bankrupt). If she applies a bankruptcy prediction model, she finds that 70 percent of the bonds will receive a "good" rating, implying that they are less likely to fail. Of the bonds that failed, only 50 percent had a "good" rating. Using Bayes' formula, what is the predicted probability of failure given a "good" rating? (Hint, let $P(A)$ be the probability of failure, $P(B)$ be the probability of a "good" rating, $P(B \mid A)$ be the likelihood of a "good" rating given failure, and $P(A \mid B)$ be the likelihood of failure given a "good" rating.)

   A. 5.7 percent

   B. 14.3 percent

   C. 28.6 percent

Solution:

B is correct. With Bayes' formula, the probability of failure given a "good" rating is

$$P(A|B) = \frac{P(B|A)}{P(B)}P(A)$$

where

$P(A) = 0.20$ = probability of failure

$P(B) = 0.70$ = probability of a "good" rating

$P(B \mid A) = 0.50$ = probability of a "good" rating given failure

   With these estimates, the probability of failure given a "good" rating is

$$P(A|B) = \frac{P(B|A)}{P(B)}P(A) = \frac{0.50}{0.70} \times 0.20 = 0.143$$

If the analyst uses the bankruptcy prediction model as a guide, the probability of failure declines from 20 percent to 14.3 percent.

4. In a typical year, 5 percent of all CEOs are fired for "performance" reasons. Assume that CEO performance is judged according to stock performance and that 50 percent of stocks have above-average returns or "good" performance. Empirically, 30 percent of all CEOs who were fired had "good" performance. Using Bayes' formula, what is the probability that a CEO will be fired given "good" performance? (Hint, let $P(A)$ be the probability of a CEO being fired, $P(B)$ be the probability of a "good" performance rating, $P(B \mid A)$ be the likelihood of a "good" performance rating given that the CEO was fired, and $P(A \mid B)$ be the likelihood of the CEO being fired given a "good" performance rating.)

   A. 1.5 percent

   B. 2.5 percent

   C. 3.0 percent

   Solution:

   C is correct. With Bayes' formula, the probability of the CEO being fired given a "good" rating is

   $$P(A|B) = \frac{P(B|A)}{P(B)}P(A)$$

   where

   $P(A) = 0.05 =$ probability of the CEO being fired

   $P(B) = 0.50 =$ probability of a "good" rating

   $P(B \mid A) = 0.30 =$ probability of a "good" rating given that the CEO is fired

   With these estimates, the probability of the CEO being fired given a "good" rating is

   $$P(A|B) = \frac{P(B|A)}{P(B)}P(A) = \frac{0.30}{0.50} \times 0.05 = 0.03$$

   Although 5 percent of all CEOs are fired, the probability of being fired given a "good" performance rating is 3 percent.

PRACTICE PROBLEMS

1. An analyst developed two scenarios with respect to the recovery of USD100,000 principal from defaulted loans:

Scenario	Probability of Scenario (%)	Amount Recovered (USD)	Probability of Amount (%)
1	40	50,000	60
		30,000	40
2	60	80,000	90
		60,000	10

The amount of the expected recovery is *closest* to which of the following?

   A. USD36,400.

   B. USD55,000.

   C. USD63,600.

2. The probability distribution for a company's sales is:

Probability	Sales (USD, millions)
0.05	70
0.70	40
0.25	25

The standard deviation of sales is *closest* to which of the following?

   A. USD9.81 million.

   B. USD12.20 million.

   C. USD32.40 million.

SOLUTIONS

1. C is correct. If Scenario 1 occurs, the expected recovery is 60% (USD50,000) + 40% (USD30,000) = USD42,000, and if Scenario 2 occurs, the expected recovery is 90% (USD80,000) + 10% (USD60,000) = USD78,000. Weighting by the probability of each scenario, the expected recovery is 40% (USD42,000) + 60% (USD78,000) = USD63,600. Alternatively, first calculating the probability of each amount occurring, the expected recovery is (40%)(60%)(USD50,000) + (40%)(40%)(USD30,000) + (60%)(90%)(USD80,000) + (60%)(10%)(USD60,000) = USD63,600.

2. A is correct. The analyst must first calculate expected sales as $0.05 \times USD70 + 0.70 \times USD40 + 0.25 \times USD25 = USD3.50$ million + USD28.00 million + USD6.25 million = USD37.75 million.

   After calculating expected sales, we can calculate the variance of sales:

   σ^2 (Sales)

   $= P(USD70)[USD70 - E(Sales)]^2 + P(USD40)[USD40 - E(Sales)]^2 + P(USD25)[USD25 - E(Sales)]^2$

   $= 0.05(USD70 - 37.75)^2 + 0.70(USD40 - 37.75)^2 + 0.25(USD25 - 37.75)^2$

   = USD52.00 million + USD3.54 million + USD40.64 million

   = USD96.18 million.

   The standard deviation of sales is thus $\sigma = (USD96.18)^{1/2} = USD9.81$ million.

5

Portfolio Mathematics

by Richard A. DeFusco, PhD, CFA, Dennis W. McLeavey, DBA, CFA, Jerald
E. Pinto, PhD, CFA, and David E. Runkle, PhD, CFA.

Richard A. DeFusco, PhD, CFA, is at the University of Nebraska-Lincoln (USA). Dennis W. McLeavey, DBA, CFA, is at the University of Rhode Island (USA). Jerald E. Pinto, PhD, CFA, is at CFA Institute (USA). David E. Runkle, PhD, CFA, is at Jacobs Levy Equity Management (USA).

LEARNING OUTCOMES

Mastery	The candidate should be able to:
☐	calculate and interpret the expected value, variance, standard deviation, covariances, and correlations of portfolio returns
☐	calculate and interpret the covariance and correlation of portfolio returns using a joint probability function for returns
☐	define shortfall risk, calculate the safety-first ratio, and identify an optimal portfolio using Roy's safety-first criterion

INTRODUCTION

1

Modern portfolio theory makes frequent use of the idea that investment opportunities can be evaluated using expected return as a measure of reward and variance of return as a measure of risk. In Lesson 1, we will develop an understanding of portfolio return and risk metrics. The forecast expected return and variance of return are functions of the returns on the individual portfolio holdings. To begin, the expected return on a portfolio is a weighted average of the expected returns on the securities in the portfolio. When we have estimated the expected returns on the individual securities, we immediately have portfolio expected return. Lesson 2 focuses on forecasting certain portfolio metrics, such as correlations and covariances by looking at the risk and return on the individual components of a portfolio. Lesson 3 introduces various portfolio risk metrics widely used in portfolio management.

LEARNING MODULE OVERVIEW

- A portfolio's variance measures its expected investment risk and is defined as $\sigma^2(R_p) = E\{[R_p E(R_p)]^2\}$. A portfolio's expected return $(E(Rp))$ is a weighted average of the expected returns $(R_1$ to $R_n)$ on the component securities using their respective proportions of the portfolio in currency units as weights $(w_1$ to $w_n)$:

$$E(R_p) = E(w_1 R_1 + w_2 R_2 + \ldots + w_n R_n)$$
$$= w_1 E(R_1) + w_2 E(R_2) + \ldots + w_n E(R_n)$$

- Portfolio variance is affected by both the risk of the individual component assets and their combined risks together as measured by their covariance, which is defined as

$$\sigma^2(R_p) = \sum_{i=1}^{n} \sum_{j=1}^{n} w_i w_j \text{Cov}(R_i, R_j).$$

- Covariance of returns can be negative (an average negative relationship between returns), zero if returns on the assets are unrelated, or positive (an average positive relationship between returns). Correlation, like covariance, measures linear association and ranges between −1 (strongly inverse) to +1 (strongly direct), with 0 indicating no relationship.

- The covariance of portfolio returns can be estimated using a joint probability function of random variables. Defined on variables X and Y, as P(X,Y), which gives the probability of joint occurrences of their values. For example, P(X=3, Y=2), is the probability X equals 3 and Y equals 2.

- A formula for computing the covariance between random variables R_A and R_B, such as the different assets of a portfolio, is

$$\text{Cov}(R_A, R_B) = \sum_i \sum_j P(R_{A,i}, R_{B,j})(R_{A,i} - E R_A)(R_{B,j} - E R_B).$$

  The value is derived by summing all possible deviation cross-products weighted by the appropriate joint probability.

- The joint probability function simplifies for independent variables, defined for two random variables X and Y if and only if $P(X,Y) = P(X) P(Y)$. The expected value of the product of both independent and uncorrelated random variables is the product of their expected values.

- An application of normal distribution theory to practical investment problems involves safety-first rules. These focus on reducing the shortfall risk, defined as portfolio value (or portfolio return) falling below some minimum acceptable level over some time horizon,

- The safety-first ratio is defined as (SFRatio = $[E(R_p) - R_L]/\sigma_P$, where $E(R_p)$ is expected portfolio return, R_L is a predetermined minimum threshold level for a variable of interest like portfolio return, and σ_P is portfolio standard deviation. When R_L is the risk-free rate, the safety-first ratio is equivalent to the Sharpe ratio.

- Roy's safety-first criterion states that the optimal portfolio minimizes the probability that portfolio return, R_P, will fall below R_L. For a portfolio with a given safety-first ratio (SFratio), the probability that its return will be less than R_L is *Normal*(–SFRatio), and the safety-first optimal portfolio has the lowest such probability. The criterion is implemented by first calculating each potential portfolio's SFRatio and then choosing the portfolio with the highest SFRatio.

PORTFOLIO EXPECTED RETURN AND VARIANCE OF RETURN

2

☐ | calculate and interpret the expected value, variance, standard deviation, covariances, and correlations of portfolio returns

The **expected return on the portfolio** ($E(Rp)$) is a weighted average of the expected returns (R_1 to R_n) on the component securities using their respective proportions of the portfolio in currency units as weights (w_1 to w_n):

$$\begin{aligned} E(R_p) &= E(w_1 R_1 + w_2 R_2 + \ldots + w_n R_n) \\ &= w_1 E(R_1) + w_2 E(R_2) + \ldots + w_n E(R_n) \end{aligned} \tag{1}$$

Suppose we have estimated expected returns on assets in the three-asset portfolio shown in Exhibit 1.

Exhibit 1: Weights and Expected Returns of Sample Portfolio

Asset Class	Weight	Expected Return (%)
S&P 500	0.50	13
US long-term corporate bonds	0.25	6
MSCI EAFE	0.25	15

We calculate the expected return on the portfolio as 11.75 percent:

$$\begin{aligned} E(R_p) &= w_1 E(R_1) + w_2 E(R_2) + w_3 E(R_3) \\ &= 0.50(13\%) + 0.25(6\%) + 0.25(15\%) = 11.75\% \end{aligned}$$

Here we are interested in portfolio variance of return as a measure of investment risk. Accordingly, portfolio variance is as follows:

$$\sigma^2(R_p) = E\{[R_p E(R_p)]^2\}. \tag{2}$$

This is expected variance or variance in a forward-looking sense. To implement this definition of portfolio variance, we use information about the individual assets in the portfolio, but we also need the concept of covariance. To avoid notational clutter, we write ER_p for $E(R_p)$.

Covariance

Given two random variables R_i and R_j, the **covariance** between R_i and R_j is as follows:

$$Cov(R_i, R_j) = E[(R_i - ER_i)(R_j - ER_j)]. \tag{3}$$

Alternative notations are $\sigma(R_i,R_j)$ and σ_{ij}. Equation 3 states that the covariance between two random variables is the probability-weighted average of the cross-products of each random variable's deviation from its own expected value. The previous measure is the population covariance and is forward-looking. The sample covariance between two random variables R_i and R_j, based on a sample of past data of size n is as follows:

$$\text{Cov}\left(R_i, R_j\right) = \left. \sum\nolimits_{n=1}^{n} \left(R_{i,t}, \overline{R}_i\right)\left(R_{j,t} - E\overline{R}_j\right) \right/ (n-1).$$ (4)

Start with the definition of variance for a three-asset portfolio and see how it decomposes into three variance terms and six covariance terms. Dispensing with the derivation, the result is Equation 5:

$$
\begin{aligned}
\sigma^2\left(R_p\right) &= E\left[\left(R_p - ER_p\right)^2\right] \\
&= E\left\{\left[w_1 R_1 + w_2 R_2 + w_3 R_3 - E(w_1 R_1 + w_2 R_2 + w_3 R_3)\right]^2\right\} \\
&= E\left\{\left[w_1 R_1 + w_2 R_2 + w_3 R_3 - w_1 ER_1 - w_2 ER_2 - w_3 ER_3\right]^2\right\}.
\end{aligned}
$$ (5)

$$
\begin{aligned}
&= w_1^2 \sigma^2(R_1) + w_1 w_2 \text{Cov}(R_1, R_2) + w_1 w_3 \text{Cov}(R_1, R_3) \\
&+ w_1 w_2 \text{Cov}(R_1, R_2) + w_2^2 \sigma^2(R_2) + w_2 w_3 \text{Cov}(R_2, R_3) \\
&+ w_1 w_3 \text{Cov}(R_1, R_3) + w_2 w_3 \text{Cov}(R_2, R_3) + w_3^2 \sigma^2(R_3).
\end{aligned}
$$

Noting that the order of variables in covariance does not matter, for example, $\text{Cov}(R_2,R_1)$ = $\text{Cov}(R_1,R_2)$, and that diagonal variance terms $\sigma^2(R_1)$, $\sigma^2(R_2)$, and $\sigma^2(R_3)$ can be expressed as $\text{Cov}(R_1,R_1)$, $\text{Cov}(R_2,R_2)$, and $\text{Cov}(R_3,R_3)$, respectively, the most compact way to state Equation 5 is

$$\sigma^2\left(R_p\right) = \sum\nolimits_{i=1}^{3} \sum\nolimits_{j=1}^{3} w_i w_j \text{Cov}\left(R_i, R_j\right).$$

Moreover, this expression generalizes for a portfolio of any size n to

$$\sigma^2\left(R_p\right) = \sum\nolimits_{i=1}^{n} \sum\nolimits_{j=1}^{n} w_i w_j \text{Cov}\left(R_i, R_j\right).$$ (6)

Equation 6 shows that individual variances of return constitute part, but not all, of portfolio variance. The three variances are outnumbered by the six covariance terms off the diagonal. If there are 20 assets, there are 20 variance terms and 20(20) – 20 = 380 off-diagonal covariance terms. A first observation is that as the number of holdings increases, covariance becomes increasingly important, all else equal.

The covariance terms capture how the co-movements of returns affect aggregate portfolio variance. From the definition of covariance, we can establish two essential observations about covariance.

1. We can interpret the sign of covariance as follows:

   - Covariance of returns is negative if, when the return on one asset is above its expected value, the return on the other asset tends to be below its expected value (an average inverse relationship between returns).

   - Covariance of returns is 0 if returns on the assets are unrelated.

   Covariance of returns is positive when the returns on both assets tend to be on the same side (above or below) their expected values at the same time (an average positive relationship between returns). The covariance of a random variable with itself (*own covariance*) is its own variance: $\text{Cov}(R,R) = E\{[RE(R)][RE(R)]\} = E\{[RE(R)]^2\} = \sigma^2(R)$.

Exhibit 2 summarizes the inputs for portfolio expected return (Panel A) and variance of return (Panel B). A complete list of the covariances constitutes all the statistical data needed to compute portfolio variance of return as shown in the covariance matrix in Panel B.

Exhibit 2: Inputs to Portfolio Expected Return and Variance

A. Inputs to Portfolio Expected Return

Asset	A	B	C
	$E(R_A)$	$E(R_B)$	$E(R_C)$

B. Covariance Matrix: The Inputs to Portfolio Variance of Return

Asset	A	B	C
A	$\mathbf{Cov(R_A R_A, R_A R_A)}$	$Cov(R_A, R_B)$	$Cov(R_A, R_C)$
B	$Cov(R_B, R_A)$	$\mathbf{Cov(R_B R_B, R_B R_B)}$	$Cov(R_B, R_C)$
C	$Cov(R_C, R_A)$	$Cov(R_C, R_B)$	$\mathbf{Cov(R_C R_C, R_C R_C)}$

With three assets, the covariance matrix has $3^2 = 3 \times 3 = 9$ entries, but the diagonal terms, the variances (bolded in Exhibit 2), are treated separately from the off-diagonal terms. So, there are $9 - 3 = 6$ covariances, excluding variances. But $Cov(R_B, R_A) = Cov(R_A, R_B)$, $Cov(R_C, R_A) = Cov(R_A, R_C)$, and $Cov(R_C, R_B) = Cov(R_B, R_C)$. The covariance matrix below the diagonal is the mirror image of the covariance matrix above the diagonal, so you only need to use one (i.e., either below or above the diagonal). As a result, there are only $6/2 = 3$ distinct covariance terms to estimate. In general, for n securities, there are $n(n - 1)/2$ distinct covariances and n variances to estimate.

Suppose we have the covariance matrix shown in Exhibit 3 with returns expressed as a percentage. The table entries are shown as return percentages squared ($\%^2$). The terms $38\%^2$ and $400\%^2$ are 0.0038 and 0.0400, respectively, stated as decimals; the correct usage of percents and decimals leads to identical answers.

Exhibit 3: Covariance Matrix

	S&P 500	US Long-Term Corporate Bonds	MSCI EAFE
S&P 500	400	45	189
US long-term corporate bonds	45	81	38
MSCI EAFE	189	38	441

Taking Equation 5 and grouping variance terms together produces the following:

$$\sigma^2(R_p) = w_1^2 \sigma^2(R_1) + w_2^2 \sigma^2(R_2) + w_3^2 \sigma^2(R_3) + 2w_1 w_2 Cov(R_1, R_2)$$
$$+ 2w_1 w_3 Cov(R_1, R_3) + 2w_2 w_3 Cov(R_2, R_3)$$
$$= (0.50)^2(400) + (0.25)^2(81) + (0.25)^2(441)$$
$$+ 2(0.50)(0.25)(45) + 2(0.50)(0.25)(189)$$
$$+ 2(0.25)(0.25)(38)$$
$$= 100 + 5.0625 + 27.5625 + 11.25 + 47.25 + 4.75 = 195.875.$$

The variance is 195.875. Standard deviation of return is $195.875^{1/2}$ = 14%. To summarize, the portfolio has an expected annual return of 11.75 percent and a standard deviation of return of 14 percent.

Looking at the first three terms in the calculation above, their sum (100 + 5.0625 + 27.5625) is 132.625, the contribution of the individual variances to portfolio variance. If the returns on the three assets were independent, covariances would be 0 and the standard deviation of portfolio return would be $132.625^{1/2}$ = 11.52 percent as compared to 14 percent before, so a less risky portfolio. If the covariance terms were negative, then a negative number would be added to 132.625, so portfolio variance and risk would be even smaller, while expected return would not change. For the same expected portfolio return, the portfolio has less risk. This risk reduction is a diversification benefit, meaning a risk-reduction benefit from holding a portfolio of assets. The diversification benefit increases with decreasing covariance. This observation is a key insight of modern portfolio theory. This insight is even more intuitively stated when we can use the concept of correlation.

Correlation

The **correlation** between two random variables, R_i and R_j, is defined as follows:

$$\rho(R_i,R_j) = Cov(R_i,R_j)/[\sigma(R_i)\sigma(R_j)]. \tag{7}$$

Alternative notations are $Corr(R_i,R_j)$ and ρ_{ij}.

The above definition of correlation is forward-looking because it involves dividing the forward-looking covariance by the product of forward-looking standard deviations. Frequently, covariance is substituted out using the relationship $Cov(R_i,R_j) = \rho(R_i,R_j)\sigma(R_i)\sigma(R_j)$. Like covariance, the correlation coefficient is a measure of linear association. However, the division in the definition makes correlation a pure number (without a unit of measurement) and places bounds on its largest and smallest possible values, which are +1 and −1, respectively.

If two variables have a strong positive linear relation, then their correlation will be close to +1. If two variables have a strong negative linear relation, then their correlation will be close to −1. If two variables have a weak linear relation, then their correlation will be close to 0. Using the previous definition, we can state a correlation matrix from data in the covariance matrix alone. Exhibit 4 shows the correlation matrix.

Exhibit 4: Correlation Matrix of Returns

	S&P 500	US Long-Term Corporate Bonds	MSCI EAFE
S&P 500	1.00	0.25	0.45
US long-term corporate bonds	0.25	1.00	0.20
MSCI EAFE	0.45	0.20	1.00

For example, from Exhibit 3, we know the covariance between long-term bonds and MSCI EAFE is 38. The standard deviation of long-term bond returns is $81^{1/2}$ = 9 percent, that of MSCI EAFE returns is $441^{1/2}$ = 21 percent, from diagonal terms in Exhibit 3. The correlation $\rho(R_{\text{long-term bonds}}, R_{\text{EAFE}})$ is 38/[(9%)(21%)] = 0.201, rounded to 0.20. The correlation of the S&P 500 with itself equals 1: The calculation is its own covariance divided by its standard deviation squared.

EXAMPLE 1

Portfolio Expected Return and Variance of Return with Varying Portfolio Weights

Anna Cintara is constructing different portfolios from the following two stocks:

Exhibit 5: Description of Two-Stock Portfolio

	Stock 1	Stock 2
Expected return	4%	8%
Standard deviation	6%	15%
Current portfolio weights	0.40	0.60
Correlation between returns		0.30

1. Calculate the covariance between the returns on the two stocks.

   Solution:

   The correlation between two stock returns is $\rho(R_i,R_j) = Cov(R_i,R_j)/[\sigma(R_i) \sigma(R_j)]$, so the covariance is $Cov(R_i,R_j) = \rho(R_i,R_j) \sigma(R_i) \sigma(R_j)$. For these two stocks, the covariance is $Cov(R_1,R_2) = \rho(R_1,R_2) \sigma(R_1) \sigma(R_2) = 0.30 (6) (15) = 27$.

2. What is the portfolio expected return and standard deviation if Cintara puts 100 percent of her investment in Stock 1 ($w_1 = 1.00$ and $w_2 = 0.00$)? What is the portfolio expected return and standard deviation if Cintara puts 100 percent of her investment in Stock 2 ($w_1 = 0.00$ and $w_2 = 1.00$)?

   Solution:

   If the portfolio is 100 percent invested in Stock 1, the portfolio has an expected return of 4 percent and a standard deviation of 6 percent. If the portfolio is 100 percent invested in Stock 2, the portfolio has an expected return of 8 percent and a standard deviation of 15 percent.

3. What are the portfolio expected return and standard deviation using the current portfolio weights?

   Solution:

   For the current 40/60 portfolio, the expected return is

   $$E(R_p) = w_1 E(R_1) + (1 - w_1)E(R_2) = 0.40(4\%) + 0.60(8\%) = 6.4\%$$

   The portfolio variance and standard deviation are as follows:

   $$\sigma^2(R_p) = w_1^2 \sigma^2(R_1) + w_2^2 \sigma^2(R_2) + 2 w_1 w_2 Cov(R_1, R_2)$$

   $$= (0.40)^2(36) + (0.60)^2(225) + 2(0.40)(0.60)(27)$$

   $$= 5.76 + 81 + 12.96 = 99.72$$

   $$\sigma(R_p) = 99.72^{1/2}$$

   $$= 9.99\%$$

4. Calculate the expected return and standard deviation of the portfolios when w_1 goes from 0.00 to 1.00 in 0.10 increments (and $w_2 = 1 - w_1$). Place the

results (stock weights, portfolio expected return, and portfolio standard deviation) in a table, and then sketch a graph of the results with the standard deviation on the horizontal axis and expected return on the vertical axis.

Solution:

The portfolio expected returns, variances, and standard deviations for the different sets of portfolio weights are given in the following table. Three of the rows are already computed in the solutions to 2 and 3, and the other rows are computed using the same expected return, variance, and standard deviation formulas as in the solution to 3:

Stock 1 weight	Stock 2 weight	Expected return (%)	Variance (%²)	Standard deviation (%)
1.00	0.00	4.00	36.00	6.00
0.90	0.10	4.40	36.27	6.02
0.80	0.20	4.80	40.68	6.38
0.70	0.30	5.20	49.23	7.02
0.60	0.40	5.60	61.92	7.87
0.50	0.50	6.00	78.75	8.87
0.40	0.60	6.40	99.72	9.99
0.30	0.70	6.80	124.83	11.17
0.20	0.80	7.20	154.08	12.41
0.10	0.90	7.60	187.47	13.69
0.00	1.00	8.00	225.00	15.00

The graph of the expected return and standard deviation follows:

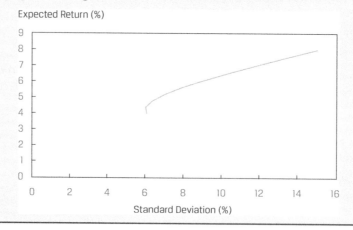

QUESTION SET

1. US and Spanish bonds returns measured in the same currency units have standard deviations of 0.64 and 0.56, respectively. If the correlation between the two bonds is 0.24, the covariance of returns is *closest* to:

   A. 0.086.

   B. 0.335.

C. 0.390.
Solution:

A is correct. The covariance is the product of the standard deviations and correlation using the formula Cov(US bond returns, Spanish bond returns) = σ(US bonds) × σ (Spanish bonds) × ρ(US bond returns, Spanish bond returns) = 0.64 × 0.56 × 0.24 = 0.086.

2. The covariance of returns is positive when the returns on two assets tend to:

   A. have the same expected values.

   B. be above their expected value at different times.

   C. be on the same side of their expected value at the same time.
   Solution:

   C is correct. The covariance of returns is positive when the returns on both assets tend to be on the same side (above or below) their expected values at the same time, indicating an average positive relationship between returns.

3. Which of the following correlation coefficients indicates the weakest linear relationship between two variables?

   A. −0.67

   B. −0.24

   C. 0.33
   Solution:

   B is correct. Correlations near +1 exhibit strong positive linearity, whereas correlations near −1 exhibit strong negative linearity. A correlation of 0 indicates an absence of any linear relationship between the variables. The closer the correlation is to 0, the weaker the linear relationship.

4. An analyst develops the following covariance matrix of returns:

	Hedge Fund	**Market Index**
Hedge fund	256	110
Market index	110	81

   The correlation of returns between the hedge fund and the market index is *closest* to:

   A. 0.005.

   B. 0.073.

   C. 0.764.
   Solution:

   C is correct. The correlation between two random variables R_i and R_j is defined as $\rho(R_i,R_j) = Cov(R_i,R_j)/[\sigma(R_i)\sigma(R_j)]$. Using the subscript i to represent hedge funds and the subscript j to represent the market index, the standard deviations are $\sigma(R_i) = 256^{1/2} = 16$ and $\sigma(R_j) = 81^{1/2} = 9$. Thus, $\rho(R_i,R_j) = Cov(R_i,R_j)/[\sigma(R_i) \sigma(R_j)] = 110/(16 \times 9) = 0.764$.

5. All else being equal, as the correlation between two assets approaches +1.0, the diversification benefits:

    A. decrease.

    B. stay the same.

    C. increase.

    Solution:

    A is correct. As the correlation between two assets approaches +1, diversification benefits decrease. In other words, an increasingly positive correlation indicates an increasingly strong positive linear relationship and fewer diversification benefits.

6. Given a portfolio of five stocks, how many unique covariance terms, excluding variances, are required to calculate the portfolio return variance?

    A. 10

    B. 20

    C. 25

    Solution:

    A is correct. A covariance matrix for five stocks has 5 × 5 = 25 entries. Subtracting the 5 diagonal variance terms results in 20 off-diagonal entries. Because a covariance matrix is symmetrical, only 10 entries are unique (20/2 = 10).

7. Which of the following statements is *most* accurate? If the covariance of returns between two assets is 0.0023, then the:

    A. assets' risk is near zero.

    B. asset returns are unrelated.

    C. asset returns have a positive relationship.

    Solution:

    C is correct. The covariance of returns is positive when the returns on both assets tend to be on the same side (above or below) their expected values at the same time.

8. A two-stock portfolio includes stocks with the following characteristics:

	Stock 1	Stock 2
Expected return	7%	10%
Standard deviation	12%	25%
Portfolio weights	0.30	0.70
Correlation	0.20	

    What is the standard deviation of portfolio returns?

    A. 14.91 percent

    B. 18.56 percent

C. 21.10 percent

Solution:

B is correct. The covariance between the returns for the two stocks is $\text{Cov}(R_1, R_2) = \rho(R_1, R_2) \, \sigma(R_1) \, \sigma(R_2) = 0.20 \, (12) \, (25) = 60$. The portfolio variance is

$$\sigma^2(R_p) = w_1^2 \sigma^2(R_1) + w_2^2 \sigma^2(R_2) + 2 w_1 w_2 \text{Cov}(R_1, R_2)$$

$$= (0.30)^2 (12)^2 + (0.70)^2 (25)^2 + 2(0.30)(0.70)(60)$$

$$= 12.96 + 306.25 + 25.2 = 344.41.$$

The portfolio standard deviation is

$$\sigma^2(R_p) = 344.41^{\frac{1}{2}} = 18.56\%.$$

9. Lena Hunziger has designed the following three-asset portfolio:

	Asset 1	Asset 2	Asset 3
Expected return	5%	6%	7%
Portfolio weight	**0.20**	0.30	0.50

Variance-Covariance Matrix			
	Asset 1	Asset 2	Asset 3
Asset 1	196	105	140
Asset 2	105	225	150
Asset 3	140	150	400

Hunziger estimated the portfolio return to be 6.3 percent. What is the portfolio standard deviation?

A. 13.07 percent

B. 13.88 percent

C. 14.62 percent

Solution:

C is correct. For a three-asset portfolio, the portfolio variance is

$$\sigma^2(R_p) = w_1^2 \sigma^2(R_1) + w_2^2 \sigma^2(R_2) + w_3^2 \sigma^2(R_3) + 2 w_1 w_2 \text{Cov}(R_1, R_2)$$

$$+ 2 w_1 w_3 \text{Cov}(R_1, R_3) + 2 w_2 w_3 \text{Cov}(R_2, R_3)$$

$$= (0.20)^2 (196) + (0.30)^2 (225) + (0.50)^2 (400) + 2(0.20)(0.30)(105)$$

$$+ 2(0.20)(0.50)(140) + 2(0.30)(0.50)(150)$$

$$= 7.84 + 20.25 + 100 + 12.6 + 28 + 45 = 213.69.$$

The portfolio standard deviation is

$$\sigma^2(R_p) = 213.69^{1/2} = 14.62\%.$$

3   FORECASTING CORRELATION OF RETURNS: COVARIANCE GIVEN A JOINT PROBABILITY FUNCTION

☐ | calculate and interpret the covariance and correlation of portfolio returns using a joint probability function for returns

How do we estimate return covariance and correlation? Frequently, we make forecasts on the basis of historical covariance or use other methods such as a market model regression based on historical return data. We can also calculate covariance using the **joint probability function** of the random variables, if that can be estimated. The joint probability function of two random variables X and Y, denoted $P(X,Y)$, gives the probability of joint occurrences of values of X and Y. For example, $P(X=3, Y=2)$, is the probability that X equals 3 and Y equals 2.

Suppose that the joint probability function of the returns on BankCorp stock (R_A) and the returns on NewBank stock (R_B) has the simple structure given in Exhibit 6.

Exhibit 6: Joint Probability Function of BankCorp and NewBank Returns (Entries Are Joint Probabilities)

	$R_B = 20\%$	$R_B = 16\%$	$R_B = 10\%$
$R_A = 25\%$	0.20	0	0
$R_A = 12\%$	0	0.50	0
$R_A = 10\%$	0	0	0.30

The expected return on BankCorp stock is 0.20(25%) + 0.50(12%) + 0.30(10%) = 14%. The expected return on NewBank stock is 0.20(20%) + 0.50(16%) + 0.30(10%) = 15%. The joint probability function above might reflect an analysis based on whether banking industry conditions are good, average, or poor. Exhibit 7 presents the calculation of covariance.

Exhibit 7: Covariance Calculations

Banking Industry Condition	Deviations BankCorp	Deviations NewBank	Product of Deviations	Probability of Condition	Probability-Weighted Product
Good	25–14	20–15	55	0.20	11
Average	12–14	16–15	–2	0.50	–1
Poor	10–14	10–15	20	0.30	6
					$\text{Cov}(R_A, R_B)$ = 16

Note: Expected return for BankCorp is 14% and for NewBank, 15%.

The first and second columns of numbers show, respectively, the deviations of BankCorp and NewBank returns from their mean or expected value. The next column shows the product of the deviations. For example, for good industry conditions, (25 – 14)(20 – 15) = 11(5) = 55. Then, 55 is multiplied or weighted by 0.20, the probability that banking industry conditions are good: 55(0.20) = 11. The calculations for average and poor banking conditions follow the same pattern. Summing up these probability-weighted products, we find $Cov(R_A, R_B) = 16$.

A formula for computing the covariance between random variables R_A and R_B is

$$Cov(R_A, R_B) = \sum_i \sum_j P(R_{A,i}, R_{B,j})(R_{A,i} - ER_A)(R_{B,j} - ER_B). \tag{8}$$

The formula tells us to sum all possible deviation cross-products weighted by the appropriate joint probability.

Next, we take note of the fact that when two random variables are independent, their joint probability function simplifies.

Two random variables X and Y are **independent** if and only if $P(X,Y) = P(X)P(Y)$.

For example, given independence, $P(3,2) = P(3)P(2)$. We multiply the individual probabilities to get the joint probabilities. *Independence* is a stronger property than *uncorrelatedness* because correlation addresses only linear relationships. The following condition holds for independent random variables and, therefore, also holds for uncorrelated random variables.

The expected value of the product of uncorrelated random variables is the product of their expected values.

$E(XY) = E(X)E(Y)$ if X and Y are uncorrelated.

Many financial variables, such as revenue (price times quantity), are the product of random quantities. When applicable, the previous rule simplifies the calculation of the expected value of a product of random variables.

EXAMPLE 2

Covariances and Correlations of Security Returns

Isabel Vasquez is reviewing the correlations between four of the asset classes in her company portfolio. In Exhibit 8, she plots 24 recent monthly returns for large-cap US stocks versus for large-cap world ex-US stocks (Panel 1) and the 24 monthly returns for intermediate-term corporate bonds versus long-term corporate bonds (Panel 2). Vasquez presents the returns, variances, and covariances in decimal form instead of percentage form. Note the different ranges of their vertical axes (Return %).

Exhibit 8: Monthly Returns for Four Asset Classes

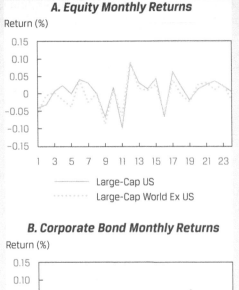

A. Equity Monthly Returns

Return (%)

Large-Cap US

Large-Cap World Ex US

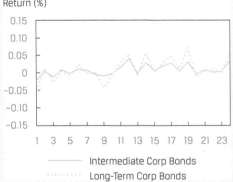

B. Corporate Bond Monthly Returns

Return (%)

Intermediate Corp Bonds

Long-Term Corp Bonds

1. Selected data for the four asset classes are shown in Exhibit 9.

Exhibit 9: Selected Data for Four Asset Classes

Asset Classes	Large-Cap US Equities	World (ex US) Equities	Intermediate Corp Bonds	Long-Term Corp Bonds
Variance	0.001736	0.001488	0.000174	0.000699
Standard deviation	0.041668	0.038571	0.013180	0.026433
Covariance	0.001349		0.000318	
Correlation	0.87553		0.95133	

Vasquez noted, as shown in Exhibit 9, that although the two equity classes had much greater variances and covariance than the two bond classes, the correlation between the two equity classes was lower than the correlation between the two bond classes. She also noted that long-term bonds were more volatile (higher variance) than intermediate-term bonds; however, long- and intermediate-term bond returns still had a high correlation.

PORTFOLIO RISK MEASURES: APPLICATIONS OF THE NORMAL DISTRIBUTION

4

☐ | define shortfall risk, calculate the safety-first ratio, and identify an optimal portfolio using Roy's safety-first criterion

Modern portfolio theory (MPT) often involves valuing investment opportunities using mean return and variance of return measures. In economic theory, **mean–variance analysis** holds exactly when investors are risk averse; when they choose investments to maximize expected utility or satisfaction; and when either (assumption 1) returns are normally distributed or (assumption 2) investors have quadratic utility functions (a concept used in economics for a mathematical representation of risk and return trade-offs). Mean–variance analysis, however, can still be useful—that is, it can hold approximately—when either assumption 1 or 2 is violated. Because practitioners prefer to work with observables, such as returns, the proposition that returns are at least approximately normally distributed has played a key role in much of MPT.

To illustrate this concept, assume an investor is saving for retirement. Although her goal is to earn the highest real return possible, she believes that the portfolio should at least achieve real capital preservation over the long term. Assuming a long-term expected inflation rate of 2 percent, the minimum acceptable return would be 2 percent. Exhibit 10 compares three investment alternatives in terms of their expected returns and standard deviation of returns. The probability of falling below 2 percent is calculated on basis of the assumption of normally distributed returns. In Exhibit 10, we see that Portfolio II, which combines the highest expected return and the lowest volatility, has the lowest probability of earning less than 2 percent (or equivalently, the highest probability of earning at least 2 percent). This also can be seen in Panel B, which shows that Portfolio II has the smallest shaded area to the left of 2 percent (the probability of earning less than the minimum acceptable return).

Exhibit 10: Probability of Earning a Minimum Acceptable Return

Panel A: Alternative Portfolio Characteristics

Portfolio	I	II	II
Expected return	5%	8%	5%
Standard deviation of return	8%	8%	12%
Probability of earning < 2% [$P(x < 2)$]	37.7%	24.6%	41.7%
Probability of earning ≥ 2% [$P(x ≥ 2)$]	62.3%	75.4%	58.3%

Panel B: Likelihoods of Attainting Minimal Acceptable Return

A. Portfolio I

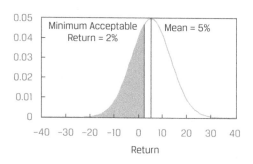

B. Portfolio II

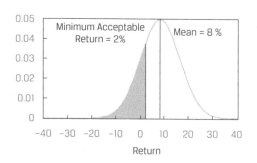

C. Portfolio III

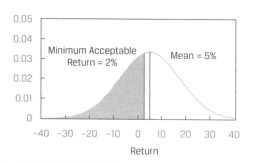

Mean–variance analysis generally considers risk symmetrically in the sense that standard deviation captures variability both above and below the mean. An alternative approach evaluates only downside risk. We discuss one such approach, safety-first rules, because they provide an excellent illustration of the application of normal distribution theory to practical investment problems. **Safety-first rules** focus on **shortfall risk**, the risk that portfolio value (or portfolio return) will fall below some minimum acceptable level over some time horizon. The risk that the assets in a defined benefit plan will fall below plan liabilities is an example of a shortfall risk.

Suppose an investor views any return below a level of R_L as unacceptable. Roy's safety-first criterion (Roy 1952) states that the optimal portfolio minimizes the probability that portfolio return, R_P, will fall below the threshold level, R_L. That is, the investor's objective is to choose a portfolio that minimizes $P(R_P < R_L)$. When portfolio returns are normally distributed, we can calculate $P(R_P < R_L)$ using the number of standard deviations that R_L lies below the expected portfolio return, $E(R_P)$. The portfolio for which $E(R_P) - R_L$ is largest relative to standard deviation minimizes $P(R_P < R_L)$. Therefore, if returns are normally distributed, the safety-first optimal portfolio *maximizes* the safety-first ratio (SFRatio), as follows:

$$\text{SFRatio} = [E(R_P) - R_L]/\sigma_P. \tag{9}$$

The quantity $E(R_P) - R_L$ is the distance from the mean return to the shortfall level. Dividing this distance by σ_P gives the distance in units of standard deviation. When choosing among portfolios using Roy's criterion (assuming normality), follow these two steps:

1. Calculate each portfolio's SFRatio.
2. Choose the portfolio with the highest SFRatio.

For a portfolio with a given safety-first ratio, the probability that its return will be less than R_L is *Normal*($-$SFRatio), and the safety-first optimal portfolio has the lowest such probability. For example, suppose an investor's threshold return, R_L, is 2 percent. He is presented with two portfolios. Portfolio 1 has an expected return of 12 percent, with a standard deviation of 15 percent. Portfolio 2 has an expected return of 14 percent, with a standard deviation of 16 percent. The SFRatios, using Equation 9, are $0.667 = (12 - 2)/15$ and $0.75 = (14 - 2)/16$ for Portfolios 1 and 2, respectively. For the superior Portfolio 2, the probability that portfolio return will be less than 2 percent is $N(-0.75) = 1 - N(0.75) = 1 - 0.7734 = 0.227$, or about 23 percent, assuming that portfolio returns are normally distributed.

You may have noticed the similarity of the SFRatio to the Sharpe ratio. If we substitute the risk-free rate, R_F, for the critical level R_L, the SFRatio becomes the Sharpe ratio. The safety-first approach provides a new perspective on the Sharpe ratio: When we evaluate portfolios using the Sharpe ratio, the portfolio with the highest Sharpe ratio is the one that minimizes the probability that portfolio return will be less than the risk-free rate (given a normality assumption).

EXAMPLE 3

The Safety-First Optimal Portfolio for a Client

You are researching asset allocations for a client in Canada with a CAD800,000 portfolio. Although her investment objective is long-term growth, at the end of a year, she may want to liquidate CAD30,000 of the portfolio to fund educational expenses. If that need arises, she would like to be able to take out the CAD30,000 without invading the initial capital of CAD800,000. Exhibit 11 shows three alternative allocations.

Exhibit 11: Mean and Standard Deviation for Three Allocations (in Percent)

Allocation	A	B	C
Expected annual return	25	11	14
Standard deviation of return	27	8	20

Address these questions (assume normality for Questions 2 and 3):

1. Given the client's desire not to invade the CAD800,000 principal, what is the shortfall level, R_L? Use this shortfall level to answer question 2.

   Solution:

   Because CAD30,000/CAD800,000 is 3.75 percent, for any return less than 3.75 percent the client will need to invade principal if she takes out CAD30,000. So, R_L = 3.75%.

2. According to the safety-first criterion, which of the three allocations is the best?

   (Hint, to decide which of the three allocations is safety-first optimal, select the alternative with the highest ratio $[E(R_P) - R_L]/\sigma_P$.)

   A. 0.787037 = (25 – 3.75)/27

   B. 0.90625 = (11 – 3.75)/8

   C. 0.5125 = (14 – 3.75)/20

   Solution:

   B is correct. Allocation B, with the largest ratio (0.90625), is the best alternative according to the safety-first criterion.

3. What is the probability that the return on the safety-first optimal portfolio will be less than the shortfall level?

   Solution:

   To answer this question, note that $P(R_B < 3.75) = Normal(-0.90625)$. We can round 0.90625 to 0.91 for use with tables of the standard normal CDF. First, we calculate $Normal(-0.91) = 1 - Normal(0.91) = 1 - 0.8186 = 0.1814$, or about 18.1 percent. Using a spreadsheet function for the standard normal CDF on –0.90625 without rounding, we get 0.182402, or about 18.2 percent. The safety-first optimal portfolio has a roughly 18 percent chance of not meeting a 3.75 percent return threshold. This can be seen in the following graphic, in which Allocation B has the smallest area under the distribution curve to the left of 3.75 percent.

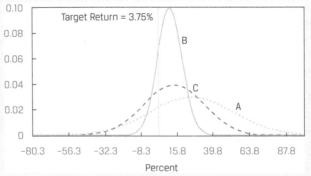

   Several points are worth noting. First, if the inputs were slightly different, we could get a different ranking. For example, if the mean return on B were 10 percent rather than 11 percent, Allocation A would be superior to B. Second, if meeting the 3.75 percent return threshold were a necessity rather than a wish, CAD830,000 in one year could be modeled as a liability. Fixed-income strategies, such as cash flow matching, could be used to offset or immunize the CAD830,000 quasi-liability.

In many investment contexts besides Roy's safety-first criterion, we use the normal distribution to estimate a probability. Another arena in which the normal distribution plays an important role is financial risk management. Financial institutions, such as investment banks, security dealers, and commercial banks, have formal systems to measure and control financial risk at various levels, from trading positions to the overall risk for the firm. Two mainstays in managing financial risk are value at risk (VaR) and stress testing/scenario analysis. **Stress testing** and **scenario analysis** refer to a set of techniques for estimating losses in extremely unfavorable combinations of events or scenarios. **Value at risk** (VaR) is a money measure of the minimum value of losses expected over a specified time period (e.g., a day, a quarter, or a year) at a given level of probability (often 0.05 or 0.01). Suppose we specify a one-day time horizon and a level of probability of 0.05, which would be called a 95 percent one-day VaR. If this VaR equaled EUR5 million for a portfolio, there would be a 0.05 probability that the portfolio would lose EUR5 million or more in a single day (assuming our assumptions were correct). One of the basic approaches to estimating VaR, the variance–covariance or analytical method, assumes that returns follow a normal distribution.

QUESTION SET

A client has a portfolio of common stocks and fixed-income instruments with a current value of GBP1,350,000. She intends to liquidate GBP50,000 from the portfolio at the end of the year to purchase a partnership share in a business. Furthermore, the client would like to be able to withdraw the GBP50,000 without reducing the initial capital of GBP1,350,000. The following table shows four alternative asset allocations.

Mean and Standard Deviation for Four Allocations (in Percent)

	A	B	C	D
Expected annual return	16	12	10	9
Standard deviation of return	24	17	12	11

1. Address the following questions (assume normality for Parts B and C):

   A. Given the client's desire not to invade the GBP1,350,000 principal, what is the shortfall level, R_L? Use this shortfall level to answer Question 2.

   B. According to the safety-first criterion, which of the allocations is the best?

   C. What is the probability that the return on the safety-first optimal portfolio will be less than the shortfall level, R_L?

   Solution:

   A. Because GBP50,000/GBP1,350,000 is 3.7 percent, for any return less than 3.7 percent the client will need to invade principal if she takes out GBP50,000. So R_L = 3.7 percent.

   B. To decide which of the allocations is safety-first optimal, select the alternative with the highest ratio $[E(R_P) - R_L]/\sigma_P$:

   Allocation 1   0.5125 = (16 − 3.7)/24.

   Allocation 2   0.488235 = (12 − 3.7)/17.

Allocation 3 $0.525 = (10 - 3.7)/12.$

Allocation 4 $0.481818 = (9 - 3.7)/11.$

Allocation C, with the largest ratio (0.525), is the best alternative according to the safety-first criterion.

C. To answer this question, note that $P(R_C < 3.7) = N(0.037 - 0.10)/0.12)$ = *Normal*(−0.525). By using Excel's NORM.S.DIST() function, we get NORM.S.DIST((0.037 − 0.10)/0.12) = 29.98%, or about 30 percent. The safety-first optimal portfolio has a roughly 30 percent chance of not meeting a 3.7 percent return threshold.

2. A client holding a GBP2,000,000 portfolio wants to withdraw GBP90,000 in one year without invading the principal. According to Roy's safety-first criterion, which of the following portfolio allocations is optimal?

	Allocation A	Allocation B	Allocation C
Expected annual return	6.5%	7.5%	8.5%
Standard deviation of returns	8.35%	10.21%	14.34%

A. Allocation A

B. Allocation B

C. Allocation C

Solution:

B is correct. Allocation B has the highest safety-first ratio. The threshold return level, R_L, for the portfolio is GBP90,000/GBP2,000,000 = 4.5 percent; thus, any return less than R_L = 4.5% will invade the portfolio principal. To compute the allocation that is safety-first optimal, select the alternative with the highest ratio:

$$\frac{[E(R_P - R_L)]}{\sigma_P}.$$

Allocation A $= \frac{6.5 - 4.5}{8.35} = 0.240.$

Allocation B $= \frac{7.5 - 4.5}{10.21} = 0.294.$

Allocation C $= \frac{8.5 - 4.5}{14.34} = 0.279.$

REFERENCES

Roy, A. D. 1952. "Safety First and the Holding of Assets." Econometrica20 (3): 431–49. 10.2307/1907413

PRACTICE PROBLEMS

1. An analyst produces the following joint probability function for a foreign index (FI) and a domestic index (DI).

	$R_{DI} = 30\%$	$R_{DI} = 25\%$	$R_{DI} = 15\%$
$R_{FI} = 25\%$	0.25		
$R_{FI} = 15\%$		0.50	
$R_{FI} = 10\%$			0.25

The covariance of returns on the foreign index and the returns on the domestic index is *closest* to:

A. 26.39.

B. 26.56.

C. 28.12.

SOLUTIONS

1. B is correct. The covariance is 26.56, calculated as follows. First, expected returns are

$E(R_{FI}) = (0.25 \times 25) + (0.50 \times 15) + (0.25 \times 10)$

$= 6.25 + 7.50 + 2.50 = 16.25$ and

$E(R_{DI}) = (0.25 \times 30) + (0.50 \times 25) + (0.25 \times 15)$

$= 7.50 + 12.50 + 3.75 = 23.75.$

Covariance is

$\text{Cov}(R_{FI},R_{DI}) = \sum_i \sum_j P(R_{FI,i}, R_{DI,j})(R_{FI,i} - ER_{FI})(R_{DI,j} - ER_{DI})$

$= 0.25[(25 - 16.25)(30 - 23.75)] + 0.50[(15 - 16.25)(25 - 23.75)] + 0.25[(10 - 16.25)(15 - 23.75)]$

$= 13.67 + (-0.78) + 13.67 = 26.56.$

Simulation Methods

by Kobor Adam, PhD, CFA.

Adam Kobor, PhD, CFA, at New York University Investment Office (USA)

LEARNING OUTCOMES

Mastery	The candidate should be able to:
☐	explain the relationship between normal and lognormal distributions and why the lognormal distribution is used to model asset prices when using continuously compounded asset returns
☐	describe Monte Carlo simulation and explain how it can be used in investment applications
☐	describe the use of bootstrap resampling in conducting a simulation based on observed data in investment applications

INTRODUCTION

1

The understanding and application of probability distributions is a critical component of forecasting financial variables and asset prices. This learning module provides a foundation for understanding important concepts related to probability distributions. Regarding the application of probability distributions, this learning module explains how to construct and interpret a Monte Carlo simulation analysis. Bootstrapping, with some similarities to Monte Carlo simulations, is also demonstrated to illustrate the use and application of this statistical sampling approach.

LEARNING MODULE OVERVIEW

- The lognormal distribution is widely used for modeling the probability distribution of financial asset prices because the distribution is bounded from below by 0 as asset prices and usually describes accurately the statistical distribution properties of financial assets prices. Lognormal distribution is typically skewed to the right.

- Continuously compounded returns play a role in many asset pricing models, as well as in risk management.

- Monte Carlo simulation is widely used to estimate risk and return in investment applications. Specifically, it is commonly used to value securities with complex features, such as embedded options, where no analytic pricing formula is available

- A Monte Carlo simulation generates a large number of random samples from a specified probability distribution or a series of distributions to obtain the likelihood of a range of results.

- Bootstrapping mimics the process of performing random sampling from a population to construct the sampling distribution by treating the randomly drawn sample as if it were the population.

- Because a random sample offers a good representation of the population, bootstrapping can simulate sampling from the population by sampling from the observed sample.

2   LOGNORMAL DISTRIBUTION AND CONTINUOUS COMPOUNDING

☐ | explain the relationship between normal and lognormal distributions and why the lognormal distribution is used to model asset prices when using continuously compounded asset returns

The Lognormal Distribution

Closely related to the normal distribution, the lognormal distribution is widely used for modeling the probability distribution of share and other asset prices. For example, the lognormal distribution appears in the Black–Scholes–Merton option pricing model. The Black–Scholes–Merton model assumes that the price of the asset underlying the option is lognormally distributed.

A random variable Y follows a lognormal distribution if its natural logarithm, ln Y, is normally distributed. The reverse is also true: If the natural logarithm of random variable Y, ln Y, is normally distributed, then Y follows a lognormal distribution. If you think of the term lognormal as "the log is normal," you will have no trouble remembering this relationship.

The two most noteworthy observations about the lognormal distribution are that it is bounded below by 0 and it is skewed to the right (it has a long right tail). Note these two properties in the graphs of the probability density functions (pdfs) of two lognormal distributions in Exhibit 1. Asset prices are bounded from below by 0. In practice, the lognormal distribution has been found to be a usefully accurate description of the distribution of prices for many financial assets. However, the normal distribution is often a good approximation for returns. For this reason, both distributions are very important for finance professionals.

Exhibit 1: Two Lognormal Distributions

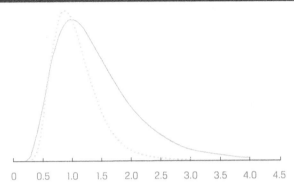

Like the normal distribution, the lognormal distribution is completely described by two parameters. Unlike many other distributions, a lognormal distribution is defined in terms of the parameters of a *different* distribution. The two parameters of a lognormal distribution are the mean and standard deviation (or variance) of its associated normal distribution: the mean and variance of ln Y, given that Y is lognormal. So, we must keep track of two sets of means and standard deviations (or variances): (1) the mean and standard deviation (or variance) of the associated normal distribution (these are the parameters) and (2) the mean and standard deviation (or variance) of the lognormal variable itself.

To illustrate this relationship, we simulated 1,000 scenarios of yearly asset returns, assuming that returns are normally distributed with 7 percent mean and 12 percent standard deviation. For each scenario i, we converted the simulated continuously compounded returns (r_i) to future asset prices with the formula Price(1 year later)$_i$ = USD1 × exp(r_i), where exp is the exponential function and assuming that the asset's price is USD1 today. In Exhibit 2, Panel A shows the distribution of the simulated returns together with the fitted normal pdf, whereas Panel B shows the distribution of the corresponding future asset prices together with the fitted lognormal pdf. Again, note that the lognormal distribution of future asset prices is bounded below by 0 and has a long right tail.

Exhibit 2: Simulated Returns (Normal PDF) and Asset Prices (Lognormal PDF)

A. Normal PDF

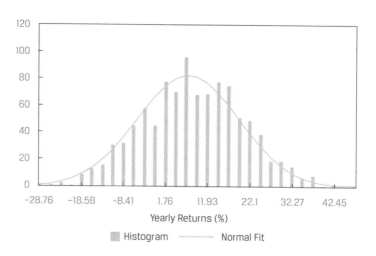

B. Lognormal PDF

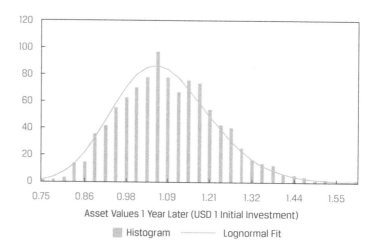

The expressions for the mean and variance of the lognormal variable are challenging. Suppose a normal random variable X has expected value μ and variance σ^2. Define $Y = \exp(X)$. Remember that the operation indicated by $\exp(X)$ or e^X (where $e \approx 2.7183$) is the opposite operation from taking logs. Because $\ln Y = \ln [\exp(X)] = X$ is normal (we assume X is normal), Y is lognormal. What is the expected value of $Y = \exp(X)$? A guess might be that the expected value of Y is $\exp(\mu)$. The expected value is actually $\exp(\mu + 0.50\sigma^2)$, which is larger than $\exp(\mu)$ by a factor of $\exp(0.50\,\sigma^2) > 1$. To get some insight into this concept, think of what happens if we increase σ^2. The distribution spreads out; it can spread upward, but it cannot spread downward past 0. As a result, the center of its distribution is pushed to the right: The distribution's mean increases.

The expressions for the mean and variance of a lognormal variable are summarized below, where μ and σ^2 are the mean and variance of the associated normal distribution (refer to these expressions as needed, rather than memorizing them):

- Mean (μ_L) of a lognormal random variable = $\exp(\mu + 0.50\sigma^2)$.

- Variance ($\sigma_L{}^2$) of a lognormal random variable = $\exp(2\mu + \sigma^2) \times [\exp(\sigma^2) - 1]$.

Continuously Compounded Rates of Return

We now explore the relationship between the distribution of stock return and stock price. In this section, we show that if a stock's continuously compounded return is normally distributed, then future stock price is necessarily lognormally distributed. Furthermore, we show that stock price may be well described by the lognormal distribution even when continuously compounded returns do not follow a normal distribution. These results provide the theoretical foundation for using the lognormal distribution to model asset prices.

Showing that the stock price at some future time T, P_T, equals the current stock price, P_0, multiplied by e raised to power $r_{0,T}$, the continuously compounded return from 0 to T:

$$P_T = P_0 \exp(r_{0,T}).$$

We showed in an earlier lesson that $r_{0,T}$, the continuously compounded return to time T, is the sum of the one-period continuously compounded returns, as follows:

$$r_{0,T} = r_{T-1,T} + r_{T-2,T-1} + \ldots + r_{0,1}. \tag{1}$$

If these shorter-period returns are normally distributed, then $r_{0,T}$ is normally distributed (given certain assumptions) or approximately normally distributed (not making those assumptions). As P_T is proportional to the log of a normal random variable, P_T is lognormal.

A key assumption in many investment applications is that returns are **independently and identically distributed** (i.i.d.). Independence captures the proposition that investors cannot predict future returns using past returns. Identical distribution captures the assumption of stationarity, a property implying that the mean and variance of return do not change from period to period.

Assume that the one-period continuously compounded returns (such as $r_{0,1}$) are i.i.d. random variables with mean μ and variance σ^2 (but making no normality or other distributional assumption). Then,

$$E(r_{0,T}) = E(r_{T-1,T}) + E(r_{T-2,T-1}) + \ldots + E(r_{0,1}) = \mu T, \tag{2}$$

(we add up μ for a total of T times), and

$$\sigma^2(r_{0,T}) = \sigma^2 T \tag{3}$$

(as a consequence of the independence assumption).

The variance of the T holding period continuously compounded return is T multiplied by the variance of the one-period continuously compounded return; also, $\sigma(r_{0,T}) = \sigma\sqrt{T}$. If the one-period continuously compounded returns on the right-hand side of Equation 1 are normally distributed, then the T holding period continuously compounded return, $r_{0,T}$, is also normally distributed with mean μT and variance $\sigma^2 T$. This is because a linear combination of normal random variables is also a normal random variable.

Even if the one-period continuously compounded returns are not normal, their sum, $r_{0,T}$, is approximately normal according to the central limit theorem. Now compare $P_T = P_0 \exp(r_{0,T})$ to $Y = \exp(X)$, where X is *normal* and Y is lognormal (as we discussed previously). Clearly, we can model future stock price P_T as a lognormal random variable because $r_{0,T}$ should be at least approximately *normal*. This assumption of normally distributed returns is the basis in theory for the lognormal distribution as a model for the distribution of prices of shares and other financial assets.

Continuously compounded returns play a role in many asset pricing models, as well as in risk management. **Volatility** measures the standard deviation of the continuously compounded returns on the underlying asset; by convention, it is stated as an annualized measure. In practice, we often estimate volatility using a historical series of continuously compounded daily returns. We gather a set of daily holding period returns, convert them into continuously compounded daily returns and then compute the standard deviation of the continuously compounded daily returns and annualize that number using Equation 3.

Annualizing is typically done based on 250 days in a year, the approximate number of business days that financial markets are typically open for trading. Thus, if daily volatility were 0.01, we would state volatility (on an annual basis) as $0.01\sqrt{250} = 0.1581$. Example 1 illustrates the estimation of volatility for the shares of Astra International.

EXAMPLE 1

Volatility of Share Price

Suppose you are researching Astra International (Indonesia Stock Exchange: ASII) and are interested in Astra's price action in a week in which international economic news had significantly affected the Indonesian stock market. You decide to use volatility as a measure of the variability of Astra shares during that week. Exhibit 3 shows closing prices during that week.

Exhibit 3: Astra International Daily Closing Prices

Day	Closing Price (Indonesian rupiah, IDR)
Monday	6,950
Tuesday	7,000
Wednesday	6,850
Thursday	6,600
Friday	6,350

Use the data provided to do the following:

1. Estimate the volatility of Astra shares. (Annualize volatility on the basis of 250 trading days in a year.)

   Solution:

   First, calculate the continuously compounded daily returns; then, find their standard deviation in the usual way. In calculating sample variance, to get sample standard deviation, the divisor is sample size minus 1.

   $\ln(7{,}000/6{,}950) = 0.007168$.

   $\ln(6{,}850/7{,}000) = -0.021661$.

   $\ln(6{,}600/6{,}850) = -0.037179$.

   $\ln(6{,}350/6{,}600) = -0.038615$.

   Sum $= -0.090287$.

   Mean $= -0.022572$.

   Variance $= 0.000452$.

   Standard deviation $= 0.021261$.

   The standard deviation of continuously compounded daily returns is 0.021261. Equation 3 states that $\hat{\sigma}(r_{0,T}) = \hat{\sigma}\sqrt{T}$. In this example, $\hat{\sigma}$ is the sample standard deviation of one-period continuously compounded returns. Thus, $\hat{\sigma}$ refers to 0.021261. We want to annualize, so the horizon T corresponds to one year. Because $\hat{\sigma}$ is in days, we set T equal to the number of trading days in a year (250).
   Therefore, we find that annualized volatility for Astra stock that week was 33.6 percent, calculated as $0.021261\sqrt{250} = 0.336165$.

2. Calculate an estimate of the expected continuously compounded annual return for Astra.

   Solution:

   Note that the sample mean, -0.022572 (from the Solution to 1), is a sample estimate of the mean, μ, of the continuously compounded one-period or daily returns. The sample mean can be translated into an estimate of the expected continuously compounded annual return using Equation 2, $\hat{\mu} T = -0.022572(250)$ (using 250 to be consistent with the calculation of volatility).

3. Discuss why it may not be prudent to use the sample mean daily return to estimate the expected continuously compounded annual return for Astra.

   Solution:

   Four daily return observations are far too few to estimate expected returns. Further, the variability in the daily returns overwhelms any information about expected return in a series this short.

4. Identify the probability distribution for Astra share prices if continuously compounded daily returns follow the normal distribution.

   Solution:

   Astra share prices should follow the lognormal distribution if the continuously compounded daily returns on Astra shares follow the normal distribution.

We have shown that the distribution of stock price is lognormal, given certain assumptions. Earlier we gave bullet-point expressions for the mean and variance of a lognormal random variable. In the context of a stock price, the $\hat{\mu}$ and $\hat{\sigma}^2$ in these expressions would refer to the mean and variance of the T horizon, not the one-period, continuously compounded returns compatible with the horizon of P_T.

3   MONTE CARLO SIMULATION

☐ | describe Monte Carlo simulation and explain how it can be used in investment applications

After gaining an understanding of probability distributions used to characterize asset prices and asset returns, we explore a technique called **Monte Carlo simulation** in which probability distributions play an integral role. A characteristic of Monte Carlo simulation is the generation of a very large number of random samples from a specified probability distribution or distributions to obtain the likelihood of a range of results.

Monte Carlo simulation is widely used to estimate risk and return in investment applications. In this setting, we simulate the portfolio's profit and loss performance for a specified time horizon, either on an asset-by-asset basis or an aggregate, portfolio basis. Repeated trials within the simulation, each trial involving a draw of random observations from a probability distribution, produce a simulated frequency distribution of portfolio returns from which performance and risk measures are derived.

Another important use of Monte Carlo simulation in investments is as a tool for valuing complex securities for which no analytic pricing formula is available. For other securities, such as mortgage-backed securities with complex embedded options, Monte Carlo simulation is also an important modeling resource. Because we control the assumptions when we carry out a simulation, we can run a model for valuing such securities through a Monte Carlo simulation to examine the model's sensitivity to a change in key assumptions.

To understand the technique of Monte Carlo simulation, we present the process as a series of steps; these can be viewed as providing an overview rather than a detailed recipe for implementing a Monte Carlo simulation in its many varied applications.

To illustrate the steps, we use Monte Carlo simulation to value an option, **contingent claim**, whose value is based on some other underlying security. For this option, no analytic pricing formula is available. For our purposes, the value of this contingent claim (an Asian option), equals the difference between the underlying stock price at that maturity and the *average* stock price during the life of the contingent claim or USD 0, whichever is greater. For instance, if the final underlying stock price is USD 34 and the average value over the life of the claim is USD 31, the value of the contingent claim at its maturity is USD 3 (the greater of USD 34 − USD 31 = USD 3 and USD 0).

Assume that the maturity of the claim is one year from today; we will simulate stock prices in monthly steps over the next 12 months and will generate 1,000 scenarios to value this claim. The payoff diagram of this contingent claim security is depicted in Panel A of Exhibit 4, a histogram of simulated average and final stock prices is shown in Panel B, and a histogram of simulated payoffs of the contingent claim is presented in Panel C.

The payoff diagram (Panel A) is a snapshot of the contingent claim at maturity. If the stock's final price is less than or equal to its average over the life of the contingent claim, then the payoff would be zero. However, if the final price exceeds the average price, the payoff is equal to this difference. Panel B shows histograms of the simulated final and average stock prices. Note that the simulated final price distribution is wider than the simulated average price distribution. Also, note that the contingent claim's value depends on the difference between the final and average stock prices, which cannot be directly inferred from these histograms.

Exhibit 4: Payoff Diagram, Histogram of Simulated Average, and Final Stock Prices, and Histogram of Simulated Payoffs for Contingent Claim

A. Contingent Claim Payoff Diagram

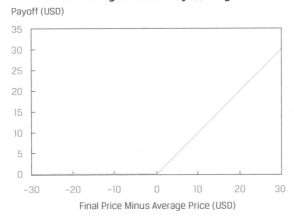

B. Histogram of Simulated Average and Final Stock Prices

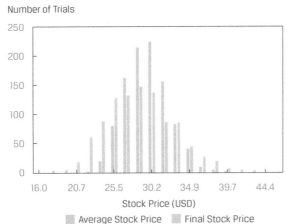

C. Histogram of Simulated Contingent Claim Payoffs

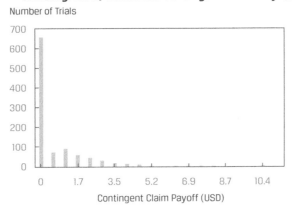

Finally, Panel C shows the histogram of the contingent claim's simulated payoffs. In 654 of 1,000 total trials, the final stock price was less than or equal to the average price, so in 65.4 percent of the trials the contingent claim paid off zero. In the remaining 34.6 percent of the trials, however, the claim paid the positive difference between the final and average prices, with the maximum payoff being USD 11.

The process flowchart in Exhibit 5 shows the steps for implementing the Monte Carlo simulation for valuing this contingent claim. Steps 1 through 3 of the process describe specifying the simulation; Steps 4 through 6 describe running the simulation.

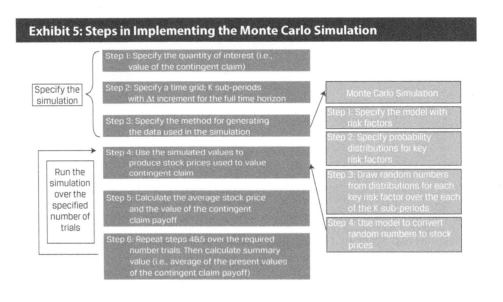

Exhibit 5: Steps in Implementing the Monte Carlo Simulation

The mechanics of implementing the Monte Carlo simulation for valuing the contingent claim using the six-step process are described as follows:

1. Specify the quantity of interest in terms of underlying variables. The quantity of interest is the contingent claim value, and the underlying variable is the stock price. Then, specify the starting value(s) of the underlying variable(s).

   We use C_{iT} to represent the value of the claim at maturity, T. The subscript i in C_{iT} indicates that C_{iT} is a value resulting from the ith **simulation trial**, each simulation trial involving a drawing of random values (an iteration of Step 4).

2. Specify a time grid. Take the horizon in terms of calendar time and split it into a number of subperiods—say, K in total. Calendar time divided by the number of subperiods, K, is the time increment, Δt. In our example, calendar time is one year and K is 12, so Δt equals one month.

3. Specify the method for generating the data used in the simulation. This step will require that distributional assumptions be made for the key risk factors that drive the underlying variables. For example, stock price is the underlying variable for the contingent claim, so we need a model for stock price movement, effectively a period return. We choose the following model for changes in stock price, where Z_k stands for the standard normal random variable:

ΔStock price $= (\mu \times$ Prior stock price $\times \Delta t) + (\sigma \times$ Prior stock price $\times Z_k)$.

The term Z_k is the key risk factor in the simulation. Through our choice of μ (mean) and σ (standard deviation), we control the distribution of the stock price variable. Although this example has one key risk factor, a given simulation may have multiple key risk factors.

Then, using a computer program or spreadsheet function, draw K random values of each risk factor. In our example, the spreadsheet function would produce a draw of K (= 12) values of the standard normal variable Z_k: Z_1, Z_2, Z_3 . . ., Z_K. We will discuss generating standard normal random numbers (or, in fact, random numbers with any kind of distribution) after describing the sequence of simulation steps.

4. Use the simulated values to produce stock prices used to value the contingent claim. This step will convert the standard normal random numbers generated in Step 3 into stock price changes (ΔStock price) by using the model of stock price dynamics from Step 3. The result is K observations on possible changes in stock price over the K subperiods (remember, K = 12). An additional calculation is needed to convert those changes into a sequence of K stock prices, with the initial stock price as the starting value over the K subperiods. This is an important step: we rely on the distributional assumptions of the Monte Carlo simulation to randomly create a very large number of stock price processes.

5. Calculate the average stock price and the value of the contingent claim. This calculation produces the average stock price during the life of the contingent claim (the sum of K stock prices divided by K). Then, compute the value of the contingent claim at maturity, C_{iT}, and then calculate its present value, C_{i0}, by discounting this terminal value using an appropriate interest rate as of today. (The subscript i in C_{i0} stands for the ith simulation trial, as it does in C_{iT}.) We have now completed one simulation trial.

6. Repeat steps 4 and 5 over the required number of trials. Iteratively, go back to Step 4 until the specified number of trials, I, is completed. Finally, produce summary values and statistics for the simulation. The quantity of interest in our example is the mean value of C_{i0} for the total number of simulation trials (I = 1,000). This mean value is the Monte Carlo estimate of the value of our contingent claim.

In Example 2, we continue with the application of Monte Carlo simulation to value another type of contingent claim.

EXAMPLE 2

Valuing a Lookback Contingent Claim Using Monte Carlo Simulation

1. A standard lookback contingent claim on a stock has a value at maturity equal to (Value of the stock at maturity – Minimum value of stock during the life of the claim prior to maturity) or USD 0, whichever is greater. If the minimum value reached prior to maturity was USD 20.11 and the value of

the stock at maturity is USD 23, for example, the contingent claim is worth USD 23 − USD 20.11 = USD 2.89.

How might you use Monte Carlo simulation in valuing a lookback contingent claim?

Solution:

We previously described how to use Monte Carlo simulation to value a certain type of contingent claim. Just as we can calculate the average value of the stock over a simulation trial to value that claim, for a lookback contingent claim, we can also calculate the minimum value of the stock over a simulation trial. Then, for a given simulation trial, we can calculate the terminal value of the claim, given the minimum value of the stock for the simulation trial. We can then discount this terminal value back to the present to get the value of the claim today ($t = 0$). The average of these $t = 0$ values over all simulation trials is the Monte Carlo simulated value of the lookback contingent claim.

Finally, note that Monte Carlo simulation is a complement to analytical methods. It provides only statistical estimates, not exact results. Analytical methods, where available, provide more insight into cause-and-effect relationships. However, as financial product innovations proceed, the applications for Monte Carlo simulation in investment management continue to grow.

QUESTION SET

1. Define Monte Carlo simulation and explain its use in investment management.

   Solution:

   A Monte Carlo simulation generates of a large number of random samples from a specified probability distribution (or distributions) to represent the role of risk in the system. Monte Carlo simulation is widely used to estimate risk and return in investment applications. In this setting, we simulate the portfolio's profit and loss performance for a specified time horizon. Repeated trials within the simulation produce a simulated frequency distribution of portfolio returns from which performance and risk measures are derived. Another important use of Monte Carlo simulation in investments is as a tool for valuing complex securities for which no analytic pricing formula is available. It is also an important modeling resource for securities with complex embedded options.

2. Compared with analytical methods, what are the strengths and weaknesses of using Monte Carlo simulation for valuing securities?

   Solution:

   - *Strengths:* Monte Carlo simulation can be used to price complex securities for which no analytic expression is available, particularly European-style options.
   - *Weaknesses:* Monte Carlo simulation provides only statistical estimates, not exact results. Analytic methods, when available, provide more insight into cause-and-effect relationships than does Monte Carlo simulation.

3. A Monte Carlo simulation can be used to:

   A. directly provide precise valuations of call options.

   B. simulate a process from historical records of returns.

   C. test the sensitivity of a model to changes in assumptions—for example, on distributions of key variables.

   Solution:

   C is correct. A characteristic feature of Monte Carlo simulation is the generation of a large number of random samples from a specified probability distribution or distributions to represent the role of risk in the system. Therefore, it is very useful for investigating the sensitivity of a model to changes in assumptions—for example, on distributions of key variables.

4. A limitation of Monte Carlo simulation is:

   A. its failure to do "what if" analysis.

   B. that it requires historical records of returns.

   C. its inability to independently specify cause-and-effect relationships.

   Solution:

   C is correct. Monte Carlo simulation is a complement to analytical methods. Monte Carlo simulation provides statistical estimates and not exact results. Analytical methods, when available, provide more insight into cause-and-effect relationships.

BOOTSTRAPPING

4

☐ | describe the use of bootstrap resampling in conducting a simulation based on observed data in investment applications

Earlier, we demonstrated how to find the standard error of the sample mean, which can be computed based on the central limit theorem. We now introduce a computational tool called **resampling**, which repeatedly draws samples from the original observed data sample for the statistical inference of population parameters. **Bootstrap**, one of the most popular resampling methods, uses computer simulation for statistical inference without using an analytical formula such as a z-statistic or t-statistic.

The idea behind bootstrap is to mimic the process of performing random sampling from a population to construct the sampling distribution. The difference lies in the fact that we have no knowledge of what the population looks like, except for a sample with size n drawn from the population. Because a random sample offers a good representation of the population, we can simulate sampling from the population by sampling from the observed sample. In other words, the bootstrap mimics the process by treating the randomly drawn sample as if it were the population.

Both the bootstrap and the Monte Carlo simulation build on repetitive sampling. Bootstrapping resamples a dataset as the true population, and infers from the sampling statistical distribution parameter values (i.e., mean, variance, skewness, and kurtosis) for the population. Monte Carlo simulation builds on generating random data with certain known statistical distribution of parameter values.

The right-hand side of Exhibit 6 illustrates the process. In bootstrap, we repeatedly draw samples from the original sample, and each resample is of the same size as the original sample. Note that each item drawn is replaced for the next draw (i.e., the identical element is put back into the group so that it can be drawn more than once). Although some items may appear several times in the resamples, other items may not appear at all.

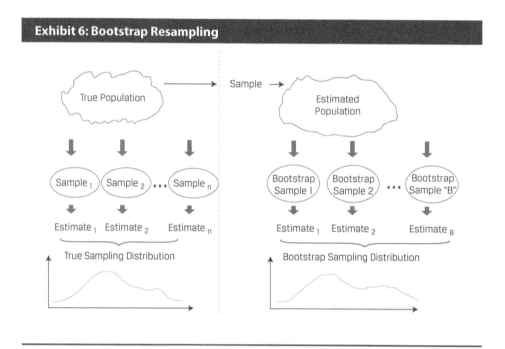

Exhibit 6: Bootstrap Resampling

The mechanics of implementing the simulation for valuing the contingent claim used in the previous lesson using the bootstrap differ only in the source of the random variable used. Instead of being drawn from a probability distribution, under bootstrapping, the random variable is drawn from the sample as described in the discussion related to Exhibit 6. Exhibit 7 shows the steps for the bootstrap process highlighting the differences between the bootstrap process and the Monte Carlo simulation from Exhibit 6.

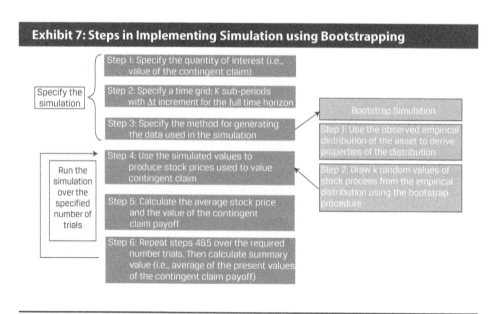

Exhibit 7: Steps in Implementing Simulation using Bootstrapping

The steps in using bootstrap to simulate the contingent claim are then (with the first two steps and the last three steps) the same for bootstrapping as they are for the Monte Carlo simulation:

1. Specify the quantity of interest in terms of underlying variables. The quantity of interest is the contingent claim value, and the underlying variable is the stock price. Then, specify the starting value(s) of the underlying variable(s).

   We use C_{iT} to represent the value of the claim at maturity, T. The subscript i in C_{iT} indicates that C_{iT} is a value resulting from the ith simulation trial, each simulation trial involving a drawing of random values (an iteration of Step 4).

2. Specify a time grid that is consistent with the periodicity of the sample observations. Take the horizon in terms of calendar time and split it into a number of subperiods—say, K in total. Calendar time divided by the number of subperiods, K, is the time increment, Δt. In the example, calendar time was one year, and K is 12, so Δt equals one month.

3. Specify the method for generating the data used in the simulation. In our example, stock price is the underlying variable for the contingent claim, so we use the observed changes in stock price as our empirical distribution. We use the observed historical behavior of stock price processes: price changes or price returns.

4. Use the simulated values to produce stock prices used to value the contingent claim. Using a computer program or spreadsheet function, draw K random values of stock process from the empirical distribution using the bootstrap procedure. Then, convert the stock price changes (ΔStock price) from Step 3 into the stock price dynamics. The calculation is necessary to convert those changes into a sequence of K stock prices, with the initial stock price as the starting value over the K subperiods. This is an important step: we rely on the distribution of the bootstrapped trials drawn from observed, historical stock price processes.

5. Calculate the average stock price and the value of the contingent claim. Another calculation produces the average stock price during the life of the contingent claim (the sum of K stock prices divided by K). Then, compute the value of the contingent claim at maturity, C_{iT}, and then calculate its present value, C_{i0}, by discounting this terminal value using an appropriate interest rate as of today. (The subscript i in C_{i0} stands for the ith simulation trial, as it does in C_{iT}.) We have now completed one simulation trial.

6. Repeat steps 4 and 5 over the required number of trials. Iteratively, go back to Step 4 until the specified number of trials, I, is completed. Finally, produce summary values and statistics for the simulation. The quantity of interest in our example is the mean value of C_{i0} for the total number of bootstrapping runs ($I = 1{,}000$). This mean value is the bootstrap estimate of the value of our contingent claim based on the observed empirical distribution.

Again, note that bootstrap simulation is a complement to analytical methods. It provides only statistical estimates based on the empirical distribution created by the bootstrapping process from observed, historical prices and price processes; these are not exact results. Analytical methods, where available, provide more insight into cause-and-effect relationships.

QUESTION SET

1. What are the main strengths and weaknesses of bootstrapping?

Solution:

Strengths:

- Bootstrapping is simple to perform.
- Bootstrapping offers a good representation of the statistical features of the population and can simulate sampling from the population by sampling from the observed sample.

Weaknesses:

- Bootstrapping provides only statistical estimates, not exact results.

PRACTICE PROBLEMS

1. The weekly closing prices of Mordice Corporation shares are as follows:

Exhibit 1: Mordice Corporation Shares	
Date	Closing Price (euros)
1 August	112
8 August	160
15 August	120

The continuously compounded return of Mordice Corporation shares for the period August 1 to August 15 is *closest* to:

   A. 6.90 percent.

   B. 7.14 percent.

   C. 8.95 percent.

2. In contrast to normal distributions, lognormal distributions:

   A. are skewed to the left.

   B. have outcomes that cannot be negative.

   C. are more suitable for describing asset returns than asset prices.

3. The lognormal distribution is a more accurate model for the distribution of stock prices than the normal distribution because stock prices are:

   A. symmetrical.

   B. unbounded.

   C. non-negative.

4. Analysts performing bootstrap:

   A. seek to create statistical inferences of population parameters from a single sample.

   B. repeatedly draw samples of the same size, with replacement, from the original population.

   C. must specify probability distributions for key risk factors that drive the underlying random variables.

SOLUTIONS

1. A is correct. The continuously compounded return of an asset over a period is equal to the natural log of the asset's price change during the period. In this case, $\ln(120/112) = 6.90\%$.

   Note that the continuously compounded return from period 0 to period T is the sum of the incremental one-period continuously compounded returns, which in this case are weekly returns. Specifically:

   Week 1 return: $\ln(160/112) = 35.67\%$.

   Week 2 return: $\ln(120/160) = -28.77\%$.

   Continuously compounded return = $35.67\% + -28.77\% = 6.90\%$.

2. B is correct. By definition, lognormal random variables cannot have negative values (bounded below by 0) and have distributions that are skewed to the right.

3. C is correct. A lognormal distributed variable has a lower bound of zero. The lognormal distribution is also right skewed, which is a useful property in describing asset prices.

4. A is correct. Bootstrapping through random sampling generates the observed variable from a random sampling with unknown population parameters. The analyst does not know the true population distribution, but through sampling can infer the population parameters from the randomly generated sample. B is incorrect because, when performing bootstrap, the analyst repeatedly draws samples from the original sample and not population, where each individual resample has the same size as the original sample and each item drawn is replaced for the next draw. C is incorrect because, when performing bootstrap, analysts simply use the observed empirical distribution of the underlying variables. In a Monte Carlo simulation, in contrast, the analyst would specify probability distributions for key risk factors that drive the underlying variables.

7

Estimation and Inference

by Wu Jian, PhD.

Jian Wu, PhD, is at State Street (USA).

LEARNING OUTCOMES

Mastery	The candidate should be able to:
☐	compare and contrast simple random, stratified random, cluster, convenience, and judgmental sampling and their implications for sampling error in an investment problem
☐	explain the central limit theorem and its importance for the distribution and standard error of the sample mean
☐	describe the use of resampling (bootstrap, jackknife) to estimate the sampling distribution of a statistic

INTRODUCTION

1

In this Learning Module, we present the various methods for obtaining information on a population (all members of a specified group) through samples (part of the population). The information on a population that we seek usually concerns the value of a **parameter**, a quantity computed from or used to describe a population of data. In Lesson 1 we introduce sampling, which we use a sample to estimate a parameter; we make use of sample statistics. A statistic is a quantity computed from or used to describe a sample of data.

Supposing that a sample is representative of the underlying population, how can the analyst assess the sampling error in estimating a population parameter? In Lesson 2, the Central Limit Theorem helps us understand the sampling distribution of the sample mean in many of the estimation problems we face. This provides guidance on how closely a sample mean can be expected to match its underlying population mean, allowing an analyst to use the sampling distribution to assess the accuracy of the sample and test hypotheses about the underlying parameter. Lesson 3 covers various resampling approaches.

LEARNING MODULE OVERVIEW

- Of the two types of sampling methods, probability sampling includes simple random sampling and stratified random sampling, and non-probability sampling includes convenience sampling and judgmental sampling. Probability sampling involves equal chance of sample selection, while non-probability sampling has a significant risk of being non-representative.

- Sampling error is the difference between the observed value of a statistic and the quantity it is intended to estimate as a result of using subsets of the population.

- Non-probability sampling methods rely not on a fixed selection process but instead on a researcher's sample selection capabilities. Its advantages include quick and low-cost data collection, and can apply expert judgment for efficient sample selection.

- The Central Limit Theorem is defined as follows: Given a population described by any probability distribution with mean μ and finite variance σ^2, the sampling distribution of the sample mean $\overline{X}$ computed from random samples of size n from this population will be approximately normal with mean μ (the population mean) and variance σ^2/n (the population variance divided by n) when the sample size n is large.

- The standard error of the sample mean is an important quantity in applying the central limit theorem in practice. It is typically estimated using the square root of the sample variance, calculated as follows:

$$s^2 = \frac{\sum_{i=1}^{n}(X_i - \overline{X})^2}{n-1}.$$

- The central limit theorem shows that when sampling from any distribution, the sample mean distribution will have these two properties when the sample size is large: (1) the distribution of the sample mean $\overline{X}$ will be approximately normal, and (2) the mean of the distribution of $\overline{X}$ will be equal to the mean of the population from which samples are drawn.

- Bootstrap, a popular resampling method which repeatedly draws samples of the same size as the original sample, uses computer simulation for statistical inference without using an analytical formula such as a z-statistic or t-statistic. It can be used as a simple but powerful method for any complicated estimators such as the standard error of a sample mean.

- Bootstrap has potential advantages in accuracy. Given these advantages, it can be applied widely in finance, such as for historical simulations in asset allocation or in gauging an investment strategy's performance against a benchmark.

- Jackknife is another resampling technique with samples selected by taking the original observed data sample and leaving out one observation at a time from the set (and not replacing it). Jackknife is often used to reduce the bias of an estimator, and other applications include finding the standard error and confidence interval of an estimator.

2

☐ | compare and contrast simple random, stratified random, cluster, convenience, and judgmental sampling and their implications for sampling error in an investment problem

We take samples for one of two reasons. In some cases, we cannot possibly examine every member of the population. In other cases, examining every member of the population would not be economically efficient. Thus, savings of time and money are two primary factors that cause an analyst to use sampling to answer a question about a population.

There are two types of sampling methods: **probability sampling** and **non-probability sampling**. Probability sampling gives every member of the population an equal chance of being selected. Hence it can create a sample that is representative of the population. In contrast, non-probability sampling depends on factors other than probability considerations, such as a sampler's judgment or the convenience to access data. Consequently, there is a significant risk that non-probability sampling might generate a non-representative sample. In general, all else being equal, probability sampling can yield more accuracy and reliability compared with non-probability sampling.

We first focus on probability sampling, particularly the widely used **simple random sampling** and **stratified random sampling**. We then turn our attention to non-probability sampling.

Simple Random Sampling

Suppose a wireless equipment analyst wants to know how much major customers will spend on average for equipment during the coming year. One strategy is to survey the population of wireless equipment customers and inquire what their purchasing plans are. Surveying all companies, however, would be very costly in terms of time and money.

Alternatively, the analyst can collect a representative sample of companies and survey them about upcoming wireless equipment expenditures. In this case, the analyst will compute the sample mean expenditure, $\overline{X}$, a statistic. This strategy has a substantial advantage over polling the whole population because it can be accomplished more quickly and at lower cost.

Sampling, however, introduces error. The error arises because not all of the companies in the population are surveyed. The analyst who decides to sample is trading time and money for sampling error.

When an analyst chooses to sample, they must formulate a sampling plan. A **sampling plan** is the set of rules used to select a sample. The basic type of sample from which we can draw statistically sound conclusions about a population is the simple random sample.

A **simple random sample** is a subset of a larger population created in such a way that each element of the population has an equal probability of being selected to the subset.

The procedure of drawing a sample to satisfy the definition of a simple random sample is called **simple random sampling**. Simple random sampling is particularly useful when data in the population is homogeneous—that is, the characteristics of the data or observations (e.g., size or region) are broadly similar. If this condition is not satisfied, other types of sampling may be more appropriate.

Systematic sampling can be used when we cannot code (or even identify) all the members of a population. With systematic sampling, we select every kth member until we have a sample of the desired size. The sample that results from this procedure should be approximately random.

Suppose the wireless equipment analyst polls a random sample of wireless equipment customers to determine the average equipment expenditure. The derived sample mean will provide the analyst with an estimate of the population mean expenditure. The mean obtained from the sample this way will differ from the population mean that we are trying to estimate. It is subject to error. An important part of this error is known as sampling error, which comes from sampling variation and occurs because we have data on only a subset of the population.

Sampling error is the difference between the observed value of a statistic and the quantity it is intended to estimate as a result of using subsets of the population.

A random sample reflects the properties of the population in an unbiased way, and sample statistics, such as the sample mean, computed on the basis of a random sample are valid estimates of the underlying population parameters. Thus a sample statistic is a random variable. In other words, not only do the original data from the population have a distribution but so does the sample statistic. This distribution is the statistic's sampling distribution.

Sampling distribution of a statistic is the distribution of all the distinct possible values that the statistic can assume when computed from samples of the same size randomly drawn from the same population.

In the case of the sample mean, for example, we refer to the "sampling distribution of the sample mean" or the distribution of the sample mean. We will have more to say about sampling distributions later in this text. Next, we look at another sampling method that is useful in investment analysis.

Stratified Random Sampling

The simple random sampling method just discussed may not be the best approach in all situations. One frequently used alternative is stratified random sampling.

In **stratified random sampling**, the population is divided into subpopulations (strata) based on one or more classification criteria. Simple random samples are then drawn from each stratum in sizes proportional to the relative size of each stratum in the population. These samples are then pooled to form a stratified random sample.

In contrast to simple random sampling, stratified random sampling guarantees that population subdivisions of interest are represented in the sample. Another advantage is that estimates of parameters produced from stratified sampling have greater precision—that is, smaller variance or dispersion—than estimates obtained from simple random sampling.

Bond indexing is one area in which stratified sampling is frequently applied. **Indexing** is an investment strategy in which an investor constructs a portfolio to mirror the performance of a specified index. In pure bond indexing, also called the full-replication approach, the investor attempts to fully replicate an index by owning all the bonds in the index in proportion to their market value weights. Many bond indexes consist of thousands of issues, however, so pure bond indexing is difficult to implement. In addition, transaction costs would be high because many bonds do not have liquid markets.

Although a simple random sample could be a solution to the cost problem, the sample would probably not match the index's major risk factors, such as interest rate sensitivity. Because the major risk factors of fixed-income portfolios are well known and quantifiable, stratified sampling offers a more effective approach. In this approach, we divide the population of index bonds into groups of similar duration (interest rate sensitivity), cash flow distribution, sector, credit quality, and call exposure. We refer to each group as a stratum or cell (a term frequently used in this context). Then, we choose a sample from each stratum proportional to the relative market weighting of the stratum in the index to be replicated.

Bond Indexes and Stratified Sampling

Suppose you are the manager of a portfolio of bonds indexed to the Bloomberg Barclays US Government/Credit Index, meaning that the portfolio returns should be similar to those of the index. You are exploring several approaches to indexing, including a stratified sampling approach. You first distinguish among agency bonds, US Treasury bonds, and investment-grade corporate bonds. For each of these three groups, you define 10 maturity intervals—1 to 2 years, 2 to 3 years, 3 to 4 years, 4 to 6 years, 6 to 8 years, 8 to 10 years, 10 to 12 years, 12 to 15 years, 15 to 20 years, and 20 to 30 years—and also separate the bonds with coupons (annual interest rates) of 6 percent or less from the bonds with coupons of more than 6 percent.

1. How many cells or strata does this sampling plan entail?

   Solution:

   We have 3 issuer classifications, 10 maturity classifications, and 2 coupon classifications. So, in total, this plan entails $3(10)(2) = 60$ different strata or cells.

2. If you use this sampling plan, what is the minimum number of issues the indexed portfolio can have?

   Solution:

   One cannot have less than 1 issue for each cell, so the portfolio must include at least 60 issues.

3. Suppose that in selecting among the securities that qualify for selection within each cell, you apply a criterion concerning the liquidity of the security's market. Is the sample obtained random? Explain your answer.

   Solution

   Applying any additional criteria to the selection of securities for the cells, not every security that might be included has an equal probability of being selected. There is no proportionality in the selection, and as a result, the sampling is not random. In practice, indexing using stratified sampling usually does not strictly involve random sampling because the selection of bond issues within cells is subject to various additional criteria. Because the purpose of sampling in this application is not to make an inference about a population parameter but rather to index a portfolio, lack of randomness is not in itself a problem in this application of stratified sampling.

Cluster Sampling

Another sampling method, **cluster sampling**, also requires the division or classification of the population into subpopulation groups, called clusters. In this method, the population is divided into clusters, each of which is essentially a mini-representation of the entire populations. Then certain clusters are chosen as a whole using simple random sampling. If all the members in each sampled cluster are sampled, this sample plan is referred to as one-stage cluster sampling. If a subsample is randomly selected from each selected cluster, then the plan is referred as two-stage cluster sampling. Exhibit 1 (bottom-right panel) shows how cluster sampling works and how it compares with the other probability sampling methods.

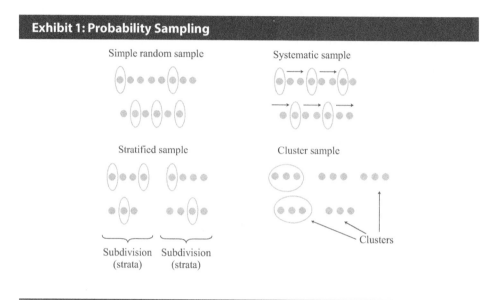

Exhibit 1: Probability Sampling

A major difference between cluster and stratified random samples is that in cluster sampling, a whole cluster is regarded as a sampling unit and only sampled clusters are included. In stratified random sampling, however, all the strata are included and only specific elements within each stratum are then selected as sampling units.

Cluster sampling is commonly used for broad market surveys, and the most popular version identifies clusters based on geographic parameters. For example, a research institute is looking to survey if individual investors in the United States are bullish, bearish, or neutral on the stock market. It would be impossible to carry out the research by surveying all the individual investors in the country. The two-stage cluster sampling is a good solution in this case. In the first stage, a researcher can group the population by states and all the individual investors of each state represent a cluster. A handful of the clusters are then randomly selected. At the second stage, a simple random sample of individual investors is selected from each sampled cluster to conduct the survey.

Compared with other probability sampling methods, given equal sample size, cluster sampling usually yields lower accuracy because a sample from a cluster might be less representative of the entire population. Its major advantage, however, is offering the most time-efficient and cost-efficient probability sampling plan for analyzing a vast population.

Non-Probability Sampling

Non-probability sampling methods rely not on a fixed selection process but instead on a researcher's sample selection capabilities. We introduce two major types of non-probability sampling methods here.

- **Convenience Sampling:** In this method, an element is selected from the population based on whether or not it is accessible to a researcher or on how easy it is for a researcher to access the element. The samples are not necessarily representative of the entire population, and hence the level of sampling accuracy could be limited. The advantage of **convenience sampling** is that data can be collected quickly at a low cost. In situations such as the preliminary stage of research or in circumstances subject to cost constraints, convenience sampling is often used as a time-efficient and cost-effective sampling plan for a small-scale pilot study before testing a large-scale and more representative sample.

- **Judgmental Sampling:** This sampling process involves selectively handpicking elements from the population based on a researcher's knowledge and professional judgment. Sample selection under **judgmental sampling** can be affected by the bias of the researcher and might lead to skewed results that do not represent the whole population. In circumstances where there is a time constraint, however, or when the specialty of researchers is critical to select a more representative sample than by using other probability or non-probability sampling methods, judgmental sampling allows researchers to go directly to the target population of interest. For example, when auditing financial statements, seasoned auditors can apply their sound judgment to select accounts or transactions that can provide sufficient audit coverage. Example 2 illustrates an application of these sampling methods.

EXAMPLE 2

Demonstrating the Power of Sampling

To demonstrate the power of sampling, we conduct two sampling experiments on a large dataset. The full dataset is the "population," representing daily returns of the fictitious Euro-Asia-Africa (EAA) Equity Index. This dataset spans a five-year period and consists of 1,258 observations of daily returns with a minimum value of −4.1 percent and a maximum value of 5.0 percent.

First, we calculate the mean daily return of the EAA Equity Index (using the population).

By taking the average of all the data points, the mean of the entire daily return series is computed as 0.035 percent.

First Experiment: Random Sampling

The sample size m is set to 5, 10, 20, 50, 100, 200, 500, and 1,000. At each sample size, we run random sampling multiple times ($N = 100$) to collect 100 samples to compute mean absolute error. The aim is to compute and plot the mean error versus the sample size.

For a given sample size m, we use a random sampling procedure to compute mean absolute error in order to measure sampling error.

By applying this procedure, we compute mean absolute errors for eight different sample sizes: m = 5, 10, 20, 50, 100, 200, 500, and 1000.

Second Experiment: Stratified Random Sampling

We now conduct stratified random sampling by dividing daily returns into groups by year. The sample size m is again set to 5, 10, 20, 50, 100, 200, 500, and 1,000. At each sample size, we run random sampling multiple times ($N = 100$) to collect 100 samples to compute mean absolute error.

We follow the same steps as before, except for the first step. Rather than running a simple random sampling, we conduct stratified random sampling—that is, randomly selecting subsamples of equal number from daily return groups by year to generate a full sample. For example, for a sample of 50, 10 data points are randomly selected from daily returns of each year from 2014 to 2018, respectively. Exhibit 2 summarizes the results.

Exhibit 2: Mean Absolute Errors under Different Sampling Procedures

Mean Absolute Error of Random Sampling

Sample size	5	10	20	50	100	200	500	1,000
Mean absolute error	0.297%	0.218%	0.163%	0.091%	0.063%	0.039%	0.019%	0.009%

Mean Absolute Error of Stratified Random Sampling

Sample size	5	10	20	50	100	200	500	1,000
Mean absolute error	0.294%	0.205%	0.152%	0.083%	0.071%	0.051%	0.025%	0.008%

Under both random sampling and stratified sampling mean absolute errors quickly shrink as sample size increases. Stratified sampling produces smaller mean absolute errors as it more accurately reflects the character of the population, but this difference shrinks—and in this case actually expands—as the sample size increases.

Exhibit 2 also indicates that a minimum sample size is needed to limit sample error and achieve a certain level of accuracy. After a certain size, however, there is little incremental benefit from adding more observations (200 to 400 in this case).

Sampling from Different Distributions

In practice, in addition to selecting appropriate sampling methods, we also need to be careful when sampling from a population that is not under one single distribution. Example 3 illustrates the problems that can arise when sampling from more than one distribution.

EXAMPLE 3

Calculating Sharpe Ratios: One or Two Years of Quarterly Data

Analysts often use the Sharpe ratio to evaluate the performance of a managed portfolio. The Sharpe ratio is the average return in excess of the risk-free rate divided by the standard deviation of returns. This ratio measures the return of a fund or a security above the risk-free rate (the excess return) earned per unit of standard deviation of return.

To compute the Sharpe ratio, suppose that an analyst collects eight quarterly excess returns (i.e., total return in excess of the risk-free rate). During the first year, the investment manager of the portfolio followed a low-risk strategy, and during the second year, the manager followed a high-risk strategy. For each of these years, the analyst also tracks the quarterly excess returns of some benchmark against which the manager will be evaluated. For each of the two years, the Sharpe ratio for the benchmark is 0.21. Exhibit 3 gives the calculation of the Sharpe ratio of the portfolio.

Exhibit 3: Calculation of Sharpe Ratios: Low-Risk and High-Risk Strategies

Quarter/Measure	Year 1 Excess Returns	Year 2 Excess Returns
Quarter 1	–3%	–12%
Quarter 2	5	20
Quarter 3	–3	–12
Quarter 4	5	20
Quarterly average	1%	4%
Quarterly standard deviation	4.62%	18.48%

Sharpe ratio = 0.22 = 1/4.62 = 4/18.48

For the first year, during which the manager followed a low-risk strategy, the average quarterly return in excess of the risk-free rate was 1 percent with a standard deviation of 4.62 percent. The Sharpe ratio is thus 1/4.62 = 0.22. The second year's results mirror the first year except for the higher average return and volatility. The Sharpe ratio for the second year is 4/18.48 = 0.22. The Sharpe ratio for the benchmark is 0.21 during the first and second years. Because larger Sharpe ratios are better than smaller ones (providing more return per unit of risk), the manager appears to have outperformed the benchmark.

Now, suppose the analyst believes a larger sample to be superior to a small one. She thus decides to pool the two years together and calculate a Sharpe ratio based on eight quarterly observations. The average quarterly excess return for the two years is the average of each year's average excess return. For the two-year period, the average excess return is (1 + 4)/2 = 2.5% per quarter. The standard deviation for all eight quarters measured from the sample mean of 2.5 percent is 12.57 percent. The portfolio's Sharpe ratio for the two-year period is now 2.5/12.57 = 0.199; the Sharpe ratio for the benchmark remains 0.21. Thus, when returns for the two-year period are pooled, the manager appears to have provided less return per unit of risk than the benchmark and less when compared with the separate yearly results.

The problem with using eight quarters of return data is that the analyst has violated the assumption that the sampled returns come from the same population. As a result of the change in the manager's investment strategy, returns in Year 2 followed a different distribution than returns in Year 1. Clearly, during Year 1, returns were generated by an underlying population with lower mean and variance than the population of the second year. Combining the results for the first and second years yielded a sample that was representative of no population. Because the larger sample did not satisfy model assumptions, any conclusions the analyst reached based on the larger sample are incorrect. For this example, she was better off using a smaller sample than a larger sample because the smaller sample represented a more homogeneous distribution of returns.

QUESTION SET

An analyst is studying research and development (R&D) spending by pharmaceutical companies around the world. She considers three sampling methods for understanding a company's level of R&D. Method 1 is to simply use all the data available to her from an internal database that she and her colleagues built while researching several dozen representative stocks in the sector. Method 2 involves relying on a commercial database provided by a data vendor. She would select every fifth pharmaceutical company on the list to pull the data. Method 3 is to first divide pharmaceutical companies in the commercial database into three groups according to the region where a company is headquartered (e.g., Asia, Europe, or North America) and then randomly select a subsample of companies from each group, with the sample size proportional to the size of its associated group in order to form a complete sample.

1. Method 1 is an example of:

   A. simple random sampling.

   B. stratified random sampling.

   C. convenience sampling.

   Solution:

   C is correct. The analyst selects the data from the internal database because they are easy and convenient to access.

2. Method 2 is an example of:

   A. judgmental sampling.

   B. systematic sampling.

   C. cluster sampling.

   Solution:

   B is correct. The sample elements are selected with a fixed interval ($k = 5$) from the large population provided by data vendor.

3. Method 3 is an example of:

   A. simple random sampling.

   B. stratified random sampling.

   C. cluster sampling.

   Solution:

   B is correct. The population of pharmaceutical companies is divided into three strata by region to perform random sampling individually.

4. Perkiomen Kinzua, a seasoned auditor, is auditing last year's transactions for Conemaugh Corporation. Unfortunately, Conemaugh had a very large number of transactions, and Kinzua is under a time constraint to finish the audit. He decides to audit only the small subset of the transaction population that is of interest and to use sampling to create that subset.

The most appropriate sampling method for Kinzua to use is:

A. judgmental sampling.

B. systematic sampling.

C. convenience sampling.

Solution:

A is correct. With judgmental sampling, Kinzua will use his knowledge and professional judgment as a seasoned auditor to select transactions of interest from the population. This approach will allow Kinzua to create a sample that is representative of the population and that will provide sufficient audit coverage. Judgmental sampling is useful in cases that have a time constraint or in which the specialty of researchers is critical to select a more representative sample than by using other probability or non-probability sampling methods. Judgment sampling, however, entails the risk that Kinzua is biased in his selections, leading to skewed results that are not representative of the whole population.

CENTRAL LIMIT THEOREM AND INFERENCE

3

☐ | explain the central limit theorem and its importance for the distribution and standard error of the sample mean

Earlier we presented a wireless equipment analyst who decided to sample in order to estimate mean planned capital expenditures by the customers of wireless equipment vendors. Supposing that the sample is representative of the underlying population, how can the analyst assess the sampling error in estimating the population mean?

The sample mean is itself a random variable with a probability distribution called the statistic's sampling distribution. To estimate how closely the sample mean can be expected to match the underlying population mean, the analyst needs to understand the sampling distribution of the mean. The central limit theorem helps us understand the sampling distribution of the mean in many of the estimation problems we face.

The Central Limit Theorem

To explain the central limit theorem, we will revisit the daily returns of the fictitious Euro-Asia-Africa Equity Index shown earlier. The dataset (the population) consists of daily returns of the index over a five-year period. The 1,258 return observations have a population mean of 0.035 percent.

We conduct four different sets of random sampling from the population. We first draw a random sample of 10 daily returns and obtain a sample mean. We repeat this exercise 99 more times, drawing a total of 100 samples of 10 daily returns. We plot the sample mean results in a histogram, as shown in the top left panel of Exhibit 4. We then repeat the process with a larger sample size of 50 daily returns. We draw 100 samples of 50 daily returns and plot the results (the mean returns) in the histogram shown in the top-right panel of Exhibit 4. We then repeat the process for sample sizes of 100 and 300 daily returns, respectively, again drawing 100 samples in each case. These results appear in the bottom-left and bottom-right panels of Exhibit 4. Looking at all four panels together, we observe that the larger the sample size, the more closely the histogram follows the shape of normal distribution.

Exhibit 4: Sampling Distribution with Increasing Sample Size

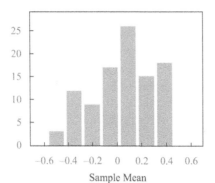

A. Sample Size $n = 10$

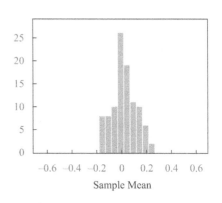

B. Sample Size $n = 50$

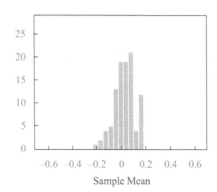

C. Sample Size $n = 100$

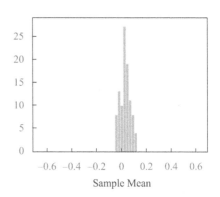

D. Sample Size $n = 300$

The results of this exercise show that as we increase the size of a random sample, the distribution of the sample means tends towards a normal distribution and the sampling error of the sample mean is reduced. This is a significant outcome and brings us to the central limit theorem concept, one of the most practically useful theorems in probability theory. It has important implications for how we construct confidence intervals and test hypotheses. Formally, the **central limit theorem** is stated as follows:

- **Central Limit Theorem.** Given a population described by any probability distribution having mean μ and finite variance σ^2, the sampling distribution of the sample mean $\overline{X}$ computed from random samples of size n from this population will be approximately normal with mean μ (the population mean) and variance σ^2/n (the population variance divided by n) when the sample size n is large.

Consider what the expression σ^2/n signifies. Variance (σ^2) stays the same, but as n increases, the size of the fraction decreases. This suggests that it becomes progressively less common to obtain a sample mean that is far from the true population mean with progressively larger sample sizes.

The central limit theorem allows us to make quite precise probability statements about the population mean by using the sample mean, *regardless of the population distribution* (so long as it has finite variance), because the sample mean follows an approximate normal distribution for large-size samples. The obvious question is, "When is a sample's size large enough that we can assume the sample mean is normally distributed?" In general, when sample size n is greater than or equal to 30, we can assume that the sample mean is approximately normally distributed. When the underlying population is very non-normal, a sample size well in excess of 30 may be required for the normal distribution to be a good description of the sampling distribution of the mean.

Standard Error of the Sample Mean

The central limit theorem states that the variance of the distribution of the sample mean is σ^2/n. The positive square root of variance is standard deviation. The standard deviation of a sample statistic is known as the standard error of the statistic. The standard error of the sample mean is an important quantity in applying the central limit theorem in practice.

- **Definition of the Standard Error of the Sample Mean.** For sample mean $\overline{X}$ calculated from a sample generated by a population with standard deviation σ, the standard error of the sample mean is given by one of two expressions:

$$\sigma_{\overline{X}} = \frac{\sigma}{\sqrt{n}}, \tag{1}$$

  when we know σ, the population standard deviation, or by

$$s_{\overline{X}} = \frac{s}{\sqrt{n}}, \tag{2}$$

  when we do not know the population standard deviation and need to use the sample standard deviation, s, to estimate it.

In practice, we almost always need to use Equation 2. The estimate of s is given by the square root of the sample variance, s^2, calculated as follows:

$$s^2 = \frac{\sum_{i=1}^{n}(X_i - \overline{X})^2}{n-1}. \tag{3}$$

Note that although the standard error is the standard deviation of the sampling distribution of the parameter, "standard deviation" in general and "standard error" are two distinct concepts, and the terms are not interchangeable.

Simply put, standard deviation measures the dispersion of the data from the mean, whereas standard error measures how much inaccuracy of a population parameter estimate comes from sampling. The contrast between standard deviation and standard error reflects the distinction between data description and inference. If we want to draw conclusions about how spread out the data are, standard deviation is the statistic to use. If we want to find out how precise the estimate of a population parameter from sampled data is relative to its true value, standard error is the statistic to use.

In another learning module we will see how the sample mean and its standard error are used in hypothesis testing to make probability statements about the population mean. To summarize, the central limit theorem tells us that when we sample from any distribution, the distribution of the sample mean will have the following properties as long as our sample size is large:

- The distribution of the sample mean $\overline{X}$ will be approximately normal.
- The mean of the distribution of $\overline{X}$ will be equal to the mean of the population from which the samples are drawn.
- The variance of the distribution of $\overline{X}$ will be equal to the variance of the population divided by the sample size.

QUESTION SET

A research analyst makes two statements about repeated random sampling:

Statement 1   When repeatedly drawing large samples from datasets, the sample means are approximately normally distributed.

Statement 2   The underlying population from which samples are drawn must be normally distributed in order for the sample mean to be normally distributed.

---

1. Which of the following best describes the validity of the analyst's statements?

   A. Statement 1 is false; Statement 2 is true.

   B. Both statements are true.

   C. Statement 1 is true; Statement 2 is false.

   Solution:

   C is correct. According to the central limit theorem, Statement 1 is true. Statement 2 is false because the underlying population does not need to be normally distributed in order for the sample mean to be normally distributed.

---

2. Although he knows security returns are not independent, a colleague makes the claim that because of the central limit theorem, if we diversify across a large number of investments, the portfolio standard deviation will eventually approach zero as *n* becomes large. Is he correct?

   Solution:

   No. First the conclusion on the limit of zero is wrong; second, the support cited for drawing the conclusion (i.e., the central limit theorem) is not relevant in this context.

---

3. Why is the central limit theorem important?

   Solution:

   In many instances, the distribution that describes the underlying population is not normal or the distribution is not known. The central limit theorem states that if the sample size is large, regardless of the shape of the underlying population, the distribution of the sample mean is approximately normal. Therefore, even in these instances, we can still construct confidence intervals (and conduct tests of inference) as long as the sample size is large (generally $n \geq 30$).

4. What is wrong with the following statement of the central limit theorem?

Central Limit Theorem. "If the random variables $X_1, X_2, X_3, ..., X_n$ are a random sample of size n from any distribution with finite mean μ and variance σ^2, then the distribution of $\overline{X}$ will be approximately normal, with a standard deviation of $\sigma/\sqrt{n}$."

Solution:

The statement makes the following mistakes:
• Given the conditions in the statement, the distribution of $\overline{X}$ will be approximately normal only for large sample sizes.
• The statement omits the important element of the central limit theorem that the distribution of $\overline{X}$ will have mean μ.

5. Peter Biggs wants to know how growth managers performed last year. Biggs assumes that the population cross-sectional standard deviation of growth manager returns is 6 percent and that the returns are independent across managers.

   A. How large a random sample does Biggs need if he wants the standard deviation of the sample means to be 1 percent?

   B. How large a random sample does Biggs need if he wants the standard deviation of the sample means to be 0.25 percent?

Solution:

A. The standard deviation or standard error of the sample mean is $\sigma_{\overline{X}} = \sigma/\sqrt{n}$. Substituting in the values for $\sigma_{\overline{X}}$ and σ, we have $1\% = 6\%/\sqrt{n}$, or $\sqrt{n} = 6$. Squaring this value, we get a random sample of $n = 36$.

B. As in Part A, the standard deviation of sample mean is $\sigma_{\overline{X}} = \sigma/\sqrt{n}$. Substituting in the values for $\sigma_{\overline{X}}$ and σ, we have $0.25\% = 6\%/\sqrt{n}$, or $\sqrt{n} = 24$. Squaring this value, we get a random sample of $n = 576$, which is substantially larger than for Part A of this question.

BOOTSTRAPPING AND EMPIRICAL SAMPLING DISTRIBUTIONS

4

☐ | describe the use of resampling (bootstrap, jackknife) to estimate the sampling distribution of a statistic

We demonstrated how to find the standard error of the sample mean, based on the central limit theorem. We return to the computational tool called **resampling**, which repeatedly draws samples from the original observed data sample for the statistical inference of population parameters. **Bootstrap**, one of the most popular resampling methods, uses computer simulation for statistical inference without using an analytical formula such as a z-statistic or t-statistic.

In bootstrap, we repeatedly draw samples from the original sample, and each resample is of the same size as the original sample. Note that each item drawn is replaced for the next draw (i.e., the identical element is put back into the group so that it can be drawn more than once). Assuming we are looking to find the standard error of sample mean, we take many resamples and then compute the mean of each resample. Note that although some items may appear several times in the resamples, other items may not appear at all.

Exhibit 5: Bootstrap Resampling

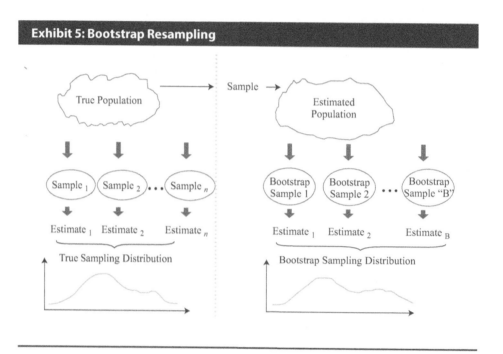

Subsequently, we construct a sampling distribution with these resamples. The bootstrap sampling distribution (right-hand side of Exhibit 5) will approximate the true sampling distribution. We estimate the standard error of the sample mean using Equation 4. Note that to distinguish the foregoing resampling process from other types of resampling, it is often called model-free resampling or non-parametric resampling.

$$s_{\overline{X}} = \sqrt{\frac{1}{B-1} \sum_{b=1}^{B} \left(\hat{\theta}_b - \overline{\theta} \right)^2}, \tag{4}$$

where:

$S_{\overline{X}}$ = the estimate of the standard error of the sample mean,

B = the number of resamples drawn from the original sample,

$\hat{\theta}_b$ = the mean of a resample, and

$\overline{\theta}$ = the mean across all the resample means.

Bootstrap is one of the most powerful and widely used tools for statistical inference. As we have explained, it can be used to estimate the standard error of a sample mean. Similarly, bootstrap can be used to find the standard error or construct confidence intervals for the statistic of other population parameters, such as the median, which does not apply to the previously discussed methodologies. Compared with conventional statistical methods, bootstrap does not rely on an analytical formula to estimate the distribution of the estimators. It is a simple but powerful method for any complicated estimators and particularly useful when no analytical formula is available.

In addition, bootstrap has potential advantages in accuracy. Given these advantages, bootstrap can be applied widely in finance, such as for historical simulations in asset allocation or in gauging an investment strategy's performance against a benchmark.

EXAMPLE 4

Bootstrap Resampling Illustration

Exhibit 6 displays a set of 12 monthly returns of a rarely traded stock, shown in Column A. Our aim is to calculate the standard error of the sample mean. Using the bootstrap resampling method, a series of bootstrap samples, labelled as "resamples" (with replacement) are drawn from the sample of 12 returns. Notice how some of the returns from data sample in Column A feature more than once in some of the resamples (e.g., 0.055 features twice in Resample 1).

Exhibit 6: Rarely Traded Stock, 12 Monthly Returns

Column A	Resample 1	Resample 2	Resample 3		Resample 1,000
−0.096	0.055	−0.096	−0.033	...	−0.072
−0.132	−0.033	0.055	−0.132	...	0.255
−0.191	0.255	0.055	−0.157	...	0.055
−0.096	−0.033	−0.157	0.255	...	0.296
0.055	0.255	−0.096	−0.132	...	0.055
−0.053	−0.157	−0.053	−0.191	...	−0.096
−0.033	−0.053	−0.096	0.055	...	0.296
0.296	−0.191	−0.132	0.255	...	−0.132
0.055	−0.132	−0.132	0.296	...	0.055
−0.072	−0.096	0.055	−0.096	...	−0.096
0.255	0.055	−0.072	0.055	...	−0.191
−0.157	−0.157	−0.053	−0.157	...	0.055
Sample mean	−0.019	−0.060	0.001	...	0.040

Drawing 1,000 such samples, we obtain 1,000 sample means. The mean across all resample means is −0.01367. The sum of squares of the differences between each sample mean and the mean across all resample means ($\sum_{b=1}^{B}(\hat{\theta}_b - \bar{\theta})^2$) is 1.94143. Using Equation 4, we calculate an estimate of the standard error of the sample mean:

$$s_{\bar{X}} = \sqrt{\frac{1}{B-1}\sum_{b=1}^{B}(\hat{\theta}_b - \bar{\theta})^2} = \sqrt{\frac{1}{999} \times 1.94143} = 0.04408.$$

Jackknife is another resampling technique for statistical inference of population parameters. Unlike bootstrap, which repeatedly draws samples with replacement, jackknife samples are selected by taking the original observed data sample and leaving out one observation at a time from the set (and not replacing it). Jackknife method is often used to reduce the bias of an estimator, and other applications include finding the standard error and confidence interval of an estimator. According to its computation procedure, we can conclude that jackknife produces similar results for every run, whereas bootstrap usually gives different results because bootstrap resamples are randomly drawn. For a sample of size n, jackknife usually requires n repetitions, whereas with bootstrap, we are left to determine how many repetitions are appropriate.

QUESTION SET

1. An analyst in a real estate investment company is researching the housing market of the Greater Boston area. From a sample of collected house sale price data in the past year, she estimates the median house price of the area. To find the standard error of the estimated median, she is considering two options:

   Option 1: The standard error of the sample median can be given by $\frac{s}{\sqrt{n}}$, where s denotes the sample standard deviation and n denotes the sample size.

   Option 2: Apply the bootstrap method to construct the sampling distribution of the sample median, and then compute the standard error using Equation 7.

   Which of the following statements is accurate?

   A. Option 1 is suitable to find the standard error of the sample median.

   B. Option 2 is suitable to find the standard error of the sample median.

   C. Both options are suitable to find the standard error of the sample median.

   Solution:

   B is correct. Option 1 is valid for estimating the standard error of the sample mean but not for that of the sample median, which is not based on the given formula. Thus, both A and C are incorrect. The bootstrap method is a simple way to find the standard error of an estimator even if no analytical formula is available or it is too complicated.

   Having covered many of the fundamental concepts of sampling and estimation, we now focus on sampling issues of special concern to analysts. The quality of inferences depends on the quality of the data as well as on the quality of the sampling plan used. Financial data pose special problems, and sampling plans frequently reflect one or more biases. The next section examines these issues.

2. Otema Chi has a spreadsheet with 108 monthly returns for shares in Marunou Corporation. He writes a software program that uses bootstrap resampling to create 200 resamples of this Marunou data by sampling with replacement. Each resample has 108 data points. Chi's program calculates the mean of each of the 200 resamples, and then it calculates that the mean of these 200 resample means is 0.0261. The program subtracts 0.0261 from each of the 200 resample means, squares each of these 200 differences, and adds the squared differences together. The result is 0.835. The program then calculates an estimate of the standard error of the sample mean.

   The estimated standard error of the sample mean is closest to:

   A. 0.0115

B. 0.0648

C. 0.0883

Solution:

B is correct. The estimate of the standard error of the sample mean with bootstrap resampling is calculated as follows:

$$s_{\overline{X}} = \sqrt{\frac{1}{B-1}\sum_{b=1}^{B}\left(\hat{\theta}_b - \overline{\theta}\right)^2} = \sqrt{\frac{1}{200-1}\sum_{b=1}^{200}\left(\hat{\theta}_b - 0.0261\right)^2} = \sqrt{0.004196}.$$

$$s_{\overline{X}} = 0.0648$$

PRACTICE PROBLEMS

1. Which one of the following statements is true about non-probability sampling?

    A. There is significant risk that the sample is not representative of the population.

    B. Every member of the population has an equal chance of being selected for the sample.

    C. Using judgment guarantees that population subdivisions of interest are represented in the sample.

2. The *best* approach for creating a stratified random sample of a population involves:

    A. drawing an equal number of simple random samples from each subpopulation.

    B. selecting every kth member of the population until the desired sample size is reached.

    C. drawing simple random samples from each subpopulation in sizes proportional to the relative size of each subpopulation.

3. A population has a non-normal distribution with mean μ and variance σ^2. The sampling distribution of the sample mean computed from samples of large size from that population will have:

    A. the same distribution as the population distribution.

    B. its mean approximately equal to the population mean.

    C. its variance approximately equal to the population variance.

4. A sample mean is computed from a population with a variance of 2.45. The sample size is 40. The standard error of the sample mean is *closest* to:

    A. 0.039.

    B. 0.247.

    C. 0.387.

5. Compared with bootstrap resampling, jackknife resampling:

    A. is done with replacement.

    B. usually requires that the number of repetitions is equal to the sample size.

    C. produces dissimilar results for every run because resamples are randomly drawn.

SOLUTIONS

1. A is correct. Because non-probability sampling is dependent on factors other than probability considerations, such as a sampler's judgment or the convenience to access data, there is a significant risk that non-probability sampling might generate a non-representative sample.

2. C is correct. Stratified random sampling involves dividing a population into subpopulations based on one or more classification criteria. Then, simple random samples are drawn from each subpopulation in sizes proportional to the relative size of each subpopulation. These samples are then pooled to form a stratified random sample.

3. B is correct. Given a population described by any probability distribution (normal or non-normal) with finite variance, the central limit theorem states that the sampling distribution of the sample mean will be approximately normal, with the mean approximately equal to the population mean, when the sample size is large.

4. B is correct. Taking the square root of the known population variance to determine the population standard deviation (σ) results in

$$\sigma = \sqrt{2.45} = 1.565.$$

The formula for the standard error of the sample mean (σ_X), based on a known sample size (n), is

$$\sigma_X = \frac{\sigma}{\sqrt{n}}.$$

Therefore,

$$\sigma_X = \frac{1.565}{\sqrt{40}} = 0.247.$$

5. B is correct. For a sample of size n, jackknife resampling usually requires n repetitions. In contrast, with bootstrap resampling, we are left to determine how many repetitions are appropriate.

8

Hypothesis Testing

by Pamela Peterson Drake, PhD, CFA.

Pamela Peterson Drake, PhD, CFA, is at James Madison University (USA).

LEARNING OUTCOMES

Mastery	The candidate should be able to:
☐	explain hypothesis testing and its components, including statistical significance, Type I and Type II errors, and the power of a test.
☐	construct hypothesis tests and determine their statistical significance, the associated Type I and Type II errors, and power of the test given a significance level
☐	compare and contrast parametric and nonparametric tests, and describe situations where each is the more appropriate type of test

INTRODUCTION

1

Hypothesis testing is covered extensively in the pre-read. This learning module builds on that coverage and assumes a functional understanding of the topic gained there or elsewhere.

Lesson 1 summaries the hypothesis testing process by exemplifying its use in finance and investment management. Lesson 2 brings forward the impact of errors in the hypothesis testing process. Lesson 3 introduces nonparametric tests and their applications in investment management.

LEARNING MODULE OVERVIEW

- The steps in testing a hypothesis are as follows:
  1. State the hypotheses.
  2. Identify the appropriate test statistic and its probability distribution.
  3. Specify the significance level.
  4. State the decision rule.
  5. Collect the data and calculate the test statistic.
  6. Make a decision.

- A test statistic is a quantity, calculated using a sample, whose value is the basis for deciding whether to reject or not reject the null hypothesis. We compare the computed value of the test statistic to a critical value for the same test statistic to determine whether to reject or not reject the null hypothesis.

- In reaching a statistical decision, two possible errors can be made: reject a true null hypothesis (a Type I error, or false positive), or fail to reject a false null hypothesis (a Type II error, or false negative).

- The level of significance of a test is the probability of a Type I error when conducting a hypothesis test. The standard approach to hypothesis testing involves specifying a level of significance (i.e., the probability of a Type I error). The complement of the level of significance is the confidence level.

- For hypothesis tests concerning the population mean of a normally distributed population with an unknown variance, the theoretically correct test statistic is the t-statistic.

- To test whether the observed difference between two means is statistically significant, the analyst must first decide whether the samples are independent or dependent (related). If the samples are independent, a test concerning differences between means is employed. If the samples are dependent, a test of mean differences (paired comparisons test) is employed.

- To determine whether the difference between two population means from normally distributed populations with unknown but equal variances, the appropriate test is a t-test based on pooling the observations of the two samples to estimate the common but unknown variance. This test is based on an assumption of independent samples.

- In tests concerning two means based on two samples that are not independent, the data are often arranged in paired observations and a test of mean differences (a paired comparisons test) is conducted. When the samples are from normally distributed populations with unknown variances, the appropriate test statistic is t-distributed.

- In tests concerning the variance of a single normally distributed population, the test statistic is chi-square with $n - 1$ degrees of freedom, where n is sample size.

- For tests concerning differences between the variances of two normally distributed populations based on two random, independent samples, the appropriate test statistic is based on an F-test (the ratio of the sample variances). The degrees of freedom for this F-test are $n1 - 1$ and $n2 - 1$, where $n1$ corresponds to the number of observations in the calculation of the numerator, and $n2$ is the number of observations in the calculation of the denominator of the F-statistic.

- A parametric test is a hypothesis test concerning a population parameter, or a hypothesis test based on specific distributional assumptions. In contrast, a nonparametric test either is not concerned with a parameter or makes minimal assumptions about the population from which the sample was taken.

- A nonparametric test is primarily used when data do not meet distributional assumptions, when there are outliers, when data are given in ranks, or when the hypothesis we are addressing does not concern a parameter.

HYPOTHESIS TESTS FOR FINANCE

☐ | explain hypothesis testing and its components, including statistical significance, Type I and Type II errors, and the power of a test.

We use **hypothesis testing** to make decisions using data. Hypothesis testing is part of statistical inference, the process of making judgments about a larger group (a population) based on a smaller group of observations (a sample).

In hypothesis testing, we test to determine whether a sample statistic is likely to come from a population with the hypothesized value of the population parameter.

The concepts and tools of hypothesis testing provide an objective means to gauge whether the available evidence supports the hypothesis. After applying a statistical test, we should have a clearer idea of the probability that a hypothesis is true or not, although our conclusion always stops short of certainty.

The main focus of this lesson is on the framework of hypothesis testing and tests concerning mean and variance, two measures frequently used in investments.

The Process of Hypothesis Testing

Hypothesis testing is part of the branch of statistics known as statistical inference. In statistical inference, there is estimation and hypothesis testing. Estimation involves point estimates and interval estimates. Consider a sample mean, which is a point estimate, that we can use to form a confidence interval. In hypothesis testing, the focus is examining how a sample statistic informs us about a population parameter. A **hypothesis** is a statement about one or more populations that we test using sample statistics.

The process of hypothesis testing begins with the formulation of a theory to organize and explain observations. We judge the correctness of the theory by its ability to make accurate predictions—for example, to predict the results of new observations. If the predictions are correct, we continue to maintain the theory as a possibly correct explanation of our observations. Risk plays a role in the outcomes of observations in finance, so we can only try to make unbiased, probability-based judgments about whether the new data support the predictions. Statistical hypothesis testing fills that key role of testing hypotheses when there is uncertainty. When an analyst correctly formulates the question into a testable hypothesis and carries out a test of hypotheses, the use of well-established scientific methods supports the conclusions and decisions made on the basis of this test.

We organize this introduction to hypothesis testing around the six steps presented in Exhibit 1, which illustrate the standard approach to hypothesis testing.

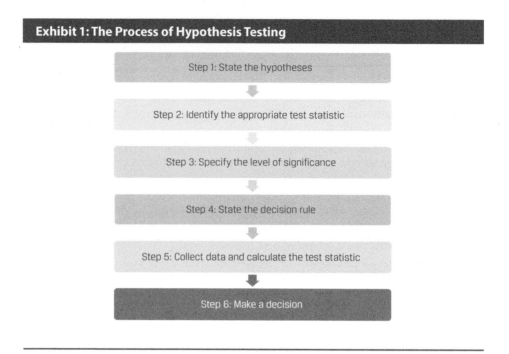

Exhibit 1: The Process of Hypothesis Testing

Step 1: State the hypotheses

Step 2: Identify the appropriate test statistic

Step 3: Specify the level of significance

Step 4: State the decision rule

Step 5: Collect data and calculate the test statistic

Step 6: Make a decision

Stating the Hypotheses

For each hypothesis test, we always state two hypotheses: the **null hypothesis** (or null), designated H_0, and the **alternative hypothesis**, designated H_a. The null hypothesis is a statement concerning a population parameter or parameters considered to be true unless the sample we use to conduct the hypothesis test gives convincing evidence that the null hypothesis is false. In fact, the null hypothesis is what we want to reject. If there is sufficient evidence to indicate that the null hypothesis is not true, we reject it in favor of the alternative hypothesis.

Importantly, the null and alternative hypotheses are stated in terms of population parameters, and we use sample statistics to test these hypotheses.

Second, the null and alternative hypotheses must be mutually exclusive and collectively exhaustive; in other words, all possible values are contained in either the null or the alternative hypothesis.

Identify the Appropriate Test Statistic and Distribution

A test statistic is a value calculated on the basis of a sample that, when used in conjunction with a decision rule, is the basis for deciding whether to reject the null hypothesis.

The focal point of our statistical decision is the value of the test statistic. The test statistic that we use depends on what we are testing.

Following the identification of the appropriate test statistic, we must be concerned with the distribution of the test statistic. We show examples of test statistics, and their corresponding distributions, in Exhibit 2.

Exhibit 2: Test Statistics and Their Distribution

What We Want to Test	Test Statistic	Probability Distribution of the Statistic	Degrees of Freedom
Test of a single mean	$t = \dfrac{\overline{X} - \mu_0}{s / \sqrt{n}}$	t-distributed	$n - 1$
Test of the difference in means	$t = \dfrac{(\overline{X}_{d1} - \overline{X}_{d2}) - (\mu_{d1} - \mu_{d2})}{\sqrt{\dfrac{s_p^2}{n_{d1}} + \dfrac{s_p^2}{n_{d2}}}}$	t-distributed	$n_1 + n_2 - 2$
Test of the mean of differences	$t = \dfrac{\overline{d} - \mu_{d0}}{s_{\overline{d}}}$	t-distributed	$n - 1$
Test of a single variance	$\chi^2 = \dfrac{(n-1)s^2}{\sigma_0^2}$	Chi-square distributed	$n - 1$
Test of the difference in variances	$F = \dfrac{s_{Before}^2}{s_{After}^2}$	F-distributed	$n_1 - 1, n_2 - 1$
Test of a correlation	$t = \dfrac{r\sqrt{n-2}}{\sqrt{1 - r^2}}$	t-Distributed	$n - 2$
Test of independence (categorical data)	$\chi^2 = \displaystyle\sum_{i=1}^{m} \dfrac{\left(O_{ij} - E_{ij}\right)^2}{E_{ij}}$	Chi-square distributed	$(r-1)(c-1)$

Note: μ_0, μ_{d0}, and σ_0^2 denote hypothesized values of the mean, mean difference, and variance, respectively. The $\overline{x}$, $\overline{d}$, s^2, s, and r denote for a sample the mean, mean of the differences, variance, standard deviation, and correlation, respectively, with subscripts indicating the sample, if appropriate. The sample size is indicated as n, and the subscript indicates the sample, if appropriate. O_{ij} and E_{ij} are observed and expected frequencies, respectively, with r indicating the number of rows and c indicating the number of columns in the contingency table.

Specify the Level of Significance

The level of significance reflects how much sample evidence we require to reject the null hypothesis. The required standard of proof can change according to the nature of the hypotheses and the seriousness of the consequences of making a mistake.

There are four possible outcomes when we test a null hypothesis, as shown in Exhibit 3. A **Type I error** is a false positive (reject when the null is true), whereas a **Type II error** is a false negative (fail to reject when the null is false).

Exhibit 3: Correct and Incorrect Decisions in Hypothesis Testing

Decision	H_0 True	H_0 False
Fail to reject H_0	Correct decision: Do not reject a true null hypothesis.	Type II error: Fail to reject a false null hypothesis. False negative
Reject H_0	Type I error: Reject a true null hypothesis. False positive	Correct decision: Reject a false null hypothesis.

When we make a decision in a hypothesis test, we run the risk of making either a Type I or a Type II error. As shown in Exhibit 3, these errors are mutually exclusive: If we mistakenly reject the true null, we can only be making a Type I error; if we mistakenly fail to reject the false null, we can only be making a Type II error.

The probability of a Type I error is denoted by the lowercase Greek letter alpha, α. This probability is also known as the **level of significance** of the test, and its complement, $(1 - \alpha)$, is the **confidence level**. For example, a level of significance of 5 percent for a test means that there is a 5 percent probability of rejecting a true null hypothesis and corresponds to the 95 percent confidence level.

Controlling the probabilities of the two types of errors involves a trade-off. All else equal, if we decrease the probability of a Type I error by specifying a smaller significance level (say, 1 percent rather than 5 percent), we increase the probability of making a Type II error because we will reject the null less frequently, including when it is false. Both Type I and Type II errors are risks of being wrong. Whether to accept more of one type versus the other depends on the consequences of the errors, such as costs. This trade-off weighs the impact of errors we are willing to accept and if so, at what cost. The only way to reduce the probabilities of both types of errors simultaneously is to increase the sample size, n.

Whereas the significance level of a test is the probability of incorrectly rejecting the true null, the **power of a test** is the probability of *correctly* rejecting the null—that is, the probability of rejecting the null when it is false. The power of a test is, in fact, the complement of the Type II error. The probability of a Type II error is often denoted by the lowercase Greek letter beta, β. We can classify the different probabilities in Exhibit 4 to reflect the notation that is often used.

Exhibit 4: Probabilities Associated with Hypothesis Testing Decisions

Decision	H_0 True	H_0 False
Fail to reject H_0	$1 - \alpha$	β
Reject H_0	α	$1 - \beta$

State the Decision Rule

The fourth step in hypothesis testing is stating the decision rule: When do we reject the null hypothesis, and when do we not? The action we take is based on comparing the calculated sample test statistic with a specified value or values, which are referred to as **critical values**.

The critical value or values we choose are based on the level of significance and the probability distribution associated with the test statistic. If we find that the calculated value of the test statistic is more extreme than the critical value or values, then we reject the null hypothesis; we say the result is **statistically significant**. Otherwise, we fail to reject the null hypothesis; there is not sufficient evidence to reject the null hypothesis. Recall that the smallest level of significance at which the null hypothesis can be rejected is the **p-value**, the area in the probability distribution outside the calculated test statistic.

QUESTION SET

1. Willco is a manufacturer in a mature cyclical industry. During the most recent industry cycle, its net income averaged USD30 million per year with a standard deviation of USD10 million ($n = 6$ observations). Management claims that Willco's performance during the most recent cycle results from new approaches and that Willco's profitability will exceed the average of USD24 million per year observed in prior cycles.

   A. With μ as the population value of mean annual net income, formulate null and alternative hypotheses consistent with testing Willco management's claim.

   B. Assuming that Willco's net income is at least approximately normally distributed, identify the appropriate test statistic and calculate the degrees of freedom.

   C. Based on a critical value of 2.015, determine whether to reject the null hypothesis.

   Solution:

   A. We often set up the "hoped for" or "suspected" condition as the alternative hypothesis. Here, that condition is that the population value of Willco's mean annual net income exceeds USD24 million. Thus, we have $H_0: \mu \le 24$ versus $H_a: \mu > 24$.

   B. Given that net income is normally distributed with unknown variance, the appropriate test statistic is a t-statistic with $n - 1 = 6 - 1 = 5$ degrees of freedom.

   C. We reject the null if the calculated t-statistic is greater than 2.015. The calculated t-statistic is

$$t = \frac{30 - 24}{10 / \sqrt{6}} = 1.4697.$$

   D. Because the calculated test statistic does not exceed 2.015, we fail to reject the null hypothesis. There is not sufficient evidence to indicate that the mean net income is greater than USD24 million.

2. All else equal, is specifying a smaller significance level in a hypothesis test likely to increase the probability of a:

	Type I error?	Type II error?
A.	No	No
B.	No	Yes
C.	Yes	No

   Solution:

   B is correct. Specifying a smaller significance level decreases the probability of a Type I error (rejecting a true null hypothesis) but increases the probability of a Type II error (not rejecting a false null hypothesis). As the level of significance decreases, the null hypothesis is less frequently rejected.

3. For each of the following hypothesis tests concerning the population mean, μ, state the conclusion regarding the test of the hypotheses.

  A. $H_0: \mu = 10$ versus $H_a: \mu \neq 10$, with a calculated t-statistic of 2.05 and critical t-values of ± 1.984.

  B. $H_0: \mu \leq 10$ versus $H_a: \mu > 10$, with a calculated t-statistic of 2.35 and a critical t-value of $+1.679$

  C. $H_0: \mu = 10$ versus $H_a: \mu \neq 10$, with a calculated t-statistic of 2.05, a p-value of 4.6352%, and a level of significance of 5%.

  D. $H_0: \mu \leq 10$ versus $H_a: \mu > 10$, with a 2% level of significance and a calculated test statistic with a p-value of 3%.

Solution:

We make the decision either by comparing the calculated test statistic with the critical values or by comparing the p-value for the calculated test statistic with the level of significance.

  A. Reject the null hypothesis because the calculated test statistic of 2.05 is outside the bounds of the critical values of ± 1.984.

  B. Reject the null hypothesis because the calculated test statistic of 2.35 is outside the bounds of the critical value of $+1.679$.

  C. The p-value corresponding to the calculated test statistic of 4.6352% is less than the level of significance (5%), so we reject the null hypothesis.

  D. We fail to reject because the p-value for the calculated test statistic of 3% is greater than the level of significance (2%).

---

3   TESTS OF RETURN AND RISK IN FINANCE

☐ | construct hypothesis tests and determine their statistical significance, the associated Type I and Type II errors, and power of the test given a significance level

Hypothesis tests concerning return and risk are among the most common in finance. The sampling distribution of the mean, when the population standard deviation is unknown, is t-distributed, and when the population standard deviation is known, it is normally distributed, or z-distributed. Since the population standard deviation is unknown in almost all cases, we will focus on the use of a t-distributed test statistic.

TEST OF A SINGLE MEAN: RISK AND RETURN CHARACTERISTICS OF AN EQUITY MUTUAL FUND

Suppose you are analyzing Sendar Equity Fund,. During the past 24 months, it has achieved a mean monthly return of 1.50%, with a sample standard deviation of monthly returns of 3.60 percent. Given its level of market risk and according to a pricing model, this mutual fund was expected to have earned a 1.10 percent mean monthly return during that time period.

Assuming returns are normally distributed, are the actual results consistent with a population mean monthly return of 1.10 percent?

Formulate and test a hypothesis that the fund's performance was different than the mean return of 1.1 percent inferred from the pricing model. Use a 5 percent level of significance.

Exhibit 5: Test of a Single Mean

Step 1	State the hypotheses.	$H_0: \mu = 1.1\%$ versus $H_a: \mu \neq 1.1\%$
Step 2	Identify the appropriate test statistic.	$t = \dfrac{\overline{X} - \mu_0}{s/\sqrt{n}}$
		with $24 - 1 = 23$ degrees of freedom.
Step 3	Specify the level of significance.	$\alpha = 5\%$ (two tailed).
Step 4	State the decision rule.	Critical t-values $= \pm 2.069$.
		Reject the null if the calculated t-statistic is less than -2.069, and reject the null if the calculated t-statistic is greater than $+2.069$.
		Excel
		Lower: `T.INV(0.025,23)`
		Upper: `T.INV(0.975,23)`
		R `qt(c(.025,.975),23)`
		Python `from scipy.stats import t`
		Lower: `t.ppf(.025,23)`
		Upper: `t.ppf(.975,23)`
Step 5	Calculate the test statistic.	$t = \dfrac{1.5 - 1.1}{3.6/\sqrt{24}} = 0.54433$
Step 6	Make a decision.	Fail to reject the null hypothesis because the calculated t-statistic falls between the two critical values. There is not sufficient evidence to indicate that the population mean monthly return is different from 1.10%.

Test the hypothesis using the 95 percent confidence interval.

The 95 percent confidence interval is $\overline{X} \pm$ Critical value$\left(\dfrac{s}{\sqrt{n}}\right)$, so

$$\left\{ 1.5 - 2.069\left(\dfrac{3.6}{\sqrt{24}}\right), \; 1.5 + 2.069\left(\dfrac{3.6}{\sqrt{24}}\right) \right\}$$
$$\{1.5 - 1.5204, \; 1.5 + 1.5204\}$$
$$\{-0.0204, \; 3.0204\}$$

The hypothesized value of 1.1 percent is within the bounds of the 95 percent confidence interval, so we fail to reject the null hypothesis.

TEST OF A SINGLE VARIANCE: RISK CHARACTERISTICS OF AN EQUITY MUTUAL FUND

Suppose we want to use the observed sample variance of the fund to test whether the true variance of the fund is less than some trigger level, say 4 percent. Performing a test of a population variance requires specifying the hypothesized value of the variance. We can formulate hypotheses concerning whether the variance is equal to a specific value or whether it is greater than or less than a hypothesized value:

One-sided alternative (left tail): $H_0: \sigma^2 \geq \sigma_0^2$ versus $H_a: \sigma^2 < \sigma_0^2$.

Note that the fund's variance is less than the trigger level $\sigma_0^2 = 4\%$ if the null hypothesis is rejected in favor of the alternative hypothesis. In tests concerning the variance of a single normally distributed population, we make use of a chi-square test statistic, denoted χ^2.

You continue with your analysis of Sendar Equity Fund, a midcap growth fund that has been in existence for only 24 months. During this period, Sendar Equity achieved a mean monthly return of 1.50 percent and a standard deviation of monthly returns of 3.60 percent. Using a 5 percent level of significance, test whether the standard deviation of returns is less than 4 percent. Recall that the standard deviation is the square root of the variance, hence a standard deviation of 4 percent or 0.04, is a variance of 0.0016.

Exhibit 6: Test of Single Variance

Step 1	State the hypotheses.	H_0: $\sigma^2 \geq 16$ versus H_a: $\sigma^2 < 16$
Step 2	Identify the appropriate test statistic.	$\chi^2 = \frac{(n-1)s^2}{\sigma_0^2}$
Step 3	Specify the level of significance.	5%
Step 4	State the decision rule.	With 24 − 1 = 23 degrees of freedom, the critical value is 13.09051.
		We reject the null hypothesis if the calculated χ^2 statistic is less than 13.09051.
		Excel `CHISQ.INV(0.05,23)`
		R `qchisq(.05,23)`
		Python
		`from scipy.stats import chi2`
		`chi2.ppf(.05,23)`
Step 5	Calculate the test statistic.	$\chi^2 = \frac{(24-1)12.96}{16} = 18.63000$
Step 6	Make a decision.	Fail to reject the null hypothesis because the calculated χ^2 statistic is greater than the critical value. There is insufficient evidence to indicate that the variance is less than 16% (or, equivalently, that the standard deviation is less than 4%).

TEST CONCERNING DIFFERENCES BETWEEN MEANS WITH INDEPENDENT SAMPLES

We often want to know whether a mean value—for example, a mean return—differs for two groups. Is an observed difference due to chance or to different underlying values for the mean? We test this by drawing a sample from each group. When it is reasonable to believe that the samples are from populations that are approximately normally distributed and that the samples are also independent of each other, we use the test of the difference in the means. We may assume that population variances are equal or unequal. However, our focus in discussing the test of the difference of means is using the assumption that the population variances are equal. In the calculation of the test statistic, we combine the observations from both samples to obtain a pooled estimate of the common population variance.

Let μ1 and μ2 represent, respectively, the population means of the first and second populations, respectively. Most often we want to test whether the population means are equal or whether one is larger than the other. Thus, we formulate the following hypotheses:

$H_0: \mu_1 - \mu_2 = 0$ versus $H_a: \mu_1 - \mu_2 \neq 0$.

EXAMPLE 1

Comparison of Returns on the ACE High Yield Index for Two Periods

Suppose we want to test whether the returns of the ACE High Yield Total Return Index, shown in Exhibit 7, are different for two different time periods, Period 1 and Period 2.

Exhibit 7: Descriptive Statistics for ACE High Yield Total Return Index for Periods 1 and 2

	Period 1	Period 2
Mean	0.01775%	0.01134%
Standard deviation	0.31580%	0.38760%
Sample size	445 days	859 days

Note that these periods are of different lengths and the samples are independent; that is, there is no pairing of the days for the two periods.

1. Is there a difference between the mean daily returns in Period 1 and in Period 2, using a 5% level of significance?

   Solution:

Step 1	State the hypotheses.	$H_0: \mu_{Period1} = \mu_{Period2}$ versus Ha: $\mu_{Period1} \neq \mu_{Period2}$
Step 2	Identify the appropriate test statistic.	$t = \dfrac{(\overline{X}_{Period1} - \overline{X}_{Period2}) - (\mu_{Period1} - \mu_{Period2})}{\sqrt{\dfrac{s_p^2}{n_{period1}} + \dfrac{s_p^2}{n_{Period}}}}$, where $s_p^2 = \dfrac{(n_{period1} - 1)s_{period2}^2 + (n_{period2} - 1)s_{Period2}^2}{n_{period1} + n_{period2} - 2}$ with $445 + 859 - 2 = 1{,}302$ degrees of freedom.
Step 3	Specify the level of significance.	$\alpha = 5\%$
Step 4	State the decision rule.	Critical t-values = ±1.962

Reject the null if the calculated t-statistic is less than −1.962, and reject the null if the calculated t-statistic is greater than +1.962.

Excel

  Lower: `T.INV(0.025,1302)`

  Upper: `T.INV(0.975,1302)`

R `qt(c(.025,.975),1302)`

Python `from scipy.stats import t`

  Lower: `t.ppf(.025,1302)`

  Upper: `t.ppf(.975,1302)`

Step 5	Calculate the test statistic.	$s_p^2 = \dfrac{(445-1)0.09973 + (859-1)0.15023}{445+859-2} = 0.1330$
		$t = \dfrac{(0.01775 - 0.01134) - 0}{\sqrt{\dfrac{0.1330}{445} + \dfrac{0.1330}{859}}} = \dfrac{0.0064}{0.0213} = 0.3009.$
Step 6	Make a decision.	Fail to reject the null because the calculated t-statistic falls within the bounds of the two critical values. We conclude that there is insufficient evidence to indicate that the returns are different for the two time periods.

Test Concerning Differences between Means with Dependent Samples

When we compare two independent samples, we use a t-distributed test statistic that uses the difference in the means and a pooled variance. An assumption for the validity of those tests is that the samples are independent—that is, unrelated to each other. When we want to conduct tests on two means based on samples that we believe are dependent, we use the **test of the mean of the differences** (a paired comparisons test).

How is this test of paired differences different from the test of the difference in means in independent samples? The test of paired comparisons is more powerful than the test of the difference in the means because by using the common element (such as the same periods or companies), we eliminate the variation between the samples that could be caused by something other than what we are testing.

EXAMPLE 2

A Comparison of the Returns of Two Indexes

Suppose we want to compare the returns of the ACE High Yield Index with those of the ACE BBB Index. We collect data over the same 1,304 days for both indexes and calculate their means and standard deviations as shown in Exhibit 8.

Exhibit 8: Mean and Standard Deviations for the ACE High Yield Index and the ACE BBB Index

	ACE High Yield Index (%)	ACE BBB Index (%)	Difference (%)
Mean return	0.0157	0.0135	−0.0021
Standard deviation	0.3157	0.3645	0.3622

1. Using a 5 percent level of significance, is the mean of the differences is different from zero?

    Solution:

Step 1	State the hypotheses.	$H_0: \mu_{d0} = 0$ versus $H_a: \mu_{d0} \neq 0$
Step 2	Identify the appropriate test statistic.	$t = \dfrac{\bar{d} - \mu_{d0}}{s_{\bar{d}}}$
Step 3	Specify the level of significance.	5%

Step 4	State the decision rule.	With $1{,}304 - 1 = 1{,}303$ degrees of freedom, the critical values are ± 1.962.

We reject the null hypothesis if the calculated t-statistic is less than -1.962 or greater than $+1.962$.

Excel

  Lower: `T.INV(0.025,1303)`

  Upper: `T.INV(0.975,1303)`

R `qt(c(.025,.975),1303`

Python `from scipy.stats import t`

  Lower: `t.ppf(.025,1303)`

  Upper: `t.ppf(.975,1303)`

Step 5	Calculate the test statistic.	

$$\bar{d} = -0.0021\%$$

$$s_{\bar{d}} = \frac{s_d}{\sqrt{n}} = \frac{0.3622}{\sqrt{1{,}304}} = 0.01003\%$$

$$t = \frac{-0.00210 - 0}{0.01003} = -0.20937$$

Step 6	Make a decision.	Fail to reject the null hypothesis because the calculated t-statistic falls within the bounds of the two critical values. There is insufficient evidence to indicate that the mean of the differences of returns is different from zero.C

Test Concerning the Equality of Two Variances

There are many instances in which we want to compare the volatility of two samples, in which case we can test for the equality of two variances. Examples include comparisons of baskets of securities against indexes or benchmarks, as well as comparisons of volatility in different periods.

EXAMPLE 3

Volatility and Regulation

You are investigating whether the population variance of returns on a stock market index changed after a change in market regulation. The first 418 weeks occurred before the regulation change, and the second 418 weeks occurred after the regulation change. You gather the data in Exhibit 9 for 418 weeks of returns both before and after the change in regulation. You have specified a 5 percent level of significance.

Exhibit 9: Index Returns and Variances before and after the Market Regulation Change

	N	Mean Weekly Return (%)	Variance of Returns
Before regulation change	418	0.250	4.644
After regulation change	418	0.110	3.919

1. Are the variance of returns different before the regulation change versus after the regulation change?

   Solution:

Step 1	State the hypotheses.	$H_0 : \sigma^2_{Before} = \sigma^2_{After}$ versus $H_a : \sigma^2_{Before} \neq \sigma^2_{After}$
Step 2	Identify the appropriate test statistic.	$F = \dfrac{s^2_{Before}}{s^2_{After}}$
Step 3	Specify the level of significance.	5%
Step 4	State the decision rule.	With $418 - 1 = 417$ and $418 - 1 = 417$ degrees of freedom, the critical values are 0.82512 and 1.21194.

Reject the null if the calculated F-statistic is less than 0.82512 or greater than 1.21194.

Excel

   Left side: `F.INV(0.025,417,417)`

   Right side: `F.INV(0.975,417,417)`

R `qf(c(.025,.975),417,417)`

Python `from scipy.stats import f`

   Left side: `f.ppf(.025,417,417)`

   Right side: `f.ppf(.975,417,417)`

Step 5	Calculate the test statistic.	$F = \dfrac{4.644}{3.919} = 1.18500$
Step 6	Make a decision.	Fail to reject the null hypothesis since the calculated F-statistic falls within the bounds of the two critical values. There is not sufficient evidence to indicate that the weekly variances of returns are different in the periods before and after the regulation change.

2. Is the variance of returns greater before the regulation change versus after the regulation change?

Solution:

Step 1	State the hypotheses.	$H_0 : \sigma^2_{Before} \leq \sigma^2_{After}$ versus $H_a : \sigma^2_{Before} > \sigma^2_{After}$
Step 2	Identify the appropriate test statistic.	$F = \dfrac{s^2_{Before}}{s^2_{After}}$
Step 3	Specify the level of significance.	5%
Step 4	State the decision rule.	With $418 - 1 = 417$ and $418 - 1 = 417$ degrees of freedom, the critical value is 1.17502.

We reject the null hypothesis if the calculated F-statistic is greater than 1.17502.

Excel `F.INV(0.95,417,417)`

R `qf(.95,417,417)`

Python
```
from scipy.stats import f
f.ppf(.95,417,417)
```

Step 5	Calculate the test statistic.	$F = \dfrac{4.644}{3.919} = 1.18500$
Step 6	Make a decision.	Reject the null hypothesis since the calculated F-statistic is greater than 1.17502. There is sufficient evidence to indicate that the weekly variances of returns before the regulation change are greater than the variances after the regulation change.

QUESTION SET

Investment analysts often use earnings per share (EPS) forecasts. One test of forecasting quality is the zero-mean test, which states that optimal forecasts should have a mean forecasting error of zero. The forecasting error is the difference between the predicted value of a variable and the actual value of the variable.

You have collected data (shown in Exhibit 10) for two analysts who cover two different industries: Analyst A covers the telecom industry; Analyst B covers automotive parts and suppliers.

Exhibit 10: Test of Return and Risk

Performance in Forecasting Quarterly Earnings per Share

	Number of Forecasts	Mean Forecast Error (Predicted – Actual)	Standard Deviation of Forecast Errors
Analyst A	10	0.05	0.10
Analyst B	15	0.02	0.09

Critical t-values:

Degrees of Freedom	Area in the Right-Side Rejection Area	
	$p = 0.05$	$p = 0.025$
8	1.860	2.306
9	1.833	2.262
10	1.812	2.228
11	1.796	2.201
12	1.782	2.179
13	1.771	2.160
14	1.761	2.145
15	1.753	2.131
16	1.746	2.120
17	1.740	2.110
18	1.734	2.101
19	1.729	2.093
20	1.725	2.086
21	1.721	2.080
22	1.717	2.074
23	1.714	2.069
24	1.711	2.064
25	1.708	2.060
26	1.706	2.056
27	1.703	2.052

1. With μ as the population mean forecasting error, formulate null and alternative hypotheses for a zero-mean test of forecasting quality.

   A. For Analyst A, determine whether to reject the null at the 0.05 level of significance.

   B. For Analyst B, determine whether to reject the null at the 0.05 level of significance.

   Solution:

   H_0: $\mu = 0$ versus H_a: $\mu \neq 0$.

   A. The t-test is based on $t = \dfrac{\overline{X} - \mu_0}{s/\sqrt{n}}$ with n – 1 = 10 – 1 = 9 degrees of freedom. At the 0.05 significance level, we reject the null if the calculated t-statistic is outside the bounds of ±2.262 (from the table for 9 degrees of freedom and 0.025 in the right side of the distribution). For Analyst A, we have a calculated test statistic of

   $$t = \frac{0.05 - 0}{0.10 / \sqrt{10}} = 1.58114.$$

   We, therefore, fail to reject the null hypothesis at the 0.05 level.

   B. For Analyst B, the t-test is based on t with 15 – 1 = 14 degrees of freedom. At the 0.05 significance level, we reject the null if the calculated t-statistic is outside the bounds of ±2.145 (from the table for 14 degrees of freedom). The calculated test statistic is

   $$t = \frac{0.02 - 0}{0.09 / \sqrt{15}} = 0.86066.$$

   Because 0.86066 is within the range of ±2.145, we fail to reject the null at the 0.05 level.

2. Reviewing the EPS forecasting performance data for Analysts A and B, you want to investigate whether the larger average forecast errors of Analyst A relative to Analyst B are due to chance or to a higher underlying mean value for Analyst A. Assume that the forecast errors of both analysts are normally distributed and that the samples are independent.

   A. Formulate null and alternative hypotheses consistent with determining whether the population mean value of Analyst A's forecast errors (μ_1) are larger than Analyst B's (μ_2).

   B. Identify the test statistic for conducting a test of the null hypothesis formulated in Part A.

   C. Identify the rejection point or points for the hypotheses tested in Part A at the 0.05 level of significance.

   D. Determine whether to reject the null hypothesis at the 0.05 level of significance.

   Solution:

   A. Stating the suspected condition as the alternative hypothesis, we have

   $$H_0: \mu_A - \mu_B \leq 0 \text{ versus } H_a: \mu_A - \mu_B > 0,$$

   where

   μ_A = the population mean value of Analyst A's forecast errors

   μ_B = the population mean value of Analyst B's forecast errors

B. We have two normally distributed populations with unknown variances. Based on the samples, it is reasonable to assume that the population variances are equal. The samples are assumed to be independent; this assumption is reasonable because the analysts cover different industries. The appropriate test statistic is t using a pooled estimate of the common variance:

$$t = \frac{(\bar{X}_1 - \bar{X}_2) - (\mu_1 - \mu_2)}{\sqrt{\frac{s_p^2}{n_1} + \frac{s_p^2}{n_2}}}, \text{ where } s_p^2 = \frac{(n_1 - 1)s_1^2 + (n_2 - 1)s_2^2}{n_1 + n_2 - 2}.$$

The number of degrees of freedom is $n_A + n_B - 2 = 10 + 15 - 2 = 23$.

C. For df = 23, according to the table, the rejection point for a one-sided (right side) test at the 0.05 significance level is 1.714.

D. We first calculate the pooled estimate of variance:

$$s_p^2 = \frac{(10 - 1)0.01 + (15 - 1)0.0081}{10 + 15 - 2} = 0.0088435.$$

We then calculate the t-distributed test statistic:

$$t = \frac{(0.05 - 0.02) - 0}{\sqrt{\frac{0.0088435}{10} + \frac{0.0088435}{15}}} = \frac{0.03}{0.0383916} = 0.78142.$$

Because $0.78142 < 1.714$, we fail to reject the null hypothesis. There is not sufficient evidence to indicate that the mean for Analyst A exceeds that for Analyst B.

An investment consultant gathers two independent random samples of five-year performance data for US and European absolute return hedge funds. Noting a return advantage of 50 bps for US managers, the consultant decides to test whether the two means are different from one another at a 0.05 level of significance. The two populations are assumed to be normally distributed with unknown but equal variances. Results of the hypothesis test are contained in the Exhibit 11.

Exhibit 11: Hypothesis Test Results

	Sample Size	Mean Return (%)	Standard Deviation
US managers	50	4.7	5.4
European managers	50	4.2	4.8
Null and alternative hypotheses		H_0: $\mu_{US} - \mu_E = 0$; H_a: $\mu_{US} - \mu_E \neq 0$	
Calculated test statistic		0.4893	
Critical value rejection points		±1.984	

Note: The mean return for US funds is μ_{US}, and μ_E is the mean return for European funds.

3. The consultant should conclude that the:

A. null hypothesis is not rejected.

B. alternative hypothesis is statistically confirmed.

C. difference in mean returns is statistically different from zero.

Solution:

A is correct. The calculated t-statistic value of 0.4893 falls within the bounds of the critical t-values of ±1.984. Thus, H_0 cannot be rejected; the result is not statistically significant at the 0.05 level.

4. During a 10-year period, the standard deviation of annual returns on a portfolio you are analyzing was 15 percent a year. You want to see whether this record is sufficient evidence to support the conclusion that the portfolio's underlying variance of return was less than 400, the return variance of the portfolio's benchmark.

   A. Formulate null and alternative hypotheses consistent with your objective.

   B. Identify the test statistic for conducting a test of the hypotheses in Part A, and calculate the degrees of freedom.

   C. Determine whether the null hypothesis is rejected or not rejected at the 0.05 level of significance using a critical value of 3.325.

   Solution:

   A. We have a "less than" alternative hypothesis, where σ^2 is the variance of return on the portfolio. The hypotheses are H_0: $\sigma^2 \geq 400$ versus H_a: $\sigma^2 < 400$, where 400 is the hypothesized value of variance. This means that the rejection region is on the left side of the distribution.

   B. The test statistic is chi-square distributed with $10 - 1 = 9$ degrees of freedom.

   C. The test statistic is calculated as

   $$\chi^2 = \frac{(n-1)s^2}{\sigma_0^2} = \frac{9 \times 15^2}{400} = \frac{2,025}{400} = 5.0625 \text{ , or } 5.06.$$

Because 5.06 is not less than 3.325, we do not reject the null hypothesis; the calculated test statistic falls to the right of the critical value, where the critical value separates the left-side rejection region from the region where we fail to reject.

We can determine the critical value for this test using software:

Excel `[CHISQ.INV(0.05,9)]`

`[qchisq(.05,9)]`

Python

`[from scipy.stats import chi2 and chi2.ppf(.05,9)]`

We can determine the p-value for the calculated test statistic of 17.0953 using software:

Excel `[CHISQ.DIST(5.06,9,TRUE)]`

`[pchisq(5.06,9,lower.tail=TRUE)]`

Python

`[from scipy.stats import chi2 and chi2.cdf(5.06,9)]`

5. You are investigating whether the population variance of returns on an index changed subsequent to a market disruption. You gather the following data for 120 months of returns before the disruption and for 120 months of returns after the disruption. You have specified a 0.05 level of significance.

Exhibit 12: Data for 120 Months of Returns

Time Period	N	Mean Monthly Return (%)	Variance of Returns
Before disruption	120	1.416	22.367
After disruption	120	1.436	15.795

A. Formulate null and alternative hypotheses consistent with the research goal.

B. Identify the test statistic for conducting a test of the hypotheses in Part A, and calculate the degrees of freedom.

C. Determine whether to reject the null hypothesis at the 0.05 level of significance if the critical values are 0.6969 and 1.4349.

Solution:

A. We have a "not equal to" alternative hypothesis:

$$H_0 : \sigma^2_{Before} = \sigma^2_{After} \text{ versus } H_a : \sigma^2_{Before} \neq \sigma^2_{After}.$$

B. To test a null hypothesis of the equality of two variances, we use an F-test:

$$F = \frac{s_1^2}{s_2^2}.$$

$F = 22.367/15.795 = 1.416$, with $120 - 1 = 119$ numerator and $120 - 1 = 119$ denominator degrees of freedom.

C. Because this is a two-tailed test, we use critical values for the $0.05/2 = 0.025$ level. The calculated test statistic falls within the bounds of the critical values (i.e., between 0.6969 and 1.4349), so we fail to reject the null hypothesis; there is not enough evidence to indicate that the variances are different before and after the disruption. Note that we could also have formed the F-statistic as $15.796/22.367 = 0.706$ and draw the same conclusion.

We could also use software to calculate the critical values:

Excel

```
[F.INV(0.025,119,119)   and

F.INV(0.975,119,119)]

[qf(c(.025,.975),119,119)]
```

Python

```
from scipy.stats import f and f.ppf

[(.025,119,119)  and

f.ppf(.975,119,119)]
```

> Additionally, we could use software to calculate the *p*-value of the calculated test statistic, which is 5.896 percent, and then compare it with the level of significance:
>
> **Excel**
>
> ```
> [(1-F.DIST(22.367/15.796,119,119,TRUE))*2 or
> F.DIST(15.796/22.367,119,119,TRUE)*2]
> ```
>
> **R**
>
> ```
> [(1-pf(22.367/15.796,119,119))*2 or
> pf(15.796/22.367,119,119)*2]
> ```
>
> **Python**
>
> ```
> from scipy.stats import f and f.cdf
> [(15.796/22.367,119,119)*2 or
> (1-f.cdf(22.367/15.796,119,119))*2]
> ```

4   PARAMETRIC VERSUS NONPARAMETRIC TESTS

☐ | compare and contrast parametric and nonparametric tests, and describe situations where each is the more appropriate type of test

The hypothesis testing procedures we have discussed up to this point have two characteristics in common. First, they are concerned with parameters, and second, their validity depends on a definite set of assumptions. Mean and variance, for example, are two parameters, or defining quantities, of a normal distribution. The tests also make specific assumptions—in particular, assumptions about the distribution of the population producing the sample. Any test or procedure with either of these two characteristics is a **parametric test** or procedure.

In some cases, however, we are concerned about quantities other than parameters of distributions. In other cases, we may believe that the assumptions of parametric tests do not hold. In cases where we are examining quantities other than population parameters or where assumptions of the parameters are not satisfied, a nonparametric test or procedure can be useful.

A **nonparametric test** is a test that is not concerned with a parameter or a test that makes minimal assumptions about the population from which the sample comes. Exhibit 13 presents examples of nonparametric alternatives to the parametric, *t*-distributed tests concerning means.

Exhibit 13: Nonparametric Alternatives to Parametric Tests Concerning Means

	Parametric	Nonparametric
Tests concerning a single mean	*t*-distributed test *z*-distributed test	Wilcoxon signed-rank test

| Tests concerning differences between means | t-distributed test | Mann–Whitney U test (Wilcoxon rank sum test) |
| Tests concerning mean differences (paired comparisons tests) | t-distributed test | Wilcoxon signed-rank test Sign test |

Uses of Nonparametric Tests

Nonparametric procedures are primarily used in four situations: (1) when the data do not meet distributional assumptions, (2) when there are outliers, (3) when the data are given in ranks or use an ordinal scale, or (4) when the relevant hypotheses do not concern a parameter.

The first situation occurs when the data available for analysis suggest that the distributional assumptions of the parametric test are not satisfied. For example, we may want to test a hypothesis concerning the mean of a population but believe that neither t- nor z-distributed tests are appropriate because the sample is small and may come from a markedly non-normally distributed population. In that case, we may use a nonparametric test. The nonparametric test will frequently involve the conversion of observations (or a function of observations) into ranks according to magnitude, and sometimes it will involve working with only "greater than" or "less than" relationships (using the + and – signs to denote those relationships). Characteristically, one must refer to specialized statistical tables to determine the rejection points of the test statistic, at least for small samples. Such tests, then, typically interpret the null hypothesis as a hypothesis about ranks or signs.

Second, whereas the underlying distribution of the population may be normal, there may be extreme values or outliers that influence the parametric statistics but not the nonparametric statistics. For example, we may want to use a nonparametric test of the median, in the case of outliers, instead of a test of the mean.

Third, we may have a sample in which observations are ranked. In those cases, we also use nonparametric tests because parametric tests generally require a stronger measurement scale than ranks. For example, if our data were the rankings of investment managers, we would use nonparametric procedures to test the hypotheses concerning those rankings.

A fourth situation in which we use nonparametric procedures occurs when our question does not concern a parameter. For example, if the question concerns whether a sample is random or not, we use the appropriate nonparametric test (a "runs test"). The nonparametric runs test is used to test whether stock price changes can be used to forecast future stock price changes—in other words, a test of the random walk theory. Another type of question that nonparametric methods can address is whether a sample came from a population following a particular probability distribution.

Nonparametric Inference: Summary

Nonparametric statistical procedures extend the reach of inference because they make few assumptions, can be used on ranked data, and may address questions unrelated to parameters. Quite frequently, nonparametric tests are reported alongside parametric tests; the user can then assess how sensitive the statistical conclusion is to the assumptions underlying the parametric test. However, if the assumptions of the parametric test are met, the parametric test (where available) is generally preferred over the nonparametric test because the parametric test may have more power—that is, a greater ability to reject a false null hypothesis.

PRACTICE PROBLEMS

1. An analyst suspects that, in the most recent year, excess returns on stocks have fallen below 5%. She wants to study whether the excess returns are less than 5%. Designating the population mean as μ, which hypotheses are most appropriate for her analysis?

   A. $H_0: \mu = 5\%$ versus $H_a: \mu \neq 5\%$

   B. $H_0: \mu \geq 5\%$ versus $H_a: \mu < 5\%$

   C. $H_0: \mu \leq 5\%$ versus $H_a: \mu > 5\%$

2. Which of the following statements about hypothesis testing is correct?

   A. The null hypothesis is the condition a researcher hopes to support.

   B. The alternative hypothesis is the proposition considered true without conclusive evidence to the contrary.

   C. The alternative hypothesis exhausts all potential parameter values not accounted for by the null hypothesis.

3. Which of the following statements regarding the null hypothesis is correct?

   A. It can be stated as "not equal to" provided the alternative hypothesis is stated as "equal to."

   B. Along with the alternative hypothesis, it considers all possible values of the population parameter.

   C. In a two-tailed test, it is rejected when evidence supports equality between the hypothesized value and the population parameter.

4. Which of the following statements regarding a one-tailed hypothesis test is correct?

   A. The rejection region increases in size as the level of significance becomes smaller.

   B. A one-tailed test more strongly reflects the beliefs of the researcher than a two-tailed test.

   C. The absolute value of the critical value is larger than that for a two-tailed test at the same level of significance.

5. If a researcher selects a 5 percent level of significance for a hypothesis test, the confidence level is:

   A. 2.5 percent.

   B. 5 percent.

   C. 95 percent.

6. A hypothesis test for a normally distributed population, at a 0.05 significance

level, implies a:

   A. 95 percent probability of rejecting a true null hypothesis.

   B. 95 percent probability of a Type I error for a two-tailed test.

   C. 5 percent critical value rejection region for a one-tailed test.

7. The value of a test statistic is *best* described as the basis for deciding whether to:

   A. reject the null hypothesis.

   B. accept the null hypothesis.

   C. reject the alternative hypothesis.

8. Which of the following *best* describes a Type I error?

   A. Rejecting a true null hypothesis

   B. Rejecting a false null hypothesis

   C. Failing to reject a false null hypothesis

9. A Type II error is *best* described as:

   A. rejecting a true null hypothesis.

   B. failing to reject a false null hypothesis.

   C. failing to reject a false alternative hypothesis.

10. The level of significance of a hypothesis test is *best* used to:

   A. calculate the test statistic.

   B. define the test's rejection points.

   C. specify the probability of a Type II error.

11. The probability of correctly rejecting the null hypothesis is the:

   A. *p*-value.

   B. power of a test.

   C. level of significance.

12. The power of a hypothesis test is:

   A. equivalent to the level of significance.

   B. the probability of not making a Type II error.

   C. unchanged by increasing a small sample size.

13. In the step "stating a decision rule" in testing a hypothesis, which of the following elements must be specified?

   A. Critical value

   B. Power of a test

    C. Value of a test statistic

14. A pooled estimator is used when testing a hypothesis concerning the:

    A. equality of the variances of two normally distributed populations.

    B. difference between the means of two approximately normally distributed populations with unknown but assumed equal variances.

    C. difference between the means of two at least approximately normally distributed populations with unknown and assumed unequal variances.

15. When evaluating mean differences between two dependent samples, the *most* appropriate test is a:

    A. *z*-test.

    B. chi-square test.

    C. paired comparisons test.

16. A chi-square test is *most* appropriate for tests concerning:

    A. a single variance.

    B. differences between two population means with variances assumed to be equal.

    C. differences between two population means with variances not assumed to be equal.

17. Which of the following tests should be used to test the difference between the variances of two normally distributed populations with random independent samples?

    A. *t*-test

    B. *F*-test

    C. Paired comparisons test

18. A nonparametric test is most appropriate when the:

    A. data consist of ranked values.

    B. validity of the test depends on many assumptions.

    C. sample sizes are large but are drawn from a population that may be non-normal.

19. In which of the following situations would a nonparametric test of a hypothesis *most likely* be used?

    A. The sample data are ranked according to magnitude.

    B. The sample data come from a normally distributed population.

    C. The test validity depends on many assumptions about the nature of the population.

20. An analyst is examining the monthly returns for two funds over one year. Both funds' returns are non-normally distributed. To test whether the mean return of one fund is greater than the mean return of the other fund, the analyst can use:

    A. a parametric test only.

    B. a nonparametric test only.

    C. both parametric and nonparametric tests.

SOLUTIONS

1. B is correct. The null hypothesis is what she wants to reject in favor of the alternative, which is that population mean excess return is less than 5%. This is a one-sided (left-side) alternative hypothesis.

2. C is correct. Together, the null and alternative hypotheses account for all possible values of the parameter. Any possible values of the parameter not covered by the null must be covered by the alternative hypothesis (e.g., $H_0: \mu \le 5$ versus $H_a: \mu > 5$). A is incorrect because the null hypothesis is what the researcher wants to reject; the "hoped for" or "suspected" condition is often set up as the alternative hypothesis. B is incorrect because the null (not the alternative) hypothesis is considered to be true unless the sample used to conduct the hypothesis test gives convincing evidence that the null hypothesis is false.

3. B is correct. The null and alternative hypotheses are complements of one another and must be both mutually and collectively exhaustive. Differently put: all possible values or outcomes need to be contained in either the null or the alternative hypothesis.

    A is incorrect because the null hypothesis must always include the equality sign (less than or equal to, equal to, or greater than or equal to). C is incorrect because, in a two-tailed test, the null hypothesis is generally set up as equality between the hypothesized value and the population parameter. If evidence supports equality, then the null hypothesis would not be rejected.

4. B is correct. One-tailed tests in which the alternative is "greater than" or "less than" represent the beliefs of the researcher more firmly than a "not equal to" alternative hypothesis.

    A is incorrect because a smaller significance level implies a smaller rejection region. C is incorrect because the absolute value of the critical value for a one-tailed hypothesis test is smaller than that of a two-tailed test.

    For example, for a two-tailed t-test with 30 degrees of freedom at the 5% significance level, the corresponding critical value is ±2.042 (2.5% in each tail) whereas the corresponding critical value for a one-tailed t-test is +1.697 or −1.697 (5% in the left or right tail). Thus, the absolute value of the critical value is smaller for the one-tailed test than it is for the two-tailed test for the same level of significance.

5. C is correct. The 5 percent level of significance (i.e., probability of a Type I error) corresponds to 1 − 0.05 = 0.95, or a 95 percent confidence level (i.e., probability of not rejecting a true null hypothesis). The level of significance is the complement to the confidence level; in other words, they sum to 1.00, or 100 percent.

6. C is correct. For a one-tailed hypothesis test, there is a 5 percent rejection region in one tail of the distribution. A is incorrect because a 5 percent significance level implies a 5 percent probability of rejecting the null hypothesis and a 95 percent confidence interval. B is incorrect because the probability of a Type I error (mistakenly rejecting a true null) is the stated 5 percent significance level.

7. A is correct. In hypothesis testing, a test statistic is a quantity whose value is the basis for deciding whether to reject the null hypothesis.

8. A is correct. The definition of a Type I error is when a true null hypothesis is rejected.

9. B is correct. A Type II error occurs when a false null hypothesis is not rejected.

10. B is correct. The level of significance is used to establish the rejection points of the hypothesis test. A is correct because the significance level is not used to calculate the test statistic; rather, it is used to determine the critical value. C is incorrect because the significance level specifies the probability of making a Type I error.

11. B is correct. The power of a test is the probability of rejecting the null hypothesis when it is false. A is incorrect because the p-value is the smallest level of significance at which the null hypothesis can be rejected. C is incorrect because the level of significance is the probability of mistakenly rejecting the null hypothesis (Type I error).

12. B is correct. The power of a hypothesis test is the probability of correctly rejecting the null when it is false. Failing to reject the null when it is false is a Type II error. Thus, the power of a hypothesis test is the probability of not committing a Type II error.

13. A is correct. The critical value in a decision rule is the rejection point for the test. It is the point with which the test statistic is compared to determine whether to reject the null hypothesis, which is part of the fourth step in hypothesis testing. B is incorrect because the power of a test refers to the probability of rejecting the null hypothesis when it is false. C is incorrect because the value of the test statistic is specified in the 'Identify the appropriate test statistic and its probability distribution" step.

14. B is correct. The assumption that the variances are equal allows for the combining of both samples to obtain a pooled estimate of the common variance.

15. C is correct. A paired comparisons test is appropriate to test the mean differences of two samples believed to be dependent. A is incorrect because a z-test is used to determine whether two population means are different when the variances are known and the sample size is large. B is incorrect because a chi-square test is used for tests concerning the variance of a single normally distributed population.

16. A is correct. A chi-square test is used for tests concerning the variance of a single normally distributed population.

17. B is correct. An F-test is used to conduct tests concerning the difference between the variances of two normally distributed populations with random independent samples.

18. A is correct. When the samples consist of ranked values, parametric tests are not appropriate. In such cases, nonparametric tests are most appropriate.

19. A is correct. A nonparametric test is used when the data are given in ranks.

20. B is correct. There are only 12 (monthly) observations over the one year of the sample and thus the samples are small. Additionally, the funds' returns are non-normally distributed. Therefore, the samples do not meet the distributional assumptions for a parametric test. The Mann–Whitney U test (a nonparametric test) could be used to test the differences between population means.

9

Parametric and Non-Parametric Tests of Independence

by Pamela Peterson Drake, PhD, CFA.

Pamela Peterson Drake, PhD, CFA, is at James Madison University (USA).

LEARNING OUTCOMES

Mastery	The candidate should be able to:
☐	explain parametric and nonparametric tests of the hypothesis that the population correlation coefficient equals zero, and determine whether the hypothesis is rejected at a given level of significance
☐	explain tests of independence based on contingency table data

INTRODUCTION

1

In many contexts in investments, we want to assess the strength of the linear relationship between two variables—that is, we want to evaluate the **correlation** between them. A significance test of a correlation coefficient allows us to assess whether the relationship between two random variables is the result of chance. Lesson 1 covers a parametric and a non-parametric approach to testing the correlation between two variables. If we decide that the relationship does not result from chance, then we can use this information in modeling or forecasting using regression models or machine learning covered in later Learning Modules.

When faced with categorical or discrete data, however, we cannot use the methods discussed in the first lesson to test whether the classifications of such data are independent. If we want to test whether there is a relationship between categorical or discreet data, we can perform a test of independence using a nonparametric test statistic. The second lesson covers the use of contingency tables in implementing this non-parametric test.

LEARNING MODULE OVERVIEW

- There are three ways to formulate hypotheses. Let θ indicate the population parameters:

  1. Two-sided alternative: $H_0: \theta = \theta_0$ versus $Ha: \theta \neq \theta_0$
  2. One-sided alternative (right side): $H_0: \theta \leq \theta_0$ versus $Ha: \theta > \theta_0$

3. One-sided alternative (left side): H_0: $\theta \geq \theta_0$ versus Ha: $\theta < \theta_0$

where θ_0 is a hypothesized value of the population parameter and θ is the true value of the population parameter.

- A parametric test is a hypothesis test concerning a population parameter or a hypothesis test based on specific distributional assumptions. In contrast, a nonparametric test either is not concerned with a parameter or makes minimal assumptions about the population from which the sample comes.

- A nonparametric test is primarily used when data do not meet distributional assumptions, when there are outliers, when data are given in ranks, or when the hypothesis we are addressing does not concern a parameter.

- In tests concerning correlation, we use a t-statistic to test whether a population correlation coefficient is different from zero. If we have n observations for two variables, this test statistic has a t-distribution with $n - 2$ degrees of freedom.

- The Spearman rank correlation coefficient is calculated on the ranks of two variables within their respective samples.

- A chi-square distributed test statistic is used to test for independence of two categorical variables. This nonparametric test compares actual frequencies with those expected on the basis of independence. This test statistic has degrees of freedom of $(r - 1)(c - 2)$, where r is the number of categories for the first variable and c is the number of categories of the second variable.

---

2   TESTS CONCERNING CORRELATION

☐ | explain parametric and nonparametric tests of the hypothesis that the population correlation coefficient equals zero, and determine whether the hypothesis is rejected at a given level of significance

The most common hypotheses concerning correlation occur when comparing the population correlation coefficient with zero because we often ask whether a relationship exists, which implies a null of the correlation coefficient equal to zero (i.e., no relationship). Hypotheses concerning the population correlation coefficient may be two- or one-sided, as we have seen in other tests. Let ρ represent the population correlation coefficient. The possible hypotheses are as follows:

Two sided: H_0: $\rho = 0$ versus H_a: $\rho \neq 0$

One sided (right side): H_0: $\rho \leq 0$ versus H_a: $\rho > 0$

One sided (left side): H_0: $\rho \geq 0$ versus H_a: $\rho < 0$

We use the sample correlation to test these hypotheses on the population correlation.

Parametric Test of a Correlation

The parametric pairwise correlation coefficient is often referred to as **Pearson correlation**, the **bivariate correlation**, or simply the correlation. Our focus is on the testing of the correlation and not the actual calculation of this statistic, but it helps distinguish this correlation from the nonparametric correlation if we look at the formula for the sample correlation. Consider two variables, X and Y. The sample correlation, r_{XY}, is as follows:

$$r_{XY} = \frac{s_{XY}}{s_X s_Y}, \tag{1}$$

where s_{XY} is the sample covariance between the X and Y variables, s_X is the standard deviation of the X variable, and s_Y is the standard deviation of the Y variable. We often drop the subscript to represent the correlation as simply r.

Therefore, you can see from this formula that each observation is compared with its respective variable mean and that, because of the covariance, it matters how much each observation differs from its respective variable mean. Note that the covariance drives the sign of the correlation.

If the two variables are normally distributed, we can test to determine whether the null hypothesis (H_0: $\rho = 0$) should be rejected using the sample correlation, r. The formula for the t-test is as follows:

$$t = \frac{r\sqrt{n-2}}{\sqrt{1-r^2}}. \tag{2}$$

This test statistic is t-distributed with $n - 2$ degrees of freedom. One practical observation concerning Equation 2 is that the magnitude of r needed to reject the null hypothesis decreases as sample size n increases, for two reasons. First, as n increases, the number of degrees of freedom increases and the absolute value of the critical value of the t-statistic decreases. Second, the absolute value of the numerator increases with larger n, resulting in a larger magnitude of the calculated t-statistic. For example, with sample size $n = 12$, $r = 0.35$ results in a t-statistic of 1.182, which is not different from zero at the 0.05 level ($t_{\alpha/2} = \pm 2.228$). With a sample size of $n = 32$, the same sample correlation, $r = 0.35$, yields a t-statistic of 2.046, which is just significant at the 0.05 level ($t_{\alpha/2} = \pm 2.042$).

Another way to make this point is that when sampling from the same population, a false null hypothesis is more likely to be rejected (i.e., the power of the test increases) as we increase the sample size, all else equal, because a higher number of observations increases the numerator of the test statistic. We show this in Exhibit 1 for three different sample correlation coefficients, with the corresponding calculated t-statistics and significance at the 5 percent level for a two-sided alternative hypothesis. As the sample size increases, significance is more likely to be indicated, but the rate of achieving this significance depends on the sample correlation coefficient; the higher the sample correlation, the faster significance is achieved when increasing the sample size. As the sample sizes increase as ever-larger datasets are examined, the null hypothesis is almost always rejected and other tools of data analysis must be applied.

Exhibit 1: Calculated Test Statistics for Different Sample Sizes and Sample Correlations with a 5 Percent Level of Significance

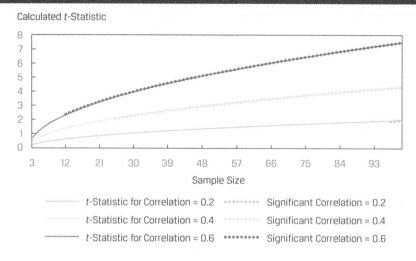

Calculated *t*-Statistic

———— *t*-Statistic for Correlation = 0.2   ·········· Significant Correlation = 0.2

———— *t*-Statistic for Correlation = 0.4   ·········· Significant Correlation = 0.4

———— *t*-Statistic for Correlation = 0.6   •••••••• Significant Correlation = 0.6

EXAMPLE 1

Examining the Relationship between Returns on Investment One and Investment Two

An analyst is examining the annual returns for Investment One and Investment Two over 33 years, as displayed in Exhibit 2.

Exhibit 2: Returns for Investments One and Two over 33 Years

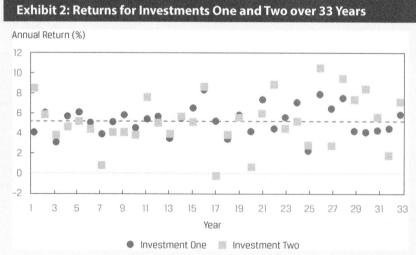

Annual Return (%)

● Investment One   ■ Investment Two

Although this time series plot provides some useful information, the analyst is most interested in quantifying how the returns of these two series are related, so she calculates the correlation coefficient, equal to 0.43051, between these series.

1. Is there a significant positive correlation between these two return series if she uses a 1 percent level of significance?

Solution:

Step 1	State the hypotheses.	$H_0: \rho \leq 0$ versus $H_a: \rho > 0$
Step 2	Identify the appropriate test statistic.	$t = \dfrac{r\sqrt{n-2}}{\sqrt{1-r^2}}$
Step 3	Specify the level of significance.	1%
Step 4	State the decision rule.	With 33 − 2 = 31 degrees of freedom and a one-sided test with a 1% level of significance, the critical value is 2.45282. We reject the null hypothesis if the calculated t-statistic is greater than 2.45282.
Step 5	Calculate the test statistic.	$t = \dfrac{0.43051\sqrt{33-2}}{\sqrt{1-0.18534}}$ $= 2.65568$
Step 6	Make a decision.	Reject the null hypothesis because the calculated t-statistic is greater than 2.45282. Evidence is sufficient to reject the H_0 in favor of H_a, that the correlation between the annual returns of these two investments is positive.

EXAMPLE 2

Correlation with the S&P 500 Returns

1. Exhibit 3 shows the sample correlations between the monthly returns for four different mutual funds and the S&P 500. The correlations are based on 36 monthly observations. The funds are as follows:

Exhibit 3: Sample Correlations between Monthly Returns and the S&P 500

Fund 1	Large-cap fund
Fund 2	Mid-cap fund
Fund 3	Large-cap value fund
Fund 4	Emerging market fund
S&P 500	US domestic stock index

	Fund 1	Fund 2	Fund 3	Fund 4	S&P 500
Fund 1	1				
Fund 2	0.9231	1			
Fund 3	0.4771	0.4156	1		

Fund 4	0.7111	0.7238	0.3102	1	
S&P 500	0.8277	0.8223	0.5791	0.7515	1

Test the null hypothesis that each of these correlations, individually, is equal to zero against the alternative hypothesis that it is not equal to zero. Use a 5 percent significance level and critical t-values of ±2.032.

Solution:

The hypotheses are H_0: $\rho = 0$ and H_a: $\rho \neq 0$. The calculated test statistics are based on the formula

$$t = \frac{r\sqrt{n-2}}{\sqrt{1-r^2}}.$$

For example, the calculated t-statistic for the correlation of Fund 3 and Fund 4 is as follows

$$t = \frac{r\sqrt{n-2}}{\sqrt{1-r^2}} = \frac{0.3102\sqrt{36-2}}{\sqrt{1-0.3102^2}} = 1.903.$$

Repeating this calculation for the entire matrix of correlations gives the following:

Calculated t-Statistics for Correlations

	Fund 1	Fund 2	Fund 3	Fund 4	S&P 500
Fund 1					
Fund 2	13.997				
Fund 3	3.165	2.664			
Fund 4	5.897	6.116	1.903		
S&P 500	8.600	8.426	4.142	6.642	

With critical values of ±2.032, with the exception of the correlation between Fund 3 and Fund 4 returns, we reject the null hypothesis for these correlations. In other words, evidence is sufficient to indicate that the correlations are different from zero, with the exception of the correlation of returns between Fund 3 and Fund 4.

We could use software to determine the critical values:

Excel

```
[T.INV(0.025,34) and T.INV(0.975,34)]
```

R

```
[qt(c(.025,.975),34)]
```

Python

```
[from scipy.stats import t and t.ppf(.025,34)
and t.ppf(.975,34)]
```

We also could use software to determine the p-value for the calculated test statistic to enable a comparison with the level of significance. For example, for $t = 2.664$, the p-value is 0.01172:

Excel

```
[(1-T.DIST(2.664,34,TRUE))*2]
```

R

```
[(1-pt(2.664,34))*2]
```

Python

```
[from scipy.stats import t

(1-t.cdf(2.664,34))*2]
```

Non-Parametric Test of Correlation: The Spearman Rank Correlation Coefficient

When we believe that the population under consideration meaningfully departs from normality, we can use a test based on the **Spearman rank correlation coefficient**, r_S. The Spearman rank correlation coefficient is essentially equivalent to the Pearson correlation coefficient as defined earlier, but it is calculated on the *ranks* of the two variables (e.g., X and Y) within their respective samples. The calculation of r_S requires the following steps:

1. Rank the observations on X from largest to smallest. Assign the number 1 to the observation with the largest value, the number 2 to the observation with second largest value, and so on. In case of ties, assign to each tied observation the average of the ranks that they jointly occupy. For example, if the third and fourth largest values are tied, we assign both observations the rank of 3.5 (the average of 3 and 4). Perform the same procedure for the observations on Y.

2. Calculate the difference, d_i, between the ranks for each pair of observations on X and Y, and then calculate d_i^2 (the squared difference in ranks).

3. With n as the sample size, the Spearman rank correlation is given as follows:

$$r_s = 1 - \frac{6\sum_{i=1}^{n} d_i^2}{n(n^2 - 1)}. \tag{3}$$

Suppose an analyst is examining the relationship between returns for two investment funds, A and B, of similar risk over 35 years. She is concerned that the assumptions for the parametric correlation may not be met, so she decides to test Spearman rank correlations. Her hypotheses are H_0: $r_S = 0$ and H_a: $r_S \neq 0$. She gathers the returns, ranks the returns for each fund, and calculates the difference in ranks and the squared differences. A partial table is provided in Exhibit 4.

Exhibit 4: Differences and Squared Differences in Ranks for Fund A and Fund B over 35 Years						
Year	Fund A	Fund B	Rank of A	Rank of B	d	d^2
1	2.453	1.382	27	31	−4	16
2	3.017	3.110	24	24	0	0
3	4.495	6.587	19	7	12	144
4	3.627	3.300	23	23	0	0

Year	Fund A	Fund B	Rank of A	Rank of B	d	d^2
⋮						
30	2.269	0.025	28	35	−7	49
31	6.354	4.428	10	19	−9	81
32	6.793	4.165	8	20	−12	144
33	7.300	7.623	5	5	0	0
34	6.266	4.527	11	18	−7	49
35	1.257	4.704	34	16	18	324
					Sum =	2,202

The Spearman rank correlation is as follows:

$$r_s = 1 - \frac{6\sum_{i=1}^{n} d_i^2}{n(n^2 - 1)} = 1 - \frac{6(2,202)}{35(1,225 - 1)} = 0.6916.$$

The test of hypothesis for the Spearman rank correlation depends on whether the sample is small or large ($n > 30$). For small samples, the researcher requires a specialized table of critical values, but for large samples, we can conduct a t-test using the test statistic in Equation 2, which is t-distributed with $n - 2$ degrees of freedom.

In this example, for a two-tailed test with a 5 percent significance level, the critical values for $n - 2 = 35 - 2 = 33$ degrees of freedom are ±2.0345. For the sample information in Exhibit 4, the calculated test statistic is as follows:

$$t = \frac{0.6916\sqrt{33}}{\sqrt{1 - (0.6916^2)}} = 5.5005$$

Accordingly, we reject the null hypothesis ($H_0: r_S = 0$), concluding that evidence is sufficient to indicate that the correlation between the returns of Fund A and Fund B is different from zero.

EXAMPLE 3

Testing the Exchange Rate Correlation

An analyst gathers exchange rate data for five currencies relative to the US dollar. Upon inspection of the distribution of these exchange rates, she observes a departure from normality, especially with negative skewness for four of the series and positive skewness for the fifth. Therefore, she decides to examine the relationships among these currencies using Spearman rank correlations. She calculates these correlations between the currencies over 180 days, which are shown in the correlogram in Exhibit 5. In this correlogram, the lower triangle reports the pairwise correlations and the upper triangle provides a visualization of the magnitude of the correlations, with larger circles indicating the larger absolute value of the correlations and darker circles indicating correlations that are negative.

Exhibit 5: Spearman Rank Correlations between Exchanges Rates Relative to the US Dollar

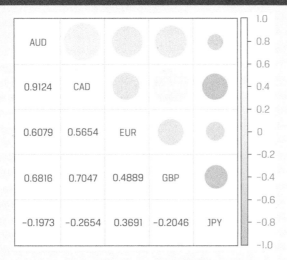

1. For any of these pairwise Spearman rank correlations, can we reject the null hypothesis of no correlation (H_0: $r_S = 0$ and H_a: $r_S \neq 0$) at the 5 percent level of significance?

   Solution:

   The critical t-values for 2.5 percent in each tail of the distribution are ±1.97338.

   There are five exchange rates, so there are 5C2 = {5! / [2!(5 -2)!]}, or 10, unique correlation pairs. Therefore, we need to calculate 10 t-statistics. For example, the correlation between EUR/USD and AUD/USD is 0.6079. The calculated t-statistic is

   $$\frac{0.6079\sqrt{180 - 2}}{\sqrt{1 - 0.6079^2}} = \frac{8.11040}{0.79401} = 10.2144.$$

   Repeating this t-statistic calculation for each pair of exchange rates yields the test statistics shown in Exhibit 6.

   Exhibit 6: Calculated Test Statistics for Test of Spearman Rank Correlations

	AUD/USD	CAD/USD	EUR/USD	GBP/USD
CAD/USD	29.7409			
EUR/USD	10.2144	9.1455		
GBP/USD	12.4277	13.2513	7.4773	
JPY/USD	−2.6851	−3.6726	5.2985	−2.7887

   The analyst should reject all 10 null hypotheses, because the calculated t-statistics for all exchange rate pairs fall outside the bounds of the two critical values. She should conclude that all the exchange rate pair correlations are different from zero at the 5 percent level.

QUESTION SET

You are interested in whether excess risk-adjusted return (alpha) is correlated with mutual fund expense ratios for US large-cap growth funds. The following table presents the sample.

Mutual Fund	Alpha	Expense Ratio
1	−0.52	1.34
2	−0.13	0.40
3	−0.50	1.90
4	−1.01	1.50
5	−0.26	1.35
6	−0.89	0.50
7	−0.42	1.00
8	−0.23	1.50
9	−0.60	1.45

1. Formulate null and alternative hypotheses consistent with the verbal description of the research goal.

   Solution:

   We have a "not equal to" alternative hypothesis:

   $H_0: \rho = 0$ versus $H_a: \rho \neq 0$

2. Identify and justify the test statistic for conducting a test of the hypotheses in Part A.

   Solution:

   Mutual fund expense ratios are bounded from above and below; in practice, there is at least a lower bound on alpha (as any return cannot be less than −100 percent), and expense ratios cannot be negative. These variables may not be normally distributed, and the assumptions of a parametric test are not likely to be fulfilled. Thus, a nonparametric test appears to be appropriate.

   We would use the nonparametric Spearman rank correlation coefficient to conduct the test:

   $$r_s = 1 - \frac{6 \sum_{i=1}^{n} d_i^2}{n(n^2 - 1)}$$

   with the t-distributed test statistic of

   $$t = \frac{r\sqrt{n-2}}{\sqrt{1-r^2}}.$$

   The calculation of the Spearman rank correlation coefficient is given in the following table.

Mutual Fund	Alpha	Expense Ratio	Rank by Alpha	Rank by Expense Ratio	Difference in Rank	Difference Squared
1	−0.52	1.34	6	6	0	0
2	−0.13	0.40	1	9	−8	64
3	−0.50	1.90	5	1	4	16
4	−1.01	1.50	9	2.5	6.5	42.25
5	−0.26	1.35	3	5	−2	4
6	−0.89	0.50	8	8	0	0
7	−0.42	1.00	4	7	−3	9
8	−0.23	1.50	2	2.5	−0.5	0.25
9	−0.60	1.45	7	4	3	9
						144.5

$$r_s = 1 - \frac{6(144.5)}{9(80)} = -0.20416.$$

3. Determine whether to reject the null hypothesis at the 0.05 level of significance if the critical values are ±2.306.

The calculated test statistic, using the t-distributed test statistic

$$t = \frac{r\sqrt{n-2}}{\sqrt{1-r^2}} \text{ is } t = \frac{-0.2416\sqrt{7}}{\sqrt{1-0.041681}} = \frac{-0.540156}{0.978937} = -0.55177.$$

On the basis of this value falling within the range of ±2.306, we fail to reject the null hypothesis that the Spearman rank correlation coefficient is zero.

TESTS OF INDEPENDENCE USING CONTINGENCY TABLE DATA

3

☐ | explain tests of independence based on contingency table data

When faced with categorical or discrete data, we cannot use the methods that we have discussed up to this point to test whether the classifications of such data are independent. Suppose we observe the following **frequency table** of 1,594 exchange-traded funds (ETFs) based on two classifications: size (i.e., market capitalization) and investment type (value, growth, or blend), as shown in Exhibit 7. The classification of the investment type is discrete, so we cannot use correlation to assess the relationship between size and investment type.

Exhibit 7: Size and Investment Type Classifications of 1,594 ETFs				
	Size Based on Market Capitalization			
Investment Type	Small	Medium	Large	Total
Value	50	110	343	503
Growth	42	122	202	366
Blend	56	149	520	725
Total	148	381	1,065	1,594

Exhibit 7 is called a **contingency table** or a **two-way table** (because there are two classifications, or classes—size and investment type).

If we want to test whether a relationship exists between the size and investment type, we can perform a test of independence using a nonparametric test statistic that is chi-square distributed:

$$\chi^2 = \sum_{i=1}^{m} \frac{(O_{ij} - E_{ij})^2}{E_{ij}}, \tag{4}$$

where:

m = the number of cells in the table, which is the number of groups in the first class multiplied by the number of groups in the second class;

O_{ij} = the number of observations in each cell of row i and column j (i.e., observed frequency); and

E_{ij} = the expected number of observations in each cell of row i and column j, assuming independence (i.e., expected frequency).

This test statistic has $(r - 1)(c - 1)$ degrees of freedom, where r is the number of rows and c is the number of columns.

In Exhibit 7, size class has three groups (small, medium, and large) and investment type class has three groups (value, growth, and blend), so m is 9 (= 3 × 3). The number of ETFs in each cell (O_{ij}), the observed frequency, is given, so to calculate the chi-square test statistic, we need to estimate E_{ij}, the expected frequency, which is the number of ETFs we would expect to be in each cell if size and investment type are completely independent. The expected number of ETFs (E_{ij}) is calculated using the following:

$$E_{ij} = \frac{(\text{Total row } i) \times (\text{Total column } j)}{\text{Overall total}}. \tag{5}$$

Consider one combination of size and investment type, small-cap value:

$$E_{ij} = \frac{503 \times 148}{1,594} = 46.703.$$

We repeat this calculation for each combination of size and investment type (i.e., m = 9 pairs) to arrive at the expected frequencies, shown in Panel A of Exhibit 8.

Next, we calculate

$$\frac{(O_{ij} - E_{ij})^2}{E_{ij}},$$

the squared difference between observed and expected frequencies scaled by expected frequency, for each cell as shown in Panel B of Exhibit 8. Finally, by summing the values of

$$\frac{(O_{ij} - E_{ij})^2}{E_{ij}}$$

for each of the m cells, we calculate the chi-square statistic as 32.08025.

Exhibit 8: Inputs to Chi-Square Test Statistic Calculation for 1,594 ETFs Assuming Independence of Size and Investment Type

A. Expected Frequency of ETFs by Size and Investment Type

Investment Type	Size Based on Market Capitalization		
	Small	Medium	Large
Value	46.703	120.228	336.070
Growth	33.982	87.482	244.536
Blend	67.315	173.290	484.395
Total	148.000	381.000	1,065.000

B. Scaled Squared Deviation for Each Combination of Size and Investment Type

Investment Type	Size Based on Market Capitalization		
	Small	Medium	Large
Value	0.233	0.870	0.143
Growth	1.892	13.620	7.399
Blend	1.902	3.405	2.617

In our ETF example, we test the null hypothesis of independence between the two classes (i.e., no relationship between size and investment type) versus the alternative hypothesis of dependence (i.e., a relationship between size and investment type) using a 5 percent level of significance, as shown in Exhibit 9. If the observed values are equal to the expected values, the calculated test statistic would be zero. If, however, the observed and expected values are different, these differences are squared, so the calculated chi-square statistic will be positive. Therefore, for the test of independence using a contingency table, there is only one rejection region, on the right side.

Exhibit 9: Test of Independence of Size and Investment Type for 1,594 ETFs

Step 1	State the hypotheses.	H_0: ETF size and investment type are not related, so these classifications are independent; H_a: ETF size and investment type are related, so these classifications are not independent.
Step 2	Identify the appropriate test statistic.	$\chi^2 = \sum_{i=1}^{m} \frac{(O_{ij} - E_{ij})^2}{E_{ij}}$
Step 3	Specify the level of significance.	5%

Step 4	State the decision rule.	With $(3 - 1) \times (3 - 1) = 4$ degrees of freedom and a one-sided test with a 5% level of significance, the critical value is 9.4877.
		We reject the null hypothesis if the calculated $\div^2$ statistic is greater than 9.4877.
		Excel `CHISQ.INV(0.95,4)`
		R `qchisq(.95,4)`
		Python `from scipy.stats import chi2` `chi2.ppf(.95,4)`
Step 5	Calculate the test statistic.	$\chi^2 = 32.08025$
Step 6	Make a decision.	Reject the null hypothesis of independence because the calculated $\div^2$ test statistic is greater than 9.4877. Evidence is sufficient to conclude that ETF size and investment type are related (i.e., not independent).

We can visualize the contingency table in a graphic referred to as a mosaic. In a mosaic, a grid reflects the comparison between the observed and expected frequencies. Consider Exhibit 10, which represents the ETF contingency table.

Exhibit 10: Mosaic of the ETF Contingency Table

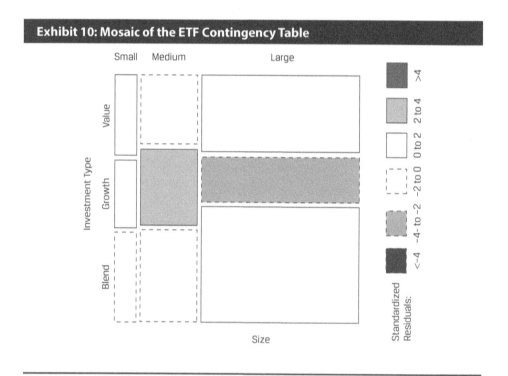

The width of the rectangles in Exhibit 10 reflect the proportion of ETFs that are small, medium, and large, whereas the height reflects the proportion that are value, growth, and blend. The darker shading indicates whether the number of observations is more than expected under the null hypothesis of independence, whereas the lighter shading indicates that the number of observations is less than expected, with "more than" and "less than" determined by reference to the standardized residual boxes. The standardized residual, also referred to as a Pearson residual, is as follows:

$$\text{Standardized residual} = \frac{O_{ij} - E_{ij}}{\sqrt{E_{ij}}}.$$

(6)

The interpretation for this ETF example is that there are more medium-size growth ETFs (standardized residual of 3.69) and fewer large-size growth ETFs (standardized residual of –2.72) than would be expected if size and investment type were independent.

EXAMPLE 4

Using Contingency Tables to Test for Independence

Consider the contingency table in Exhibit 11, which classifies 500 randomly selected companies on the basis of two environmental, social, and governance (ESG) rating dimensions: environmental rating and governance rating.

Exhibit 11: Classification of 500 Randomly Selected Companies Based on Environmental and Governance Ratings

| | Governance Rating | | | |
Environmental Rating	Progressive	Average	Poor	Total
Progressive	35	40	5	80
Average	80	130	50	260
Poor	40	60	60	160
Total	155	230	115	500

1. What are the expected frequencies for these two ESG rating dimensions if these categories are independent?

Solution:

The expected frequencies based on independence of the governance rating and the environmental rating are shown in Panel A of Exhibit 12. For example, using Equation 5, the expected frequency for the combination of progressive governance and progressive environmental ratings is

$$E_{ij} = \frac{155 \times 80}{500} = 24.80.$$

The scaled squared deviations for each combination of environmental and governance rating are shown in Panel B of Exhibit 12. For example, using Equation 4, the scaled squared deviation for the combination of progressive governance and progressive environmental ratings is as follows:

$$= \frac{(35 - 24.8)^2}{24.8} = 4.195.$$

> ### Exhibit 12: Inputs to Chi-Square Test Statistic Calculation Assuming Independence of Environmental and Governance Ratings
>
> **A. Expected Frequencies of Environmental and Governance Ratings Assuming Independence**
>
> | | Governance Rating | | |
> |---|---|---|---|
> | **Environmental Rating** | **Progressive** | **Average** | **Poor** |
> | Progressive | 24.8 | 36.8 | 18.4 |
> | Average | 80.6 | 119.6 | 59.8 |
> | Poor | 49.6 | 73.6 | 36.8 |
>
> **B. Scaled Squared Deviation for Each Combination of Environmental and Governance Ratings**
>
> | | Governance Rating | | |
> |---|---|---|---|
> | **Environmental Rating** | **Progressive** | **Average** | **Poor** |
> | Progressive | 4.195 | 0.278 | 9.759 |
> | Average | 0.004 | 0.904 | 1.606 |
> | Poor | 1.858 | 2.513 | 14.626 |

2. Using a 5 percent level of significance, determine whether these two ESG rating dimensions are independent of one another.

   Solution:

Step 1	State the hypotheses.	H_0: Governance and environmental ratings are not related, so these ratings are independent; H_a: Governance and environmental ratings are related, so these ratings are not independent.
Step 2	Identify the appropriate test statistic.	$\chi^2 = \sum_{i=1}^{m} \frac{(O_{ij} - E_{ij})^2}{E_{ij}}$
Step 3	Specify the level of significance.	5%
Step 4	State the decision rule.	With $(3 - 1) \times (3 - 1) = 4$ degrees of freedom and a one-sided test with a 5% level of significance, the critical value is 9.487729.

We reject the null hypothesis if the calculated $\div^2$ statistic is greater than 9.487729.

Excel
```
CHISQ.INV(0.95,4)
```
R
```
qchisq(.95,4)
```
Python
```
from scipy.stats import chi2
chi2.ppf(.95,4)
```

Step 5	Calculate the test statistic.	$\chi^2 = 35.74415$
		To calculate the test statistic, we first calculate the squared difference between observed and expected frequencies scaled by expected frequency for each cell, as shown in Panel B of Exhibit 12. Then, summing the values in each of the m cells (see Equation 4), we calculate the chi-square statistic as 35.74415.
Step 6	Make a decision.	Reject the null hypothesis because the calculated $\div^2$ test statistic is greater than 9.487729. Evidence is sufficient to indicate that the environmental and governance ratings are related, so they are not independent.

QUESTION SET

An analyst group follows 250 firms and classifies them in two dimensions. First, they use dividend payment history and earnings forecasts to classify firms into one of three groups, with 1 indicating the dividend stars and 3 the dividend laggards. Second, they classify firms on the basis of financial leverage, using debt ratios, debt features, and corporate governance to classify the firms into three groups, with 1 indicating the least risky firms based on financial leverage and 3 indicating the riskiest. The classification of the 250 firms is as follows:

Financial Leverage Group	Dividend Group		
	1	2	3
1	40	40	40
2	30	10	20
3	10	50	10

Using the classification of the 250 firms, answer the following questions:

1. What are the null and alternative hypotheses to test whether the dividend and financial leverage groups are independent of one another?

Solution:

The hypotheses are as follows:

H_0: Dividend and financial leverage ratings are not related, so these groupings are independent.

H_a: Dividend and financial leverage ratings are related, so these groupings are not independent.

2. What is the appropriate test statistic to use in this type of test?

Solution:

The appropriate test statistic is

$$\chi^2 = \sum_{i=1}^{m} \frac{(O_{ij} - E_{ij})^2}{E_{ij}},$$

where O_{ij} represents the observed frequency for the i and j group and E_{ij} represents the expected frequency for the i and j group if the groupings are independent.

The expected frequencies based on independence are as follows:

Financial Leverage Group	Dividend Group			Sum
	1	2	3	
1	38.4	48	33.6	120
2	19.2	24	16.8	60
3	22.4	28	19.6	70
Sum	80	100	70	250

The scaled squared deviations for each combination of financial leverage and dividend grouping are:

Financial Leverage Group	Dividend Group		
	1	2	3
1	0.06667	1.33333	1.21905
2	6.07500	8.16667	0.60952
3	6.86429	17.28571	4.70204

3. If the critical value for the 0.05 level of significance is 9.4877, what is your conclusion?

Solution:

The sum of these scaled squared deviations is the calculated chi-square statistic of 46.3223. Because this calculated value exceeds the critical value of 9.4877, we reject the null hypothesis that these groupings are independent.

PRACTICE PROBLEMS

1. Jill Batten is analyzing how the returns on the stock of Stellar Energy Corp. are related with the previous month's percentage change in the US Consumer Price Index for Energy (CPIENG). Based on 248 observations, she has computed the sample correlation between the Stellar and CPIENG variables to be –0.1452. She also wants to determine whether the sample correlation is significantly different from zero. The critical value for the test statistic at the 0.05 level of significance is approximately 1.96. Batten should conclude that the statistical relationship between Stellar and CPIENG is:

   A. significant, because the calculated test statistic is outside the bounds of the critical values for the test statistic.

   B. significant, because the calculated test statistic has a lower absolute value than the critical value for the test statistic.

   C. insignificant, because the calculated test statistic is outside the bounds of the critical values for the test statistic.

2. Which of the following statements is correct regarding the chi-square test of independence?

   A. The test has a one-sided rejection region.

   B. The null hypothesis is that the two groups are dependent.

   C. If there are two categories, each with three levels or groups, there are six degrees of freedom.

SOLUTIONS

1. A is correct. The calculated test statistic is

$$t = \frac{r\sqrt{n-2}}{\sqrt{1-r^2}}$$
$$= \frac{-0.1452\sqrt{248-2}}{\sqrt{1-(-0.1452)^2}} = -2.30177.$$

Because the value of $t = -2.30177$ is outside the bounds of ± 1.96, we reject the null hypothesis of no correlation and conclude that evidence is sufficient to indicate that the correlation is different from zero.

2. A is correct. The test statistic includes squared differences between the observed and expected values, so the test involves only one side, the right side. B is incorrect because the null hypothesis is that the groups are independent, and C is incorrect because with three levels of groups for the two categorical variables, there are four degrees of freedom.

Simple Linear Regression

by Pamela Peterson Drake, PhD, CFA.

Pamela Peterson Drake, PhD, CFA, is at James Madison University (USA).

LEARNING OUTCOMES

Mastery	The candidate should be able to:
☐	describe a simple linear regression model, how the least squares criterion is used to estimate regression coefficients, and the interpretation of these coefficients
☐	explain the assumptions underlying the simple linear regression model, and describe how residuals and residual plots indicate if these assumptions may have been violated
☐	calculate and interpret measures of fit and formulate and evaluate tests of fit and of regression coefficients in a simple linear regression
☐	describe the use of analysis of variance (ANOVA) in regression analysis, interpret ANOVA results, and calculate and interpret the standard error of estimate in a simple linear regression
☐	calculate and interpret the predicted value for the dependent variable, and a prediction interval for it, given an estimated linear regression model and a value for the independent variable
☐	describe different functional forms of simple linear regressions

INTRODUCTION

1

☐	describe a simple linear regression model, how the least squares criterion is used to estimate regression coefficients, and the interpretation of these coefficients

Financial analysts often need to examine whether a variable is useful for explaining another variable. For example, the analyst may want to know whether earnings or cash flow growth help explain a company's market value. **Regression analysis** is a tool for examining this type of issue.

Linear regression allows us to test hypotheses about the relationship between two variables by quantifying the strength of the relationship between the two variables, and to use one variable to make predictions about the other variable. Our focus is on linear regression with a single independent variable—that is, simple linear regression.

LEARNING MODULE OVERVIEW

- Simple linear regression is a mathematical process for determining how the variation in one variable can explain the variation in another variable.

- The variable we wish to explain is called the dependent variable, and the variable that we use to explain the dependent variable is called the independent variable.

- Simple linear regression uses the ordinary least squares approach to calculate the slope and intercept parameters that characterize a linear relationship between the two variables.

- Simple linear regression requires that we make four assumptions: linearity, homoskedasticity, independence, and normality.

- Linearity requires that the regression residuals be random and that the independent variable not be random. Homoskedasticity, which refers to variance being constant across observations, cannot be assumed when we see residuals clustering in multiple groups because the clustering indicates multiple regimes with different variances within our time period.

- Independence means that the X-Y pairs are uncorrelated; a pattern in a plot of the residuals (e.g., seasonality) suggests that there is autocorrelation across observations and that we cannot assume independence. Normality means that residuals must be normally distributed and does not require that the data itself be normally distributed. Non-normality is of particular concern for small sample sizes, but for large sample sizes, the central limit theorem tells us that we may be able to relax the normality requirement.

- The total variation in the dependent variable, called the sum of squares total (SST), can be decomposed into two parts: the explained variation, called the sum of squares regression (SSR), and the unexplained variation, called the sum of squares error (SSE).

- There are several ways to measure a regression model's goodness of fit. These include the coefficient of determination, the F-statistic for the test of fit, and the standard error of the regression.

- Hypothesis testing can be used to determine, at a specified confidence level, whether the slope or intercept differs from zero or another specified value, or whether the slope is positive or negative. We can use indicator variables to determine whether our regression parameters differ between data points that either have or do not have a particular characteristic (e.g., monthly price data in cases in which only some months have earnings announcements).

- An analysis of variance (ANOVA) table presents the sums of squares, degrees of freedom, mean squares, and F-statistic for a regression model.

- The standard error of the estimate is a measure of the distance between the observed values of the dependent variable and those predicted from the estimated regression. The smaller this value, the better the fit of the model.

- The standard error of the forecast is used to provide an interval estimate around the estimated regression line. It is necessary because the regression line does not describe the relationship between the dependent and independent variables perfectly.

- The simple linear regression model on non-linear data can be adjusted by using different functional forms that transform the dependent or independent variables.

- Three common functional forms for transforming data include the log-lin model, the lin-log model, and the log-log model.

- The key to fitting the appropriate functional form of a simple linear regression is examining the goodness-of-fit measures—the coefficient of determination (R^2), the F-statistic, and the standard error of the estimate (s_e)—as well as examining whether there are patterns in the residuals.

ESTIMATION OF THE SIMPLE LINEAR REGRESSION MODEL

2

☐ describe a simple linear regression model, how the least squares criterion is used to estimate regression coefficients, and the interpretation of these coefficients

Introduction to Linear Regression

Suppose an analyst is examining the return on assets (ROA) for an industry and observes the ROA for the six companies shown in Exhibit 1. The average of these ROAs is 12.5 percent, but the range is from 4 percent to 20 percent.

Exhibit 1: Return on Assets of Selected Companies	
Company	**ROA (%)**
A	6.0
B	4.0
C	15.0
D	20.0
E	10.0
F	20.0

In trying to understand why the ROAs differ among these companies, we could look at why the ROA of Company A differs from that of Company B, why the ROA of Company A differs from that of Company D, why the ROA of Company F differs from that of Company C, and so on, comparing each pair of ROAs. We can simplify this exercise by instead comparing each company's ROA to the mean ROA of 12.5 percent. To do this, we look at the sum of the squared deviations of the observations from the mean to capture variations in ROA from their mean. Let Y represent the variable that we would like to explain, which in this case is the ROA. Let Y_i represent an observation of a company's ROA, and let $\overline{Y}$ represent the mean ROA for the sample of size n. We can describe the variation of the ROAs as follows:

$$\text{Variation of } Y = \sum_{i=1}^{n} (Y_i - \overline{Y})^2. \tag{1}$$

Our goal is to understand what drives these ROAs or, in other words, what explains the variation of Y. The variation of Y is often referred to as the **sum of squares total (SST)**, or the total sum of squares.

We now ask whether it is possible to explain the variation of the ROA using another variable that also varies among the companies; note that if this other variable is constant or random, it would not explain the ROA differences. Suppose the analyst believes that the capital expenditures in the previous period, scaled by the prior period's beginning property, plant, and equipment, are a driver for the ROA variable. Let us represent this scaled capital expenditures variable as CAPEX, as we show in Exhibit 2.

Exhibit 2: Return on Assets and Scaled Capital Expenditures		
Company	**ROA (%)**	**CAPEX (%)**
A	6.0	0.7
B	4.0	0.4
C	15.0	5.0
D	20.0	10.0
E	10.0	8.0
F	20.0	12.5
Arithmetic mean	12.5	6.1

Let X represent the explanatory variable, in this case, CAPEX. Then X_i will represent an observation of our explanatory variable, and $\overline{X}$ will represent the mean value for the explanatory variable, that is, the mean of all of our CAPEX values. The variation of X is calculated as follows:

$$\text{Variation of } X = \sum_{i=1}^{n} (X_i - \overline{X})^2. \tag{2}$$

We can see the relation between ROA and CAPEX in the **scatter plot** (or scattergram) in Exhibit 3, which represents the two variables in two dimensions. Typically, we present the variable whose variation we want to explain along the vertical axis and the variable whose variation we want to use to explain that variation along the horizontal axis. Each point in this scatter plot represents a paired observation that consists of CAPEX and ROA. From a casual visual inspection, a positive relation is apparent between ROA and CAPEX: Companies with higher CAPEX tend to have a higher ROA.

Exhibit 3: Scatter Plot of ROA and CAPEX

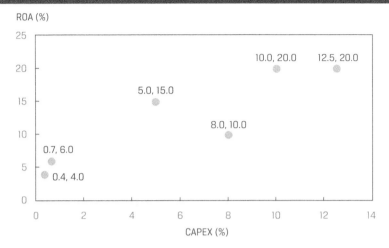

In the ROA example, we use the capital expenditures to explain the ROAs. We refer to the variable whose variation is being explained as the **dependent variable**, or the explained variable; it is typically denoted by Y. We refer to the variable whose variation is being used to explain the variation of the dependent variable as the **independent variable**, or the explanatory variable; it is typically denoted by X. Therefore, in our example, the ROA is the dependent variable (Y) and CAPEX is the independent variable (X).

A common method used to relate the dependent and independent variables is through the estimation of a linear relationship, which implies describing the relation between the two variables as represented by a straight line. If we have only one independent variable, we refer to the method as **simple linear regression (SLR)**, or linear regression; if we have more than one independent variable, we refer to the method as multiple regression.

Linear regression allows us to test hypotheses about the relationship between two variables by quantifying the strength of the relationship between the two variables and to use one variable to make predictions about the other variable.

IDENTIFYING THE DEPENDENT AND INDEPENDENT VARIABLES IN A REGRESSION

An analyst is researching the relationship between corporate earnings growth and stock returns. Specifically, she is interested in whether earnings revisions are correlated with stock price returns in the same period. She collects five years of monthly data on earnings per share (EPS) revisions and stock price returns for a sample of 100 companies.

1. What are the dependent and independent variables in her model?

Solution:

The dependent variable is monthly stock price returns, and the independent variable is EPS revisions. In the analyst's model, the variation in monthly stock price returns is being explained by the variation in EPS revisions.

Estimating the Parameters of a Simple Linear Regression

The Basics of Simple Linear Regression

Regression analysis begins with the dependent variable, the variable whose variation you are seeking to explain. The independent variable is the variable whose variation you are using to explain changes in the dependent variable. For example, you might try to explain small-stock returns (the dependent variable) using returns to the S&P 500 Index (the independent variable). Or you might try to explain a country's inflation rate (the dependent variable) as a function of growth in its money supply (the independent variable).

As the name implies, linear regression assumes a linear relationship between the dependent and the independent variables. The goal is to fit a line to the observations on Y and X to minimize the squared deviations from the line; this is the least squares criterion—hence, the name least squares regression. Because of its common use, linear regression is often referred to as ordinary least squares (OLS) regression.

Using notation, the linear relation between the dependent and independent variables is described as follows:

$$Y_i = b_0 + b_1 X_i + \varepsilon_i, \; i = 1, \ldots, n. \tag{3}$$

Equation 3 is a model that does not require that every (X, Y) pair for an observation fall on the regression line. This equation states that the dependent variable, Y, is equal to the **intercept**, b_0, plus a **slope coefficient**, b_1, multiplied by the independent variable, X, plus an **error term**, ε. The error term, or simply the error, represents the difference between the observed value of Y and that expected from the true underlying population relation between Y and X. We refer to the intercept, b_0, and the slope coefficient, b_1, as the **regression coefficients**? A way that we often describe this simple linear regression relation is that Y is regressed on X.

Consider the ROA and CAPEX scatter diagram from Exhibit 3, which we elaborate on in Exhibit 4 by including the fitted regression line. This line represents the average relationship between ROA and CAPEX; not every observation falls on the line, but the line describes the mean relation between ROA and CAPEX.

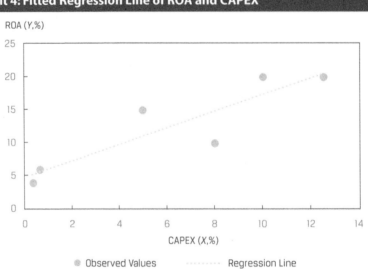

Exhibit 4: Fitted Regression Line of ROA and CAPEX

Estimating the Regression Line

We cannot observe the population parameter values b_0 and b_1 in a regression model. Instead, we observe only $\hat{b}_0$ and $\hat{b}_1$, which are estimates (as indicated by the "hats" above the coefficients) of the population parameters based on the sample. Thus, predictions must be based on the parameters' estimated values, and testing is based on estimated values in relation to the hypothesized population values.

We estimate the regression line as the line that best fits the observations. In simple linear regression, the estimated intercept, $\hat{b}_0$, and slope, $\hat{b}_1$, are such that the sum of the squared vertical distances from the observations to the fitted line is minimized. The focus is on the sum of the squared differences between the observations on Y_i and the corresponding estimated value, $\hat{Y}_i$, on the regression line.

We represent the value of the dependent variable for the ith observation that falls on the line as $\hat{Y}_i$, which is equal to $\hat{b}_0 + \hat{b}_1 X_i$. $\hat{Y}_i$ is what the estimated value of the Y variable would be for the ith observation based on the mean relationship between Y and X. The **residual** for the ith observation, e_i, is how much the observed value of Y_i differs from the $\hat{Y}_i$ estimated using the regression line: $e_i = Y_i - \hat{Y}_i$. Note the subtle difference between the error term and the residual: The error term refers to the true underlying population relationship, whereas the residual refers to the fitted linear relation based on the sample.

Fitting the line requires minimizing the sum of the squared residuals, the **sum of squares error (SSE)**, also known as the residual sum of squares:

$$
\begin{aligned}
\text{Sum of squares error} &= \sum_{i=1}^{n} (Y_i - \hat{Y}_i)^2 \\
&= \sum_{i=1}^{n} \left[Y_i - (\hat{b}_0 + \hat{b}_1 X_i) \right]^2 \\
&= \sum_{i=1}^{n} e_i^2.
\end{aligned}
\tag{4}
$$

Using least squares regression to estimate the values of the population parameters of b_0 and b_1, we can fit a line through the observations of X and Y that explains the value that Y takes for any particular value of X.

As seen in Exhibit 5, the residuals are represented by the vertical distances from the fitted line (see the third and fifth observations, Companies C and E, respectively) and are, therefore, in the units of measurement represented by the dependent variable. The residual is in the same unit of measurement as the dependent variable: If the dependent variable is in euros, the error term is in euros, and if the dependent variable is in growth rates, the error term is in growth rates.

Exhibit 5: Residuals of the Linear Regression

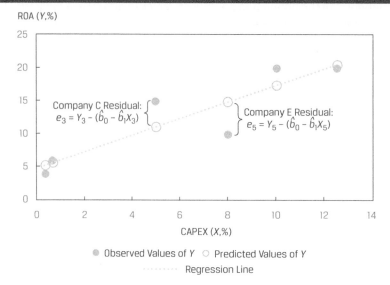

ROA (Y,%)

Company C Residual:
$e_3 = Y_3 - (\hat{b}_0 - \hat{b}_1 X_3)$

Company E Residual:
$e_5 = Y_5 - (\hat{b}_0 - \hat{b}_1 X_5)$

CAPEX (X,%)

● Observed Values of Y   ○ Predicted Values of Y
.... Regression Line

How do we calculate the intercept $(\hat{b}_0)$ and the slope $(\hat{b}_1)$ for a given sample of (Y, X) pairs of observations? The slope is the ratio of the covariance between Y and X to the variance of X, where $\bar{Y}$ is the mean of the Y variable and $\bar{X}$ is the mean of X variable:

$$\hat{b}_1 = \frac{\text{Covariance of } Y \text{ and } X}{\text{Variance of } X} = \frac{\frac{\sum_{i=1}^{n}(Y_i - \bar{Y})(X_i - \bar{X})}{n-1}}{\frac{\sum_{i=1}^{n}(X_i - \bar{X})^2}{n-1}}.$$

Simplifying,

$$\hat{b}_1 = \frac{\sum_{i=1}^{n}(Y_i - \bar{Y})(X_i - \bar{X})}{\sum_{i=1}^{n}(X_i - \bar{X})^2}. \tag{5}$$

Once we estimate the slope, we can then estimate the intercept using the mean of Y and the mean of X:

$$\hat{b}_0 = \bar{Y} - \hat{b}_1 \bar{X}. \tag{6}$$

Incremental values to calculate the slope and the intercept are in Exhibit 6.

Exhibit 6: Estimating Slope and Intercept for the ROA Model

Company	ROA (Yi)	CAPEX (Xi)	$(Y_i - \bar{Y})^2$	$(X_i - \bar{X})^2$	$(Y_i - \bar{Y})(X_i - \bar{X})$
A	6.0	0.7	42.25	29.16	35.10
B	4.0	0.4	72.25	32.49	48.45
C	15.0	5.0	6.25	1.21	−2.75
D	20.0	10.0	56.25	15.21	29.25
E	10.0	8.0	6.25	3.61	−4.75
F	20.0	12.5	56.25	40.96	48.00

Company	ROA (Yi)	CAPEX (Xi)	$(Y_i - \bar{Y})^2$	$(X_i - \bar{X})^2$	$(Y_i - \bar{Y})(X_i - \bar{X})$
Sum	75.0	36.6	239.50	122.64	153.30
Arithmetic mean	12.5	6.1			

Slope coefficient: $\hat{b}_1 = \frac{153.30}{122.64} = 1.25.$

Intercept: $\hat{b}_0 = 12.5 - (1.25 \times 6.10) = 4.875.$

ROW regression model: $\hat{Y}_i = 4.875 + 1.25X_i + \varepsilon_i.$

Notice the similarity of the formula for the slope coefficient and that of the pairwise correlation. The sample correlation, r, is the ratio of the covariance to the product of the standard deviations:

$$r = \frac{\text{Covariance of } Y \text{ and } X}{(\text{Standard deviation of } Y)(\text{Standard deviation of } X)} \tag{7}$$

The subtle difference between the slope and the correlation formulas is in the denominator: For the slope, this is the variance of the independent variable, but for the correlation, the denominator is the product of the standard deviations. For our ROA and CAPEX analysis,

$$\text{Covariance of } Y \text{ and } X: \text{cov}_{XY} = \frac{\sum_{i=1}^{n}(Y_i - \bar{Y})(X_i - \bar{X})}{n - 1} = \frac{153.30}{5} = 30.6600.$$

Standard deviation of Y and X:

$$S_Y = \sqrt{\frac{\sum_{i=1}^{n}(Y_i - \bar{Y})^2}{n - 1}} = \sqrt{\frac{239.50}{5}} = 6.9210 \;;$$

$$S_X = \sqrt{\frac{\sum_{i=1}^{n}(X_i - \bar{X})^2}{n - 1}} = \sqrt{\frac{122.64}{5}} = 4.9526.$$

$$r = \frac{30.66}{(6.9210)(4.9526)} = 0.8945.$$

Because the denominators of both the slope and the correlation are positive, the sign of the slope and the correlation are driven by the numerator: If the covariance is positive, both the slope and the correlation are positive, and if the covariance is negative, both the slope and the correlation are negative.

EXAMPLE 1

How Do Analysts Perform Simple Linear Regression?

Typically, an analyst will use the data analysis functions on a spreadsheet, such as Microsoft Excel, or a statistical package in the R or Python programming languages to perform linear regression analysis. The following are some of the more common choices in practice.

Simple Linear Regression: Intercept and Slope

- *Excel*: Use the INTERCEPT, SLOPE functions.
- *R*: Use the lm function.
- *Python*: Use the sm.OLS function in the statsmodels package.

Correlations

- *Excel*: Use the CORREL function.
- *R*: Use the cor function in the stats library.
- *Python*: Use the corrcoef function in the numpy library.

Note that in R and Python, there are many choices for regression and correlation analysis.

Interpreting the Regression Coefficients

What is the meaning of the regression coefficients? The intercept is the value of the dependent variable if the value of the independent variable is zero. Importantly, this does not make sense in some contexts, especially if it is unrealistic that the independent variable would be zero. For example, if we have a model in which money supply explains GDP growth, the intercept has no meaning because, practically speaking, zero money supply is not possible. If the independent variable were money supply growth, however, the intercept is meaningful. The slope is the change in the dependent variable for a one-unit change in the independent variable. If the slope is positive, then the change in the independent variable and that of the dependent variable will be in the same direction; if the slope is negative, the change in the independent variable and that of the dependent variable will be in opposite directions.

EXAMPLE 2

Interpreting Positive and Negative Slopes

Suppose the dependent variable (Y) is in millions of euros and the independent variable (X) is in millions of US dollars.

If the slope is positive 1.2, then

$\uparrow$ USD1 million $\rightarrow$ $\uparrow$ EUR1.2 million

$\downarrow$ USD1 million $\rightarrow$ $\downarrow$ EUR1.2 million

If the slope is negative 1.2, then

$\uparrow$ USD1 million $\rightarrow$ $\downarrow$ EUR1.2 million

$\downarrow$ USD1 million $\rightarrow$ $\uparrow$ EUR1.2 million

Using the ROA regression model from Exhibit 6, we would interpret the estimated coefficients as follows:

- The return on assets for a company is 4.875% if the company makes no capital expenditures.
- If CAPEX increases by one unit—say, from 4% to 5%—ROA increases by 1.25%.

Using the estimated regression coefficients, we can determine the values of the dependent variable if they follow the average relationship between the dependent and independent variables. A result of the mathematics of the least squares fitting of the regression line is that the expected value of the residual term is zero: $E(\varepsilon) = 0$.

We show the calculation of the predicted dependent variable and residual term for each observation in the ROA example in Exhibit 7. Note that the sum and average of Y_i and $\hat{Y}_1$ are the same, and the sum of the residuals is zero.

Exhibit 7: Calculation of the Dependent Variable and Residuals for the ROA and CAPEX Model

Company	(1) ROA (Y_i)	(2) CAPEX(X_i)	(3) Predicted ROA ($\hat{Y}_i$)	(4) (1) – (3) (2) Residual (e_i)
A	6.0	0.7	5.750	0.250
B	4.0	0.4	5.375	−1.375
C	15.0	5.0	11.125	3.875
D	20.0	10.0	17.375	2.625
E	10.0	8.0	14.875	−4.875
F	20.0	12.5	20.500	−0.500
Sum	75.0	36.6	75.000	0.000
Average	12.5	6.1	12.5	0.000

For Company C (i = 3),
$\hat{Y}_i = \hat{b}_0 + \hat{b}_1 X_i + \varepsilon_i = 4.875 + 1.25 X_i + \varepsilon_i$
$\hat{Y}_i = 4.875 + (1.25 \times 5.0) = 4.875 + 6.25 = 11.125$
$Y_i - \hat{Y}_i = e_i = 15.0 - 11.125 = 3.875,$ *the vertical distance in Exhibit 5.*

Whereas the sum of the residuals must equal zero by design, the focus of fitting the regression line in a simple linear regression is minimizing the sum of the squared residual terms.

Cross-Sectional versus Time-Series Regressions

Regression analysis uses two principal types of data: cross sectional and time series. A cross-sectional regression involves many observations of X and Y for the same time period. These observations could come from different companies, asset classes, investment funds, countries, or other entities, depending on the regression model. For example, a cross-sectional model might use data from many companies to test whether predicted EPS growth explains differences in price-to-earnings ratios during a specific time period. Note that if we use cross-sectional observations in a regression, we usually denote the observations as $i = 1, 2, \ldots, n$.

Time-series data use many observations from different time periods for the same company, asset class, investment fund, country, or other entity, depending on the regression model. For example, a time-series model might use monthly data from many years to test whether a country's inflation rate determines its short-term interest rates. If we use time-series data in a regression, we usually denote the observations as $t = 1, 2, \ldots, T$. Note that in the sections that follow, we primarily use the notation $i = 1, 2, \ldots, n$, even for time series.

QUESTION SET

An analyst is exploring the relationship between a company's net profit margin and research and development expenditures. He collects data for an industry and calculates the ratio of research and development expenditures to revenues (RDR) and the net profit margin (NPM) for eight companies.

Specifically, he wants to explain the net profit margin variation by using the variation observed in the companies' research and development spending. He reports the data in Exhibit 8.

Exhibit 8: Observations on NPM and RDR for Eight Companies

Company	NPM (%)	RDR (%)
1	4	8
2	5	10
3	10	6
4	9	5
5	5	7
6	6	9
7	12	5
8	3	10

1. What is the slope coefficient for this simple linear regression model?

Solution:

The slope coefficient for the regression model is –1.3, and the details for the inputs to this calculation are in Exhibit 9.

Exhibit 9: Details of Calculation of Slope of NPM Regressed on RDR

Company	NPM (%) (Y_i)	RDR (%) (X_i)	$Y_i - \bar{Y}$	$X_i - \bar{X}$	$(Y_i - \bar{Y})^2$	$(X_i - \bar{X})^2$	$(Y_i - \bar{Y})(X_i - \bar{X})$
1	4	8	–2.8	0.5	7.5625	0.25	–1.375
2	5	10	–1.8	2.5	3.0625	6.25	–4.375
3	10	6	3.3	–1.5	10.5625	2.25	–4.875
4	9	5	2.3	–2.5	5.0625	6.25	–5.625
5	5	7	–1.8	–0.5	3.0625	0.25	0.875
6	6	9	–0.8	1.5	0.5625	2.25	–1.125
7	12	5	5.3	–2.5	27.5625	6.25	–13.125
8	3	10	–3.8	2.5	14.0625	6.25	–9.375
Sum	54	60	0.0	0.0	71.5000	30.00	–39.000
Average	6.75	7.5					

Slope coefficient: $\hat{b}_1 = \frac{-39}{30} = -1.3$.

2. What is the intercept for this regression model?

Solution:

The intercept of the regression model is 16.5:

Intercept: $\hat{b}_0 = 6.75 - (-1.3 \times 7.5) = 6.75 + 9.75 = 16.5$

3. How is this estimated linear regression model represented?

Solution:

The regression model is represented by $\hat{Y}_i = 16.5 - 1.3X_i + \varepsilon_i$.

4. What is the pairwise correlation between NPM and RDR?

Solution:

The pairwise correlation is −0.8421:

$$r = \frac{-39/7}{\sqrt{71.5/7}\sqrt{30/7}} = \frac{-5.5714}{(3.1960)(2.0702)} = -0.8421.$$

ASSUMPTIONS OF THE SIMPLE LINEAR REGRESSION MODEL

3

☐ explain the assumptions underlying the simple linear regression model, and describe how residuals and residual plots indicate if these assumptions may have been violated

We have discussed how to interpret the coefficients in a simple linear regression model. Now we turn to the statistical assumptions underlying this model. Suppose that we have n observations of both the dependent variable, Y, and the independent variable, X, and we want to estimate the simple linear regression of Y regressed on X. We need to make the following four key assumptions to be able to draw valid conclusions from a simple linear regression model:

1. Linearity: The relationship between the dependent variable, Y, and the independent variable, X, is linear.

2. Homoskedasticity: The variance of the regression residuals is the same for all observations.

3. Independence: The observations, pairs of Ys and Xs, are independent of one another. This implies the regression residuals are uncorrelated across observations.

4. Normality: The regression residuals are normally distributed.

Now we take a closer look at each of these assumptions and introduce the "best practice" of examining residual plots of regression results to identify potential violations of these key assumptions.

Assumption 1: Linearity

We are fitting a linear model, so we must assume that the true underlying relationship between the dependent and independent variables is linear. If the relationship between the independent and dependent variables is nonlinear in the parameters, estimating that relation with a simple linear regression model will produce invalid results: The model will be biased, because it will under- and overestimate the dependent variable at certain points. For example, $Y_i = b_0 e^{b_1 X_i} + \varepsilon_i$ is nonlinear in b_1, so we should not apply the linear regression model to it. Exhibit 10 shows an example of this exponential model, with a regression line indicated. You can see that this line does not fit this relationship well: For lower and higher values of X, the linear model underestimates the Y, whereas for the middle values, the linear model overestimates Y.

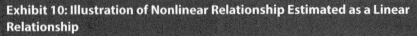

Exhibit 10: Illustration of Nonlinear Relationship Estimated as a Linear Relationship

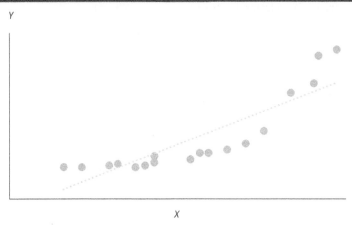

Another implication of this assumption is that the independent variable, X, must not be random; that is, it is non-stochastic. If the independent variable is random, there would be no linear relation between the dependent and independent variables. Although we may initially assume that the independent variable in the regression model is not random, that assumption may not always be true.

When we look at the residuals of a model, what we would like to see is that the residuals are random. The residuals should not exhibit a pattern when plotted against the independent variable. As we show in Exhibit 11, the residuals from the Exhibit 10 linear regression do not appear to be random but, rather, they exhibit a relationship with the independent variable, X, falling for some range of X and rising in another.

Exhibit 11: Illustration of Residuals in a Nonlinear Relationship Estimated as a Linear Relationship

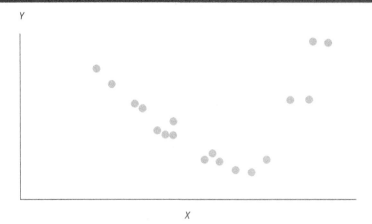

Assumption 2: Homoskedasticity

Assumption 2, that the variance of the residuals is the same for all observations, is known as the **homoskedasticity** assumption. In terms of notation, this assumption relates to the squared residuals:

$$E\left(\varepsilon_i^2\right) = \sigma_\varepsilon^2, i = 1, \ldots, n. \tag{8}$$

If the residuals are not homoskedastic, that is, if the variance of residuals differs across observations, then we refer to this as **heteroskedasticity**.

Suppose you are examining a time series of short-term interest rates as the dependent variable and inflation rates as the independent variable over 16 years. We may believe that short-term interest rates (Y) and inflation rates (X) should be related (i.e., interest rates are higher with higher rates of inflation). If this time series spans many years, with different central bank actions that force short-term interest rates to be (artificially) low for the last eight years of the series, then it is likely that the residuals in this estimated model will appear to come from two different models. We will refer to the first eight years as Regime 1 (normal rates) and the second eight years as Regime 2 (low rates). If the model fits differently in the two regimes, the residuals and their variances will be different.

You can see this situation in Exhibit 12, which shows a scatter plot with an estimated regression line. The slope of the regression line over all 16 years is 1.1979.

Exhibit 12: Scatter Plot of Interest Rates (*Y*) and Inflation Rates (*X*)

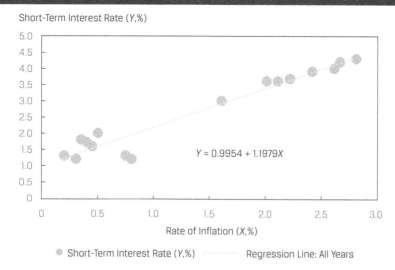

We plot the residuals of this model in Exhibit 13 against the years. In this plot, we indicate the distance that is two standard deviations from zero (the mean of the residuals) for the first eight years' residuals and then do the same for the second eight years. As you can see, the residuals appear different for the two regimes: the variation in the residuals for the first eight years is much smaller than the variation for the second eight years.

Exhibit 13: Residual Plot for Interest Rates (*Y*) vs. Inflation Rates (*X*) Model

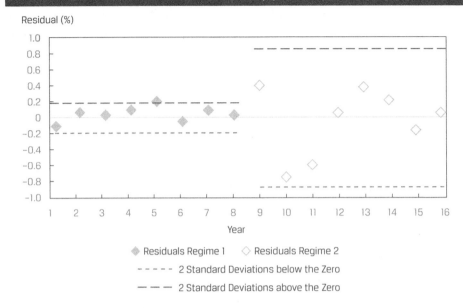

Why does this happen? The model seems appropriate, but when we examine the residuals (Exhibit 13), an important step in assessing the model fit, we see that the model fits better in some years compared with others. The difference in variance of residuals between the two regimes is apparent from the much wider band around residuals for Regime 2 (the low-rate period). This indicates a clear violation of the homoskedasticity assumption.

If we estimate a regression line for each regime, we can see that the model for the two regimes is quite different, as we show in Exhibit 14. In the case of Regime 1 (normal rates), the slope is 1.0247, whereas in Regime 2 (low rates) the slope is −0.2805. In sum, the clustering of residuals in two groups with much different variances clearly indicates the existence of distinct regimes for the relationship between short-term interest rates and the inflation rate.

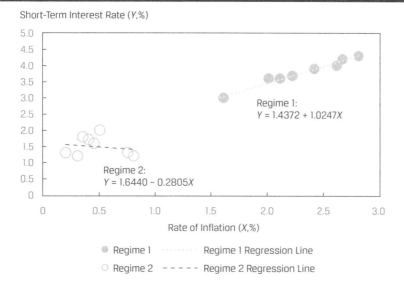

Exhibit 14: Fitted Regression Lines for the Two Regimes

Assumption 3: Independence

We assume that the observations (Y and X pairs) are uncorrelated with one another, meaning they are independent. If there is correlation between observations (i.e., autocorrelation), they are not independent and the residuals will be correlated. The assumption that the residuals are uncorrelated across observations is also necessary for correctly estimating the variances of the **estimated parameters** of b_0 and b_1 (i.e., $\hat{b}_0$ and $\hat{b}_1$) that we use in hypothesis tests of the intercept and slope, respectively. It is important to examine whether the residuals exhibit a pattern, suggesting a violation of this assumption. Therefore, we need to visually and statistically examine the residuals for a regression model.

Consider the quarterly revenues of a company regressed over 40 quarters, as shown in Exhibit 15, with the regression line included. It is clear that these revenues display a seasonal pattern, an indicator of autocorrelation.

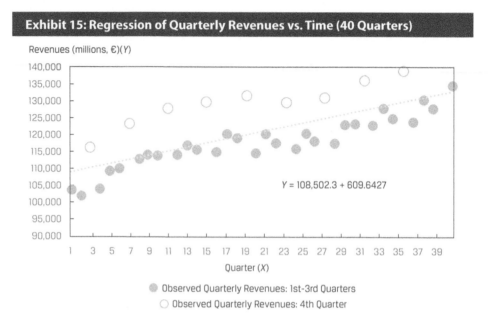

Exhibit 15: Regression of Quarterly Revenues vs. Time (40 Quarters)

$Y = 108,502.3 + 609.6427$

In Exhibit 16, we plot the residuals from this model and see that there is a pattern. These residuals are correlated, specifically jumping up in Quarter 4 and then falling back the subsequent quarter. In sum, the patterns in both Exhibit 15 and Exhibit 16 indicate a violation of the assumption of independence.

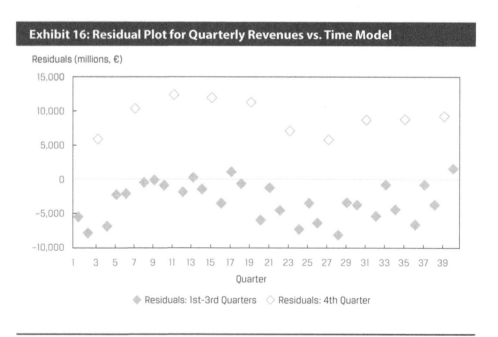

Exhibit 16: Residual Plot for Quarterly Revenues vs. Time Model

Assumption 4: Normality

The assumption of normality requires that the residuals be normally distributed. This does not mean that the dependent and independent variables must be normally distributed; it only means that the residuals from the model are normally distributed. However, in estimating any model, it is good practice to understand the distribution of the dependent and independent variables to explore for outliers. An outlier in either or both variables can substantially influence the fitted line such that the estimated model will not fit well for most of the other observations.

With normally distributed residuals, we can test a particular hypothesis about a linear regression model. For large sample sizes, we may be able to drop the assumption of normality by appealing to the central limit theorem; asymptotic theory (which deals with large samples) shows that in many cases, the test statistics produced by standard regression programs are valid even if the model's residuals are not normally distributed.

QUESTION SET

An analyst is investigating a company's revenues and estimates a simple linear time-series model by regressing revenues against time, where time—1, 2, . . . , 15—is measured in years. She plots the company's observed revenues and the estimated regression line, as shown in Exhibit 17. She also plots the residuals from this regression model, as shown in Exhibit 18.

Exhibit 17: Revenues vs. Time Using Simple Linear Regression

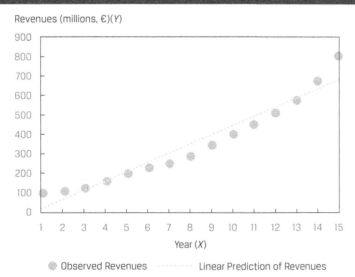

Exhibit 18: Residual Plot for Revenues vs. Time

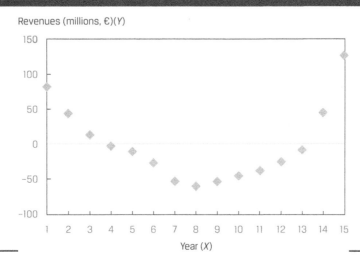

1. Based on Exhibit 17 and Exhibit 18, describe which assumption(s) of simple linear regression the analyst's model may be violating.

   Solution:

   The correct model is not linear, as evident from the pattern of the revenues in Exhibit 17. In the earlier years (i.e., 1 and 2) and later years (i.e., 14 and 15), the linear model underestimates revenues, whereas for the middle years (i.e., 7–11), the linear model overestimates revenues. Moreover, the curved pattern of residuals in Exhibit 18 indicates potential heteroskedasticity (residuals have unequal variances), lack of independence of observations, and non-normality (a concern given the small sample size of $n = 15$). In sum, the analyst should be concerned that her model violates all the assumptions governing simple linear regression (linearity, homoskedasticity, independence, and normality).

---

4 HYPOTHESIS TESTS IN THE SIMPLE LINEAR REGRESSION MODEL

calculate and interpret measures of fit and formulate and evaluate tests of fit and of regression coefficients in a simple linear regression

Analysis of Variance

The simple linear regression model sometimes describes the relationship between two variables quite well, but sometimes it does not. We must be able to distinguish between these two cases to use regression analysis effectively. Remember our goal is to explain the variation of the dependent variable. So, how well has this goal been achieved, given our choice of independent variable?

Breaking Down the Sum of Squares Total into Its Components

We begin with the sum of squares total and then break it down into two parts: the sum of squares error and the **sum of squares regression (SSR)**. The sum of squares regression is the sum of the squared differences between the predicted value of the dependent variable, $\hat{Y}_i$, based on the estimated regression line, and the mean of the dependent variable, $\bar{Y}$:

$$\sum_{i=1}^{n} \left(\hat{Y}_i - \bar{Y}\right)^2. \tag{9}$$

We have already defined the sum of squares total, which is the total variation in Y, and the sum of squares error, the unexplained variation in Y. Note that the sum of squares regression is the explained variation in Y. So, as illustrated in Exhibit 19, SST = SSR + SSE, meaning total variation in Y equals explained variation in Y plus unexplained variation in Y.

Exhibit 19: Breakdown of Variation of Dependent Variable

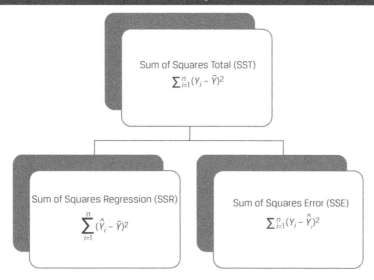

We show the breakdown of the sum of squares total formula for our ROA regression example in Exhibit 20. The total variation of ROA that we want to explain (SST) is 239.50. This number includes the variation unexplained (SSE), 47.88, and the variation explained (SSR), 191.63. These sum of squares values are important inputs into measures of the fit of the regression line.

Exhibit 20: Breakdown of the Sum of Squares Total for ROA Model

Company	ROA (Y_i)	CAPEX (X_i)	Predicted ROA $(\hat{Y})$	Variation to Be Explained $(Y_i - \bar{Y})^2$	Variation Unexplained $(Y_i - \hat{Y}_i)$	Variation Explained $(\hat{Y}_i - \bar{Y})^2$
A	6.0	0.7	5.750	42.25	0.063	45.563
B	4.0	0.4	5.375	72.25	1.891	50.766
C	15.0	5.0	11.125	6.25	15.016	1.891
D	20.0	10.0	17.375	56.25	6.891	23.766
E	10.0	8.0	14.875	6.25	23.766	5.641
F	20.0	12.5	20.500	56.25	0.250	64.000
				239.50	47.88	191.625
Mean	12.50					

Sum of squares total = 239.50.
Sum of squares error = 47.88.
Sum of squares regression = 191.63.

Measures of Goodness of Fit

We can use several measures to evaluate goodness of fit—that is, how well the regression model fits the data. These include the coefficient of determination, the F-statistic for the test of fit, and the standard error of the regression.

The **coefficient of determination (R²)**, also referred to as the *R*-squared or R^2, is the percentage of the variation of the dependent variable that is explained by the independent variable:

$$\text{Coefficient of determination} = \frac{\text{Sum of squares regression}}{\text{Sum of squares total}}$$

$$\text{Coefficient of determination} = \frac{\sum_{i=1}^{n}(\widehat{Y}_i - \overline{Y})^2}{\sum_{i=1}^{n}(Y_i - \overline{Y})^2}. \tag{10}$$

By construction, the coefficient of determination ranges from 0 percent to 100 percent. In our ROA example, the coefficient of determination is 191.625 ÷ 239.50, or 0.8001, so 80.01 percent of the variation in ROA is explained by CAPEX. In a simple linear regression, the square of the pairwise correlation is equal to the coefficient of determination:

$$r^2 = \frac{\sum_{i=1}^{n}(\widehat{Y}_i - \overline{Y})^2}{\sum_{i=1}^{n}(Y_i - \overline{Y})^2} = R^2. \tag{11}$$

In our earlier ROA regression analysis, $r = 0.8945$, so we now see that r^2 is indeed equal to the coefficient of determination (R^2), since $(0.8945)^2 = 0.8001$.

Whereas the coefficient of determination—the portion of the variation of the dependent variable explained by the independent variable—is descriptive, it is not a statistical test. To see if our regression model is likely to be statistically meaningful, we will need to construct an *F*-distributed test statistic.

In general, we use an *F*-distributed test statistic to compare two variances. In regression analysis, we can use an *F*-distributed test statistic to test whether the slopes in a regression are equal to zero, with the slopes designated as b_i, against the alternative hypothesis that at least one slope is not equal to zero:

H_0: $b_1 = b_2 = b_3 = \ldots = b_k = 0$.

H_a: At least one b_k is not equal to zero.

For simple linear regression, these hypotheses simplify to

H_0: $b_1 = 0$.

H_a: $b_1 \neq 0$.

The *F*-distributed test statistic is constructed by using the sum of squares regression and the sum of squares error, each adjusted for degrees of freedom; in other words, it is the ratio of two variances. We divide the sum of squares regression by the number of independent variables, represented by k. In the case of a simple linear regression, k = 1, so we arrive at the **mean square regression (MSR)**, which is the same as the sum of squares regression:

$$\text{MSR} = \frac{\text{Sum of squares regression}}{k} = \frac{\sum_{i=1}^{n}(\widehat{Y}_i - \overline{Y})^2}{1}. \tag{12}$$

So, for simple linear regression,

$$\text{MSR} = \sum_{i=1}^{n}(\widehat{Y}_i - \overline{Y})^2. \tag{13}$$

Next, we calculate the **mean square error (MSE)**, which is the sum of squares error divided by the degrees of freedom, which are $n - k - 1$. In simple linear regression, $n - k - 1$ becomes $n - 2$:

$$\text{MSE} = \frac{\text{Sum of squares error}}{n - k - 1},$$

$$MSE = \frac{\sum_{i=1}^{n}(Y_i - \widehat{Y}_i)^2}{n-2}.$$ (14)

Therefore, the F-distributed test statistic (MSR/MSE) is

$$F = \frac{\dfrac{\text{Sum of squares regression}}{k}}{\dfrac{\text{Sum of squares error}}{n-k-1}} = \frac{\text{MSR}}{\text{MSE}},$$

$$F = \frac{\dfrac{\sum_{i=1}^{n}(\widehat{Y}_i - \overline{Y})^2}{1}}{\dfrac{\sum_{i=1}^{n}(Y_i - \widehat{Y}_i)^2}{n-2}},$$ (15)

which is distributed with 1 and $n-2$ degrees of freedom in simple linear regression. The F-statistic in regression analysis is one sided, with the rejection region on the right side, because we are interested in whether the variation in Y explained (the numerator) is larger than the variation in Y unexplained (the denominator).

Hypothesis Testing of Individual Regression Coefficients

Hypothesis Tests of the Slope Coefficient

We can use the F-statistic to test for the significance of the slope coefficient (i.e., whether it is significantly different from zero), but we also may want to perform other hypothesis tests for the slope coefficient—for example, testing whether the population slope is different from a specific value or whether the slope is positive. We can use a t-distributed test statistic to test such hypotheses about a regression coefficient.

Suppose we want to check a stock's valuation using the market model; we hypothesize that the stock has an average systematic risk (i.e., risk similar to that of the market), as represented by the coefficient on the market returns variable. Or we may want to test the hypothesis that economists' forecasts of the inflation rate are unbiased (i.e., on average, not overestimating or underestimating actual inflation rates). In each case, does the evidence support the hypothesis? Such questions as these can be addressed with hypothesis tests on the regression slope. To test a hypothesis about a slope, we calculate the test statistic by subtracting the hypothesized population slope (B_1) from the estimated slope coefficient ($\widehat{b}_1$) and then dividing this difference by the standard error of the slope coefficient, $s_{\widehat{b}_1}$:

$$t = \frac{\widehat{b}_1 - B_1}{s_{\widehat{b}_1}}.$$ (16)

This test statistic is t-distributed with $n-k-1$ or $n-2$ degrees of freedom because two parameters (an intercept and a slope) were estimated in the regression.

The **standard error of the slope coefficient** ($s_{\widehat{b}_1}$) for a simple linear regression is the ratio of the model's standard error of the estimate (s_e), introduced later, to the square root of the variation of the independent variable:

$$s_{\widehat{b}_1} = \frac{s_e}{\sqrt{\sum_{i=1}^{n}(X_i - \overline{X})^2}}.$$ (17)

We compare the calculated t-statistic with the critical values to test hypotheses. Note that the greater the variability of the independent variable, the lower the standard error of the slope (Equation 17) and hence the greater the calculated t-statistic (Equation 16). If the calculated t-statistic is outside the bounds of the critical t-values, we reject the null hypothesis, but if the calculated t-statistic is within the bounds of the critical values, we fail to reject the null hypothesis. Similar to tests of the mean, the alternative hypothesis can be two sided or one sided.

Consider our previous simple linear regression example with ROA as the dependent variable and CAPEX as the independent variable. Suppose we want to test whether the slope coefficient of CAPEX is different from zero to confirm our intuition of a significant relationship between ROA and CAPEX. We can test the hypothesis concerning the slope using the six-step process, as we show in Exhibit 21. As a result of this test, we conclude that the slope is different from zero; that is, CAPEX is a significant explanatory variable of ROA.

Exhibit 21: Test of the Slope for the Regression of ROA on CAPEX

Step 1	State the hypotheses.	$H_0: b_1 = 0$ versus $H_a: b_1 \neq 0$
Step 2	Identify the appropriate test statistic.	$t = \dfrac{\hat{b}_1 - B_1}{s_{\hat{b}_1}}$ with $6 - 2 = 4$ degrees of freedom.
Step 3	Specify the level of significance.	$\alpha = 5\%$.
Step 4	State the decision rule.	Critical t-values = ±2.776. We can determine this from **Excel** *Lower:* `T.INV(0.025,4)` *Upper:* `T.INV(0.975,4)` **R:** `qt(c(.025,.975),4)` **Python:** `from scipy.stats import t` *Lower:* `t.ppf(.025,4)` *Upper:* `t.ppf(.975,4)` We reject the null hypothesis if the calculated t-statistic is less than −2.776 or greater than +2.776.
Step 5	Calculate the test statistic.	The slope coefficient is 1.25 (Exhibit 6). The mean square error is 11.96875 (Exhibit 39). The variation of CAPEX is 122.640 (Exhibit 6). $s_e = \sqrt{11.96875} = 3.459588$.
Step 6	Make a decision.	Reject the null hypothesis of a zero slope. There is sufficient evidence to indicate that the slope is different from zero.

A feature of simple linear regression is that the t-statistic used to test whether the slope coefficient is equal to zero and the t-statistic to test whether the pairwise correlation is zero (i.e., $H_0: \rho = 0$ versus $H_a: \rho \neq 0$) are the same value. Just as with a test of a slope, both two-sided and one-sided alternatives are possible for a test of a correlation—for example, $H_0: \rho \leq 0$ versus $H_a: \rho > 0$. The test-statistic to test whether the correlation is equal to zero is as follows:

$$t = \frac{r\sqrt{n-2}}{\sqrt{1-r^2}}. \tag{18}$$

In our example of ROA regressed on CAPEX, the correlation (r) is 0.8945. To test whether this correlation is different from zero, we perform a test of hypothesis, shown in Exhibit 22. As you can see, we draw a conclusion similar to that for our test of the slope, but it is phrased in terms of the correlation between ROA and CAPEX: There is a significant correlation between ROA and CAPEX.

Exhibit 22: Test of the Correlation between ROA and CAPEX

Step 1	State the hypotheses.	H_0: $\rho = 0$ versus H_a: $\rho \neq 0$
Step 2	Identify the appropriate test statistic.	$t = \frac{r\sqrt{n-2}}{\sqrt{1-r^2}}$. with $6 - 2 = 4$ degrees of freedom.
Step 3	Specify the level of significance.	$\alpha = 5\%$.
Step 4	State the decision rule.	Critical t-values = ±2.776. Reject the null if the calculated t-statistic is less than −2.776 or greater than +2.776.
Step 5	Calculate the test statistic.	$t = \frac{0.8945\sqrt{4}}{\sqrt{1-0.8001}} = 4.00131$.
Step 6	Make a decision.	Reject the null hypothesis of no correlation. There is sufficient evidence to indicate that the correlation between ROA and CAPEX is different from zero.

Another interesting feature of simple linear regression is that the test-statistic used to test the fit of the model (i.e., the F-distributed test statistic) is related to the calculated t-statistic used to test whether the slope coefficient is equal to zero: $t^2 = F$; therefore, $4.00131^2 = 16.0104$.

What if instead we want to test whether there is a one-to-one relationship between ROA and CAPEX, implying a slope coefficient of 1.0. The hypotheses become H_0: $b_1 = 1$ and H_a: $b_1 \neq 1$. The calculated t-statistic is as follows:

$$t = \frac{1.25 - 1}{0.312398} = 0.80026.$$

This calculated test statistic falls within the bounds of the critical values, ±2.776, so we fail to reject the null hypothesis: There is not sufficient evidence to indicate that the slope is different from 1.0.

What if instead we want to test whether there is a positive slope or positive correlation, as our intuition suggests? In this case, all the steps are the same as in Exhibit 21 and Exhibit 22 except the critical values because the tests are one sided. For a test of a positive slope or positive correlation, the critical value for a 5 percent level of significance is +2.132. We show the test of hypotheses for a positive slope and a positive correlation in Exhibit 23. Our conclusion is that evidence is sufficient to support both a positive slope and a positive correlation.

Exhibit 23: One-Sided Tests for the Slope and Correlation

		Test of the Slope	Test of the Correlation
Step 1	State the hypotheses.	H_0: $b_1 \leq 0$ versus H_a: $b_1 > 0$	H_0: $\rho \leq 0$ versus H_a: $\rho > 0$
Step 2	Identify the appropriate test statistic.	$t = \frac{\hat{b}_1 - B_1}{s_{\hat{b}_1}}$ with $6 - 2 = 4$ degrees of freedom.	$t = \frac{r\sqrt{n-2}}{\sqrt{1-r^2}}$. with $6 - 2 = 4$ degrees of freedom.
Step 3	Specify the level of significance.	$\alpha = 5\%$.	$\alpha = 5\%$.
Step 4	State the decision rule.	Critical t-value = 2.132. Reject the null if the calculated t-statistic is greater than 2.132.	Critical t-value = 2.132. Reject the null if the calculated t-statistic is greater than 2.132.

Step 5	Calculate the test statistic.	$t = \frac{1.25 - 0}{0.312398} = 4.00131$	$t = \frac{0.8945\sqrt{4}}{\sqrt{1 - 0.8001}} = 4.00131$
Step 6	Make a decision.	Reject the null hypothesis. Evidence is sufficient to indicate that the slope is greater than zero.	Do *not* reject the null hypothesis. There is *not* sufficient evidence to indicate that the correlation is greater than zero.

Hypothesis Tests of the Intercept

We may want to test whether the population intercept is a specific value. As a reminder on how to interpret the intercept, consider the simple linear regression with a company's revenue growth rate as the dependent variable (Y), and the GDP growth rate of its home country as the independent variable (X). The intercept is the company's revenue growth rate if the GDP growth rate is 0 percent.

The equation for the standard error of the intercept, $s_{\hat{b}_0}$, is as follows:

$$s_{\hat{b}_0} = S_e \sqrt{\frac{1}{n} + \frac{\bar{X}^2}{\sum_{i=1}^{n}(X_i - \bar{X})^2}}. \tag{19}$$

We can test whether the intercept is different from the hypothesized value, B_0, by comparing the estimated intercept ($\hat{b}_0$) with the hypothesized intercept and then dividing the difference by the standard error of the intercept:

$$t_{intercept} = \frac{\hat{b}_0 - B_0}{s_{\hat{b}_0}} = \frac{\hat{b}_0 - B_0}{\sqrt{\frac{1}{n} + \frac{\bar{X}^2}{\sum_{i-1}^{n}(X_i - \bar{X})^2}}}. \tag{20}$$

In the ROA regression example, the intercept is 4.875 percent. Suppose we want to test whether the intercept is greater than 3 percent. The one-sided hypothesis test is shown in Exhibit 24. As you can see, we reject the null hypothesis. In other words, evidence is sufficient that if there are no capital expenditures (CAPEX = 0), ROA is greater than 3 percent.

Exhibit 24: Test of Hypothesis for Intercept for Regression of ROA on CAPEX

Step 1	State the hypotheses.	$H_0: b_0 \leq 3\%$ versus $H_a: b_0 > 3\%$
Step 2	Identify the appropriate test statistic.	$t_{intercept} = \frac{\hat{b}_0 - B_0}{s_{\hat{b}_0}}$ with 6 − 2 = 4 degrees of freedom.
Step 3	Specify the level of significance.	$\alpha = 5\%$.
Step 4	State the decision rule.	Critical t-value = 2.132. Reject the null if the calculated t-statistic is greater than 2.132.
Step 5	Calculate the test statistic.	$t_{intercept} = \frac{4.875 - 3.0}{3.4596 \times \sqrt{\frac{1}{6} + \frac{6.1^2}{122.64}}} = \frac{1.875}{3.4596 \times 0.68562}$ = 0.7905
Step 6	Make a decision.	Reject the null hypothesis. There is sufficient evidence to indicate that the intercept is greater than 3%.

Hypothesis Tests of Slope When the Independent Variable Is an Indicator Variable

Suppose we want to examine whether a company's quarterly earnings announcements influence its monthly stock returns. In this case, we could use an **indicator variable**, or dummy variable, that takes on only the values 0 or 1 as the independent variable. Consider the case of a company's monthly stock returns over a 30-month period. A simple linear regression model for investigating this question would be monthly returns, RET, regressed on the indicator variable, EARN, that takes on a value of 0 if there is no earnings announcement that month and 1 if there is an earnings announcement:

$$RET_i = b_0 + b_1 EARN_i + \varepsilon_i. \tag{21}$$

This regression setup allows us to test whether there are different returns for earnings-announcement months versus non-earnings-announcement months. The observations and regression results are shown graphically in Exhibit 25.

Exhibit 25: Earnings Announcements, Dummy Variable, and Stock Returns

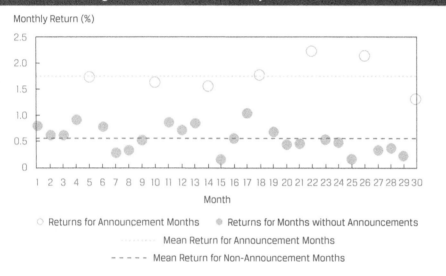

Clearly there are some months in which the returns are different from other months, and these correspond to months in which there was an earnings announcement. We estimate the simple linear regression model and perform hypothesis testing in the same manner as if the independent variable were a continuous variable. In a simple linear regression, the interpretation of the intercept is the predicted value of the dependent variable if the indicator variable is zero. Moreover, the slope when the indicator variable is 1 is the difference in the means if we grouped the observations by the indicator variable. The results of the regression are given in Panel A of Exhibit 26.

Exhibit 26: Regression and Test of Differences Using an Indicator Variable

A. Regression Estimation Results

	Estimated Coefficients	Standard Error of Coefficients	Calculated Test Statistic
Intercept	0.5629	0.0560	10.0596
EARN	1.2098	0.1158	10.4435

Regression Estimation Results
Degrees of freedom = 28.

Critical t-values = +2.0484 (5% significance).

B. Test of Differences in Means

	RET for Earnings-Announcement Months	RET for Non-Earnings-Announcement Months	Difference in Means
Mean	1.7727	0.5629	1.2098
Variance	0.1052	0.0630	
Observations	7	23	
Pooled variance			0.07202
Calculated test statistic			10.4435

Test of Differences in Means
Degrees of freedom = 28.
Critical t-values = +2.0484 (5% significance).

We can see the following from Panel A of Exhibit 26:

- The intercept (0.5629) is the mean of the returns for non-earnings-announcement months.

- The slope coefficient (1.2098) is the difference in means of returns between earnings-announcement and non-earnings-announcement months.

- We reject the null hypothesis that the slope coefficient on EARN is equal to zero. We also reject the null hypothesis that the intercept is zero. The reason is that in both cases, the calculated test statistic exceeds the critical *t*-value.

We could also test whether the mean monthly return is the same for both the non-earnings-announcement months and the earnings-announcement months by testing the following:

$$H_0: \mu_{RETearnings} = \mu_{RETNon-earnings} \text{ and } H_a: \mu_{RETearnings} \neq \mu_{RETNon-earnings}$$

The results of this hypothesis test are gleaned from Panel B of Exhibit 26. As you can see, we reject the null hypothesis that there is no difference in the mean RET for the earnings-announcement and non-earnings-announcements months at the 5 percent level of significance, because the calculated test statistic (10.4435) exceeds the critical value (2.0484).

Test of Hypotheses: Level of Significance and p-Values

The choice of significance level in hypothesis testing is always a matter of judgment. Analysts often choose the 0.05 level of significance, which indicates a 5 percent chance of rejecting the null hypothesis when, in fact, it is true (a Type I error, or false positive). Of course, decreasing the level of significance from 0.05 to 0.01 decreases the probability of a Type I error, but it also increases the probability of a Type II error—failing to reject the null hypothesis when, in fact, it is false (i.e., a false negative).

The *p*-value is the smallest level of significance at which the null hypothesis can be rejected. The smaller the *p*-value, the smaller the chance of making a Type I error (i.e., rejecting a true null hypothesis), so the greater the likelihood the regression model is valid. For example, if the *p*-value is 0.005, we reject the null hypothesis that the true parameter is equal to zero at the 0.5 percent significance level (99.5 percent confidence). In most software packages, the p-values provided for regression coefficients are for a test of null hypothesis that the true parameter is equal to zero against the alternative that the parameter is not equal to zero.

In our ROA regression example, the calculated t-statistic for the test of whether the slope coefficient is zero is 4.00131. The p-value corresponding to this test statistic is 0.016, which means there is just a 0.16 percent chance of rejecting the null hypotheses when it is true. Comparing this p-value with the level of significance of 5 percent (and critical values of ±2.776) leads us to easily reject the null hypothesis of H_0: $b_1 = 0$.

How do we determine the p-values? Because this is the area in the distribution outside the calculated test statistic, we need to resort to software tools. For the p-value corresponding to the $t = 4.00131$ from the ROA regression example, we could use the following:

- **Excel** (1-T.DIST(4.00131,4,TRUE))*2
- **R** (1-pt(4.00131,4))*2
- **Python** from scipy.stats import t *and* (1 - t.cdf(4.00131,4))*2

QUESTION SET

The following applies to questions 1–3:

Julie Moon is an energy analyst examining electricity, oil, and natural gas consumption in different regions over different seasons. She ran a simple regression explaining the variation in energy consumption as a function of temperature. The total variation of the dependent variable was 140.58, and the explained variation was 60.16. She had 60 monthly observations.

1. Calculate the coefficient of determination.

   Solution:

   The coefficient of determination is 0.4279:

   $$\frac{\text{Explained variation}}{\text{Total variation}} = \frac{60.16}{140.58} = 0.4279.$$

2. Calculate the F-statistic to test the fit of the model.

   Solution:

   $$F = \frac{60.16 \big/ 1}{(140.58 - 60.16) \big/ (60 - 2)} = \frac{60.16}{1.3866} = 43.3882.$$

3. Calculate the sample standard deviation of monthly energy consumption.

   Solution:

   The sample variance of the dependent variable uses the total variation of the dependent variable and divides it by the number of observations less one:

   $$\sum_{i=1}^{n} \frac{(Y_i - \bar{Y})^2}{n-1} = \frac{\text{Total variation}}{n-1} = \frac{140.58}{60-1} = 2.3827.$$

   The sample standard deviation of the dependent variable is the square root of the variance, or $\sqrt{2.3827} = 1.544$.

The following applies to questions 4–6:

An analyst is interested in interpreting the results of and performing tests of hypotheses for the market model estimation that regresses the daily return on ABC stock on the daily return on the fictitious Europe–Asia–Africa (EAA) Equity Index, his proxy for the stock market. He has generated the regression results presented in Exhibit 27.

Exhibit 27: Hypothesis Testing of Simple Linear Regression Results Selected Results of Estimation of Market Model for ABC Stock

Standard error of the estimate (s_e)	1.26
Standard deviation of ABC stock returns	0.80
Standard deviation of EAA Equity Index returns	0.70
Number of observations	1,200

	Coefficients
Intercept	0.010
Slope of EAA Equity Index returns	0.982

4. If the critical t-values are ±1.96 (at the 5 percent significance level), is the slope coefficient different from zero?

   Solution:

   First, we calculate the variation of the independent variable using the standard deviation of the independent variable:

   $$\sum_{i=1}^{n} (X_i - \overline{X})^2 = \frac{\sum_{i=1}^{n} (X_i - \overline{X})^2}{n - 1} \times (n - 1).$$

   So,

   $$\sum_{i=1}^{n} (X_i - \overline{X})^2 = 0.70^2 \times 1,199 = 587.51.$$

   Next, the standard error of the estimated slope coefficient is

   $$s_{\hat{b}_1} = \frac{s_e}{\sqrt{\sum_{i=1}^{n} (X_i - \overline{X})^2}} = \frac{1.26}{\sqrt{587.51}} = 0.051983,$$

   and the test statistic is

   $$t = \frac{\hat{b}_1 - B_1}{s_{\hat{b}_1}} = \frac{0.982 - 0}{0.051983} = 18.8907.$$

   The calculated test statistic is outside the bounds of ±1.96, so we reject the null hypothesis of a slope coefficient equal to zero.

5. If the critical t-values are ±1.96 (at the 5 percent significance level), is the slope coefficient different from 1.0?

   Solution:

   The calculated test statistic for the test of whether the slope coefficient is equal to 1.0 is

$$t = \frac{0.982 - 1}{0.051983} = -0.3463.$$

The calculated test statistic is within the bounds of ±1.96, so we fail to reject the null hypothesis of a slope coefficient equal to 1.0, which is evidence that the true population slope may be 1.0.

6. An economist collected the monthly returns for KDL's portfolio and a diversified stock index. The data collected are shown in Exhibit 28:

Exhibit 28: Monthly Returns for KDL

Month	Portfolio Return (%)	Index Return (%)
1	1.11	−0.59
2	72.10	64.90
3	5.12	4.81
4	1.01	1.68
5	−1.72	−4.97
6	4.06	−2.06

The economist calculated the correlation between the two returns and found it to be 0.996. The regression results with the portfolio return as the dependent variable and the index return as the independent variable are given in Exhibit 29:

Exhibit 29: Regression Results

Regression Statistics

R^2	0.9921
Standard error	2.8619
Observations	6

Source	df	Sum of Squares	Mean Square	F	p-Value
Regression	1	4,101.6205	4,101.6205	500.7921	0.0000
Residual	4	32.7611	8.1903		
Total	5	4,134.3815			

	Coefficients	Standard Error	t-Statistic	p-Value
Intercept	2.2521	1.2739	1.7679	0.1518
Index return (%)	1.0690	0.0478	22.3784	0.0000

When reviewing the results, Andrea Fusilier suspected that they were unreliable. She found that the returns for Month 2 should have been 7.21 percent and 6.49 percent, instead of the large values shown in the first table. Correcting these values resulted in a revised correlation of 0.824 and the revised regression results in Exhibit 30:

Exhibit 30: Revised Regression Results

Regression Statistics

R^2	0.6784
Standard error	2.0624
Observations	6

Source	df	Sum of Squares	Mean Square	F	p-Value
Regression	1	35.8950	35.8950	8.4391	0.044
Residual	4	17.0137	4.2534		
Total	5	52.91			

	Coefficients	Standard Error	t-Statistic	p-Value
Intercept	2.2421	0.8635	2.5966	0.060
Slope	0.6217	0.2143	2.9050	0.044

Explain how the bad data affected the results.

Solution:

The Month 2 data point is an outlier, lying far away from the other data values. Because this outlier was caused by a data entry error, correcting the outlier improves the validity and reliability of the regression. In this case, revised R^2 is lower (from 0.9921 to 0.6784). The outliers created the illusion of a better fit from the higher R^2; the outliers altered the estimate of the slope. The standard error of the estimate is lower when the data error is corrected (from 2.8619 to 2.0624), as a result of the lower mean square error. At a 0.05 level of significance, both models fit well. The difference in the fit is illustrated in Exhibit 31.

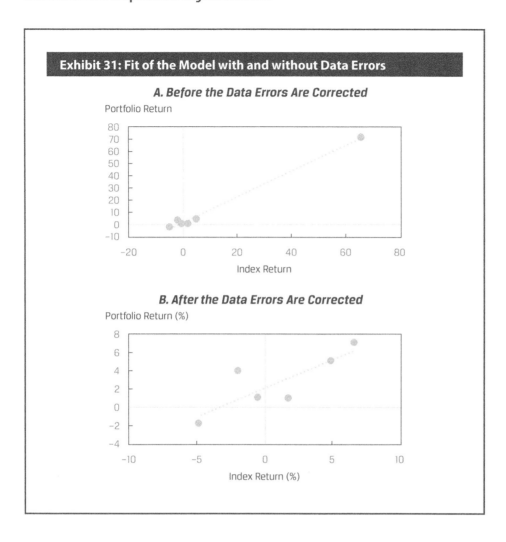

Exhibit 31: Fit of the Model with and without Data Errors

A. Before the Data Errors Are Corrected

Portfolio Return

Index Return

B. After the Data Errors Are Corrected

Portfolio Return (%)

Index Return (%)

PREDICTION IN THE SIMPLE LINEAR REGRESSION MODEL

5

☐ describe the use of analysis of variance (ANOVA) in regression analysis, interpret ANOVA results, and calculate and interpret the standard error of estimate in a simple linear regression

☐ calculate and interpret the predicted value for the dependent variable, and a prediction interval for it, given an estimated linear regression model and a value for the independent variable

ANOVA and Standard Error of Estimate in Simple Linear Regression

We often represent the sums of squares from a regression model in an **analysis of variance (ANOVA)** table, as shown in Exhibit 32, which presents the sums of squares, the degrees of freedom, the mean squares, and the F-statistic. Notice that the variance of the dependent variable is the ratio of the sum of squares total to $n - 1$.

Exhibit 32: Analysis of Variance Table for Simple Linear Regression

Source	Sum of Squares	Degrees of Freedom	Mean Square	F-Statistic
Regression	$\text{SSR} = \sum_{i=1}^{n} (\hat{Y}_i - \bar{Y})^2$	1	$\text{MSR} = \dfrac{\sum_{i=1}^{n}(\hat{Y}_i - \bar{Y})^2}{1}$	$F = \dfrac{\text{MSR}}{\text{MSE}} = \dfrac{\frac{\sum_{i=1}^{n}(\hat{Y}_i - \bar{Y})^2}{1}}{\frac{\sum_{i=1}^{n}(Y_i - \hat{Y}_i)^2}{n-2}}$
Error	$\text{SSE} = \sum_{i=1}^{n} (Y_i - \hat{Y}_i)^2$	$n - 2$	$\text{MSE} = \dfrac{\sum_{i=1}^{n}(Y_i - \hat{Y}_i)^2}{n-2}$	
Total	$\text{SST} = \sum_{i=1}^{n} (Y_i - \bar{Y})^2$	$n - 1$		

From the ANOVA table, we can also calculate the **standard error of the estimate** (s_e), which is also known as the standard error of the regression or the root mean square error. The s_e is a measure of the distance between the observed values of the dependent variable and those predicted from the estimated regression—the smaller the s_e, the better the fit of the model. The s_e, along with the coefficient of determination and the F-statistic, is a measure of the goodness of the fit of the estimated regression line. Unlike the coefficient of determination and the F-statistic, which are relative measures of fit, the standard error of the estimate is an absolute measure of the distance of the observed dependent variable from the regression line. Thus, the s_e is an important statistic used to evaluate a regression model and is used to calculate prediction intervals and to perform tests on the coefficients. The calculation of s_e is straightforward once we have the ANOVA table because it is the square root of the MSE:

$$\text{Standard error of the estimate } (s_e) = \sqrt{\text{MSE}} = \sqrt{\frac{\sum_{i=1}^{n}(Y_i - \hat{Y}_i)^2}{n-2}}. \tag{22}$$

We show the ANOVA table for our ROA regression example in Exhibit 32, using the information from Exhibit 33. For a 5 percent level of significance, the critical F-value for the test of whether the model is a good fit (i.e., whether the slope coefficient is different from zero) is 7.71. We can get this critical value in the following ways:

- *Excel* [F.INV(0.95,1,4)]
- *R* [qf(.95,1,4)]
- *Python* [from scipy.stats import f *and* f.ppf(.95,1,4)]

With a calculated F-statistic of 16.0104 and a critical F-value of 7.71, we reject the null hypothesis and conclude that the slope of our simple linear regression model for ROA is different from zero.

Exhibit 33: ANOVA Table for ROA Regression Model

Source	Sum of Squares	Degrees of Freedom	Mean Square	F-Statistic
Regression	191.625	1	191.625	16.0104
Error	47.875	4	11.96875	
Total	239.50	5		

The calculations to derive the ANOVA table and ultimately to test the goodness of fit of the regression model can be time consuming, especially for samples with many observations. However, statistical packages, such as SAS, SPSS Statistics, and Stata, as well as software, such as Excel, R, and Python, produce the ANOVA table as part of the output for regression analysis.

Prediction Using Simple Linear Regression and Prediction Intervals

Financial analysts often want to use regression results to make predictions about a dependent variable. For example, we might ask, "How fast will the sales of XYZ Corporation grow this year if real GDP grows by 4 percent?" But we are not merely interested in making these forecasts; we also want to know how certain we can be about the forecasts' results. A forecasted value of the dependent variable, $\hat{Y}_f$, is determined using the estimated intercept and slope, as well as the expected or forecasted independent variable, X_f:

$$\hat{Y}_f = \hat{b}_0 + \hat{b}_1 X_f. \tag{23}$$

In our ROA regression model, if we forecast a company's CAPEX to be 6 percent, the forecasted ROA based on our estimated equation is 12.375 percent:

$$\hat{Y}_f = 4.875 + (1.25 \times 6) = 12.375.$$

However, we need to consider that the estimated regression line does not describe the relation between the dependent and independent variables perfectly; it is an average of the relation between the two variables. This is evident because the residuals are not all zero.

Therefore, an interval estimate of the forecast is needed to reflect this uncertainty. The estimated variance of the prediction error, s_f^2, of Y, given X, is

$$s_f^2 = s_e^2 \left[1 + \frac{1}{n} + \frac{(X_f - \bar{X})^2}{(n-1)s_X^2} \right] = s_e^2 \left[1 + \frac{1}{n} + \frac{(X_f - \bar{X})^2}{\sum_{i=1}^{n}(X_i - \bar{X})^2} \right],$$

and the **standard error of the forecast** is

$$s_f = s_e \sqrt{1 + \frac{1}{n} + \frac{(X_f - \bar{X})^2}{\sum_{i=1}^{n}(X_i - \bar{X})^2}}. \tag{24}$$

The standard error of the forecast depends on the following:

- the standard error of the estimate, s_e;
- the number of observations, n;
- the forecasted value of the independent variable, X_f, used to predict the dependent variable and its deviation from the estimated mean, $\bar{X}$; and
- the variation of the independent variable.

We can see the following from the equation for the standard error of the forecast:

1. The better the fit of the regression model, the smaller the standard error of the estimate (s_e) and, therefore, the smaller standard error of the forecast.

2. The larger the sample size (n) in the regression estimation, the smaller the standard error of the forecast.

3. The closer the forecasted independent variable (X_f) is to the mean of the independent variable ($\bar{X}$) used in the regression estimation, the smaller the standard error of the forecast.

Once we have this estimate of the standard error of the forecast, determining a prediction interval around the predicted value of the dependent variable $\left(\hat{Y}_f\right)$ is very similar to estimating a confidence interval around an estimated parameter. The prediction interval is

$$\hat{Y}_f \pm t_{critical\ for\ \alpha/2} s_f.$$

We outline the steps for developing the prediction interval in Exhibit 34.

Exhibit 34: Creating a Prediction Interval around the Predicted Dependent Variable

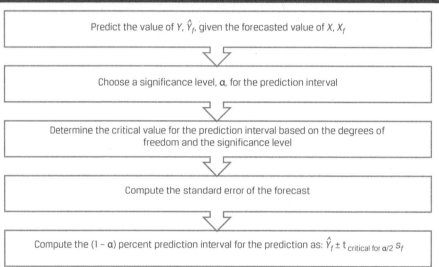

Predict the value of Y, $\hat{Y}_f$, given the forecasted value of X, X_f

Choose a significance level, α, for the prediction interval

Determine the critical value for the prediction interval based on the degrees of freedom and the significance level

Compute the standard error of the forecast

Compute the $(1 - \alpha)$ percent prediction interval for the prediction as: $\hat{Y}_f \pm t_{critical\ for\ \alpha/2}\ s_f$

For our ROA regression model, given that the forecasted value of CAPEX is 6.0, the predicted value of Y is 12.375:

$$\hat{Y}_f = 4.875 + 1.25 X_f = 4.875 + (1.25 \times 6.0) = 12.375.$$

Assuming a 5 percent significance level (α), two sided, with $n - 2$ degrees of freedom (so, df = 4), the critical values for the prediction interval are ±2.776.

The standard error of the forecast is

$$s_f = 3.459588 \sqrt{1 + \frac{1}{6} + \frac{(6 - 6.1)^2}{122.640}} = 3.459588 \sqrt{1.166748} = 3.736912.$$

The 95 percent prediction interval then becomes

$$12.375 \pm 2.776\,(3.736912)$$

$$12.375 \pm 10.3737$$

$$\left\{2.0013 < \hat{Y}_f < 22.7487\right\}$$

For our ROA regression example, we can see how the standard error of the forecast (s_f) changes as our forecasted value of the independent variable gets farther from the mean of the independent variable $\left(X_f - \overline{X}\right)$ in Exhibit 35. The mean of CAPEX is 6.1 percent, and the band that represents one standard error of the forecast, above and below the forecast, is minimized at that point and increases as simple independent variable gets farther from $\overline{X}$.

Exhibit 35: ROA Forecasts and Standard Error of the Forecast

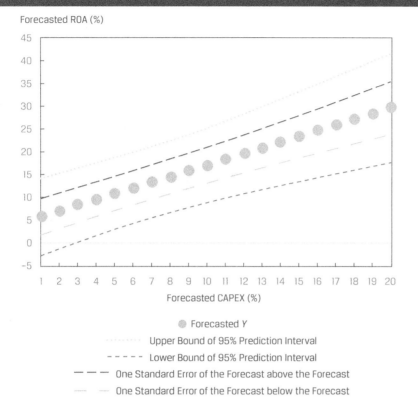

Forecasted ROA (%)

Forecasted CAPEX (%)

- ● Forecasted *Y*
- ·········· Upper Bound of 95% Prediction Interval
- − − − − − Lower Bound of 95% Prediction Interval
- − − − One Standard Error of the Forecast above the Forecast
- —— —— One Standard Error of the Forecast below the Forecast

QUESTION SET

Suppose you run a cross-sectional regression for 100 companies, where the dependent variable is the annual return on stock and the independent variable is the lagged percentage of institutional ownership (INST). The results of this simple linear regression estimation are shown in Exhibit 36. Evaluate the model by answering questions 1–4.

Exhibit 36: ANOVA Table for Annual Stock Return Regressed on Institutional Ownership

Source	Sum of Squares	Degrees of Freedom	Mean Square
Regression	576.1485	1	576.1485
Error	1,873.5615	98	19.1180
Total	2,449.7100		

1. What is the coefficient of determination for this regression model?

   Solution:

   The coefficient of determination is sum of squares regression/sum of squares total: $576.148 \div 2{,}449.71 = 0.2352$, or 23.52 percent.

2. What is the standard error of the estimate for this regression model?

    Solution:

    The standard error of the estimate is the square root of the mean square error: $\sqrt{19.1180} = 4.3724$.

3. At a 5 percent level of significance, do we reject the null hypothesis of the slope coefficient equal to zero if the critical F-value is 3.938?

    Solution:

    Using a six-step process for testing hypotheses, we get the following:

Step 1	State the hypotheses.	$H_0: b_1 = 0$ versus $H_a: b_1 \neq 0$
Step 2	Identify the appropriate test statistic.	$F = \dfrac{MSR}{MSE}$ with 1 and 98 degrees of freedom.
Step 3	Specify the level of significance.	$\alpha = 5\%$ (one tail, right side).
Step 4	State the decision rule.	Critical F-value = 3.938. Reject the null hypothesis if the calculated F-statistic is greater than 3.938.
Step 5	Calculate the test statistic.	$F = \dfrac{576.1485}{19.1180} = 30.1364$
Step 6	Make a decision.	Reject the null hypothesis because the calculated F-statistic is greater than the critical F-value. Evidence is sufficient to indicate that the slope coefficient is different from 0.0.

4. Based on your answers to the preceding questions, evaluate this simple linear regression model.

    Solution:

    The coefficient of determination indicates that variation in the independent variable explains 23.52 percent of the variation in the dependent variable. Also, the F-statistic test confirms that the model's slope coefficient is different from 0 at the 5 percent level of significance. In sum, the model seems to fit the data reasonably well.

The following applies to questions 5-11.

Suppose we want to forecast a company's net profit margin (NPM) based on its research and development expenditures scaled by revenues (RDR), using the model estimated in Example 2 and the details provided in Exhibit 8. The regression model was estimated using data on eight companies as

$$\hat{Y}_f = 16.5 - 1.3 X_f,$$

with a standard error of the estimate (s_e) of 1.8618987 and variance of RDR, $\dfrac{\sum_{i=1}^{n}(X_i - \bar{X})^2}{(n-1)}$, of 4.285714, as given.

5. What is the predicted value of NPM if the forecasted value of RDR is 5?

    Solution:

    The predicted value of NPM is 10: $16.5 - (1.3 \times 5) = 10$.

6. What is the standard error of the forecast (s_f) if the forecasted value of RDR is 5?

   Solution:

   To derive the standard error of the forecast (s_f), we first have to calculate the variation of RDR. Then, we have all the pieces to calculate s_f:

   $$\sum_{i=1}^{n} (X_i - \overline{X})^2 = 4.285714 \times 7 = 30.$$

   $$s_f = 1.8618987 \sqrt{1 + \frac{1}{8} + \frac{(5 - 7.5)^2}{30}} = 2.1499.$$

7. What is the 95 percent prediction interval for the predicted value of NPM using critical t-values (df = 6) of ±2.447?

   Solution:

   The 95 percent prediction interval for the predicted value of NPM is

   $$\{10 \pm 2.447(2.1499)\},$$

   $$\left\{ 4.7392 < \hat{Y}_f < 15.2608 \right\}.$$

8. What is the predicted value of NPM if the forecasted value of RDR is 15?

   Solution:

   The predicted value of NPM is –3: 16.5 – (1.3 × 15) = –3.

9. Referring to exhibit 9, what is the standard error of the forecast if the forecasted value of RDR is 15?

   Solution:

   To derive the standard error of the forecast, we first must calculate the variation of RDR. Then, we can calculate s_f:

   $$\sum_{i=1}^{n} (X_i - \overline{X})^2 = 4.285714 \times 7 = 30.$$

   $$s_f = 1.8618987 \sqrt{1 + \frac{1}{8} + \frac{(15 - 7.5)^2}{30}} = 3.2249.$$

10. What is the 95 percent prediction interval for the predicted value of NPM using critical t-values (df = 6) of ±2.447?

    Solution:

    The 95 percent prediction interval for the predicted value of NPM is

    $$\{-3 \pm 2.447(3.2249)\},$$

    $$\left\{ -10.8913 < \hat{Y}_f < 4.8913 \right\}.$$

The following applies to questions 12-17.

You are examining the results of a regression estimation that attempts to explain the unit sales growth of a business you are researching. The analysis of variance output for the regression is given in the Exhibit 37. The regression was based on five observations ($n = 5$).

Exhibit 37: ANOVA Output

Source	df	Sum of Squares	Mean Square	F	p-Value
Regression	1	88.0	88.0	36.667	0.00904
Residual	3	7.2	2.4		
Total	4	95.2			

11. Calculate the sample variance of the dependent variable using information in the table.

    Solution:

    The sample variance of the dependent variable is the sum of squares total divided by its degrees of freedom ($n - 1 = 5 - 1 = 4$, as given). Thus, the sample variance of the dependent variable is $95.2 \div 4 = 23.8$.

12. Calculate the coefficient of determination for this estimated model.

    Solution:

    The coefficient of determination $= 88.0 \div 95.2 = 0.92437$.

13. What hypothesis does the F-statistic test?

    Solution:

    The F-statistic tests whether all the slope coefficients in a linear regression are equal to zero.

14. Is the F-test significant at the 0.05 significance level?

    Solution:

    The calculated value of the F-statistic is 36.667, as shown in Exhibit 32. The corresponding p-value is less than 0.05, so you reject the null hypothesis of a slope equal to zero.

15. Calculate the standard error of the estimate.

    Solution:

    The standard error of the estimate is the square root of the mean square error: $s_e = \sqrt{2.4} = 1.54919$.

6   FUNCTIONAL FORMS FOR SIMPLE LINEAR REGRESSION

☐ | describe different functional forms of simple linear regressions

Not every set of independent and dependent variables has a linear relation. In fact, we often see non-linear relationships in economic and financial data. Consider the revenues of a company over time illustrated in Exhibit 38, with revenues as the dependent

(*Y*) variable and time as the independent (*X*) variable. Revenues grow at a rate of 15 percent per year for several years, but then the growth rate eventually declines to just 5 percent per year. Estimating this relationship as a simple linear model would understate the dependent variable, revenues, and, for some ranges of the independent variable, time, and would overstate it for other ranges of the independent variable.

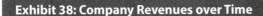

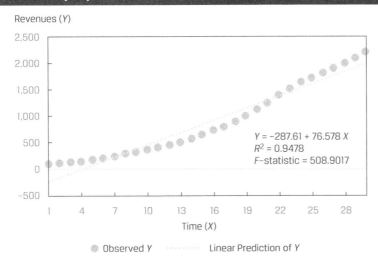

Exhibit 38: Company Revenues over Time

We can still use the simple linear regression model, but we need to modify either the dependent or the independent variables to make it work well. This is the case with many different financial or economic data that you might use as dependent and independent variables in your regression analysis.

Several different functional forms can be used to potentially transform the data to enable their use in linear regression. These transformations include using the log (i.e., natural logarithm) of the dependent variable, the log of the independent variable, the reciprocal of the independent variable, the square of the independent variable, or the differencing of the independent variable. We illustrate and discuss three often-used functional forms, each of which involves log transformation:

1. the **log-lin model**, in which the dependent variable is logarithmic but the independent variable is linear;

2. the **lin-log model**, in which the dependent variable is linear but the independent variable is logarithmic; and

3. the **log-log model**, in which both the dependent and independent variables are in logarithmic form.

The Log-Lin Model

In the log-lin model, the dependent variable is in logarithmic form and the independent variable is not, as follows:

$$\ln Y_i = b_0 + b_1 X_i. \tag{25}$$

The slope coefficient in this model is the relative change in the dependent variable for an absolute change in the independent variable. We can transform the Y variable (revenues) in Exhibit 38 into its natural log (ln) and then fit the regression line, as shown in Exhibit 39. From this chart, we see that the log-lin model is a better-fitting model than the simple linear regression model.

Exhibit 39: Log-Lin Model Applied to Company Revenues over Time

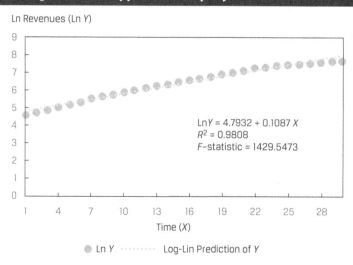

Ln Revenues (Ln Y)

$LnY = 4.7932 + 0.1087\ X$
$R^2 = 0.9808$
F-statistic = 1429.5473

Time (X)

● Ln Y ⋯⋯⋯ Log-Lin Prediction of Y

It is important to note that in working with a log-lin model, you must take care when making a forecast. For example, suppose the estimated regression model is $\ln Y = -7 + 2X$. If X is 2.5 percent, then the forecasted value of $\ln Y$ is -2. In this case, the predicted value of Y is the antilog of -2, or $e^{-2} = 0.135335$. Another caution is that you cannot directly compare a log-lin model with a lin-lin model (i.e., the regression of Y on X without any transformation) because the dependent variables are not in the same form—we would have to transform the R^2 and F-statistic to enable a comparison. Looking at the residuals, however, is helpful:

The Lin-Log Model

The lin-log model is similar to the log-lin model, but only the independent variable is in logarithmic form:

$$Y_i = b_0 + b_1 \ln X_i. \tag{26}$$

The slope coefficient in this regression model provides the absolute change in the dependent variable for a relative change in the independent variable.

Suppose an analyst is examining the cross-sectional relationship between operating profit margin, the dependent variable (Y), and unit sales, the independent variable (X), and gathers data on a sample of 30 companies. The scatter plot and regression line for these observations are shown in Exhibit 40. Although the slope is different from zero at the 5 percent level (the calculated t-statistic on the slope is 5.8616, compared with critical t-values of ±2.048), given the R^2 of 55.10 percent, the issue is whether we can get a better fit by using a different functional form.

Exhibit 40: Relationship between Operating Profit Margin and Unit Sales

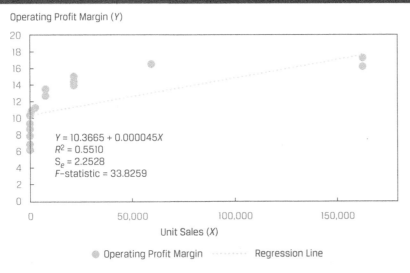

Operating Profit Margin (Y)

$Y = 10.3665 + 0.000045X$
$R^2 = 0.5510$
$S_e = 2.2528$
F–statistic = 33.8259

Unit Sales (X)

● Operating Profit Margin ⋯⋯⋯ Regression Line

If instead we use the natural log of the unit sales as the independent variable in our model, we get a very different picture, as shown in Exhibit 41. The R^2 for the model of operating profit margin regressed on the natural log of unit sales jumps to 97.17 percent. Because the dependent variable is the same in both the original and transformed models, we can compare the standard error of the estimate: 2.2528 with the original independent variable and a much lower 0.5629 with the transformed independent variable. Clearly the log-transformed explanatory variable has resulted in a better-fitting model.

Exhibit 41: Relationship Between Operating Profit Margin and Natural Logarithm of Unit Sales

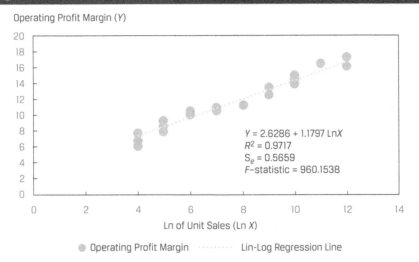

Operating Profit Margin (Y)

$Y = 2.6286 + 1.1797\,LnX$
$R^2 = 0.9717$
$S_e = 0.5659$
F–statistic = 960.1538

Ln of Unit Sales (Ln X)

● Operating Profit Margin ⋯⋯⋯ Lin-Log Regression Line

The Log-Log Model

The log-log model, in which both the dependent variable and the independent variable are linear in their logarithmic forms, is also referred to as the double-log model:

$$\ln Y_i = b_0 + b_1 \ln X_i. \tag{27}$$

This model is useful in calculating elasticities because the slope coefficient is the relative change in the dependent variable for a relative change in the independent variable. Consider a cross-sectional model of company revenues (the Y variable) regressed on advertising spending as a percentage of selling, general, and administrative expenses, ADVERT (the X variable). As shown in Exhibit 42, a simple linear regression model results in a shallow regression line, with a coefficient of determination of just 20.89 percent.

Exhibit 42: Fitting a Linear Relation Between Revenues and Advertising Spending

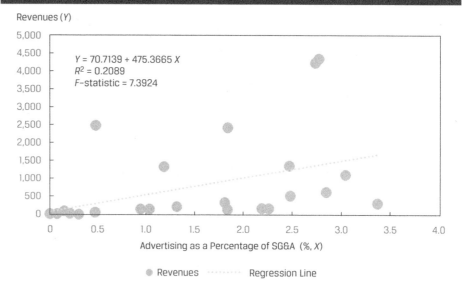

If instead we use the natural logarithms of both the revenues and ADVERT, we get a much different picture of this relationship. As shown in Exhibit 43, the estimated regression line has a significant positive slope; the log-log model's R^2 increases by more than four times, from 20.89 percent to 84.91 percent; and the F-statistic jumps from 7.39 to 157.52. So, using the log-log transformation dramatically improves the regression model fit relative to our data.

Exhibit 43: Fitting a Log-Log Model of Revenues and Advertising Spending

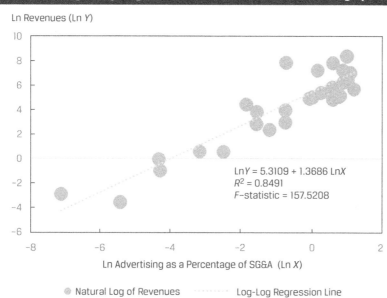

Ln Revenues (Ln *Y*)

$LnY = 5.3109 + 1.3686\ LnX$
$R^2 = 0.8491$
F-statistic = 157.5208

Ln Advertising as a Percentage of SG&A (Ln *X*)

⬤ Natural Log of Revenues ·········· Log-Log Regression Line

Selecting the Correct Functional Form

The key to fitting the appropriate functional form of a simple linear regression is examining the goodness-of-fit measures—the coefficient of determination (R^2), the F-statistic, and the standard error of the estimate (s_e)—as well as examining whether there are patterns in the residuals. In addition to fit statistics, most statistical packages provide plots of residuals as part of the regression output, which enables you to visually inspect the residuals. To reiterate an important point, what you want to see in these plots is random residuals.

As an example, consider the relationship between the monthly returns on DEF stock and the monthly returns of the EAA Equity Index, as depicted in Panel A of Exhibit 44, with the regression line indicated. Using the equation for this regression line, we calculate the residuals and plot them against the EAA Equity Index, as shown in Panel B of Exhibit 44. The residuals appear to be random, bearing no relation to the independent variable. The distribution of the residuals, shown in Panel C of Exhibit 44, shows that the residuals are approximately normal. Using statistical software, we can investigate further by examining the distribution of the residuals, including using a normal probability plot or statistics to test for normality of the residuals.

Exhibit 44: Monthly Returns on DEF Stock Regressed on Returns on the EAA Index

A. Scatterplot of Returns on DEF Stock and Return on the EAA Index

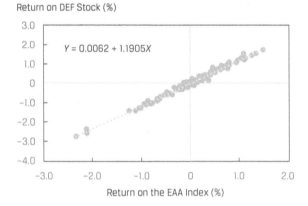

B. Scatterplot of Residuals and the Returns on the EAA Index

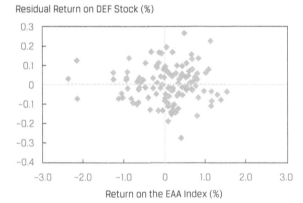

C. Histogram of Residuals

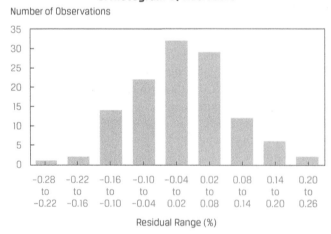

QUESTION SET

An analyst is investigating the relationship between the annual growth in consumer spending (CONS) in a country and the annual growth in the country's GDP (GGDP). The analyst estimates the two models in Exhibit 45.

Exhibit 45: Model Estimates

	Model 1	Model 2
	$GGDP_i = b_0 + b_1 CONS_i + \varepsilon_i$	$GGDP_i = b_0 + b_1 \ln(CONS_i) + \varepsilon_i$
Intercept	1.040	1.006
Slope	0.669	1.994
R^2	0.788	0.867
Standard error of the estimate	0.404	0.320
F-statistic	141.558	247.040

---

1. Identify the functional form used in these models.

   Solution:

   Model 1 is a simple linear regression model with no variable transformation, whereas Model 2 is a lin-log model with the natural log of the variable CONS as the independent variable.

---

2. Explain which model has better goodness of fit with the sample data.

   Solution:

   The lin-log model, Model 2, fits the data better. Since the dependent variable is the same for the two models, we can compare the fit of the models using either the relative measures (R^2 or F-statistic) or the absolute measure of fit, the standard error of the estimate. The standard error of the estimate is lower for Model 2, whereas the R^2 and F-statistic are higher for Model 2 compared with Model 1.

PRACTICE PROBLEMS

The following information relates to questions 1-3

An analyst has estimated a model that regresses a company's return on equity (ROE) against its growth opportunities (GO), defined as the company's three-year compounded annual growth rate in sales, over 20 years, and produces the following estimated simple linear regression:

$$ROE_i = 4 + 1.8\ GO_i + \varepsilon_i.$$

Both variables are stated in percentages, so a GO observation of 5 percent is included as 5.

1. The predicted value of the company's ROE if its GO is 10 percent is closest to:

    A. 1.8 percent.

    B. 15.8 percent.

    C. 22.0 percent.

2. The change in ROE for a change in GO from 5 percent to 6 percent is closest to:

    A. 1.8 percent.

    B. 4.0 percent.

    C. 5.8 percent.

3. The residual in the case of a *GO* of 8 percent and an observed *ROE* of 21 percent is closest to:

    A. −1.8 percent.

    B. 2.6 percent.

    C. 12.0 percent.

4. Homoskedasticity is best described as the situation in which the variance of the residuals of a regression is:

    A. zero.

    B. normally distributed.

    C. constant across observations.

The following information relates to questions 5-8

An analyst is examining the annual growth of the money supply for a country over the past 30 years. This country experienced a central bank policy shift 15 years ago, which altered the approach to the management of the money supply. The analyst estimated a model using the annual growth rate in the money supply regressed on the variable (SHIFT) that takes on a value of 0 before the policy shift and 1 after. She estimated the values in Exhibit 1:

Exhibit 1: SHIFT Estimates			
	Coefficients	Standard Error	t-Stat.
Intercept	5.767264	0.445229	12.95348
SHIFT	−5.13912	0.629649	−8.16188

Critical t-values, level of significance of 0.05:
eOne-sided, left side: −1.701
fOne-sided, right side: +1.701
gTwo-sided: ±2.048

5. The variable SHIFT is best described as:

   A. an indicator variable.

   B. a dependent variable.

   C. a continuous variable.

6. The interpretation of the intercept is the mean of the annual growth rate of the money supply:

   A. before the shift in policy.

   B. over the entire period.

   C. after the shift in policy.

7. The interpretation of the slope is the:

   A. change in the annual growth rate of the money supply per year.

   B. average annual growth rate of the money supply after the shift in policy.

   C. difference in the average annual growth rate of the money supply from before to after the shift in policy.

8. Testing whether there is a change in the money supply growth after the shift in policy, using a 0.05 level of significance, we conclude that there is:

   A. sufficient evidence that the money supply growth changed.

   B. not enough evidence that the money supply growth is different from zero.

   C. not enough evidence to indicate that the money supply growth changed.

The following information relates to questions 9-12

Kenneth McCoin, CFA, is a challenging interviewer. Last year, he handed each job applicant a sheet of paper with the information in Exhibit 1, and he then asked several questions about regression analysis. Some of McCoin's questions, along with a sample of the answers he received to each, are given below. McCoin told the applicants that the independent variable is the ratio of net income to sales for restaurants with a market cap of more than $100 million and the dependent variable is the ratio of cash flow from operations to sales for those restaurants. Which of the choices provided is the best answer to each of McCoin's questions?

Exhibit 1: Regression Analysis

Regression Statistics	
R^2	0.7436
Standard error	0.0213
Observations	24

Source	df	Sum of Squares	Mean Square	F	p-Value
Regression	1	0.029	0.029000	63.81	0
Residual	22	0.010	0.000455		
Total	23	0.040			

	Coefficients	Standard Error	t-Statistic	p-Value
Intercept	0.077	0.007	11.328	0
Net income to sales (%)	0.826	0.103	7.988	0

9. The coefficient of determination is *closest* to:

   A. 0.7436.

   B. 0.8261.

   C. 0.8623.

10. The correlation between X and Y is *closest* to:

    A. −0.7436.

    B. 0.7436.

    C. 0.8623.

11. If the ratio of net income to sales for a restaurant is 5 percent, the predicted ratio

of cash flow from operations (CFO) to sales is *closest* to:

A. −4.054.

B. 0.524.

C. 4.207.

12. Is the relationship between the ratio of cash flow to operations and the ratio of net income to sales significant at the 0.05 level?

A. No, because the R^2 is greater than 0.05

B. No, because the p-values of the intercept and slope are less than 0.05

C. Yes, because the p-values for F and t for the slope coefficient are less than 0.05

The following information relates to questions 13-17

Howard Golub, CFA, is preparing to write a research report on Stellar Energy Corp. common stock. One of the world's largest companies, Stellar is in the business of refining and marketing oil. As part of his analysis, Golub wants to evaluate the sensitivity of the stock's returns to various economic factors. For example, a client recently asked Golub whether the price of Stellar Energy Corp. stock has tended to rise following increases in retail energy prices. Golub believes the association between the two variables is negative, but he does not know the strength of the association.

Golub directs his assistant, Jill Batten, to study the relationships between (1) Stellar monthly common stock returns and the previous month's percentage change in the US Consumer Price Index for Energy (CPIENG) and (2) Stellar monthly common stock returns and the previous month's percentage change in the US Producer Price Index for Crude Energy Materials (PPICEM). Golub wants Batten to run both a correlation and a linear regression analysis. In response, Batten compiles the summary statistics shown in Exhibit 1 for 248 months. All the data are in decimal form, where 0.01 indicates a 1 percent return. Batten also runs a regression analysis using Stellar monthly returns as the dependent variable and the monthly change in CPIENG as the independent variable. Exhibit 2 displays the results of this regression model.

Exhibit 1: Descriptive Statistics

	Stellar Common Stock Monthly Return	Lagged Monthly Change	
		CPIENG	PPICEM
Mean	0.0123	0.0023	0.0042
Standard deviation	0.0717	0.0160	0.0534
Covariance, Stellar vs. CPIENG	−0.00017		

	Stellar Common Stock Monthly Return	Lagged Monthly Change	
		CPIENG	PPICEM
Covariance, Stellar vs. PPICEM	−0.00048		
Covariance, CPIENG vs. PPICEM	0.00044		
Correlation, Stellar vs. CPIENG	−0.1452		

Exhibit 2: Regression Analysis with CPIENG

Regression Statistics	
R^2	0.0211
Standard error of the estimate	0.0710
Observations	248

	Coefficients	Standard Error	*t*-Statistic
Intercept	0.0138	0.0046	3.0275
CPIENG (%)	−0.6486	0.2818	−2.3014

Critical t-values
One-sided, left side: −1.651
One-sided, right side: +1.651
Two-sided: ±1.967

13. Which of the following best describes Batten's regression?

    A. Time-series regression

    B. Cross-sectional regression

    C. Time-series and cross-sectional regression

14. Based on the regression, if the CPIENG *decreases* by 1.0 percent, the expected return on Stellar common stock during the next period is *closest* to:

    A. 0.0073 (0.73 percent).

    B. 0.0138 (1.38 percent).

    C. 0.0203 (2.03 percent).

15. Based on Batten's regression model, the coefficient of determination indicates that:

    A. Stellar's returns explain 2.11 percent of the variability in CPIENG.

    B. Stellar's returns explain 14.52 percent of the variability in CPIENG.

    C. changes in CPIENG explain 2.11 percent of the variability in Stellar's returns.

16. For Batten's regression model, 0.0710 is the standard deviation of:

    A. the dependent variable.

B. the residuals from the regression.

C. the predicted dependent variable from the regression.

17. For the analysis run by Batten, which of the following is an *incorrect* conclusion from the regression output?

A. The estimated intercept from Batten's regression is statistically different from zero at the 0.05 level of significance.

B. In the month after the CPIENG declines, Stellar's common stock is expected to exhibit a positive return.

C. Viewed in combination, the slope and intercept coefficients from Batten's regression are not statistically different from zero at the 0.05 level of significance.

The following information relates to questions 18-26

Anh Liu is an analyst researching whether a company's debt burden affects investors' decision to short the company's stock. She calculates the short interest ratio (the ratio of short interest to average daily share volume, expressed in days) for 50 companies as of the end of the year and compares this ratio with the companies' debt ratio (the ratio of total liabilities to total assets, expressed in decimal form).

Liu provides a number of statistics in Exhibit 1. She also estimates a simple regression to investigate the effect of the debt ratio on a company's short interest ratio. The results of this simple regression, including the analysis of variance (ANOVA), are shown in Exhibit 2.

In addition to estimating a regression equation, Liu graphs the 50 observations using a scatter plot, with the short interest ratio on the vertical axis and the debt ratio on the horizontal axis.

Exhibit 1: Summary Statistics

Statistic	Debt Ratio (X_i)	Short Interest Ratio (Y_i)
Sum	19.8550	192.3000
Sum of squared deviations from the mean	$\sum_{i=1}^{n}(X_i - \overline{X})^2 = 2.2225$	$\sum_{i=1}^{n}(Y_i - \overline{Y})^2 = 412.2042.$
Sum of cross-products of deviations from the mean	$\sum_{i=1}^{n}(X_i - \overline{X})(Y_i - \overline{Y}) = -9.2430.$	

Exhibit 2: Regression of the Short Interest Ratio on the Debt Ratio

ANOVA	Degrees of Freedom (df)	Sum of Squares	Mean Square
Regression	1	38.4404	38.4404
Residual	48	373.7638	7.7867
Total	49	412.2042	
Regression Statistics			
R^2	0.0933		
Standard error of estimate	2.7905		
Observations	50		

	Coefficients	Standard Error	t-Statistic
Intercept	5.4975	0.8416	6.5322
Debt ratio (%)	−4.1589	1.8718	−2.2219

Critical t-values for a 0.05 level of significance:
One-sided, left side: −1.677
One-sided, right side: +1.677
Two-sided: ±2.011

Liu is considering three interpretations of these results for her report on the relationship between debt ratios and short interest ratios:

Interpretation 1   Companies' higher debt ratios cause lower short interest ratios.

Interpretation 2   Companies' higher short interest ratios cause higher debt ratios.

Interpretation 3   Companies with higher debt ratios tend to have lower short interest ratios.

She is especially interested in using her estimation results to predict the short interest ratio for MQD Corporation, which has a debt ratio of 0.40.

18. Based on Exhibit 1 and Exhibit 2, if Liu were to graph the 50 observations, the scatter plot summarizing this relation would be *best* described as:

A. horizontal.

B. upward sloping.

C. downward sloping.

19. Based on Exhibit 1, the sample covariance is *closest to*:

A. −9.2430.

B. −0.1886.

C. 8.4123.

20. Based on Exhibit 1 and Exhibit 2, the correlation between the debt ratio and the

short interest ratio is *closest to*:

   A. −0.3054.

   B. 0.0933.

   C. 0.3054.

21. Which of the interpretations *best* describes Liu's findings?

   A. Interpretation 1

   B. Interpretation 2

   C. Interpretation 3

22. The dependent variable in Liu's regression analysis is the:

   A. intercept.

   B. debt ratio.

   C. short interest ratio.

23. Based on Exhibit 2, the number of degrees of freedom for the *t*-test of the slope coefficient in this regression is:

   A. 48.

   B. 49.

   C. 50.

24. Which of the following should Liu conclude from the results shown in Exhibit 2?

   A. The average short interest ratio is 5.4975.

   B. The estimated slope coefficient is different from zero at the 0.05 level of significance.

   C. The debt ratio explains 30.54 percent of the variation in the short interest ratio.

25. Based on Exhibit 2, the short interest ratio expected for MQD Corporation is *closest* to:

   A. 3.8339.

   B. 5.4975.

   C. 6.2462.

26. Based on Liu's regression results in Exhibit 2, the *F*-statistic for testing whether the slope coefficient is equal to zero is *closest* to:

   A. −2.2219.

   B. 3.5036.

   C. 4.9367.

The following information relates to questions 27-29

Doug Abitbol is a portfolio manager for Polyi Investments, a hedge fund that trades in the United States. Abitbol manages the hedge fund with the help of Robert Olabudo, a junior portfolio manager.

Abitbol looks at economists' inflation forecasts and would like to examine the relationship between the US Consumer Price Index (US CPI) consensus forecast and the actual US CPI using regression analysis. Olabudo estimates regression coefficients to test whether the consensus forecast is unbiased. If the consensus forecasts are unbiased, the intercept should be 0.0 and the slope will be equal to 1.0. Regression results are presented in Exhibit 1. Additionally, Olabudo calculates the 95 percent prediction interval of the actual CPI using a US CPI consensus forecast of 2.8.

Exhibit 1: Regression Output: Estimating US CPI

Regression Statistics

R^2	0.9859
Standard error of estimate	0.0009
Observations	60

	Coefficients	Standard Error	t-Statistic
Intercept	0.0001	0.0002	0.5000
US CPI consensus forecast	0.9830	0.0155	63.4194

Notes:

1. The absolute value of the critical value for the t-statistic is 2.002 at the 5 percent level of significance.
2. The standard deviation of the US CPI consensus forecast is $s_x = 0.7539$.
3. The mean of the US CPI consensus forecast is $\overline{X} = 1.3350$.

Finally, Abitbol and Olabudo discuss the forecast and forecast interval:

- Observation 1. For a given confidence level, the forecast interval is the same no matter the US CPI consensus forecast.
- Observation 2. A larger standard error of the estimate will result in a wider confidence interval.

27. Based on Exhibit 1, Olabudo should:

   A. conclude that the inflation predictions are unbiased.

   B. reject the null hypothesis that the slope coefficient equals one.

   C. reject the null hypothesis that the intercept coefficient equals zero.

28. Based on Exhibit 1, Olabudo should calculate a prediction interval for the actual US CPI *closest* to:

   A. 2.7506 to 2.7544.

   B. 2.7521 to 2.7529.

   C. 2.7981 to 2.8019.

29. Which of Olabudo's observations of forecasting is correct?

   A. Only Observation 1

   B. Only Observation 2

   C. Both Observation 1 and Observations 2

The following information relates to questions 30-34

Elena Vasileva recently joined EnergyInvest as a junior portfolio analyst. Vasileva's supervisor asks her to evaluate a potential investment opportunity in Amtex, a multinational oil and gas corporation based in the United States. Vasileva's supervisor suggests using regression analysis to examine the relation between Amtex shares and returns on crude oil.

Vasileva notes the following assumptions of regression analysis:

- Assumption 1. The error term is uncorrelated across observations.
- Assumption 2. The variance of the error term is the same for all observations.
- Assumption 3. The dependent variable is normally distributed.

Vasileva runs a regression of Amtex share returns on crude oil returns using the monthly data she collected. Selected data used in the regression are presented in Exhibit 1, and selected regression output is presented in Exhibit 2. She uses a 1 percent level of significance in all her tests.

Exhibit 1: Selected Data for Crude Oil Returns and Amtex Share Returns

	Oil Return (X_i)	Amtex Return (Y_i)	Cross-Product $(X_i - \bar{X})(Y_i - \bar{Y})$	Predicted Amtex Return $(\hat{Y}_i)$	Regression Residual $(Y_i - \hat{Y}_i)$	Squared Residual $(Y_i - \hat{Y}_i)^2$
Month 1	−0.032000	0.033145	−0.000388	0.002011	−0.031134	0.000969
⋮	⋮	⋮	⋮	⋮	⋮	⋮
Month 36	0.028636	0.062334	0.002663	0.016282	−0.046053	0.002121
Sum			0.085598			0.071475
Average	−0.018056	0.005293				

Exhibit 2: Selected Regression Output, Dependent Variable: Amtex Share Return		
	Coefficient	Standard Error
Intercept	0.0095	0.0078
Oil return	0.2354	0.0760

Critical t-values for a 1 percent level of significance:

One-sided, left side: −2.441

One-sided, right side: +2.441

Two-sided: ±2.728

Vasileva expects the crude oil return next month, Month 37, to be −0.01. She computes the standard error of the forecast to be 0.0469.

30. Which of Vasileva's assumptions regarding regression analysis is *incorrect*?

   A. Assumption 1

   B. Assumption 2

   C. Assumption 3

31. Based on Exhibit 1, the standard error of the estimate is *closest* to:

   A. 0.04456.

   B. 0.04585.

   C. 0.05018.

32. Based on Exhibit 2, Vasileva should reject the null hypothesis that:

   A. the slope is less than or equal to 0.15.

   B. the intercept is less than or equal to zero.

   C. crude oil returns do not explain Amtex share returns.

33. Based on Exhibit 2 and Vasileva's prediction of the crude oil return for Month 37, the estimate of Amtex share return for Month 37 is *closest* to:

   A. −0.0024.

   B. 0.0071.

   C. 0.0119.

34. Using information from Exhibit 2, the 99 percent prediction interval for Amtex share return for Month 37 is *best* described as:

   A. $\hat{Y}_f \pm 0.0053$.

   B. $\hat{Y}_f \pm 0.0469$.

   C. $\hat{Y}_f \pm 0.1279$.

The following information relates to questions 35-38

Espey Jones is examining the relation between the net profit margin (NPM) of companies, in percent, and their fixed asset turnover (FATO). He collected a sample of 35 companies for the most recent fiscal year and fit several different functional forms, settling on the following model:

$\ln(\text{NPM}_i) = b_0 + b_1 \text{FATO}_i$.

The results of this estimation are provided in Exhibit 1.

Exhibit 1: Results of Regressing NPM on FATO

Source	df	Sum of Squares	Mean Square	F	p-Value
Regression	1	102.9152	102.9152	1,486.7079	0.0000
Residual	32	2.2152	0.0692		
Total	33	105.1303			

	Coefficients	Standard Error	t-Statistic	p-Value
Intercept	0.5987	0.0561	10.6749	0.0000
FATO	0.2951	0.0077	38.5579	0.0000

35. The coefficient of determination is *closest* to:

   A. 0.0211.

   B. 0.9789.

   C. 0.9894.

36. The standard error of the estimate is *closest* to:

   A. 0.2631.

   B. 1.7849.

   C. 38.5579.

37. At a 0.01 level of significance, Jones should conclude that:

   A. the mean net profit margin is 0.5987 percent.

   B. the variation of the fixed asset turnover explains the variation of the natural log of the net profit margin.

   C. a change in the fixed asset turnover from three to four times is likely to result in a change in the net profit margin of 0.5987 percent.

38. The predicted net profit margin for a company with a fixed asset turnover of 2

times is *closest* to:

A. 1.1889 percent.

B. 1.8043 percent.

C. 3.2835 percent

SOLUTIONS

1. C is correct. The predicted value of ROE = 4 + (1.8 × 10) = 22.

2. A is correct. The slope coefficient of 1.8 is the expected change in the dependent variable (*ROE*) for a one-unit change in the independent variable (*GO*).

3. B is correct. The predicted value is *ROE* = 4 + (1.8 × 8) = 18.4. The observed value of *ROE* is 21, so the residual is 2.6 = 21.0 − 18.4.

4. C is correct. Homoskedasticity is the situation in which the variance of the residuals is constant across the observations.

5. A is correct. SHIFT is an indicator or dummy variable because it takes on only the values 0 and 1.

6. A is correct. In a simple regression with a single indicator variable, the intercept is the mean of the dependent variable when the indicator variable takes on a value of zero, which is before the shift in policy in this case.

7. C is correct. Whereas the intercept is the average of the dependent variable when the indicator variable is zero (i.e., before the shift in policy), the slope is the difference in the mean of the dependent variable from before to after the change in policy.

8. A is correct. The null hypothesis of no difference in the annual growth rate is rejected at the 0.05 level: The calculated test statistic of −8.16188 is outside the bounds of ±2.048.

9. A is correct. The coefficient of determination is the same as R^2, which is 0.7436 in the table.

10. C is correct. Because the slope is positive, the correlation between X and Y is simply the square root of the coefficient of determination: $\sqrt{0.7436}$ = 0.8623.

11. C is correct. To make a prediction using the regression model, multiply the slope coefficient by the forecast of the independent variable and add the result to the intercept. Expected value of CFO to sales = 0.077 + (0.826 × 5) = 4.207.

12. C is correct. The *p*-value is the smallest level of significance at which the null hypotheses concerning the slope coefficient can be rejected. In this case, the *p*-value is less than 0.05, and thus the regression of the ratio of cash flow from operations to sales on the ratio of net income to sales is significant at the 5 percent level.

13. A is correct. The data are observations over time.

14. C is correct. From the regression equation, Expected return = 0.0138 + (−0.6486 × −0.01) = 0.0138 + 0.006486 = 0.0203, or 2.03 percent.

15. C is correct. R^2 is the coefficient of determination. In this case, it shows that 2.11% of the variability in Stellar's returns is explained by changes in CPIENG.

16. B is correct. The standard error of the estimate is the standard deviation of the regression residuals.

17. C is the correct response because it is a false statement. The slope and intercept are both statistically different from zero at the 0.05 level of significance.

18. C is correct. The slope coefficient (shown in Exhibit 2) is negative.

19. B is correct. The sample covariance is calculated as follows:

$$\frac{\sum_{i=1}^{n}(X_i - \bar{X})(Y_i - \bar{Y})}{n-1} = -9.2430 \div 49 = -0.1886.$$

20. A is correct. In simple regression, the R^2 is the square of the pairwise correlation. Because the slope coefficient is negative, the correlation is the negative of the square root of 0.0933, or −0.3055.

21. C is correct. Conclusions cannot be drawn regarding causation; they can be drawn only about association; therefore, Interpretations 1 and 2 are incorrect.

22. C is correct. Liu explains the variation of the short interest ratio using the variation of the debt ratio.

23. A is correct. The degrees of freedom are the number of observations minus the number of parameters estimated, which equals 2 in this case (the intercept and the slope coefficient). The number of degrees of freedom is 50 − 2 = 48.

24. B is correct. The t-statistic is −2.2219, which is outside the bounds created by the critical t-values of ±2.011 for a two-tailed test with a 5 percent significance level. The value of 2.011 is the critical t-value for the 5 percent level of significance (2.5 percent in one tail) for 48 degrees of freedom. A is incorrect because the mean of the short interest ratio is 192.3 ÷ 50 = 3.846. C is incorrect because the debt ratio explains 9.33 percent of the variation of the short interest ratio.

25. A is correct. The predicted value of the short interest ratio = 5.4975 + (−4.1589 × 0.40) = 5.4975 − 1.6636 = 3.8339.

26. C is correct. The calculation is $F = \dfrac{\text{Mean square regression}}{\text{Mean square error}} = \dfrac{38.4404}{7.7867} = 4.9367.$

27. A is correct. We fail to reject the null hypothesis of a slope equal to one, and we fail to reject the null hypothesis of an intercept equal to zero. The test of the slope equal to 1.0 is

$$t = \frac{0.9830 - 1.000}{0.0155} = -1.09677.$$

The test of the intercept equal to 0.0 is

$$t = \frac{0.0001 - 0.0000}{.00002} = 0.5000.$$

Therefore, we conclude that the forecasts are unbiased.

28. A is correct. The forecast interval for inflation is calculated in three steps:
Step 1. Make the prediction given the US CPI forecast of 2.8:

$$\widehat{Y} = \widehat{b_0} + \widehat{b_1}X$$
$$= 0.0001 + (0.9830 \times 2.8)\cdot$$
$$= 2.7525.$$

Step 2. Compute the variance of the prediction error:

$$s_f^2 = s_e^2 \left\{ 1 + (1/n) + \left[(X_f - \overline{X})^2 \right] / \left[(n-1) \times s_x^2 \right] \right\}.$$

$$s_f^2 = 0.0009^2 \left\{ 1 + (1/60) + \left[(2.8 - 1.3350)^2 \right] / \left[(60-1) \times 0.7539^2 \right] \right\}.$$

$$s_f^2 = 0.00000088.$$

$$s_f = 0.0009.$$

Step 3. Compute the prediction interval:

$$\hat{Y} \pm t_c \times s_f.$$

$2.7525 \pm (2.0 \times 0.0009)$

Lower bound: $2.7525 - (2.0 \times 0.0009) = 2.7506$.

Upper bound: $2.7525 + (2.0 \times 0.0009) = 2.7544$.

Given the US CPI forecast of 2.8, the 95 percent prediction interval is 2.7506 to 2.7544.

29. B is correct. The confidence level influences the width of the forecast interval through the critical t-value that is used to calculate the distance from the forecasted value: The larger the confidence level, the wider the interval. Therefore, Observation 1 is not correct.

    Observation 2 is correct. The greater the standard error of the estimate, the greater the standard error of the forecast.

30. C is correct. The assumptions of the linear regression model are that (1) the relationship between the dependent variable and the independent variable is linear in the parameters b_0 and b_1, (2) the residuals are independent of one another, (3) the variance of the error term is the same for all observations, and (4) the error term is normally distributed. Assumption 3 is incorrect because the dependent variable need not be normally distributed.

31. B is correct. The standard error of the estimate for a linear regression model with one independent variable is calculated as the square root of the mean square error:

$$s_e = \sqrt{\frac{0.071475}{34}} = 0.04585.$$

32. C is correct. Crude oil returns explain the Amtex share returns if the slope coefficient is statistically different from zero. The slope coefficient is 0.2354, and the calculated t-statistic is

$$t = \frac{0.2354 - 0.0000}{0.0760} = 3.0974,$$

which is outside the bounds of the critical values of ± 2.728.

Therefore, Vasileva should reject the null hypothesis that crude oil returns do not explain Amtex share returns, because the slope coefficient is statistically different from zero.

A is incorrect because the calculated t-statistic for testing the slope against 0.15 is $t = \frac{0.2354 - 0.1500}{0.0760} = 1.1237$, which is less than the critical value of $+2.441$.

B is incorrect because the calculated t-statistic is $t = \frac{0.0095 - 0.0000}{0.0078} = 1.2179$,

which is less than the critical value of $+2.441$.

33. B is correct. The predicted value of the dependent variable, Amtex share return, given the value of the independent variable, crude oil return, -0.01, is calculated

as $\hat{Y} = \hat{b}_0 + \hat{b}_1 X_i = 0.0095 + [0.2354 \times (-0.01)] = 0.0071$.

34. C is correct. The predicted share return is $0.0095 + [0.2354 \times (-0.01)] = 0.0071$. The lower limit for the prediction interval is $0.0071 - (2.728 \times 0.0469) = -0.1208$, and the upper limit for the prediction interval is $0.0071 + (2.728 \times 0.0469) = 0.1350$.

    A is incorrect because the bounds of the interval should be based on the standard error of the forecast and the critical t-value, not on the mean of the dependent variable.

    B is incorrect because bounds of the interval are based on the product of the standard error of the forecast *and* the critical t-value, not simply the standard error of the forecast.

35. B is correct. The coefficient of determination is $102.9152 \div 105.1303 = 0.9789$.

36. A is correct. The standard error is the square root of the mean square error, or $\sqrt{0.0692} = 0.2631$.

37. B is correct. The p-value corresponding to the slope is less than 0.01, so we reject the null hypothesis of a zero slope, concluding that the fixed asset turnover explains the natural log of the net profit margin.

38. C is correct. The predicted natural log of the net profit margin is $0.5987 + (2 \times 0.2951) = 1.1889$. The predicted net profit margin is $e^{1.1889} = 3.2835\%$.

Introduction to Big Data Techniques

by Robert Kissell, PhD, and Barbara J. Mack.

Robert Kissell, PhD, is at Molloy College and Kissell Research Group (USA). Barbara J. Mack is at Pingry Hill Enterprises, Inc. (USA).

LEARNING OUTCOMES

Mastery	The candidate should be able to:
☐	describe aspects of "fintech" that are directly relevant for the gathering and analyzing of financial data.
☐	describe Big Data, artificial intelligence, and machine learning
☐	describe applications of Big Data and Data Science to investment management

INTRODUCTION

1

The meeting of finance and technology, commonly known as *fintech*, is changing the landscape of investment management. Advancements include the use of Big Data, artificial intelligence, and machine learning to evaluate investment opportunities, optimize portfolios, and mitigate risks. These developments are affecting not only quantitative asset managers but also fundamental asset managers who make use of these tools and technologies to engage in hybrid forms of investment decision making.

LEARNING MODULE OVERVIEW

- Big Data is characterized by the three Vs—volume, velocity, and variety—and includes both traditional and non-traditional (or alternative) datasets. When Big Data is used for inference or prediction, it is important to consider a fourth V: veracity.

- Among the main sources of alternative data are data generated by individuals, business processes, and sensors.

- Artificial intelligence (AI) computer systems are capable of performing tasks that traditionally required human intelligence at levels comparable (or superior) to those of human beings.

- Machine learning (ML) seeks to extract knowledge from large amounts of data by "learning" from known examples and then generating structure or predictions. Simply put, ML algorithms aim to "find the pattern, apply the pattern." Main types of ML include supervised learning, unsupervised learning, and deep learning.
- Natural language processing (NLP) is an application of text analytics that uses insight into the structure of human language to analyze and interpret text- and voice-based data.

2   HOW IS FINTECH USED IN QUANTITATIVE INVESTMENT ANALYSIS?

☐ describe aspects of "fintech" that are directly relevant for the gathering and analyzing of financial data.

☐ describe Big Data, artificial intelligence, and machine learning

In its broadest sense, the term **fintech** generally refers to technology-driven innovation occurring in the financial services industry. For our purposes, fintech refers to technological innovation in the design and delivery of financial services and products. In common usage, fintech can also refer to companies involved in developing the new technologies and their applications, as well as the business sector that includes such companies. Many of these innovations are challenging the traditional business models of incumbent financial services providers.

Early forms of fintech included data processing and the automation of routine tasks. Systems that provided execution of decisions according to specified rules and instructions followed. Fintech has advanced into decision-making applications based on complex machine-learning logic, in which computer programs are able to "learn" how to complete tasks over time. In some applications, advanced computer systems are performing tasks at levels that far surpass human capabilities. Fintech has changed the financial services industry in many ways, giving rise to new systems for investment advice, financial planning, business lending, and payments.

Whereas fintech covers a broad range of services and applications, areas of development that are more directly relevant to quantitative analysis in the investment industry include the following:

- **Analysis of large datasets.** In addition to growing amounts of traditional data, such as security prices, corporate financial statements, and economic indicators, massive amounts of **alternative data** generated from non-traditional data sources, such as social media and sensor networks, can now be integrated into a portfolio manager's investment decision-making process and used to help generate alpha and reduce losses.

- **Analytical tools.** For extremely large datasets, techniques involving **artificial intelligence (AI)**—computer systems capable of performing tasks that previously required human intelligence—might be better suited to identify complex, non-linear relationships than traditional quantitative methods and statistical analysis. Advances in AI-based techniques are enabling different data analysis approaches. For example, analysts are turning to AI to sort through the enormous amounts of data from company filings, annual reports, and earnings calls to determine which data are most important and to help uncover trends and generate insights relating to human sentiment and behavior.

Big Data

As noted, datasets are growing rapidly in terms of the size and diversity of data types that are available for analysis. The term **Big Data** has been in use since the late 1990s and refers to the vast amount of information being generated by industry, governments, individuals, and electronic devices. Big Data includes data generated from traditional sources—such as stock exchanges, companies, and governments—as well as non-traditional data types, also known as alternative data, arising from the use of electronic devices, social media, sensor networks, and company exhaust (information generated in the normal course of doing business).

Traditional data sources include corporate data in the form of annual reports, regulatory filings, sales and earnings figures, and conference calls with analysts. Traditional data also include data that are generated in the financial markets, including trade prices and volumes. Because the world has become increasingly connected, we can now obtain data from a wide range of devices, including smart phones, cameras, microphones, radio-frequency identification (RFID) readers, wireless sensors, and satellites that are now in use all over the world. As the internet and the presence of such networked devices have grown, the use of non-traditional data sources, or alternative data sources—including social media (posts, tweets, and blogs), email and text communications, web traffic, online news sites, and other electronic information sources—has risen.

The term *Big Data* typically refers to datasets that have the following characteristics:

- **Volume**: The amount of data collected in files, records, and tables is very large, representing many millions, or even billions, of data points.

- **Velocity**: The speed and frequency with which the data are recorded and transmitted has accelerated. Real-time or near-real-time data have become the norm in many areas.

- **Variety**: The data are collected from many different sources and in a variety of formats, including structured data (e.g., SQL tables), semistructured data (e.g., HTML code), and unstructured data (e.g., video messages).

Features relating to big data's volume, velocity, and variety are shown in Exhibit 1.

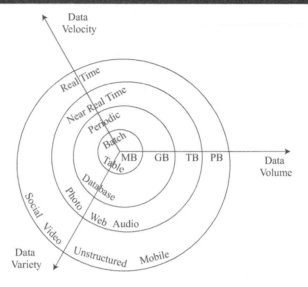

Exhibit 1: Big Data Characteristics: Volume, Velocity, and Variety

Data	Volume Key	Bytes of Information
MB	Megabyte	One Million
GB	Gigabyte	One Billion
TB	Terabyte	One Trillion
PB	Petabyte	One Quadrillion

Source: Ivy Wigmore, "Definition: 3Vs (Volume, Variety and Velocity)," WhatIs.com, last updated December 2020, http://whatis.techtarget.com/definition/3Vs.

Exhibit 1 shows that data volumes are growing from megabytes and gigabytes to far larger sizes, such as terabytes and petabytes, as more data are being generated, captured, and stored. At the same time, more data, traditional and non-traditional, are available on a real-time or near-real-time basis with far greater variety in data types than ever before.

When Big Data is used for inference or prediction, a "fourth V" comes into play—veracity—which relates to the credibility and reliability of different data sources. Determining the credibility and reliability of data sources is an important part of any empirical investigation. The issue of veracity becomes critically important for Big Data, however, because of the varied sources of these large datasets. Big Data amplifies the age-old challenge of disentangling quality from quantity.

Big Data can be structured, semi-structured, or unstructured data. Structured data items can be organized in tables and are commonly stored in a database where each field represents the same type of information. Unstructured data can be disparate, unorganized data that cannot be represented in tabular form. Unstructured data, such as those generated by social media, email, text messages, voice recordings, pictures, blogs, scanners, and sensors, often require different, specialized applications or custom programs before they can be useful to investment professionals. For example, to analyze data contained in emails or texts, specially developed or customized computer code might be required to first process these files. Semistructured data can have attributes of both structured and unstructured data.

Sources of Big Data

Big Data, therefore, encompasses data generated by the following:

- financial markets (e.g., equity, fixed income, futures, options, and other derivatives),
- businesses (e.g., corporate financials, commercial transactions, and credit card purchases),
- governments (e.g., trade, economic, employment, and payroll data),
- individuals (e.g., credit card purchases, product reviews, internet search logs, and social media posts),
- sensors (e.g., satellite imagery, shipping cargo information, and traffic patterns), and, in particular,
- the Internet of Things, or IoT (e.g., data generated by "smart" buildings, where the building is providing a steady stream of information about climate control, energy consumption, security, and other operational details).

In gathering business intelligence, historically, analysts have tended to draw on traditional data sources, using statistical methods to measure performance, predict future growth, and analyze sector and market trends. In contrast, the analysis of Big Data incorporates the use of alternative data sources.

From retail sales data to social media sentiment to satellite imagery that might reveal information about agriculture, shipping, and oil rigs, alternative datasets can provide additional insights about consumer behavior, firm performance, trends, and other factors important for investment-related activities. Such information is having a significant effect on the way that professional investors, particularly quantitative investors, approach financial analysis and decision-making processes.

The three main sources of alternative data are

- data generated by individuals,
- data generated by business processes, and
- data generated by sensors.

Data generated by individuals are often produced in text, video, photo, and audio formats and also can be generated through such means as website clicks or time spent on a webpage. This type of data tends to be unstructured. The volume of this type of data is growing dramatically as people participate in greater numbers and more frequently in online activities, such as social media and e-commerce, including online reviews of products, services, and entire companies, and as they make personal data available through web searches, email, and other electronic trails.

Business process data include information flows from corporations and other public entities. These data tend to be structured data and include direct sales information, such as credit card data, as well as corporate exhaust. Corporate exhaust includes corporate supply chain information, banking records, and retail point-of-sale scanner data. Business process data can be leading or real-time indicators of business performance, whereas traditional corporate metrics might be reported only on a quarterly or even yearly basis and typically are lagging indicators of performance.

Sensor data are collected from such devices as smart phones, cameras, RFID chips, and satellites that usually are connected to computers through wireless networks. Sensor data can be unstructured, and the volume of data is many orders of magnitude greater than that of individual or business process datastreams. This form of data is growing exponentially because microprocessors and networking technology are increasingly present in a wide array of personal and commercial electronic devices. Extended to office buildings, homes, vehicles, and many other physical forms, this culminates in a network arrangement, known as the **Internet of Things**, which is formed by the vast array of physical devices, home appliances, smart buildings, vehicles, and other items that are embedded with electronics, sensors, software, and network connections that enable the objects in the system to interact and share information.

Exhibit 2 shows a classification of alternative data sources and includes examples for each.

Exhibit 2: Classification of Alternative Data Sources

Individuals	Business Processes	Sensors
Social media	Transaction data	Satellites
News, reviews	Corporate data	Geolocation
Web searches, personal data		Internet of Things
		Other sensors

In the search to identify new factors that could affect security prices, enhance asset selection, improve trade execution, and uncover trends, alternative data are being used to support data-driven investment models and decisions. As interest in alternative data has risen, the number of specialized firms that collect, aggregate, and sell alternative datasets has grown.

Although the market for alternative data is expanding, investment professionals should understand the potential legal and ethical issues related to information that is not in the public domain. For example, the **scraping** of web data potentially could capture personal information that is protected by regulations or that might have been published or provided without the explicit knowledge and consent of the individuals involved. Best practices are still in development in many jurisdictions, and because of varying approaches taken by national regulators, the different forms of guidance could conflict.

Big Data Challenges

Big Data poses several challenges when it is used in investment analysis, including the quality, volume, and appropriateness of the data. Key issues revolve around the following questions, among others: Does the dataset have selection bias, missing data, or data outliers? Is the volume of collected data sufficient? Is the dataset well suited for the type of analysis? In most instances, the data must be sourced, cleansed, and organized before analysis can occur. This process can be extremely difficult with alternative data because of the unstructured characteristics of the data involved, which more often are qualitative (e.g., texts, photos, and videos) than quantitative in nature.

Given the size and complexity of alternative datasets, traditional analytical methods cannot always be used to interpret and evaluate these datasets. To address this challenge, AI and machine learning techniques have emerged that support work on such large and complex sources of information.

3

ADVANCED ANALYTICAL TOOLS: ARTIFICIAL INTELLIGENCE AND MACHINE LEARNING

☐ | describe Big Data, artificial intelligence, and machine learning

Artificial intelligence (AI) computer systems are capable of performing tasks that traditionally have required human intelligence. AI technology has enabled the development of computer systems that exhibit cognitive and decision-making ability comparable or superior to that of human beings.

An early example of AI was the **expert system**, a type of computer programming that attempted to simulate the knowledge base and analytical abilities of human experts in specific problem-solving contexts. This was often accomplished through the use of "if–then" rules. By the late 1990s, faster networks and more powerful processors enabled AI to be deployed in logistics, data mining, financial analysis, medical diagnosis, and other areas. Since the 1980s, financial institutions have made use of AI—particularly, **neural networks**, programming based on how our brain learns and processes information—to detect abnormal charges or claims in credit card fraud detection systems.

Machine learning (ML) involves computer-based techniques that seek to extract knowledge from large amounts of data without making any assumptions on the data's underlying probability distribution. The goal of ML algorithms is to automate decision-making processes by generalizing, or "learning," from known examples to determine an underlying structure in the data. The emphasis is on the ability of the algorithm to generate structure or predictions without any help from a human. Simply put, ML algorithms aim to "find the pattern, apply the pattern."

As it is currently used in the investing context, ML requires massive amounts of data for "training," so although some ML techniques have existed for years, insufficient data have historically limited broader application. Previously, these algorithms lacked access to the large amounts of data needed to model relationships successfully. The growth in Big Data has provided ML algorithms, including neural networks, with sufficient data to improve modeling and predictive accuracy, and greater use of ML techniques is now possible.

In ML, the computer algorithm is given "inputs" (a set of variables or datasets) and might be given "outputs" (the target data). The algorithm "learns" from the data provided how best to model inputs to outputs (if provided) or how to identify or describe underlying data structure if no outputs are given. Training occurs as the algorithm identifies relationships in the data and uses that information to refine its learning process.

ML involves splitting the dataset into three distinct subsets: a training dataset, a validation dataset, and a test dataset. The training dataset allows the algorithm to identify relationships between inputs and outputs based on historical patterns in the data. These relationships are then validated, and the model tuned, using the validation dataset. The test dataset is used to test the model's ability to predict well on new data. Once an algorithm has been trained, validated, and tested, the ML model can be used to predict outcomes based on other datasets.

ML still requires human judgment in understanding the underlying data and selecting the appropriate techniques for data analysis. Before they can be used, the data must be clean and free of biases and spurious data. As noted, ML models also require sufficiently large amounts of data and might not perform well when not enough available data are available to train and validate the model.

Analysts must be cognizant of errors that could arise from **overfitting** the data, because models that overfit the data might discover "false" relationships or "unsubstantiated" patterns that will lead to prediction errors and incorrect output forecasts. Overfitting occurs when the ML model learns the input and target dataset too precisely. In such cases, the model has been "overtrained" on the data and treats noise in the data as true parameters. An ML model that has been overfitted is not able to accurately predict outcomes using a different dataset and might be too complex. When a model has been **underfitted**, the ML model treats true parameters as if they are noise and is not able to recognize relationships within the training data. In such cases, the model could be too simplistic. Underfitted models typically will fail to fully discover patterns that underlie the data.

In addition, because they are not explicitly programmed, ML techniques can appear to be opaque or "black box" approaches, which arrive at outcomes that might not be entirely understood or explainable.

ML approaches can help identify relationships between variables, detect patterns or trends, and create structure from data, including data classification. ML can be divided broadly into three distinct classes of techniques: supervised learning, unsupervised learning, and deep learning.

In **supervised learning**, computers learn to model relationships based on labeled training data. In supervised learning, inputs and outputs are labeled, or identified, for the algorithm. After learning how best to model relationships for the labeled data, the trained algorithms are used to model or predict outcomes for new datasets. Trying to identify the best signal, or variable; to forecast future returns on a stock; or to predict whether local stock market performance will be up, down, or flat during the next business day are problems that could be approached using supervised learning techniques.

In **unsupervised learning**, computers are not given labeled data but instead are given only data from which the algorithm seeks to describe the data and their structure. For example, grouping companies into peer groups based on their characteristics rather than using standard sector or country groupings is an application of unsupervised learning techniques.

Underlying AI advances have been key developments relating to neural networks. In **deep learning** (or **deep learning nets**), computers use neural networks, often with many hidden layers, to perform multistage, non-linear data processing to identify patterns. Deep learning can use supervised or unsupervised ML approaches. By taking a layered or multistage approach to data analysis, deep learning develops an understanding of simple concepts that informs analysis of more complex concepts.

Neural networks have existed since 1958 and have been used for many applications, such as forecasting and pattern recognition. Improvements in the algorithms underlying neural networks are providing more accurate models that better incorporate and learn from data. As a result, these algorithms are now far better at such activities as image, pattern, and speech recognition. In many cases, the advanced algorithms require less computing power than the earlier neural networks, and their improved solution enables analysts to discover insights and identify relationships that were previously too difficult or too time consuming to uncover.

ADVANCES IN AI OUTSIDE FINANCE

Non-finance-related AI breakthroughs include victories in the general knowledge gameshow *Jeopardy* (by IBM's Watson in 2011) and in the ancient Chinese board game Go (by Google's DeepMind in 2016). Not only is AI providing solutions where perfect information exists (all players have equal access to the same information), such as checkers, chess, and Go, but AI is also providing insight in cases in which information might be imperfect and players have hidden information; AI successes at the game of poker (by DeepStack) are an example. AI has also been behind the rise of virtual assistants, such as Siri (from Apple), Google's Translate app, and Amazon's product recommendation engine.

The ability to analyze Big Data using ML techniques, alongside more traditional statistical methods, represents a significant development in investment research, supported by the presence of greater data availability and advances in the algorithms. Improvements in computing power and software processing speeds and falling storage costs have further supported this evolution.

ML techniques are being used for Big Data analysis to help predict trends or market events, such as the likelihood of a successful merger or an outcome to a political election. Image recognition algorithms can now analyze data from satellite-imaging systems to provide intelligence on the number of consumers in retail store parking lots, shipping activity and manufacturing facilities, and yields on agricultural crops, to name just a few examples.

Such information could provide insight into individual firms or at national or global levels and might be used as inputs into valuation or economic models.

TACKLING BIG DATA WITH DATA SCIENCE 4

☐ | describe applications of Big Data and Data Science to investment management

Data science can be defined as an interdisciplinary field that harnesses advances in computer science (including ML), statistics, and other disciplines for the purpose of extracting information from Big Data (or data in general). Companies rely on the expertise of data scientists/analysts to extract information and insights from Big Data for a wide variety of business and investment purposes.

An important consideration for the data scientist is the structure of the data. As noted in the discussion on Big Data, because of their unstructured nature, alternative data often require specialized treatment before they can be used for analysis.

Data Processing Methods

To help determine the best data management technique needed for Big Data analysis, data scientists use various data processing methods, including capture, curation, storage, search, and transfer.

- Capture—Data capture refers to how the data are collected and transformed into a format that can be used by the analytical process. Low-latency systems—systems that operate on networks that communicate high volumes of data with minimal delay (latency)—are essential for automated trading applications that make decisions based on real-time prices and market events. In contrast, high-latency systems do not require access to real-time data and calculations.

- Curation—Data curation refers to the process of ensuring data quality and accuracy through a data cleaning exercise. This process consists of reviewing all data to detect and uncover data errors—bad or inaccurate data—and making adjustments for missing data when appropriate.

- Storage—Data storage refers to how the data will be recorded, archived, and accessed and the underlying database design. An important consideration for data storage is whether the data are structured or unstructured and whether analytical needs require low-latency solutions.

- Search—Search refers to how to query data. Big Data has created the need for advanced applications capable of examining and reviewing large quantities of data to locate requested data content.

- Transfer—Transfer refers to how the data will move from the underlying data source or storage location to the underlying analytical tool. This could be through a direct data feed, such as a stock exchange's price feed.

Data Visualization

Data visualization is an important tool for understanding Big Data. Visualization refers to how the data will be formatted, displayed, and summarized in graphical form. Traditional structured data can be visualized using tables, charts, and trends, whereas non-traditional unstructured data require new techniques of data visualization. These visualization tools include, for example, interactive three-dimensional (3D) graphics, in which users can focus in on specified data ranges and rotate the data across 3D axes to help identify trends and uncover relationships. Multidimensional data analysis consisting of more than three variables requires additional data visualization techniques—for example, adding color, shapes, and sizes to the 3D charts. Furthermore, a wide variety of solutions exists to reflect the structure of the data through the geometry of the visualization, with interactive graphics allowing for especially rich possibilities. Examples include heat maps, tree diagrams, and network graphs.

Another valuable Big Data visualization technique that is applicable to textual data is a "tag cloud," in which words are sized and displayed on the basis of the frequency of the word in the data file. For example, words that appear more often are shown with a larger font, and words that appear less often are shown with a smaller font. A "mind map" is another data visualization technique; it is a variation of the tag cloud, but rather than displaying the frequency of words, a mind map shows how different concepts are related to each other.

Exhibit 3 shows an example of a "tag cloud" based on a section of this reading. The more frequently a word is found within the text, the larger it becomes in the tag cloud. As shown in the tag cloud, the words appearing most frequently in the section include "data," "ML," "learning," "AI," "techniques," "model," and "relationships."

Exhibit 3: Data Visualization Tag Cloud

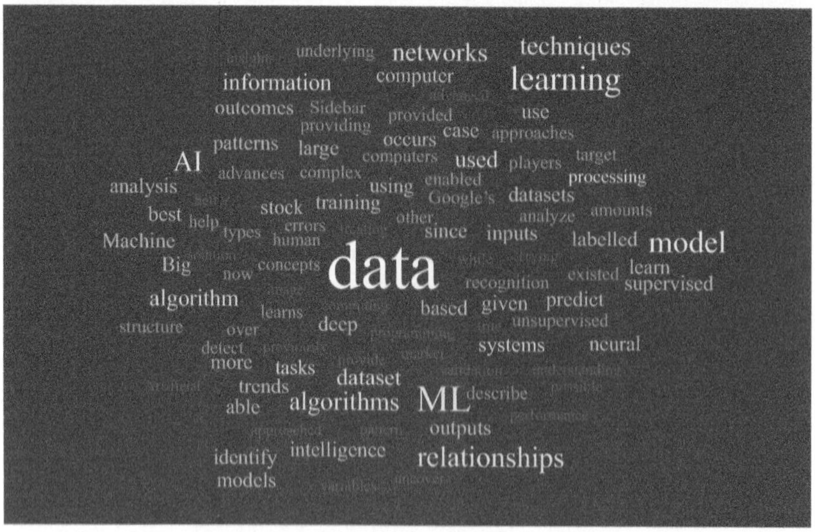

Source: "About Word Clouds," WordItOut, https://worditout.com/word-cloud/create.

Fintech is being used in numerous areas of investment management. Applications for investment management include text analytics and natural language processing, risk analysis, and algorithmic trading.

Text Analytics and Natural Language Processing

Text analytics involves the use of computer programs to analyze and derive meaning typically from large, unstructured text- or voice-based datasets, such as company filings, written reports, quarterly earnings calls, social media, email, internet postings, and surveys. Text analytics includes using computer programs to perform automated information retrieval from different, unrelated sources to aid the decision-making process. More analytical usage includes lexical analysis, or the analysis of word frequency in a document and pattern recognition based on key words and phrases. Text analytics could be used in predictive analysis to help identify indicators of future performance, such as consumer sentiment.

Natural language processing (NLP) is a field of research at the intersection of computer science, AI, and linguistics that focuses on developing computer programs to analyze and interpret human language. Within the larger field of text analytics, NLP is an important application. Automated tasks using NLP include translation, speech recognition, text mining, sentiment analysis, and topic analysis. NLP also might be used in compliance functions to review employee voice and electronic communications for adherence to company or regulatory policy, for detecting fraud or inappropriate conduct, or for ensuring private or customer information is kept confidential.

Consider that all the public corporations worldwide generate millions of pages of annual reports and tens of thousands of hours of earnings calls each year. This is more information than any individual analyst or team of researchers can assess. NLP, especially when aided by ML algorithms, can analyze annual reports, call transcripts, news articles, social media posts, and other text- and audio-based data to identify trends in shorter time spans and with greater scale and accuracy than is humanly possible.

For example, NLP can be used to monitor analyst commentary to aid investment decision making. Financial analysts might generate earnings-per-share (EPS) forecasts reflecting their views on a company's near-term prospects. Focusing on forecasted EPS numbers could mean investors miss subtleties contained in an analyst's written research report. Because analysts tend not to change their buy, hold, and sell recommendations for a company frequently, they might instead offer nuanced commentary without making a change in their investment recommendation. After analyzing analyst commentary, NLP can assign sentiment ratings ranging from very negative to very positive for each. NLP, therefore, can be used to detect, monitor, and tag shifts in sentiment, potentially ahead of an analyst's recommendation change. Machine capabilities enable this analysis to scale across thousands of companies worldwide, performing work previously done by humans.

Similarly, communications and transcripts from policy makers, such as the European Central Bank or the US Federal Reserve, offer an opportunity for NLP-based analysis because officials at these institutions might send subtle messages through their choice of topics, words, and inferred tone. NLP can analyze nuances within text to provide insights around trending or waning topics of interest, such as interest rate policy, aggregate output, or inflation expectations.

Models using NLP analysis might incorporate non-traditional information to evaluate what people are saying—through their preferences, opinions, likes, or dislikes—in an attempt to identify trends and short-term indicators—for example about a company, a stock, or an economic event—to forecast coming trends that may affect investment performance in the future. For example, past research has evaluated the predictive power of Twitter sentiment regarding initial public offering (IPO) performance as well as the effect of positive and negative news sentiment on stock returns.

PROGRAMMING LANGUAGES AND DATABASES

Some of the more common programming languages used in data science include the following:

- **Python:** Python is an open-source, free programming language that does not require an in-depth understanding of computer programming. Python allows individuals with little or no programming experience to develop computer applications for advanced analytical use and is the basis for many fintech applications.

- **R:** R is an open-source, free programming language traditionally used for statistical analysis. R has mathematical packages for statistical analysis, ML, optimization, econometrics, and financial analysis.

- **Java:** Java is a programming language that can run on different computers, servers, and operating systems. Java is the underlying program language used in many internet applications.

- **C and C++:** Both C and C++ are specialized programming languages that provide the ability to optimize source code to achieve superior calculation speed and processing performance. C and C++ is used in applications for algorithmic and high-frequency trading.

- **Excel VBA:** Excel VBA helps bridge the gap between programming and manual data processing by allowing users to run macros to automate tasks, such as updating data tables and formulas, running data queries and collecting data from different web locations, and performing calculations. Excel VBA allows users to develop customized reports and analyses that rely on data that are updated from different applications and databases.

Some of the more common types of databases in use include the following:

- **SQL:** SQL is a database query language for structured data where the data can be stored in tables with rows and columns. SQL-based databases need to be run on a server that is accessed by users using SQL queries.

- **SQLite:** SQLite is a database for structured data. SQLite databases are embedded into the program and do not need to be run on a server. It is the most common database for mobile apps that require access to data.

- **NoSQL:** NoSQL is a database used for unstructured data where the data cannot be summarized in traditional tables with rows and columns.

PRACTICE PROBLEMS

1. A characteristic of Big Data is that:

    A. it involves formats with diverse structures.

    B. one of its traditional sources is business processes.

    C. real-time communication of it is uncommon due to vast content.

2. Which of the following statements is true in the use of ML:

    A. some techniques are termed "black box" due to data biases.

    B. human judgment is not needed because algorithms continuously learn from data.

    C. training data can be learned too precisely, resulting in inaccurate predictions when used with different datasets.

3. Text analytics is appropriate for application to:

    A. large, structured datasets.

    B. public but not private information.

    C. identifying possible short-term indicators of coming trends.

SOLUTIONS

1. A is correct. Big Data is collected from many different sources and is in a variety of formats, including structured data (e.g., SQL tables), semistructured data (e.g., HTML code), and unstructured data (e.g., video messages).

2. C is correct. Overfitting occurs when the ML model learns the input and target dataset too precisely. In this case, the model has been "overtrained" on the data and is treating noise in the data as true parameters. An ML model that has been overfitted is not able to accurately predict outcomes using a different dataset and might be too complex.

3. C is correct. Through the text analytics application of NLP, models using NLP analysis might incorporate non-traditional information to evaluate what people are saying—through their preferences, opinions, likes, or dislikes— in an attempt to identify trends and short-term indicators—for example, about a company, a stock, or an economic event—to forecast coming trends that may affect investment performance in the future.

Appendices A-E

APPENDICES A-E

Appendix A
Cumulative Probabilities for a Standard Normal Distribution
$P(Z \leq x) = N(x)$ for $x \geq 0$ or $P(Z \leq z) = N(z)$ for $z \geq 0$

x or z	0	0.01	0.02	0.03	0.04	0.05	0.06	0.07	0.08	0.09
0.00	0.5000	0.5040	0.5080	0.5120	0.5160	0.5199	0.5239	0.5279	0.5319	0.5359
0.10	0.5398	0.5438	0.5478	0.5517	0.5557	0.5596	0.5636	0.5675	0.5714	0.5753
0.20	0.5793	0.5832	0.5871	0.5910	0.5948	0.5987	0.6026	0.6064	0.6103	0.6141
0.30	0.6179	0.6217	0.6255	0.6293	0.6331	0.6368	0.6406	0.6443	0.6480	0.6517
0.40	0.6554	0.6591	0.6628	0.6664	0.6700	0.6736	0.6772	0.6808	0.6844	0.6879
0.50	0.6915	0.6950	0.6985	0.7019	0.7054	0.7088	0.7123	0.7157	0.7190	0.7224
0.60	0.7257	0.7291	0.7324	0.7357	0.7389	0.7422	0.7454	0.7486	0.7517	0.7549
0.70	0.7580	0.7611	0.7642	0.7673	0.7704	0.7734	0.7764	0.7794	0.7823	0.7852
0.80	0.7881	0.7910	0.7939	0.7967	0.7995	0.8023	0.8051	0.8078	0.8106	0.8133
0.90	0.8159	0.8186	0.8212	0.8238	0.8264	0.8289	0.8315	0.8340	0.8365	0.8389
1.00	0.8413	0.8438	0.8461	0.8485	0.8508	0.8531	0.8554	0.8577	0.8599	0.8621
1.10	0.8643	0.8665	0.8686	0.8708	0.8729	0.8749	0.8770	0.8790	0.8810	0.8830
1.20	0.8849	0.8869	0.8888	0.8907	0.8925	0.8944	0.8962	0.8980	0.8997	0.9015
1.30	0.9032	0.9049	0.9066	0.9082	0.9099	0.9115	0.9131	0.9147	0.9162	0.9177
1.40	0.9192	0.9207	0.9222	0.9236	0.9251	0.9265	0.9279	0.9292	0.9306	0.9319
1.50	0.9332	0.9345	0.9357	0.9370	0.9382	0.9394	0.9406	0.9418	0.9429	0.9441
1.60	0.9452	0.9463	0.9474	0.9484	0.9495	0.9505	0.9515	0.9525	0.9535	0.9545
1.70	0.9554	0.9564	0.9573	0.9582	0.9591	0.9599	0.9608	0.9616	0.9625	0.9633
1.80	0.9641	0.9649	0.9656	0.9664	0.9671	0.9678	0.9686	0.9693	0.9699	0.9706
1.90	0.9713	0.9719	0.9726	0.9732	0.9738	0.9744	0.9750	0.9756	0.9761	0.9767
2.00	0.9772	0.9778	0.9783	0.9788	0.9793	0.9798	0.9803	0.9808	0.9812	0.9817
2.10	0.9821	0.9826	0.9830	0.9834	0.9838	0.9842	0.9846	0.9850	0.9854	0.9857
2.20	0.9861	0.9864	0.9868	0.9871	0.9875	0.9878	0.9881	0.9884	0.9887	0.9890
2.30	0.9893	0.9896	0.9898	0.9901	0.9904	0.9906	0.9909	0.9911	0.9913	0.9916
2.40	0.9918	0.9920	0.9922	0.9925	0.9927	0.9929	0.9931	0.9932	0.9934	0.9936
2.50	0.9938	0.9940	0.9941	0.9943	0.9945	0.9946	0.9948	0.9949	0.9951	0.9952
2.60	0.9953	0.9955	0.9956	0.9957	0.9959	0.9960	0.9961	0.9962	0.9963	0.9964
2.70	0.9965	0.9966	0.9967	0.9968	0.9969	0.9970	0.9971	0.9972	0.9973	0.9974
2.80	0.9974	0.9975	0.9976	0.9977	0.9977	0.9978	0.9979	0.9979	0.9980	0.9981
2.90	0.9981	0.9982	0.9982	0.9983	0.9984	0.9984	0.9985	0.9985	0.9986	0.9986
3.00	0.9987	0.9987	0.9987	0.9988	0.9988	0.9989	0.9989	0.9989	0.9990	0.9990
3.10	0.9990	0.9991	0.9991	0.9991	0.9992	0.9992	0.9992	0.9992	0.9993	0.9993
3.20	0.9993	0.9993	0.9994	0.9994	0.9994	0.9994	0.9994	0.9995	0.9995	0.9995
3.30	0.9995	0.9995	0.9995	0.9996	0.9996	0.9996	0.9996	0.9996	0.9996	0.9997
3.40	0.9997	0.9997	0.9997	0.9997	0.9997	0.9997	0.9997	0.9997	0.9997	0.9998
3.50	0.9998	0.9998	0.9998	0.9998	0.9998	0.9998	0.9998	0.9998	0.9998	0.9998
3.60	0.9998	0.9998	0.9999	0.9999	0.9999	0.9999	0.9999	0.9999	0.9999	0.9999
3.70	0.9999	0.9999	0.9999	0.9999	0.9999	0.9999	0.9999	0.9999	0.9999	0.9999
3.80	0.9999	0.9999	0.9999	0.9999	0.9999	0.9999	0.9999	0.9999	0.9999	0.9999
3.90	1.0000	1.0000	1.0000	1.0000	1.0000	1.0000	1.0000	1.0000	1.0000	1.0000
4.00	1.0000	1.0000	1.0000	1.0000	1.0000	1.0000	1.0000	1.0000	1.0000	1.0000

For example, to find the z-value leaving 2.5 percent of the area/probability in the upper tail, find the element 0.9750 in the body of the table. Read 1.90 at the left end of the element's row and 0.06 at the top of the element's column, to give 1.90 + 0.06 = 1.96. *Table generated with Excel.*

Quantitative Methods for Investment Analysis, Second Edition, by Richard A. DeFusco, CFA, Dennis W. McLeavey, CFA, Jerald E. Pinto, CFA, and David E. Runkle, CFA. Copyright © 2004 by CFA Institute.

Appendix A (continued)
Cumulative Probabilities for a Standard Normal Distribution
$P(Z \leq x) = N(x)$ for $x \leq 0$ or $P(Z \leq z) = N(z)$ for $z \leq 0$

x or z	0	0.01	0.02	0.03	0.04	0.05	0.06	0.07	0.08	0.09
0.0	0.5000	0.4960	0.4920	0.4880	0.4840	0.4801	0.4761	0.4721	0.4681	0.4641
−0.10	0.4602	0.4562	0.4522	0.4483	0.4443	0.4404	0.4364	0.4325	0.4286	0.4247
−0.20	0.4207	0.4168	0.4129	0.4090	0.4052	0.4013	0.3974	0.3936	0.3897	0.3859
−0.30	0.3821	0.3783	0.3745	0.3707	0.3669	0.3632	0.3594	0.3557	0.3520	0.3483
−0.40	0.3446	0.3409	0.3372	0.3336	0.3300	0.3264	0.3228	0.3192	0.3156	0.3121
−0.50	0.3085	0.3050	0.3015	0.2981	0.2946	0.2912	0.2877	0.2843	0.2810	0.2776
−0.60	0.2743	0.2709	0.2676	0.2643	0.2611	0.2578	0.2546	0.2514	0.2483	0.2451
−0.70	0.2420	0.2389	0.2358	0.2327	0.2296	0.2266	0.2236	0.2206	0.2177	0.2148
−0.80	0.2119	0.2090	0.2061	0.2033	0.2005	0.1977	0.1949	0.1922	0.1894	0.1867
−0.90	0.1841	0.1814	0.1788	0.1762	0.1736	0.1711	0.1685	0.1660	0.1635	0.1611
−1.00	0.1587	0.1562	0.1539	0.1515	0.1492	0.1469	0.1446	0.1423	0.1401	0.1379
−1.10	0.1357	0.1335	0.1314	0.1292	0.1271	0.1251	0.1230	0.1210	0.1190	0.1170
−1.20	0.1151	0.1131	0.1112	0.1093	0.1075	0.1056	0.1038	0.1020	0.1003	0.0985
−1.30	0.0968	0.0951	0.0934	0.0918	0.0901	0.0885	0.0869	0.0853	0.0838	0.0823
−1.40	0.0808	0.0793	0.0778	0.0764	0.0749	0.0735	0.0721	0.0708	0.0694	0.0681
−1.50	0.0668	0.0655	0.0643	0.0630	0.0618	0.0606	0.0594	0.0582	0.0571	0.0559
−1.60	0.0548	0.0537	0.0526	0.0516	0.0505	0.0495	0.0485	0.0475	0.0465	0.0455
−1.70	0.0446	0.0436	0.0427	0.0418	0.0409	0.0401	0.0392	0.0384	0.0375	0.0367
−1.80	0.0359	0.0351	0.0344	0.0336	0.0329	0.0322	0.0314	0.0307	0.0301	0.0294
−1.90	0.0287	0.0281	0.0274	0.0268	0.0262	0.0256	0.0250	0.0244	0.0239	0.0233
−2.00	0.0228	0.0222	0.0217	0.0212	0.0207	0.0202	0.0197	0.0192	0.0188	0.0183
−2.10	0.0179	0.0174	0.0170	0.0166	0.0162	0.0158	0.0154	0.0150	0.0146	0.0143
−2.20	0.0139	0.0136	0.0132	0.0129	0.0125	0.0122	0.0119	0.0116	0.0113	0.0110
−2.30	0.0107	0.0104	0.0102	0.0099	0.0096	0.0094	0.0091	0.0089	0.0087	0.0084
−2.40	0.0082	0.0080	0.0078	0.0075	0.0073	0.0071	0.0069	0.0068	0.0066	0.0064
−2.50	0.0062	0.0060	0.0059	0.0057	0.0055	0.0054	0.0052	0.0051	0.0049	0.0048
−2.60	0.0047	0.0045	0.0044	0.0043	0.0041	0.0040	0.0039	0.0038	0.0037	0.0036
−2.70	0.0035	0.0034	0.0033	0.0032	0.0031	0.0030	0.0029	0.0028	0.0027	0.0026
−2.80	0.0026	0.0025	0.0024	0.0023	0.0023	0.0022	0.0021	0.0021	0.0020	0.0019
−2.90	0.0019	0.0018	0.0018	0.0017	0.0016	0.0016	0.0015	0.0015	0.0014	0.0014
−3.00	0.0013	0.0013	0.0013	0.0012	0.0012	0.0011	0.0011	0.0011	0.0010	0.0010
−3.10	0.0010	0.0009	0.0009	0.0009	0.0008	0.0008	0.0008	0.0008	0.0007	0.0007
−3.20	0.0007	0.0007	0.0006	0.0006	0.0006	0.0006	0.0006	0.0005	0.0005	0.0005
−3.30	0.0005	0.0005	0.0005	0.0004	0.0004	0.0004	0.0004	0.0004	0.0004	0.0003
−3.40	0.0003	0.0003	0.0003	0.0003	0.0003	0.0003	0.0003	0.0003	0.0003	0.0002
−3.50	0.0002	0.0002	0.0002	0.0002	0.0002	0.0002	0.0002	0.0002	0.0002	0.0002
−3.60	0.0002	0.0002	0.0001	0.0001	0.0001	0.0001	0.0001	0.0001	0.0001	0.0001
−3.70	0.0001	0.0001	0.0001	0.0001	0.0001	0.0001	0.0001	0.0001	0.0001	0.0001
−3.80	0.0001	0.0001	0.0001	0.0001	0.0001	0.0001	0.0001	0.0001	0.0001	0.0001
−3.90	0.0000	0.0000	0.0000	0.0000	0.0000	0.0000	0.0000	0.0000	0.0000	0.0000
−4.00	0.0000	0.0000	0.0000	0.0000	0.0000	0.0000	0.0000	0.0000	0.0000	0.0000

For example, to find the z-value leaving 2.5 percent of the area/probability in the lower tail, find the element 0.0250 in the body of the table. Read −1.90 at the left end of the element's row and 0.06 at the top of the element's column, to give −1.90 − 0.06 = −1.96. *Table generated with Excel.*

Appendix B
Table of the Student's t-Distribution (One-Tailed Probabilities)

df	p = 0.10	p = 0.05	p = 0.025	p = 0.01	p = 0.005
1	3.078	6.314	12.706	31.821	63.657
2	1.886	2.920	4.303	6.965	9.925
3	1.638	2.353	3.182	4.541	5.841
4	1.533	2.132	2.776	3.747	4.604
5	1.476	2.015	2.571	3.365	4.032
6	1.440	1.943	2.447	3.143	3.707
7	1.415	1.895	2.365	2.998	3.499
8	1.397	1.860	2.306	2.896	3.355
9	1.383	1.833	2.262	2.821	3.250
10	1.372	1.812	2.228	2.764	3.169
11	1.363	1.796	2.201	2.718	3.106
12	1.356	1.782	2.179	2.681	3.055
13	1.350	1.771	2.160	2.650	3.012
14	1.345	1.761	2.145	2.624	2.977
15	1.341	1.753	2.131	2.602	2.947
16	1.337	1.746	2.120	2.583	2.921
17	1.333	1.740	2.110	2.567	2.898
18	1.330	1.734	2.101	2.552	2.878
19	1.328	1.729	2.093	2.539	2.861
20	1.325	1.725	2.086	2.528	2.845
21	1.323	1.721	2.080	2.518	2.831
22	1.321	1.717	2.074	2.508	2.819
23	1.319	1.714	2.069	2.500	2.807
24	1.318	1.711	2.064	2.492	2.797
25	1.316	1.708	2.060	2.485	2.787
26	1.315	1.706	2.056	2.479	2.779
27	1.314	1.703	2.052	2.473	2.771
28	1.313	1.701	2.048	2.467	2.763
29	1.311	1.699	2.045	2.462	2.756
30	1.310	1.697	2.042	2.457	2.750

df	p = 0.10	p = 0.05	p = 0.025	p = 0.01	p = 0.005
31	1.309	1.696	2.040	2.453	2.744
32	1.309	1.694	2.037	2.449	2.738
33	1.308	1.692	2.035	2.445	2.733
34	1.307	1.691	2.032	2.441	2.728
35	1.306	1.690	2.030	2.438	2.724
36	1.306	1.688	2.028	2.434	2.719
37	1.305	1.687	2.026	2.431	2.715
38	1.304	1.686	2.024	2.429	2.712
39	1.304	1.685	2.023	2.426	2.708
40	1.303	1.684	2.021	2.423	2.704
41	1.303	1.683	2.020	2.421	2.701
42	1.302	1.682	2.018	2.418	2.698
43	1.302	1.681	2.017	2.416	2.695
44	1.301	1.680	2.015	2.414	2.692
45	1.301	1.679	2.014	2.412	2.690
46	1.300	1.679	2.013	2.410	2.687
47	1.300	1.678	2.012	2.408	2.685
48	1.299	1.677	2.011	2.407	2.682
49	1.299	1.677	2.010	2.405	2.680
50	1.299	1.676	2.009	2.403	2.678
60	1.296	1.671	2.000	2.390	2.660
70	1.294	1.667	1.994	2.381	2.648
80	1.292	1.664	1.990	2.374	2.639
90	1.291	1.662	1.987	2.368	2.632
100	1.290	1.660	1.984	2.364	2.626
110	1.289	1.659	1.982	2.361	2.621
120	1.289	1.658	1.980	2.358	2.617
200	1.286	1.653	1.972	2.345	2.601
∞	1.282	1.645	1.960	2.326	2.576

To find a critical t-value, enter the table with df and a specified value for α, the significance level. For example, with 5 df, α = 0.05 and a one-tailed test, the desired probability in the tail would be p = 0.05 and the critical t-value would be t(5, 0.05) = 2.015. With α =0.05 and a two-tailed test, the desired probability in each tail would be p = 0.025 =α/2, giving t(0.025) = 2.571. *Table generated using Excel*

Quantitative Methods for Investment Analysis, Second Edition, by Richard A. DeFusco, CFA, Dennis W. McLeavey, CFA, Jerald E. Pinto, CFA, and David E. Runkle, CFA. Copyright © 2004 by CFA Institute.

Appendix C
Values of χ^2 (Degrees of Freedom, Level of Significance)

Degrees of Freedom	Probability in Right Tail								
	0.99	0.975	0.95	0.9	0.1	0.05	0.025	0.01	0.005
1	0.000157	0.000982	0.003932	0.0158	2.706	3.841	5.024	6.635	7.879
2	0.020100	0.050636	0.102586	0.2107	4.605	5.991	7.378	9.210	10.597
3	0.1148	0.2158	0.3518	0.5844	6.251	7.815	9.348	11.345	12.838
4	0.297	0.484	0.711	1.064	7.779	9.488	11.143	13.277	14.860
5	0.554	0.831	1.145	1.610	9.236	11.070	12.832	15.086	16.750
6	0.872	1.237	1.635	2.204	10.645	12.592	14.449	16.812	18.548
7	1.239	1.690	2.167	2.833	12.017	14.067	16.013	18.475	20.278
8	1.647	2.180	2.733	3.490	13.362	15.507	17.535	20.090	21.955
9	2.088	2.700	3.325	4.168	14.684	16.919	19.023	21.666	23.589
10	2.558	3.247	3.940	4.865	15.987	18.307	20.483	23.209	25.188
11	3.053	3.816	4.575	5.578	17.275	19.675	21.920	24.725	26.757
12	3.571	4.404	5.226	6.304	18.549	21.026	23.337	26.217	28.300
13	4.107	5.009	5.892	7.041	19.812	22.362	24.736	27.688	29.819
14	4.660	5.629	6.571	7.790	21.064	23.685	26.119	29.141	31.319
15	5.229	6.262	7.261	8.547	22.307	24.996	27.488	30.578	32.801
16	5.812	6.908	7.962	9.312	23.542	26.296	28.845	32.000	34.267
17	6.408	7.564	8.672	10.085	24.769	27.587	30.191	33.409	35.718
18	7.015	8.231	9.390	10.865	25.989	28.869	31.526	34.805	37.156
19	7.633	8.907	10.117	11.651	27.204	30.144	32.852	36.191	38.582
20	8.260	9.591	10.851	12.443	28.412	31.410	34.170	37.566	39.997
21	8.897	10.283	11.591	13.240	29.615	32.671	35.479	38.932	41.401
22	9.542	10.982	12.338	14.041	30.813	33.924	36.781	40.289	42.796
23	10.196	11.689	13.091	14.848	32.007	35.172	38.076	41.638	44.181
24	10.856	12.401	13.848	15.659	33.196	36.415	39.364	42.980	45.558
25	11.524	13.120	14.611	16.473	34.382	37.652	40.646	44.314	46.928
26	12.198	13.844	15.379	17.292	35.563	38.885	41.923	45.642	48.290
27	12.878	14.573	16.151	18.114	36.741	40.113	43.195	46.963	49.645
28	13.565	15.308	16.928	18.939	37.916	41.337	44.461	48.278	50.994
29	14.256	16.047	17.708	19.768	39.087	42.557	45.722	49.588	52.335
30	14.953	16.791	18.493	20.599	40.256	43.773	46.979	50.892	53.672
50	29.707	32.357	34.764	37.689	63.167	67.505	71.420	76.154	79.490
60	37.485	40.482	43.188	46.459	74.397	79.082	83.298	88.379	91.952
80	53.540	57.153	60.391	64.278	96.578	101.879	106.629	112.329	116.321
100	70.065	74.222	77.929	82.358	118.498	124.342	129.561	135.807	140.170

To have a probability of 0.05 in the right tail when df = 5, the tabled value is $\chi^2(5, 0.05) = 11.070$.

Quantitative Methods for Investment Analysis, Second Edition, by Richard A. DeFusco, CFA, Dennis W. McLeavey, CFA, Jerald E. Pinto, CFA, and David E. Runkle, CFA. Copyright © 2004 by CFA Institute.

Appendix D
Table of the F-Distribution

Numerator: df_1 and Denominator: df_2

Panel A. Critical values for right-hand tail area equal to 0.05

df2: \ df1:	1	2	3	4	5	6	7	8	9	10	11	12	15	20	21	22	23	24	25	30	40	60	120	∞
1	161	200	216	225	230	234	237	239	241	242	243	244	246	248	248	249	249	249	249	250	251	252	253	254
2	18.5	19.0	19.2	19.2	19.3	19.3	19.4	19.4	19.4	19.4	19.4	19.4	19.4	19.4	19.4	19.5	19.5	19.5	19.5	19.5	19.5	19.5	19.5	19.5
3	10.1	9.55	9.28	9.12	9.01	8.94	8.89	8.85	8.81	8.79	8.76	8.74	8.70	8.66	8.65	8.65	8.64	8.64	8.63	8.62	8.59	8.57	8.55	8.53
4	7.71	6.94	6.59	6.39	6.26	6.16	6.09	6.04	6.00	5.96	5.94	5.91	5.86	5.80	5.79	5.79	5.78	5.77	5.77	5.75	5.72	5.69	5.66	5.63
5	6.61	5.79	5.41	5.19	5.05	4.95	4.88	4.82	4.77	4.74	4.70	4.68	4.62	4.56	4.55	4.54	4.53	4.53	4.52	4.50	4.46	4.43	4.40	4.37
6	5.99	5.14	4.76	4.53	4.39	4.28	4.21	4.15	4.10	4.06	4.03	4.00	3.94	3.87	3.86	3.86	3.85	3.84	3.83	3.81	3.77	3.74	3.70	3.67
7	5.59	4.74	4.35	4.12	3.97	3.87	3.79	3.73	3.68	3.64	3.60	3.57	3.51	3.44	3.43	3.43	3.42	3.41	3.40	3.38	3.34	3.30	3.27	3.23
8	5.32	4.46	4.07	3.84	3.69	3.58	3.50	3.44	3.39	3.35	3.31	3.28	3.22	3.15	3.14	3.13	3.12	3.12	3.11	3.08	3.04	3.01	2.97	2.93
9	5.12	4.26	3.86	3.63	3.48	3.37	3.29	3.23	3.18	3.14	3.10	3.07	3.01	2.94	2.93	2.92	2.91	2.90	2.89	2.86	2.83	2.79	2.75	2.71
10	4.96	4.10	3.71	3.48	3.33	3.22	3.14	3.07	3.02	2.98	2.94	2.91	2.85	2.77	2.76	2.75	2.75	2.74	2.73	2.70	2.66	2.62	2.58	2.54
11	4.84	3.98	3.59	3.36	3.20	3.09	3.01	2.95	2.90	2.85	2.82	2.79	2.72	2.65	2.64	2.63	2.62	2.61	2.60	2.57	2.53	2.49	2.45	2.40
12	4.75	3.89	3.49	3.26	3.11	3.00	2.91	2.85	2.80	2.75	2.72	2.69	2.62	2.54	2.53	2.52	2.51	2.51	2.50	2.47	2.43	2.38	2.34	2.30
13	4.67	3.81	3.41	3.18	3.03	2.92	2.83	2.77	2.71	2.67	2.63	2.60	2.53	2.46	2.45	2.44	2.43	2.42	2.41	2.38	2.34	2.30	2.25	2.21
14	4.60	3.74	3.34	3.11	2.96	2.85	2.76	2.70	2.65	2.60	2.57	2.53	2.46	2.39	2.38	2.37	2.36	2.35	2.34	2.31	2.27	2.22	2.18	2.13
15	4.54	3.68	3.29	3.06	2.90	2.79	2.71	2.64	2.59	2.54	2.51	2.48	2.40	2.33	2.32	2.31	2.30	2.29	2.28	2.25	2.20	2.16	2.11	2.07
16	4.49	3.63	3.24	3.01	2.85	2.74	2.66	2.59	2.54	2.49	2.46	2.42	2.35	2.28	2.26	2.25	2.24	2.24	2.23	2.19	2.15	2.11	2.06	2.01
17	4.45	3.59	3.20	2.96	2.81	2.70	2.61	2.55	2.49	2.45	2.41	2.38	2.31	2.23	2.22	2.21	2.20	2.19	2.18	2.15	2.10	2.06	2.01	1.96
18	4.41	3.55	3.16	2.93	2.77	2.66	2.58	2.51	2.46	2.41	2.37	2.34	2.27	2.19	2.18	2.17	2.16	2.15	2.14	2.11	2.06	2.02	1.97	1.92
19	4.38	3.52	3.13	2.90	2.74	2.63	2.54	2.48	2.42	2.38	2.34	2.31	2.23	2.16	2.14	2.13	2.12	2.11	2.11	2.07	2.03	1.98	1.93	1.88
20	4.35	3.49	3.10	2.87	2.71	2.60	2.51	2.45	2.39	2.35	2.31	2.28	2.20	2.12	2.11	2.10	2.09	2.08	2.07	2.04	1.99	1.95	1.90	1.84
21	4.32	3.47	3.07	2.84	2.68	2.57	2.49	2.42	2.37	2.32	2.28	2.25	2.18	2.10	2.08	2.07	2.06	2.05	2.05	2.01	1.96	1.92	1.87	1.81
22	4.30	3.44	3.05	2.82	2.66	2.55	2.46	2.40	2.34	2.30	2.26	2.23	2.15	2.07	2.06	2.05	2.04	2.03	2.02	1.98	1.94	1.89	1.84	1.78
23	4.28	3.42	3.03	2.80	2.64	2.53	2.44	2.37	2.32	2.27	2.24	2.20	2.13	2.05	2.04	2.02	2.01	2.01	2.00	1.96	1.91	1.86	1.81	1.76
24	4.26	3.40	3.01	2.78	2.62	2.51	2.42	2.36	2.30	2.25	2.22	2.18	2.11	2.03	2.01	2.00	1.99	1.98	1.97	1.94	1.89	1.84	1.79	1.73
25	4.24	3.39	2.99	2.76	2.60	2.49	2.40	2.34	2.28	2.24	2.20	2.16	2.09	2.01	2.00	1.98	1.97	1.96	1.96	1.92	1.87	1.82	1.77	1.71
30	4.17	3.32	2.92	2.69	2.53	2.42	2.33	2.27	2.21	2.16	2.13	2.09	2.01	1.93	1.92	1.91	1.90	1.89	1.88	1.84	1.79	1.74	1.68	1.62
40	4.08	3.23	2.84	2.61	2.45	2.34	2.25	2.18	2.12	2.08	2.04	2.00	1.92	1.84	1.83	1.81	1.80	1.79	1.78	1.74	1.69	1.64	1.58	1.51
60	4.00	3.15	2.76	2.53	2.37	2.25	2.17	2.10	2.04	1.99	1.95	1.92	1.84	1.75	1.73	1.72	1.71	1.70	1.69	1.65	1.59	1.53	1.47	1.39
120	3.92	3.07	2.68	2.45	2.29	2.18	2.09	2.02	1.96	1.91	1.87	1.83	1.75	1.66	1.64	1.63	1.62	1.61	1.60	1.55	1.50	1.43	1.35	1.25
Infinity	3.84	3.00	2.60	2.37	2.21	2.10	2.01	1.94	1.88	1.83	1.79	1.75	1.67	1.57	1.56	1.54	1.53	1.52	1.51	1.46	1.39	1.32	1.22	1.00

Appendix D (continued)
Table of the *F*-Distribution

Panel B. Critical values for right-hand tail area equal to 0.025

										Numerator: df_1 and Denominator: df_2															
df2:	df1: 1	2	3	4	5	6	7	8	9	10	11	12	15	20	21	22	23	24	25	30	40	60	120	∞
1	648	799	864	900	922	937	948	957	963	969	973	977	985	993	994	995	996	997	998	1001	1006	1010	1014	1018
2	38.51	39.00	39.17	39.25	39.30	39.33	39.36	39.37	39.39	39.40	39.41	39.41	39.43	39.45	39.45	39.45	39.45	39.46	39.46	39.46	39.47	39.48	39.49	39.50
3	17.44	16.04	15.44	15.10	14.88	14.73	14.62	14.54	14.47	14.42	14.37	14.34	14.25	14.17	14.16	14.14	14.13	14.12	14.12	14.08	14.04	13.99	13.95	13.90
4	12.22	10.65	9.98	9.60	9.36	9.20	9.07	8.98	8.90	8.84	8.79	8.75	8.66	8.56	8.55	8.53	8.52	8.51	8.50	8.46	8.41	8.36	8.31	8.26
5	10.01	8.43	7.76	7.39	7.15	6.98	6.85	6.76	6.68	6.62	6.57	6.52	6.43	6.33	6.31	6.30	6.29	6.28	6.27	6.23	6.18	6.12	6.07	6.02
6	8.81	7.26	6.60	6.23	5.99	5.82	5.70	5.60	5.52	5.46	5.41	5.37	5.27	5.17	5.15	5.14	5.13	5.12	5.11	5.07	5.01	4.96	4.90	4.85
7	8.07	6.54	5.89	5.52	5.29	5.12	4.99	4.90	4.82	4.76	4.71	4.67	4.57	4.47	4.45	4.44	4.43	4.41	4.40	4.36	4.31	4.25	4.20	4.14
8	7.57	6.06	5.42	5.05	4.82	4.65	4.53	4.43	4.36	4.30	4.24	4.20	4.10	4.00	3.98	3.97	3.96	3.95	3.94	3.89	3.84	3.78	3.73	3.67
9	7.21	5.71	5.08	4.72	4.48	4.32	4.20	4.10	4.03	3.96	3.91	3.87	3.77	3.67	3.65	3.64	3.63	3.61	3.60	3.56	3.51	3.45	3.39	3.33
10	6.94	5.46	4.83	4.47	4.24	4.07	3.95	3.85	3.78	3.72	3.66	3.62	3.52	3.42	3.40	3.39	3.38	3.37	3.35	3.31	3.26	3.20	3.14	3.08
11	6.72	5.26	4.63	4.28	4.04	3.88	3.76	3.66	3.59	3.53	3.47	3.43	3.33	3.23	3.21	3.20	3.18	3.17	3.16	3.12	3.06	3.00	2.94	2.88
12	6.55	5.10	4.47	4.12	3.89	3.73	3.61	3.51	3.44	3.37	3.32	3.28	3.18	3.07	3.06	3.04	3.03	3.02	3.01	2.96	2.91	2.85	2.79	2.72
13	6.41	4.97	4.35	4.00	3.77	3.60	3.48	3.39	3.31	3.25	3.20	3.15	3.05	2.95	2.93	2.92	2.91	2.89	2.88	2.84	2.78	2.72	2.66	2.60
14	6.30	4.86	4.24	3.89	3.66	3.50	3.38	3.29	3.21	3.15	3.09	3.05	2.95	2.84	2.83	2.81	2.80	2.79	2.78	2.73	2.67	2.61	2.55	2.49
15	6.20	4.77	4.15	3.80	3.58	3.41	3.29	3.20	3.12	3.06	3.01	2.96	2.86	2.76	2.74	2.73	2.71	2.70	2.69	2.64	2.59	2.52	2.46	2.40
16	6.12	4.69	4.08	3.73	3.50	3.34	3.22	3.12	3.05	2.99	2.93	2.89	2.79	2.68	2.67	2.65	2.64	2.63	2.61	2.57	2.51	2.45	2.38	2.32
17	6.04	4.62	4.01	3.66	3.44	3.28	3.16	3.06	2.98	2.92	2.87	2.82	2.72	2.62	2.60	2.59	2.57	2.56	2.55	2.50	2.44	2.38	2.32	2.25
18	5.98	4.56	3.95	3.61	3.38	3.22	3.10	3.01	2.93	2.87	2.81	2.77	2.67	2.56	2.54	2.53	2.52	2.50	2.49	2.44	2.38	2.32	2.26	2.19
19	5.92	4.51	3.90	3.56	3.33	3.17	3.05	2.96	2.88	2.82	2.76	2.72	2.62	2.51	2.49	2.48	2.46	2.45	2.44	2.39	2.33	2.27	2.20	2.13
20	5.87	4.46	3.86	3.51	3.29	3.13	3.01	2.91	2.84	2.77	2.72	2.68	2.57	2.46	2.45	2.43	2.42	2.41	2.40	2.35	2.29	2.22	2.16	2.09
21	5.83	4.42	3.82	3.48	3.25	3.09	2.97	2.87	2.80	2.73	2.68	2.64	2.53	2.42	2.41	2.39	2.38	2.37	2.36	2.31	2.25	2.18	2.11	2.04
22	5.79	4.38	3.78	3.44	3.22	3.05	2.93	2.84	2.76	2.70	2.65	2.60	2.50	2.39	2.37	2.36	2.34	2.33	2.32	2.27	2.21	2.14	2.08	2.00
23	5.75	4.35	3.75	3.41	3.18	3.02	2.90	2.81	2.73	2.67	2.62	2.57	2.47	2.36	2.34	2.33	2.31	2.30	2.29	2.24	2.18	2.11	2.04	1.97
24	5.72	4.32	3.72	3.38	3.15	2.99	2.87	2.78	2.70	2.64	2.59	2.54	2.44	2.33	2.31	2.30	2.28	2.27	2.26	2.21	2.15	2.08	2.01	1.94
25	5.69	4.29	3.69	3.35	3.13	2.97	2.85	2.75	2.68	2.61	2.56	2.51	2.41	2.30	2.28	2.27	2.26	2.24	2.23	2.18	2.12	2.05	1.98	1.91
30	5.57	4.18	3.59	3.25	3.03	2.87	2.75	2.65	2.57	2.51	2.46	2.41	2.31	2.20	2.18	2.16	2.15	2.14	2.12	2.07	2.01	1.94	1.87	1.79
40	5.42	4.05	3.46	3.13	2.90	2.74	2.62	2.53	2.45	2.39	2.33	2.29	2.18	2.07	2.05	2.03	2.02	2.01	1.99	1.94	1.88	1.80	1.72	1.64
60	5.29	3.93	3.34	3.01	2.79	2.63	2.51	2.41	2.33	2.27	2.22	2.17	2.06	1.94	1.93	1.91	1.90	1.88	1.87	1.82	1.74	1.67	1.58	1.48
120	5.15	3.80	3.23	2.89	2.67	2.52	2.39	2.30	2.22	2.16	2.10	2.05	1.94	1.82	1.81	1.79	1.77	1.76	1.75	1.69	1.61	1.53	1.43	1.31
Infinity	5.02	3.69	3.12	2.79	2.57	2.41	2.29	2.19	2.11	2.05	1.99	1.94	1.83	1.71	1.69	1.67	1.66	1.64	1.63	1.57	1.48	1.39	1.27	1.00

Appendix D (continued)
Table of the F-Distribution

Panel C. Critical values for right-hand tail area equal to 0.01

Numerator: df_1 and Denominator: df_2

$df1$: $df2$:	1	2	3	4	5	6	7	8	9	10	11	12	15	20	21	22	23	24	25	30	40	60	120	∞
1	4052	5000	5403	5625	5764	5859	5928	5982	6023	6056	6083	6106	6157	6209	6216	6223	6229	6235	6240	6261	6287	6313	6339	6366
2	98.5	99.0	99.2	99.2	99.3	99.3	99.4	99.4	99.4	99.4	99.4	99.4	99.4	99.4	99.5	99.5	99.5	99.5	99.5	99.5	99.5	99.5	99.5	99.5
3	34.1	30.8	29.5	28.7	28.2	27.9	27.7	27.5	27.3	27.2	27.1	27.1	26.9	26.7	26.7	26.6	26.6	26.6	26.6	26.5	26.4	26.3	26.2	26.1
4	21.2	18.0	16.7	16.0	15.5	15.2	15.0	14.8	14.7	14.5	14.5	14.4	14.2	14.0	14.0	14.0	13.9	13.9	13.9	13.8	13.7	13.7	13.6	13.5
5	16.3	13.3	12.1	11.4	11.0	10.7	10.5	10.3	10.2	10.1	10.0	9.89	9.72	9.55	9.53	9.51	9.49	9.47	9.45	9.38	9.29	9.20	9.11	9.02
6	13.7	10.9	9.78	9.15	8.75	8.47	8.26	8.10	7.98	7.87	7.79	7.72	7.56	7.40	7.37	7.35	7.33	7.31	7.30	7.23	7.14	7.06	6.97	6.88
7	12.2	9.55	8.45	7.85	7.46	7.19	6.99	6.84	6.72	6.62	6.54	6.47	6.31	6.16	6.13	6.11	6.09	6.07	6.06	5.99	5.91	5.82	5.74	5.65
8	11.3	8.65	7.59	7.01	6.63	6.37	6.18	6.03	5.91	5.81	5.73	5.67	5.52	5.36	5.34	5.32	5.30	5.28	5.26	5.20	5.12	5.03	4.95	4.86
9	10.6	8.02	6.99	6.42	6.06	5.80	5.61	5.47	5.35	5.26	5.18	5.11	4.96	4.81	4.79	4.77	4.75	4.73	4.71	4.65	4.57	4.48	4.40	4.31
10	10.0	7.56	6.55	5.99	5.64	5.39	5.20	5.06	4.94	4.85	4.77	4.71	4.56	4.41	4.38	4.36	4.34	4.33	4.31	4.25	4.17	4.08	4.00	3.91
11	9.65	7.21	6.22	5.67	5.32	5.07	4.89	4.74	4.63	4.54	4.46	4.40	4.25	4.10	4.08	4.06	4.04	4.02	4.01	3.94	3.86	3.78	3.69	3.60
12	9.33	6.93	5.95	5.41	5.06	4.82	4.64	4.50	4.39	4.30	4.22	4.16	4.01	3.86	3.84	3.82	3.80	3.78	3.76	3.70	3.62	3.54	3.45	3.36
13	9.07	6.70	5.74	5.21	4.86	4.62	4.44	4.30	4.19	4.10	4.02	3.96	3.82	3.66	3.64	3.62	3.60	3.59	3.57	3.51	3.43	3.34	3.25	3.17
14	8.86	6.51	5.56	5.04	4.70	4.46	4.28	4.14	4.03	3.94	3.86	3.80	3.66	3.51	3.48	3.46	3.44	3.43	3.41	3.35	3.27	3.18	3.09	3.00
15	8.68	6.36	5.42	4.89	4.56	4.32	4.14	4.00	3.89	3.80	3.73	3.67	3.52	3.37	3.35	3.33	3.31	3.29	3.28	3.21	3.13	3.05	2.96	2.87
16	8.53	6.23	5.29	4.77	4.44	4.20	4.03	3.89	3.78	3.69	3.62	3.55	3.41	3.26	3.24	3.22	3.20	3.18	3.16	3.10	3.02	2.93	2.84	2.75
17	8.40	6.11	5.19	4.67	4.34	4.10	3.93	3.79	3.68	3.59	3.52	3.46	3.31	3.16	3.14	3.12	3.10	3.08	3.07	3.00	2.92	2.83	2.75	2.65
18	8.29	6.01	5.09	4.58	4.25	4.01	3.84	3.71	3.60	3.51	3.43	3.37	3.23	3.08	3.05	3.03	3.02	3.00	2.98	2.92	2.84	2.75	2.66	2.57
19	8.19	5.93	5.01	4.50	4.17	3.94	3.77	3.63	3.52	3.43	3.36	3.30	3.15	3.00	2.98	2.96	2.94	2.92	2.91	2.84	2.76	2.67	2.58	2.49
20	8.10	5.85	4.94	4.43	4.10	3.87	3.70	3.56	3.46	3.37	3.29	3.23	3.09	2.94	2.92	2.90	2.88	2.86	2.84	2.78	2.69	2.61	2.52	2.42
21	8.02	5.78	4.87	4.37	4.04	3.81	3.64	3.51	3.40	3.31	3.24	3.17	3.03	2.88	2.86	2.84	2.82	2.80	2.79	2.72	2.64	2.55	2.46	2.36
22	7.95	5.72	4.82	4.31	3.99	3.76	3.59	3.45	3.35	3.26	3.18	3.12	2.98	2.83	2.81	2.78	2.77	2.75	2.73	2.67	2.58	2.50	2.40	2.31
23	7.88	5.66	4.76	4.26	3.94	3.71	3.54	3.41	3.30	3.21	3.14	3.07	2.93	2.78	2.76	2.74	2.72	2.70	2.69	2.62	2.54	2.45	2.35	2.26
24	7.82	5.61	4.72	4.22	3.90	3.67	3.50	3.36	3.26	3.17	3.09	3.03	2.89	2.74	2.72	2.70	2.68	2.66	2.64	2.58	2.49	2.40	2.31	2.21
25	7.77	5.57	4.68	4.18	3.86	3.63	3.46	3.32	3.22	3.13	3.06	2.99	2.85	2.70	2.68	2.66	2.64	2.62	2.60	2.53	2.45	2.36	2.27	2.17
30	7.56	5.39	4.51	4.02	3.70	3.47	3.30	3.17	3.07	2.98	2.91	2.84	2.70	2.55	2.53	2.51	2.49	2.47	2.45	2.39	2.30	2.21	2.11	2.01
40	7.31	5.18	4.31	3.83	3.51	3.29	3.12	2.99	2.89	2.80	2.73	2.66	2.52	2.37	2.35	2.33	2.31	2.29	2.27	2.20	2.11	2.02	1.92	1.80
60	7.08	4.98	4.13	3.65	3.34	3.12	2.95	2.82	2.72	2.63	2.56	2.50	2.35	2.20	2.17	2.15	2.13	2.12	2.10	2.03	1.94	1.84	1.73	1.60
120	6.85	4.79	3.95	3.48	3.17	2.96	2.79	2.66	2.56	2.47	2.40	2.34	2.19	2.03	2.01	1.99	1.97	1.95	1.93	1.86	1.76	1.66	1.53	1.38
Infinity	6.63	4.61	3.78	3.32	3.02	2.80	2.64	2.51	2.41	2.32	2.25	2.18	2.04	1.88	1.85	1.83	1.81	1.79	1.77	1.70	1.59	1.47	1.32	1.00

Appendix D (continued)
Table of the F-Distribution

Panel D. Critical values for right-hand tail area equal to 0.005

Numerator: df₁ and Denominator: df₂

df2: \ df1:	1	2	3	4	5	6	7	8	9	10	11	12	15	20	21	22	23	24	25	30	40	60	120	∞
1	16211	20000	21615	22500	23056	23437	23715	23925	24091	24222	24334	24426	24630	24836	24863	24892	24915	24940	24959	25044	25146	25253	25359	25464
2	198.5	199.0	199.2	199.2	199.3	199.3	199.4	199.4	199.4	199.4	199.4	199.4	199.4	199.4	199.4	199.4	199.4	199.4	199.4	199.5	199.5	199.5	199.5	200
3	55.55	49.80	47.47	46.20	45.39	44.84	44.43	44.13	43.88	43.68	43.52	43.39	43.08	42.78	42.73	42.69	42.66	42.62	42.59	42.47	42.31	42.15	41.99	41.83
4	31.33	26.28	24.26	23.15	22.46	21.98	21.62	21.35	21.14	20.97	20.82	20.70	20.44	20.17	20.13	20.09	20.06	20.03	20.00	19.89	19.75	19.61	19.47	19.32
5	22.78	18.31	16.53	15.56	14.94	14.51	14.20	13.96	13.77	13.62	13.49	13.38	13.15	12.90	12.87	12.84	12.81	12.78	12.76	12.66	12.53	12.40	12.27	12.14
6	18.63	14.54	12.92	12.03	11.46	11.07	10.79	10.57	10.39	10.25	10.13	10.03	9.81	9.59	9.56	9.53	9.50	9.47	9.45	9.36	9.24	9.12	9.00	8.88
7	16.24	12.40	10.88	10.05	9.52	9.16	8.89	8.68	8.51	8.38	8.27	8.18	7.97	7.75	7.72	7.69	7.67	7.64	7.62	7.53	7.42	7.31	7.19	7.08
8	14.69	11.04	9.60	8.81	8.30	7.95	7.69	7.50	7.34	7.21	7.10	7.01	6.81	6.61	6.58	6.55	6.53	6.50	6.48	6.40	6.29	6.18	6.06	5.95
9	13.61	10.11	8.72	7.96	7.47	7.13	6.88	6.69	6.54	6.42	6.31	6.23	6.03	5.83	5.80	5.78	5.75	5.73	5.71	5.62	5.52	5.41	5.30	5.19
10	12.83	9.43	8.08	7.34	6.87	6.54	6.30	6.12	5.97	5.85	5.75	5.66	5.47	5.27	5.25	5.22	5.20	5.17	5.15	5.07	4.97	4.86	4.75	4.64
11	12.23	8.91	7.60	6.88	6.42	6.10	5.86	5.68	5.54	5.42	5.32	5.24	5.05	4.86	4.83	4.80	4.78	4.76	4.74	4.65	4.55	4.45	4.34	4.23
12	11.75	8.51	7.23	6.52	6.07	5.76	5.52	5.35	5.20	5.09	4.99	4.91	4.72	4.53	4.50	4.48	4.45	4.43	4.41	4.33	4.23	4.12	4.01	3.90
13	11.37	8.19	6.93	6.23	5.79	5.48	5.25	5.08	4.94	4.82	4.72	4.64	4.46	4.27	4.24	4.22	4.19	4.17	4.15	4.07	3.97	3.87	3.76	3.65
14	11.06	7.92	6.68	6.00	5.56	5.26	5.03	4.86	4.72	4.60	4.51	4.43	4.25	4.06	4.03	4.01	3.98	3.96	3.94	3.86	3.76	3.66	3.55	3.44
15	10.80	7.70	6.48	5.80	5.37	5.07	4.85	4.67	4.54	4.42	4.33	4.25	4.07	3.88	3.86	3.83	3.81	3.79	3.77	3.69	3.59	3.48	3.37	3.26
16	10.58	7.51	6.30	5.64	5.21	4.91	4.69	4.52	4.38	4.27	4.18	4.10	3.92	3.73	3.71	3.68	3.66	3.64	3.62	3.54	3.44	3.33	3.22	3.11
17	10.38	7.35	6.16	5.50	5.07	4.78	4.56	4.39	4.25	4.14	4.05	3.97	3.79	3.61	3.58	3.56	3.53	3.51	3.49	3.41	3.31	3.21	3.10	2.98
18	10.22	7.21	6.03	5.37	4.96	4.66	4.44	4.28	4.14	4.03	3.94	3.86	3.68	3.50	3.47	3.45	3.42	3.40	3.38	3.30	3.20	3.10	2.99	2.87
19	10.07	7.09	5.92	5.27	4.85	4.56	4.34	4.18	4.04	3.93	3.84	3.76	3.59	3.40	3.37	3.35	3.33	3.31	3.29	3.21	3.11	3.00	2.89	2.78
20	9.94	6.99	5.82	5.17	4.76	4.47	4.26	4.09	3.96	3.85	3.76	3.68	3.50	3.32	3.29	3.27	3.24	3.22	3.20	3.12	3.02	2.92	2.81	2.69
21	9.83	6.89	5.73	5.09	4.68	4.39	4.18	4.01	3.88	3.77	3.68	3.60	3.43	3.24	3.22	3.19	3.17	3.15	3.13	3.05	2.95	2.84	2.73	2.61
22	9.73	6.81	5.65	5.02	4.61	4.32	4.11	3.94	3.81	3.70	3.61	3.54	3.36	3.18	3.15	3.12	3.10	3.08	3.06	2.98	2.88	2.77	2.66	2.55
23	9.63	6.73	5.58	4.95	4.54	4.26	4.05	3.88	3.75	3.64	3.55	3.47	3.30	3.12	3.09	3.06	3.04	3.02	3.00	2.92	2.82	2.71	2.60	2.48
24	9.55	6.66	5.52	4.89	4.49	4.20	3.99	3.83	3.69	3.59	3.50	3.42	3.25	3.06	3.04	3.01	2.99	2.97	2.95	2.87	2.77	2.66	2.55	2.43
25	9.48	6.60	5.46	4.84	4.43	4.15	3.94	3.78	3.64	3.54	3.45	3.37	3.20	3.01	2.99	2.96	2.94	2.92	2.90	2.82	2.72	2.61	2.50	2.38
30	9.18	6.35	5.24	4.62	4.23	3.95	3.74	3.58	3.45	3.34	3.25	3.18	3.01	2.82	2.80	2.77	2.75	2.73	2.71	2.63	2.52	2.42	2.30	2.18
40	8.83	6.07	4.98	4.37	3.99	3.71	3.51	3.35	3.22	3.12	3.03	2.95	2.78	2.60	2.57	2.55	2.52	2.50	2.48	2.40	2.30	2.18	2.06	1.93
60	8.49	5.79	4.73	4.14	3.76	3.49	3.29	3.13	3.01	2.90	2.82	2.74	2.57	2.39	2.36	2.33	2.31	2.29	2.27	2.19	2.08	1.96	1.83	1.69
120	8.18	5.54	4.50	3.92	3.55	3.28	3.09	2.93	2.81	2.71	2.62	2.54	2.37	2.19	2.16	2.13	2.11	2.09	2.07	1.98	1.87	1.75	1.61	1.43
Infinity	7.88	5.30	4.28	3.72	3.35	3.09	2.90	2.74	2.62	2.52	2.43	2.36	2.19	2.00	1.97	1.95	1.92	1.90	1.88	1.79	1.67	1.53	1.36	1.00

With 1 degree of freedom (df) in the numerator and 3 df in the denominator, the critical F-value is 10.1 for a right-hand tail area equal to 0.05.

Quantitative Methods for Investment Analysis, Second Edition, by Richard A. DeFusco, CFA, Dennis W. McLeavey, CFA, Jerald E. Pinto, CFA, and David E. Runkle, CFA. Copyright © 2004 by CFA Institute.

Appendix E
Critical Values for the Durbin-Watson Statistic (α = .05)

n	K = 1		K = 2		K = 3		K = 4		K = 5	
	d_l	d_u	d_l	d_u	d_l	d_u	d_l	d_u	d_l	d_u
15	1.08	1.36	0.95	1.54	0.82	1.75	0.69	1.97	0.56	2.21
16	1.10	1.37	0.98	1.54	0.86	1.73	0.74	1.93	0.62	2.15
17	1.13	1.38	1.02	1.54	0.90	1.71	0.78	1.90	0.67	2.10
18	1.16	1.39	1.05	1.53	0.93	1.69	0.82	1.87	0.71	2.06
19	1.18	1.40	1.08	1.53	0.97	1.68	0.86	1.85	0.75	2.02
20	1.20	1.41	1.10	1.54	1.00	1.68	0.90	1.83	0.79	1.99
21	1.22	1.42	1.13	1.54	1.03	1.67	0.93	1.81	0.83	1.96
22	1.24	1.43	1.15	1.54	1.05	1.66	0.96	1.80	0.86	1.94
23	1.26	1.44	1.17	1.54	1.08	1.66	0.99	1.79	0.90	1.92
24	1.27	1.45	1.19	1.55	1.10	1.66	1.01	1.78	0.93	1.90
25	1.29	1.45	1.21	1.55	1.12	1.66	1.04	1.77	0.95	1.89
26	1.30	1.46	1.22	1.55	1.14	1.65	1.06	1.76	0.98	1.88
27	1.32	1.47	1.24	1.56	1.16	1.65	1.08	1.76	1.01	1.86
28	1.33	1.48	1.26	1.56	1.18	1.65	1.10	1.75	1.03	1.85
29	1.34	1.48	1.27	1.56	1.20	1.65	1.12	1.74	1.05	1.84
30	1.35	1.49	1.28	1.57	1.21	1.65	1.14	1.74	1.07	1.83
31	1.36	1.50	1.30	1.57	1.23	1.65	1.16	1.74	1.09	1.83
32	1.37	1.50	1.31	1.57	1.24	1.65	1.18	1.73	1.11	1.82
33	1.38	1.51	1.32	1.58	1.26	1.65	1.19	1.73	1.13	1.81
34	1.39	1.51	1.33	1.58	1.27	1.65	1.21	1.73	1.15	1.81
35	1.40	1.52	1.34	1.58	1.28	1.65	1.22	1.73	1.16	1.80
36	1.41	1.52	1.35	1.59	1.29	1.65	1.24	1.73	1.18	1.80
37	1.42	1.53	1.36	1.59	1.31	1.66	1.25	1.72	1.19	1.80
38	1.43	1.54	1.37	1.59	1.32	1.66	1.26	1.72	1.21	1.79
39	1.43	1.54	1.38	1.60	1.33	1.66	1.27	1.72	1.22	1.79
40	1.44	1.54	1.39	1.60	1.34	1.66	1.29	1.72	1.23	1.79
45	1.48	1.57	1.43	1.62	1.38	1.67	1.34	1.72	1.29	1.78
50	1.50	1.59	1.46	1.63	1.42	1.67	1.38	1.72	1.34	1.77
55	1.53	1.60	1.49	1.64	1.45	1.68	1.41	1.72	1.38	1.77
60	1.55	1.62	1.51	1.65	1.48	1.69	1.44	1.73	1.41	1.77
65	1.57	1.63	1.54	1.66	1.50	1.70	1.47	1.73	1.44	1.77
70	1.58	1.64	1.55	1.67	1.52	1.70	1.49	1.74	1.46	1.77
75	1.60	1.65	1.57	1.68	1.54	1.71	1.51	1.74	1.49	1.77
80	1.61	1.66	1.59	1.69	1.56	1.72	1.53	1.74	1.51	1.77
85	1.62	1.67	1.60	1.70	1.57	1.72	1.55	1.75	1.52	1.77
90	1.63	1.68	1.61	1.70	1.59	1.73	1.57	1.75	1.54	1.78
95	1.64	1.69	1.62	1.71	1.60	1.73	1.58	1.75	1.56	1.78
100	1.65	1.69	1.63	1.72	1.61	1.74	1.59	1.76	1.57	1.78

Note: K = the number of slope parameters in the model.

Source: From J. Durbin and G. S. Watson, "Testing for Serial Correlation in Least Squares Regression, II." *Biometrika* 38 (1951): 159–178.

Glossary

Abandonment option   The option to terminate an investment at some future time if the financial results are disappointing.

Abnormal return   The return on an asset in excess of the asset's required rate of return; the risk-adjusted return.

Absolute dispersion   The amount of variability present without comparison to any reference point or benchmark.

Accelerated book build   An offering of securities by an investment bank acting as principal that is accomplished in only one or two days.

Accounting profit   Income as reported on the income statement, in accordance with prevailing accounting standards, before the provisions for income tax expense. Also called *income before taxes* or *pretax income*.

Accredited investors   Investors that meet certain minimum regulatory net worth or other requirements in order to invest in certain types of alternative assets.

Accrued interest   The amount of interest in currency or par value terms of a fixed-income instrument that accumulates from the last coupon payment until the trade settlement date. The amount is paid by the buyer to the seller.

Action lag   Delay from policy decisions to implementation.

Active investment   An approach to investing in which the investor seeks to outperform a given benchmark.

Active return   The return on a portfolio minus the return on the portfolio's benchmark.

Activist   Short for "activist shareholder." Managers secure sufficient equity holdings to allow them to seek a position in a company's board and influence corporate policies or direction.

Activity ratios   Ratios that measure how well a company is managing key current assets and working capital over time.

Ad hoc committee   A small group of lenders or bondholders who negotiate with an issuer on debt restructuring and refinancing before the issuer submits a final proposal to the wider group of all lenders and bondholders.

Add-on pricing   A pricing approach based on high-margin optional features, customizations, and additional content.

Add-on rate   A yield or pricing convention for money market instrument quotations. It is the interest earned on an instrument, derived from the difference between the price and face value, expressed as a percentage of the price and multiplied by the periodicity of the annual rate.

Agency costs   Direct and indirect costs borne by the principal in a principal-agent relationship owing primarily to information asymmetries. Agency costs include the costs of monitoring and assessing the agent as well as missed opportunities.

Agency RMBS   Securities created by the pooling of residential mortgage-backed securities in the United States by either the Federal National Mortgage Association (Fannie Mae) or the Federal Home Loan Mortgage Corporation (Freddie Mac). These RMBS carry the full faith and credit of the government, essentially a guarantee with respect to timely payment of interest and repayment of principal.

All-or-nothing (AON) orders   An order that includes the instruction to trade only if the trade fills the entire quantity (size) specified.

Allocationally efficient   A characteristic of a market, a financial system, or an economy that promotes the allocation of resources to their highest value uses.

Altcoin   A cryptocurrency other than Bitcoin.

Alternative data   Data that are generated from non-traditional sources, such as social media and sensor networks.

Alternative hypothesis   The hypothesis that is accepted if the null hypothesis is rejected.

Alternative investment markets   Market for investments other than traditional securities investments (i.e., traditional common and preferred shares and traditional fixed income instruments). The term usually encompasses direct and indirect investment in real estate (including timberland and farmland) and commodities (including precious metals); hedge funds, private equity, and other investments requiring specialized due diligence.

Alternative trading systems   Trading venues that function like exchanges but that do not exercise regulatory authority over their subscribers except with respect to the conduct of the subscribers' trading in their trading systems. Also called *electronic communications networks* or *multilateral trading facilities*.

American depository receipt   A US dollar-denominated security that trades like a common share on US exchanges.

American depository share   The underlying shares on which American depository receipts are based. They trade in the issuing company's domestic market.

American options   Options that may be exercised at any time from contract inception until maturity.

American-style   Type of option contract that can be exercised at any time up to the option's expiration date.

Amortization   The process of allocating the cost of intangible long-term assets having a finite useful life to accounting periods; the allocation of the amount of a bond premium or discount to the periods remaining until bond maturity.

Amortizing debt   A loan or bond with a payment schedule that calls for periodic payments of interest and repayments of principal.

Analysis of variance (ANOVA)   A table that presents the sums of squares, degrees of freedom, mean squares, and F-statistic for a regression model.

Analytical duration   Estimates of duration using mathematical formulas. Estimates of the impact of yield changes on bond prices using analytical duration implicitly assume that benchmark yields and spreads are independent variables and are uncorrelated.

Anchoring and adjustment bias   An information-processing bias in which the use of a psychological heuristic influences the way people estimate probabilities.

Annual general meeting (AGM)   A yearly meeting of the corporate board of directors and shareholders, typically held in person and digitally, during which votes on directors, compensation plans, shareholder resolutions, and any other matters properly brought forward at the meeting are held. Issuer management may also make presentations and hold events.

Anomalies Apparent deviations from market efficiency.

Antidilutive With reference to a transaction or a security, one that would increase earnings per share (EPS) or result in EPS higher than the company's basic EPS—antidilutive securities are not included in the calculation of diluted EPS.

Arbitrage 1) The simultaneous purchase of an undervalued asset or portfolio and sale of an overvalued but equivalent asset or portfolio, in order to obtain a riskless profit on the price differential. Taking advantage of a market inefficiency in a risk-free manner. 2) The condition in a financial market in which equivalent assets or combinations of assets sell for two different prices, creating an opportunity to profit at no risk with no commitment of money. In a well-functioning financial market, few arbitrage opportunities are possible. 3) A risk-free operation that earns an expected positive net profit but requires no net investment of money.

Arbitrageurs Traders who engage in arbitrage. See *arbitrage*.

Arithmetic mean The sum of the observations divided by the number of observations.

Artificial intelligence (AI) Computer systems that are capable of performing tasks that previously required human intelligence. AI methods are sometimes better suited to identify complex, non-linear relationships than are traditional quantitative and statistical methods.

Ask The price at which a dealer or trader is willing to sell an asset, typically qualified by a maximum quantity (ask size). See *offer*.

Ask size The maximum quantity of an asset that pertains to a specific ask price from a trader. For example, if the ask for a share issue is $30 for a size of 1,000 shares, the trader is offering to sell at $30 up to 1,000 shares.

Asset allocation The process of determining how investment funds should be distributed among asset classes.

Asset class A group of assets that have similar characteristics, attributes, and risk–return relationships.

Asset utilization ratios Ratios that measure how efficiently a company performs day-to-day tasks, such as the collection of receivables and management of inventory.

Asset-backed commercial paper Secured form of commercial paper issuance. Loans or receivables are sold to a special purpose entity that issues the ABCP and makes interest and principal payments to investors from asset cash flows.

Asset-backed securities (ABS) A type of bond issued by a legal entity called a special purpose entity created solely to own assets such as loans, receivables, and mortgages and to distribute cash flows to ABS investors. Generally, ABS backed by mortgages are known as mortgage-backed securities (MBS) while ABS refer to non-mortgage ABS.

Asset-backed token A token that represents the ownership of a physical asset that does not exist on the blockchain and whose value is based on the underlying asset.

Asset-based valuation models Valuation based on estimates of the market value of a company's assets.

Asymmetric information Also known as *information asymmetry*; the differential of information between corporate insiders and outsiders regarding the company's performance and prospects. Managers typically have more information about the company's performance and prospects than owners and creditors.

At-the-money Describes a unique situation in which the price of the underlying is equal to an option's exercise price. Like an out-of-the-money option, the intrinsic value is zero.

Auction/reverse auction models Pricing models that establish prices through bidding (by sellers in the case of reverse auctions).

Autarky Countries seeking political self-sufficiency with little or no external trade or finance. State-owned enterprises control strategic domestic industries.

Automatic stabilizer A countercyclical factor that automatically comes into play as an economy slows and unemployment rises.

Availability bias An information-processing bias in which people take a heuristic approach to estimating the probability of an outcome based on how easily the outcome comes to mind.

Available-for-sale Under US GAAP, debt securities not classified as either held-to-maturity or held-for-trading securities. The investor is willing to sell but not actively planning to sell. In general, available-for-sale debt securities are reported at fair value on the balance sheet, with unrealized gains included as a component of other comprehensive income.

Average revenue (AR) Total revenue divided by quantity sold.

Backfill Bias A problem whereby certain surviving hedge funds may be added to databases and various hedge fund indexes only after they are initially successful and start to report their returns. Also see *survivorship bias*.

Backup line of credit A type of credit enhancement provided by a bank to an issuer of commercial paper to ensure that the issuer will have access to sufficient liquidity to repay maturing commercial paper if issuing new paper is not a viable option.

Backwardation A downward-sloping, or inverted, forward curve in a futures market.

Balance sheet ratios Financial ratios involving balance sheet items only.

Balanced With respect to a government budget, one in which spending and revenues (taxes) are equal.

Balloon payment A large payment required at maturity to retire a bond's outstanding principal amount.

Base rates The reference rate on which a bank bases lending rates to all other customers.

Base-rate neglect A type of representativeness bias in which the base rate or probability of the categorization is not adequately considered.

Basic EPS Net earnings available to common shareholders (i.e., net income minus preferred dividends) divided by the weighted average number of common shares outstanding.

Basis risk The possibility that the expected value of a derivative differs unexpectedly from that of the underlying.

Basket of listed depository receipts (BLDR) An exchange-traded fund (ETF) that represents a portfolio of depository receipts.

Bayes' formula The rule for updating the probability of an event of interest—given a set of prior probabilities for the event, information, and information given the event—if you receive new information.

Bearer bonds Bonds for which ownership is not recorded; only the clearing system knows who the bond owner is.

Behavioral finance A field of finance that examines the psychological variables that affect and often distort the investment decision making of investors, analysts, and portfolio managers.

Behind the market Said of prices specified in orders that are worse than the best current price; e.g., for a limit buy order, a limit price below the best bid.

Benchmark A bond used to compare against another bond to discern attributes, often a government bond with the same or similar time-to-maturity as the bond under analysis.

Benchmark spread The difference in yield-to-maturity between a bond and that of a benchmark bond.

Best bid The highest bid in the market.

Best effort offering An offering of a security using an investment bank in which the investment bank, as agent for the issuer, promises to use its best efforts to sell the offering but does not guarantee that a specific amount will be sold.

Best offer The lowest offer (ask price) in the market.

Best-in-class An ESG implementation approach that seeks to identify the most favorable companies in an industry based on ESG considerations.

Beta A measure of systematic risk that is based on the covariance of an asset's or portfolio's return with the return of the overall market; a measure of the sensitivity of a given investment or portfolio to movements in the overall market.

Bid The price at which a dealer or trader is willing to buy an asset, typically qualified by a maximum quantity.

Bid size The maximum quantity of an asset that pertains to a specific bid price from a trader.

Big data The vast amount of information being generated by both traditional sources—for example, stock exchanges, companies, governments—and non-traditional sources—for example, electronic devices, social media, sensor networks, and company exhaust.

Bilateralism The conduct of political, economic, financial, or cultural cooperation between two countries. Countries engaging in bilateralism may have relations with many different countries but in one-at-a-time agreements without multiple partners. Typically, countries exist on a spectrum between bilateralism and multilateralism.

Bimodal A distribution that has two most frequently occurring values.

Bitcoin A cryptocurrency using blockchain technology that was created in 2009.

Bivariate correlation Also known as Pearson correlation. A parametric measure of the relationship between two variables.

Black swan risk An event that is rare and difficult to predict but has an important impact.

Block brokers A broker (agent) that provides brokerage services for large-size trades.

Blockchain A type of digital ledger in which information is recorded sequentially and then linked together and secured using cryptographic methods.

Blue chip Widely held large market capitalization companies that are considered financially sound and are leaders in their respective industry or local stock market.

Board of directors A body or individual selected by a limited company's member(s) or shareholder(s), in a manner determined by the company's charter, that manages the company. Typically, for larger companies, boards of directors appoint and oversee executive management.

Bond equivalent yield A money market interest rate quoted on a 365-day add-on rate basis.

Bond indenture A legal document between a bond issuer and investors that governs each party's rights and responsibilities.

Bond market vigilantes Bond market participants who might reduce their demand for long-term bonds, thus pushing up their yields.

Bondholders Investors in an entity's securitized debt claims, such as commercial paper, notes, and bonds. Common types of bondholders include investment funds and institutional investors.

Bonds Contractual agreements between an issuer and bondholders.

Bonus issue of shares A type of dividend in which a company distributes additional shares of its common stock to shareholders instead of cash.

Book building Investment bankers' process of compiling a "book" or list of indications of interest to buy part of an offering.

Book value The net amount shown for an asset or liability on the balance sheet; book value may also refer to the company's excess of total assets over total liabilities. Also called *carrying value*.

Boom An expansionary phase characterized by economic growth "testing the limits" of the economy.

Bootstrap A resampling method that repeatedly draws samples with replacement of the selected elements from the original observed sample. Bootstrap is usually conducted by using computer simulation and is often used to find standard error or construct confidence intervals of population parameters.

Bottom-up analysis An investment selection approach that focuses on company-specific circumstances rather than emphasizing economic cycles or industry analysis.

Box and whisker plot A graphic for visualizing the dispersion of data across quartiles. It consists of a box with "whiskers" connected to the box.

Breakeven point Represents the price of the underlying in a derivative contract in which the profit to both counterparties would be zero.

Bridge financing Interim financing that provides funds until permanent financing can be arranged.

Broker An agent who executes orders to buy or sell securities on behalf of a client in exchange for a commission.

Brokered market A market in which brokers arrange trades among their clients.

Broker–dealer A financial intermediary (often a company) that may function as a principal (dealer) or as an agent (broker) depending on the type of trade.

Brownfield investments The third stage of development of an infrastructure asset. Brownfield investments involve expanding existing facilities and may involve privatization of public assets or a sale leaseback of completed greenfield projects. They are characterized by a shorter investment period with immediate cash flows and an operating history.

Budget surplus/deficit The difference between government revenue and expenditure for a stated fixed period of time.

Bullet bond A bond whose principal repayment is made entirely at maturity.

Bundling A pricing approach that refers to combining multiple products or services so that customers are incentivized or required to buy them together.

Business cycles Are recurrent expansions and contractions in economic activity affecting broad segments of the economy.

Business model A concise description of how a business works and makes revenues and profits, including its customers, products or services, channels for reaching customers, and pricing.

Businesses Organization entities formed and managed for the purpose of providing a return or economic benefits to its investors and owners.

Buy-side firm An investment management company or other investor that uses the services of brokers or dealers (i.e., the client of the sell side firms).

Buyback A transaction in which a company buys back its own shares. Unlike stock dividends and stock splits, share repurchases use corporate cash.

Cabotage The right to transport passengers or goods within a country by a foreign firm. Many countries—including those with multilateral trade agreements—impose restrictions on cabotage across transportation subsectors, meaning that shippers, airlines, and truck drivers are not allowed to transport goods and services within another country's borders.

Call market A market in which trades occur only at a particular time and place (i.e., when the market is called).

Call money rate The interest rate that buyers pay for their margin loan.

Call option The right to buy an underlying.

Call period The time during which the issuer of a callable bond can exercise the call option.

Call price The price at which the issuer of a callable bond has the right to purchase the bond from investors.

Call protection period The time during which the issuer of a callable bond is not allowed to exercise the call option.

Call risk The uncertain maturity and limited price appreciation associated with callable bonds.

Callable bond A bond containing an embedded call option that gives the issuer the right to buy the bond back from the investor at specified prices on predetermined dates.

Cannibalization A transfer of sales or market share from one product to another product owned by the same company. It tends to occur when the two products are actual or perceived substitutes.

Capacity The ability of the borrower to make its debt payments on time.

Capital Other company resources available that reduce reliance on debt.

Capital allocation The process that companies use for decision making on capital investments—those projects with a life of one year or longer.

Capital allocation line (CAL) A graph line that describes the combinations of expected return and standard deviation of return available to an investor from combining the optimal portfolio of risky assets with the risk-free asset.

Capital asset pricing model (CAPM) An equation describing the expected return on any asset (or portfolio) as a linear function of its beta relative to the market portfolio.

Capital expenditure Expenditure on physical capital (fixed assets).

Capital investments An expenditure for an asset or resource with a useful life of more than one year.

Capital market expectations (CME) Expectations concerning the risk and return prospects of asset classes.

Capital market line (CML) The line with an intercept point equal to the risk-free rate that is tangent to the efficient frontier of risky assets; represents the efficient frontier when a risk-free asset is available for investment.

Capital market securities Fixed-income securities with original maturities greater than one year.

Capital markets Financial markets that trade securities of longer duration, such as bonds and equities.

Capital restrictions Controls placed on foreigners' ability to own domestic assets and/or domestic residents' ability to own foreign assets.

Capital structure The mix of debt and equity that a company uses to finance its business; a company's specific mix of long-term financing.

Capital-indexed bond A type of index-linked bond for which changes in the index are captured with adjustments to the principal. A common example is Treasury Inflation Protected Securities (TIPS) issued by the United States government.

Capital-intensive businesses Companies or business activities that are characterized by a relatively low fixed asset turnover, a high percentage of capital expenditures to sales, or a high net-working-capital-to-sales ratio.

Capital-light businesses Also known as *asset light businesses*, companies or business activities characterized by relatively high fixed asset turnover, a low percentage of capital expenditures to sales, or a low net-working-capital-to-sales ratio.

Carried interest A performance fee (also referred to as an incentive fee, or carry) that is applied based on excess returns above a hurdle rate.

Carrying Investing and holding an asset for a period of time.

Carrying amount The amount at which an asset or liability is valued according to accounting principles.

Carrying value Of a fixed-income instrument is the purchase price plus (minus) the amortized amount of the discount (premium) if the bond is purchased at a price below (above) par value.

Cartel Participants in collusive agreements that are made openly and formally.

Cash conversion cycle The amount of time between an issuer paying its suppliers in cash and receiving cash from its customers.

Cash flow additivity principle The principle that dollar amounts indexed at the same point in time are additive.

Cash flow from operations A cash profit measure over a period for an issuer's primary business activities. It includes cash from customers as well as interest and dividends received from financial investments, less cash paid to employees and suppliers as well as taxes paid to governments and interest paid to lenders.

Cash flow hedge Refers to a specific **hedge accounting** classification in which a derivative is designated as absorbing the variable cash flow of a floating-rate asset or liability, such as foreign exchange, interest rates, or commodities.

Cash markets Markets in which specific assets are exchanged at current prices. Cash markets are often referred to as **spot markets**.

Cash prices The current prices prevailing in **cash markets**.

Cash ratio A measure of liquidity that is the ratio of cash and marketable securities to current liabilities.

Catch-up clause A clause in an agreement that favors the GP. For a GP who earns a 20% performance fee, a catch-up clause allows the GP to receive 100% of the distributions above the hurdle rate *until* she receives 20% of the profits generated, and then every excess dollar is split 80/20 between the LPs and GP.

CDS credit spread Reflects the credit spread of a credit default swap (CDS) derivative contract. As with cash bonds, CDS credit spreads depend on the probability of default (POD) and the loss given default (LGD).

Central bank digital currencies (CBDCs) A tokenized version of the currency issued by the central bank, such as a digital bank note or coin, and a digital liability of the central bank.

Central bank funds market The market in which deposit-taking banks that have an excess reserve with their national central bank can lend money to banks that need funds for maturities ranging from overnight to one year. Called the federal or fed funds market in the United States.

Central bank funds rate The interest rate at which central bank funds are bought (borrowed) and sold (lent) for maturities ranging from overnight to one year. Called federal or fed funds rate in the United States.

Central clearing mandate A requirement instituted by global regulatory authorities following the 2008 global financial crisis that most **over-the-counter (OTC)** derivatives be **cleared** by a **central counterparty (CCP)**.

Central counterparty (CCP) An economic entity that assumes the **counterparty credit risk** between derivative **counterparties**, one of which is typically a financial intermediary. CCPs provide **clearing** and **settlement** for most **derivative contracts**.

Central limit theorem The theorem that states the sum (and the mean) of a set of independent, identically distributed random variables with finite variances is normally distributed, whatever distribution the random variables follow.

Certificate of deposit (CD) An instrument that represents a specified amount of funds on deposit with a bank for a specified maturity and interest rate. CDs are issued in various denominations and can be negotiable or non-negotiable.

Channels Venues where a company markets and/or delivers its products and services.

Character The quality of a debt issuer's management.

Checking accounts Bank deposits with no stated maturity available for transactional purposes that pay little or no interest. Also known as a *demand deposit*.

Circuit breaker A pause in intraday trading for a brief period if a price limit is reached.

Classical cycle Refers to fluctuations in the level of economic activity when measured by GDP in volume terms.

Clawback A requirement that the general partner return any funds distributed as incentive fees until the limited partners have received their initial investment and a percentage of the total profit.

Clearing An exchange's process of verifying the execution of a transaction, exchange of payments, and recording of participants.

Clearing instructions Instructions that indicate how to arrange the final settlement ("clearing") of a trade.

Clearinghouse An entity associated with a futures market that acts as middleman between the contracting parties and guarantees to each party the performance of the other.

Closed-end fund A mutual fund in which no new investment money is accepted. New investors invest by buying existing shares, and investors in the fund liquidate by selling their shares to other investors.

Cluster sampling A procedure that divides a population into subpopulation groups (clusters) representative of the population and then randomly draws certain clusters to form a sample.

Co-investing In co-investing, the investor invests in assets *indirectly* through the fund but also possesses rights (known as co-investment rights) to invest *directly* in the same assets. Through co-investing, an investor is able to make an investment *alongside* a fund when the fund identifies deals.

Code of ethics An established guide that communicates an organization's values and overall expectations regarding member behavior. A code of ethics serves as a general guide for how community members should act.

Coefficient of determination (R^2) The percentage of the variation of the dependent variable that is explained by the independent variable. It is a measure of goodness of fit of a regression model.

Coefficient of variation The ratio of a set of observations' standard deviation to the observations' mean value.

Cognitive cost The effort involved in processing new information and updating beliefs.

Cognitive dissonance The mental discomfort that occurs when new information conflicts with previously held beliefs or cognitions.

Cognitive errors Behavioral biases resulting from faulty reasoning; cognitive errors stem from basic statistical, information-processing, or memory errors.

Coincident economic indicators Turning points that are usually close to those of the overall economy; they are believed to have value for identifying the economy's present state.

Collateral Assets or financial guarantees underlying a debt obligation that are above and beyond the issuer's promise to pay.

Collateral manager Buys and sells debt obligations for and from the CDO's collateral pool to generate sufficient cash flows to meet the obligations to the CDO bondholders.

Collateralized bond obligations (CBOs) CDOs backed by high-yield corporate and emerging market bonds.

Collateralized debt obligations (CDOs) Securities backed by a diversified pool of one or more debt obligations. CDOs can be backed by a broad range of debt.

Collateralized loan obligations (CLOs) CDOs backed by leveraged bank loans.

Collateralized mortgage obligations Securitize mortgage pass-through securities or multiple pools of loans. CMOs are structured to redistribute the cash flows to different bond classes or tranches and create securities that have different exposures to prepayment risk.

Commercial paper (CP) Short-term, negotiable, unsecured promissory note that represents a debt obligation of the issuer.

Committed (regular) lines of credit Bank commitments to extend credit; the commitment is considered a short-term liability and is usually in effect for 364 days (one day short of a full year).

Committed capital The amount that the limited partners have agreed to provide to the private equity fund.

Commodities A product or service from a firm that is indistinguishable from products or services of competing firms, usually conforming to a common standard or grade imposed by convention or regulation.

Commoditization A process by which competing products become less differentiated over time and become interchangeable "commodities" in the eyes of customers. This process is typically associated with declining profitability for the selling firms.

Commodity producers A firm that makes and/or sells commodities.

Commodity swap A type of swap involving the exchange of payments over multiple dates as determined by specified reference prices or indexes relating to commodities.

Common market Level of economic integration that incorporates all aspects of the customs union and extends it by allowing free movement of factors of production among members.

Common shares A type of security that represents an ownership interest in a company. Also called *common stock*.

Common stock A type of security that represents an ownership interest in a company. Also called *common shares.*

Common-size analysis The restatement of financial statement items using a common denominator or reference item that allows one to identify trends and major differences; an example is an income statement in which all items are expressed as a percent of revenue.

Companies Organization entities formed and managed for the purpose of providing a return or economic benefits to its investors and owners.

Company research report A document that presents an analyst's investment recommendation on an issuer and its securities, supported by financial modeling, industry overviews and competitive analyses, valuation scenarios, ESG considerations, and investment risks.

Complete markets Informally, markets in which the variety of distinct securities traded is so broad that any desired payoff in a future state-of-the-world is achievable.

Concession agreement A contractual arrangement under which an entity (also known as a grantor) establishes terms and conditions with a developer or operator (referred to as a concessionaire) to plan, build, operate, finance, and maintain an infrastructure asset for a specific period.

Conditional expected value The expected value of a stated event given that another event has occurred.

Conditional pass-through covered bonds Convert to pass-through securities after the original maturity date if all bond payments have not yet been made.

Conditional variances The variance of one variable, given the outcome of another.

Conditions The general economic, competitive, and business environment faced by all borrowers that may affect their ability to service or refinance debt.

Confidence level The complement of the level of significance.

Confirmation bias A belief perseverance bias in which people tend to look for and notice what confirms their beliefs, to ignore or undervalue what contradicts their beliefs, and to misinterpret information as support for their beliefs.

Consensus protocol A set of rules governing how blocks can join the blockchain that is designed to resist attempts at malicious manipulation up to a certain level of security; it can be either a proof of work or a proof of stake.

Conservatism bias A belief perseverance bias in which people maintain their prior views or forecasts by inadequately incorporating new information.

Constant yield-price trajectory A graphical depiction of the relationship between time to maturity and a bond price, assuming no default, that shows that a bond price approaches par as time passes.

Constituent securities With respect to an index, the individual securities within an index.

Contango Refers to spot price below forward price in a futures market.

Contingency provision Clause in a legal document that allows for some action if a specific event or circumstance occurs.

Contingency table A table of the frequency distribution of observations classified on the basis of two discrete variables.

Contingent claim A type of derivative in which one of the *counterparties* determines whether and when the trade will settle. An *option* is a common type of contingent claim.

Contingent convertible bonds Bonds that automatically convert to equity if a specific event or circumstance occurs, such as the issuer's equity capital falling below the minimum requirement set by regulators.

Continuous trading market A market in which trades can be arranged and executed any time the market is open.

Continuously compounded return The natural logarithm of 1 plus the holding period return, or equivalently, the natural logarithm of the ending price over the beginning price.

Contract manufacturers Companies that make products for other companies that meet specific terms and specifications.

Contract size Amount(s) used for calculation to price and value the derivative. The contract size is often referred to as "notional amount or notional principal."

Contraction The period of a business cycle after the peak and before the trough; often called a *recession* or, if exceptionally severe, called a *depression.*

Contraction risk The risk of earlier repayment of a mortgage-backed security than expected.

Contractionary Tending to cause the real economy to contract.

Contractionary fiscal policy A fiscal policy that has the objective to make the real economy contract.

Contribution margin A profitability measure using variable costs: unit price less unit variable cost. It can also be expressed as a percentage of price or sales.

Controlling shareholder An individual or entity that owns a majority of the voting rights in a corporation.

Convenience sampling A procedure of selecting an element from a population on the basis of whether or not it is accessible to a researcher or how easy it is for a researcher to access the element.

Convenience yield A non-cash benefit of holding a physical commodity versus a derivative.

Conversion price For a convertible bond, the price per share at which the bond can be converted into shares.

Conversion ratio Number of common shares received in exchange for each preferred share after a predetermined period.

Conversion value For a convertible bond, the value of the bond if it is converted at the market price of the shares. Also called *parity value.*

Convertible bond A bond that gives the bondholder the right to exchange the bond for a specified number of common shares in the issuing company.

Convertible debt A debt instrument that gives the holder the right to exchange the instrument for a specified number of common shares in the issuing company.

Convertible preference shares A type of equity security that entitles shareholders to convert their shares into a specified number of common shares.

Convexity An interest rate risk measure used in conjunction with duration; captures the degree of nonlinearity (curvature) in the relation between price change and yield change.

Convexity adjustment A measure that is used to complement modified duration to capture the second-order effect of yield changes on a bond's price. It is equal to the annual convexity statistic times one-half times the given change in the yield-to-maturity squared.

Convexity bias Refers to the difference in price changes for a given change in yield between interest rate futures and interest rate forward contracts. That is, interest rate forwards exhibit a non-linear or convex relationship between price and yield, while the price–yield relationship is linear for interest rate futures.

Cooperation   The process by which countries work together toward some shared goal or purpose. These goals may, and often do, vary widely—from strategic or military concerns, to economic influence, to cultural preferences.

Cooperative country   A country that engages and reciprocates in rules standardization; harmonization of tariffs; international agreements on trade, immigration, or regulation; and allowing the free flow of information, including technology transfer.

Core real estate strategies   Strategies with exposure to well-leased, high-quality commercial and residential real estate in the best markets, generally offered by open-end funds. Investors expect core real estate to deliver stable returns, primarily from income from the property.

Core-plus real estate strategies   Value-add investments that require modest redevelopment or upgrades to lease any vacant space together with possible alternative use of the underlying properties. Compared to core real estate strategies, these may be appealing for investors seeking higher returns and willing to accept additional risks from development, redevelopment, repositioning, and leasing.

Corporate issuers   Limited companies or corporations that seek financing in financial markets by, for example, issuing debt or equity securities.

Corporations   Another term for limited companies, though often used to refer to public limited companies. See *limited company*, *private limited company*, and *public limited company*.

Correlation   A measure of the linear relationship between two random variables.

Correlation coefficient   A number between –1 and +1 that measures the consistency or tendency for two investments to act in a similar way. It is used to determine the effect on portfolio risk when two assets are combined.

Cost averaging   The periodic investment of a fixed amount of money.

Cost of capital   The cost of financing for a company; the rate of return that suppliers of capital require as compensation for their contribution of capital (also called *opportunity cost of funds*).

Cost of carry   The net of the costs and benefits related to owning an underlying asset for a specific period.

Cost of debt   The required return on debt financing for a company, such as when it issues a bond, takes out a bank loan, or leases an asset through a finance lease.

Cost of equity   The return required by equity investors to compensate for both the time value of money and the risk. Also referred to as the required rate of return on common stock or the required return on equity.

Counterparty   Legal entities entering a **derivative contract**.

Counterparty credit risk   The likelihood that a **counterparty** is unable to meet its financial obligations under the contract.

Counterparty risk   The risk that the other party to a contract will fail to honor the terms of the contract.

Country   The geopolitical environment as well as the legal and political system faced by all issuers in a jurisdiction that may affect debt payment.

Coupon   Periodic interest payments paid by a bond issuer to investors, typically expressed as a percentage of par on an annual basis.

Cournot assumption   Assumption in which each firm determines its profit-maximizing production level assuming that the other firms' output will not change.

Covariance   A measure of the co-movement (linear association) between two random variables.

Covenants   The terms and conditions of lending agreements that the issuer must comply with; they specify the actions that an issuer is obligated to perform (affirmative covenant) or prohibited from performing (negative covenant).

Credit default swap (CDS)   A type of credit derivative in which one party, the credit protection buyer who is seeking credit protection against a third party, makes a series of regularly scheduled payments to the other party, the credit protection seller. The seller makes no payments until a credit event occurs.

Credit enhancements   Provisions or methods that allow a borrower improve their creditworthiness in a structured transaction.

Credit event   An event that defines a payout in a credit derivative. Events are usually defined as bankruptcy, failure to pay an obligation, or an involuntary debt restructuring.

Credit facilities   Loan agreements with pre-specified terms and limits but with fluctuating balances based on borrower-specific needs at different points in time, analogous to a credit card.

Credit migration risk   The risk that a bond issuer's creditworthiness deteriorates, or migrates lower, leading investors to believe the risk of default is higher. Also called **downgrade risk**.

Credit rating   Letter-grade, qualitative measures of an issuer's ability to meet its debt obligations based on both the probability of default and the expected loss under a default scenario.

Credit rating agencies   Institutions that issue and maintain credit ratings. The three largest are Standard & Poor's, Moody's, and Fitch Ratings.

Credit risk   The expected economic loss under a potential borrower default over the life of the contract

Credit spread   A premium over and above the current government bond yield.

Credit spread risk   The risk of greater expected loss due to changes in credit conditions as a result of macroeconomic, market, and/or issuer-related factors.

Credit tranching   Internal credit enhancement where cash flows into a senior/subordinate structure.

Credit-linked notes   Bonds whose coupon changes when the bonds' credit rating changes.

Critical values   Values of the test statistic at which the decision changes from fail to reject the null hypothesis to reject the null hypothesis.

Cross-default clause   Covenant or contract clause that specifies borrowers are considered in default if they default on another debt obligation.

Cross-sectional analysis   Also called relative analysis. Analysis that involves comparisons across individuals in a group over a given time period or at a given point in time.

Crossing networks   Trading systems that match buyers and sellers who are willing to trade at prices obtained from other markets.

Crowdsourcing   A business model that enables users to contribute directly to a product, service, or online content.

Cryptocurrency   An electronic medium of exchange that lacks physical form.

Cryptocurrency wallet A storage unit for public and/or private keys for cryptocurrency transactions. These wallets may be a physical device, program, or service.

Cryptography An algorithmic process to encrypt data, making the data unusable if received by unauthorized parties.

Cumulative preference shares Preference shares for which any dividends that are not paid accrue and must be paid in full before dividends on common shares can be paid.

Cumulative voting A voting process whereby shareholders can accumulate and vote all their shares for a single candidate in an election, as opposed to having to allocate their voting rights evenly among all candidates.

Currencies Monies issued by national monetary authorities.

Currency Money issued by national monetary authorities.

Currency swap A swap in which each party makes interest payments to the other in different currencies.

Current government spending With respect to government expenditures, spending on goods and services that are provided on a regular, recurring basis including health, education, and defense.

Current ratio A measure of liquidity that is the ratio of current assets to current liabilities.

Current yield The sum of the coupon payments received over the year divided by the flat price. Also called the income, interest yield, or running yield.

Customs union Extends the free trade area (FTA) by not only allowing free movement of goods and services among members, but also creating a common trade policy against nonmembers.

CVaR Conditional VaR, a tail loss measure. The weighted average of all loss outcomes in the statistical distribution that exceed the VaR loss.

Daily settlement A specific process of *mark-to-market* by a central clearing party in which the profits and losses of all counterparties to derivatives contracts are determined using settlement prices for each contract.

Dark pools Alternative trading systems that do not display the orders that their clients send to them.

Data mining The practice of determining a model by extensive searching through a dataset for statistically significant patterns.

Data science An interdisciplinary field that harnesses advances in computer science, statistics, and other disciplines for the purpose of extracting information from big data (or data in general).

Data snooping The practice of determining a model by extensive searching through a dataset for statistically significant patterns.

Day order An order that is good for the day on which it is submitted. If it has not been filled by the close of business, the order expires unfilled.

Days of inventory on hand (DOH) The average number of days it would take to sell the amount of inventory on hand. It is calculated as either the ending or average balance of inventories divided by (cost of goods sold/days in the period).

Days payable outstanding (DPO) The average number of days it takes a company to pay its suppliers. It is calculated as either the ending or average balance of accounts payable divided by (cost of goods sold/days in the period).

Days sales outstanding (DSO) The average number of days it takes for a company to receive payment from customers who purchase goods or services on credit. It is calculated as either the ending or average balance of accounts receivable divided by (revenues/days in the period).

Dealers Financial intermediaries, such as commercial banks or investment banks, who transact as **counterparties** with derivative end users.

Debt A claim against an entity to receive cash, stock, or other assets at a future date. From the perspective of the debtor or borrower, an obligation to pay cash, stock, or other assets at a future date. Generally, debt claims are unconditional and are senior to equity claims.

Debt service coverage ratio A ratio in which the net operating income of a real estate investment for a specific period is divided by the amount of debt service to be paid during the same time period.

Debt tax shield The tax benefit from interest paid on debt being tax deductible from income, equal to the marginal tax rate multiplied by the value of the debt.

Debt-to-assets ratio A solvency ratio calculated as total debt divided by total assets.

Debt-to-capital ratio A solvency ratio calculated as total debt divided by total debt plus total shareholders' equity.

Debt-to-equity ratio A solvency ratio calculated as total debt divided by total shareholders' equity.

Debt-to-income ratio (DTI) Residential lending metric that compares an individual's monthly debt payments to their monthly pre-tax, gross income.

Debut issuer An issuer approaching the bond market for the first time.

Deciles Quantiles that divide a distribution into 10 equal parts.

Declaration date The day that the corporation issues a statement declaring a specific dividend.

Decreasing returns to scale When a production process leads to increases in output that are proportionately smaller than the increase in inputs.

Deductible temporary differences Temporary differences that result in a reduction of or deduction from taxable income in a future period when the balance sheet item is recovered or settled.

Deep learning An area of artificial intelligence in which a system uses neural networks to perform multistage, non-linear data processing to identify patterns. Also called *deep learning nets*.

Deep learning nets See *Deep learning*.

Deep-in-the-money option An option that is highly likely to be exercised.

Deep-out-of-the-money option An option that is highly unlikely to be exercised.

Default When a borrower on a mortgage loan fails to meet the obligations of the loan.

Default risk premium An extra return that compensates investors for the possibility that the borrower will fail to make a promised payment at the contracted time and in the contracted amount.

Defeasance Mechanism that allows prepayment on mortgage, but the borrower must purchase a portfolio of government securities that fully replicates the cash flows of the remaining scheduled principal and interest payments, including the balloon loan balance, on the loan.

Defensive interval ratio A liquidity ratio that estimates the number of days that an entity could meet cash needs from liquid assets; calculated as (cash + short-term marketable investments + receivables) divided by daily cash expenditures.

Deferred coupon bonds Bonds that pay no coupons for their first few years but then pay a higher coupon than they otherwise normally would for the remainder of their life. Also called *split coupon bonds.*

Deferred tax assets A balance sheet asset that arises when an excess amount is paid for income taxes relative to accounting profit. The taxable income is higher than accounting profit and income tax payable exceeds tax expense. The company expects to recover the difference during the course of future operations when tax expense exceeds income tax payable.

Deferred tax liabilities A balance sheet liability that arises when a deficit amount is paid for income taxes relative to accounting profit. The taxable income is less than the accounting profit and income tax payable is less than tax expense. The company expects to eliminate the liability over the course of future operations when income tax payable exceeds tax expense.

Defined benefit pension plans (DB plans) Plans in which the company promises to pay a certain annual amount (defined benefit) to the employee after retirement. The company bears the investment risk of the plan assets.

Defined contribution pension plans Individual accounts to which an employee and typically the employer makes contributions during their working years and expect to draw on the accumulated funds at retirement. The employee bears the investment and inflation risk of the plan assets.

Deflation Negative inflation.

Degree of financial leverage The ratio of percentage change in net income to percentage change in operating income over a period. It is a measure of how sensitive net income is to changes in operating income, driven by the firm's use of debt in its capital structure.

Degree of operating leverage (DOL) The ratio of percentage change in operating income to percentage change in sales over a period. It is a measure of how sensitive operating income is to changes in sales, driven by the fixed and variable cost composition of operating expenses.

Delta The relationship between the option price and the underlying price, which reflects the sensitivity of the price of the option to changes in the price of the underlying. Delta is a good approximation of how an option price will change for a small change in the stock.

Demand shock A typically unexpected disturbance to demand, such as an unexpected interruption in trade or transportation.

Dependent variable The variable that is explained by a regression model.

Depository bank A bank that raises funds from depositors and other investors and lends it to borrowers.

Depository institutions Commercial banks, savings and loan banks, credit unions, and similar institutions that raise funds from depositors and other investors and lend it to borrowers.

Depository receipt A security that trades like an ordinary share on a local exchange and represents an economic interest in a foreign company.

Depreciation The process of systematically allocating the cost of long-lived (tangible) assets to the periods during which the assets are expected to provide economic benefits.

Derivative A financial instrument that derives its value from the performance of an underlying asset.

Derivative contract A legal agreement between counterparties with a specific **maturity**, or length of time, until the closing of the transaction, or **settlement**.

Derivative pricing rule A pricing rule used by crossing networks in which a price is taken (derived) from the price that is current in the asset's primary market.

Derivatives A financial instrument whose value depends on the value of some underlying asset or factor (e.g., a stock price, an interest rate, or exchange rate).

Differentiated products A product or service from a firm that is distinguishable or distinct from those of competing firms. It is customers who determine and value whether a product is differentiated.

Diffuse prior The assumption of equal prior probabilities.

Diffusion index Reflects the proportion of the index's components that are moving in a pattern consistent with the overall index.

Digital assets The umbrella term covering assets that can be created, stored, and transmitted electronically and have associated ownership or use rights. Digital assets include a variety of assets, such as cryptocurrencies, tokens (security and utility), and digital collectables.

Diluted EPS The EPS that would result if all dilutive securities were converted into common shares.

Dilution An increase in the number of shares outstanding from share issuance that decreases the percentage of shares owned by existing shareholders.

Direct investing Occurs when an investor makes a direct investment in an asset without the use of an intermediary.

Direct lending Providing capital directly from private debt investors.

Direct listing Where the equity of a security is floated on the public markets directly, without underwriters, reducing the complexity and cost of the transaction.

Direct sales Marketing and/or delivering products and services to customers without an intermediary or third party between the customer and seller.

Direct taxes Taxes levied directly on income, wealth, and corporate profits.

Discount factor The price equivalent of a zero rate. Also may be stated as the present value of a currency unit on a future date.

Discount rate A yield or pricing convention for money market instrument quotations. It is the interest earned on an instrument, derived from the difference between the price and face value, expressed as a percentage of the face value and multiplied by the periodicity of the annual rate.

Discounted cash flow models Valuation models that estimate the intrinsic value of a security as the present value of the future benefits expected to be received from the security.

Discriminatory pricing rule A pricing rule used in continuous markets in which the limit price of the order or quote that first arrived determines the trade price.

Diseconomies of scale Increase in cost per unit resulting from increased production.

Dispersion The variability of a population or sample of observations around the central tendency.

Display size The size of an order displayed to public view.

Disposition effect As a result of loss aversion, an emotional bias whereby investors are reluctant to dispose of losers. This results in an inefficient and gradual adjustment to deterioration in fundamental value.

Distressed debt Debt of mature companies in financial difficulty, in bankruptcy, or likely to default on debt.

Distressed/restructuring These strategies focus on securities of companies either in or perceived to be near bankruptcy. In one approach, hedge funds simply purchase fixed-income securities trading at a significant discount to par but that are still senior enough to be backed by sufficient corporate assets.

Distributed ledger A type of database that can be shared among entities in a network.

Distributed ledger technology (DLT) Technology based on a distributed ledger.

Diversification ratio The ratio of the standard deviation of an equally weighted portfolio to the standard deviation of a randomly selected security.

Dividend A distribution paid to shareholders based on the number of shares owned.

Dividend discount model (DDM) A present value model of stock value that views the intrinsic value of a stock as present value of the stock's expected future dividends.

Dividend payout ratio The ratio of cash dividends paid to earnings for a period.

Dividends Distributions of profits and/or net assets from a corporation to its shareholders. While often in cash, dividends can be also be paid in stock or assets, such as property.

Divisor A number (denominator) used to determine the value of a price return index. It is initially chosen at the inception of an index and subsequently adjusted by the index provider, as necessary, to avoid changes in the index value that are unrelated to changes in the prices of its constituent securities.

Domestic bonds A type of bond for which the issuer's domicile and jurisdiction of issuance are the same.

Domestic content provisions Stipulate that some percentage of the value added or components used in production should be of domestic origin.

Double taxation The taxation of business income at both the entity and personal or owner levels. In most jurisdictions, this taxation scheme applies to public limited companies.

Downside risk The potential for loss.

Drag on liquidity An action or event that reduces available funds or delays cash inflows.

Drivers Causative factors that explain the level of and changes in an output variable.

DSC ratio A property's annual net operating income (NOI) divided by the debt service.

Dual-class structure A capital structure that includes at least two classes of equity shares with unequal voting rights.

Dupont analysis An approach to decomposing return on investment, e.g., return on equity, as the product of other financial ratios.

Duration The percentage change in bond price given an unanticipated small change in interest rates.

Duration gap The difference between a bond's Macaulay duration and its investor's investment horizon.

Dynamic pricing A pricing approach that charges different prices at different times. Specific examples include off-peak pricing, "surge" pricing, and "congestion" pricing.

Early repayment option May entitle the borrower to prepay all or part of the outstanding mortgage principal prior to maturity. This creates a risk from the lender's or investor's viewpoint because the cash flow amounts and timing cannot be known with certainty.

Earnings surprise The portion of a company's earnings that is unanticipated by investors and, according to the efficient market hypothesis, merits a price adjustment.

Economic indicators Economic statistics provided by government and established private organizations that contain information on an economy's recent past activity or its current or future position in the business cycle.

Economic infrastructure investments A category of infrastructure investments that support economic activity through transportation assets, information and communication technology assets, and utility and energy assets.

Economic stabilization Reduction of the magnitude of economic fluctuations.

Economic union Incorporates all aspects of a common market and in addition requires common economic institutions and coordination of economic policies among members.

Economies of scale A decline in costs per unit as output grows, generally resulting from having fixed costs in the cost structure that are spread over more units of output.

Economies of scope A decline in costs per unit as the number of product or business lines increases, generally resulting from having shared costs between the product lines.

Effective annual rate An interest rate with a periodicity of one.

Effective convexity An interest rate risk statistic that measures the non-linear/second-order effect of changes in the benchmark yield curve on a bond's price.

Effective duration The sensitivity of the bond's price to an instantaneous parallel shift in a benchmark yield curve—for example, the government par curve.

Efficient market A market in which asset prices reflect new information quickly and rationally. See also, *informationally efficient market*.

Either/or fee A custom fee arrangement whereby major investors are offered a structure where managers agree to charge *either* a lower management fee *or* a higher incentive fee, whichever is greater.

Electronic communications networks (ECNs) See *alternative trading systems* and *multilateral trading facilities*.

Embedded derivative A derivative within an underlying, such as a callable, putable, or convertible bond.

Embedded options Contingency provisions found in a bond's indenture representing rights that enable their holders to take advantage of interest rate movements. They can be exercised by the issuer, by the bondholder, or automatically depending on the course of interest rates.

Emotional biases Behavioral biases resulting from reasoning influenced by feelings; emotional biases stem from impulse or intuition.

Empirical duration Estimates of duration calculated over time and in different interest rate environments. Unlike analytical duration, empirical duration estimates do not assume that benchmark yields and spreads are independent variables and are uncorrelated.

Employee stock ownership plan (ESOP) A type of employee benefit plan in which a company sets up a trust fund to receive contributions of newly issued shares or cash to buy existing shares. Contributions are tax deductible up to certain limits. Shares in the trust fund are allocated to individual employees based on relative pay or a formula.

Endowment bias An emotional bias in which people value an asset more when they hold rights to it than when they do not.

Enterprise risk management An overall assessment of a company's risk position. A centralized approach to risk management sometimes called firmwide risk management.

Enterprise value (EV)   Total company value (the market value of debt, common equity, and preferred equity) minus the value of cash and investments.

Equal weighting   An index weighting method in which an equal weight is assigned to each constituent security at inception.

Equity   Ownership interest in an entity. A residual claim on the assets of an entity after more senior claims, such as debt, have been satisfied. Also known as *net assets*.

Equity swap   A swap transaction in which at least one cash flow is tied to the return on an equity portfolio position, often an equity index.

Error term   Represents the difference between the observed value of the independent variable and that expected from the true underlying population relation between the dependent and independent variable.

Estimated parameters   In a simple linear regression, the estimated parameters are the intercept and slope of the fitted line.

Ether   A programmable cryptocurrency created on the Ethereum blockchain in 2015 that allows for the execution of smart contracts.

Ethical principles   Beliefs regarding what is good, acceptable, or obligatory behavior and what is bad, unacceptable, or forbidden behavior.

Ethics   The study of moral principles or of making good choices. Ethics encompasses a set of moral principles and rules of conduct that provide guidance for our behavior.

Eurobonds   A type of bond issued internationally, outside the jurisdiction of the country in whose currency the bond is denominated.

European options   Options that may be exercised only at contract maturity.

European-style   Said of an option contract that can only be exercised on the option's expiration date.

Event risk   Risk that evolves around set dates, such as elections, new legislation, or other date-driven milestones, such as holidays or political anniversaries, known in advance. Example: Brexit referendum.

Ex-dividend date   The first date that a share trades without (i.e., "ex") the right to receive the declared dividend for the period.

Excess kurtosis   Degree of kurtosis (fatness of tails) relative to the kurtosis of the normal distribution.

Excess spread   Surplus difference of yield remaining after payments to bondholders are made after expenses are made and losses are covered.

Exchange   A rules-based, open access market venue where financial instruments are traded, with price and volume transparency accessible by issuers, investors, and their intermediaries.

Exchange-traded derivative (ETD)   Futures, options, and other financial contracts available on exchanges.

Exchanges   Places where traders can meet to arrange their trades.

Execution instructions   Instructions that indicate how to fill an order.

Exercise   The decision to transact the underlying by an option holder.

Exercise date   The day that an option is exercised by its holder. For a call option, the day the strike price is paid and underlying is purchased. For a put option, when the strike price is received and the underlying is sold.

Exercise price   The pre-agreed execution price specified in an option contract. Sometimes, this price is referred to as the strike price.

Exogenous risk   A sudden or unanticipated risk that impacts either a country's cooperative stance, the ability of non-state actors to globalize, or both. Examples include sudden uprisings, invasions, or the aftermath of natural disasters.

Expansion   The period of a business cycle after its lowest point and before its highest point.

Expansionary   Tending to cause the real economy to grow.

Expansionary fiscal policy   Fiscal policy aimed at achieving real economic growth.

Expected exposure (EE)   The size of the investor's claim at the time of default.

Expected loss (EL)   Default probability times loss severity given default.

Expected return on the portfolio   Denoted as $(E(R_p))$. The weighted average of the expected returns (R_1 to R_n) on the component securities using their respective weights (w_1 to w_n).

Expected value of a random variable   The probability-weighted average of the possible outcomes of a random variable.

Expert system   A type of computer programming, often based on "if–then" rules, that attempts to simulate the knowledge base and analytical abilities of human experts in specific problem-solving contexts.

Export subsidy   Paid by the government to the firm when it exports a unit of a good that is being subsidized.

Exposure at default (EAD)   The size of the investor's claim at the time of default.

Extension risk   The risk of later repayment of a mortgage-backed security than expected.

External credit enhancements   Provisions or methods from a third party that allow a borrower improve their creditworthiness in a structured transaction.

External debt   Sovereign debt owed to foreign creditors.

Extra dividend   A dividend paid by a company that does not pay dividends on a regular schedule, or a dividend that supplements regular cash dividends with an extra payment.

Extraordinary general meetings (EGMs)   Meetings besides an AGM of the corporate board and shareholders, typically held to deliberate and vote on urgent matters. Corporate charters and bylaws specify who can call an EGM and under what conditions.

Extreme value theory   A branch of statistics that focuses primarily on extreme outcomes.

Face value   The amount of principal on a bond, also known as par value.

Factoring arrangement   When a company sells its accounts receivable to a lender (known as a factor) that assumes responsibility for the credit-granting and collection process.

Fair value   A market-based measure of an investment based on observable or derived assumptions to determine a price that market participants would use to exchange an asset or liability in an orderly transaction at a specific time.

Fair value hedge   Refers to a specific **hedge accounting** designation that applies when a derivative is deemed to offset the fluctuation in fair value of an asset or liability.

Fallen angels   Formerly investment-grade issuers whose credit quality has deteriorated since the time of issuance.

Fat-Tailed   Describes a distribution that has fatter tails than a normal distribution (also called leptokurtic).

Fed funds rate   The US interbank lending rate on overnight borrowings of reserves.

Federal funds rate   The US interbank lending rate on overnight borrowings of reserves. Also known as *Fed Funds rate*.

Fiat money   Money that is not convertible into any other commodity.

Fiduciary call   A combination of a purchased call option and investment in a risk-free bond with face value of the option's exercise price.

Fill or kill   See *immediate or cancel order*.

Finance lease   A type of lease which is more akin to the purchase or sale of the underlying asset.

Financial leverage   The use of debt in the capital structure. Measured using ratios such as operating income to operating income less interest expense, total assets to total equity, or debt to equity.

Financial leverage ratio   A measure of financial leverage calculated as average total assets divided by average total equity.

Financial risk   The risk arising from a company's capital structure and, specifically, from the level of debt and debt-like obligations.

Fintech   Technological innovation in the financial services industry, specifically with the design and delivery of financial services and products. It may also refer more broadly to companies involved in developing the new technologies and their applications, as well as the business sector that includes such companies.

Firm commitment   A pre-determined amount (price and quantity) is agreed to be exchanged at settlement. Examples of firm commitments include forward contracts, futures contracts, and swaps.

First lien   Security interest in a property that gives the lender the right to seize the collateral if the borrower does not pay as agreed.

First lien debt   Debt secured by a pledge of certain assets that could include buildings, but it may also include property and equipment, licenses, patents, brands, etc.

First mortgage debt   Debt secured by a pledge of a specific property.

Fiscal multiplier   The ratio of a change in national income to a change in government spending.

Fiscal policy   The use of taxes and government spending to affect the level of aggregate expenditures.

Fixed charge coverage   A solvency ratio measuring the number of times interest and lease payments are covered by operating income, calculated as (EBIT + lease payments) divided by (interest payments + lease payments).

Fixed charge coverage ratio   A measure of how well a company's earnings covers its fixed expenses, which may include debt payments, interest expense, and lease costs.

Fixed-income instruments   Debt instruments such as loans or bonds.

Fixed-income securities   Fixed-income instruments designed to be more easily tradeable than a loan, such as a bond.

Fixed-price call   A contingency provision that grants an issuer the right to buy back a bond at a predetermined price in the future.

Fixed-rate payer   The counterparty paying fixed cash flows in a swap contract. May also be referred to as the floating-rate receiver.

Flat price   The full price of a bond minus accrued interest. Flat prices are usually quoted by bond dealers.

Float-adjusted market-capitalization weighting   An index weighting method in which the weight assigned to each constituent security is determined by adjusting its market capitalization for its market float.

Floating-rate notes   Notes on which interest payments are not fixed but instead vary from period to period depending on the current level of a reference interest rate. Also known as *floaters*.

Floating-rate payer   The counterparty paying the variable cash flows in a swap contract. May also be referred to as the fixed-rate receiver.

Forecast object   A variable on or related to an issuer's financial statements that an analyst makes a projection for. Examples include drivers of financial statements, financial statement lines, and summary measures like EBITDA.

Foreclosure   Allows a lender to take possession of the property and ultimately sell the property to recover funds toward satisfying the outstanding debt obligation.

Foreign bonds   A type of bond for which the issuer's domicile and jurisdiction of issuance are different.

Foreign currency reserves   Holding by the central bank of non-domestic currency deposits and non-domestic bonds.

Foreign direct investments (FDI)   Long-term investments in the productive capacity of a foreign country.

Foreign exchange gains (or losses)   Gains (or losses) that occur when the exchange rate changes between the investor's currency and the currency that foreign securities are denominated in.

Forward contract   A **derivative contract** for the future exchange of an **underlying** at a fixed price set at contract signing.

Forward price   Represents the price agreed upon in a forward contract to be exchanged at the contract's maturity date, T. This price is shown in equations as $F_0(T)$.

Forward price-to-earnings ratio   A P/E calculated on the basis of a forecast of EPS; a stock's current price divided by next year's expected earnings.

Forward rate agreement (FRA)   An OTC derivatives contract in which counterparties agree to apply a specific interest rate to a future time period.

Founders class shares   A way to entice early participation in startup funds whereby managers offer incentives that entitle investors to a lower fee structure and/or other favorable terms.

Framing bias   An information-processing bias in which a person answers a question differently based on the way in which it is asked (framed).

Franchising   A situation where an owner of an asset and associated intellectual property divests the asset and licenses intellectual property to a third-party operator (franchisee) in exchange for royalties. Franchisees operate under the constraints of a franchise agreement.

Free cash flow   The actual cash that would be available to the company's investors after making all investments necessary to maintain the company as an ongoing enterprise (also referred to as free cash flow to the firm); the internally generated funds that can be distributed to the company's investors (e.g., shareholders and bondholders) without impairing the value of the company.

Free cash flow hypothesis   The hypothesis that higher debt levels discipline managers by forcing them to make fixed debt service payments and by reducing the company's free cash flow.

Free float   The portion of a listed company's equity securities that are not held by insiders, strategic investors, sponsors, founders, and so on, that are more freely available for trading.

Free trade areas   One of the most prevalent forms of regional integration, in which all barriers to the flow of goods and services among members have been eliminated.

Free-cash-flow-to-equity models   Valuation models based on discounting expected future free cash flow to equity.

Freemium business model   A pricing approach that allows customers a certain level of usage or functionality at no charge. Those who wish to use more must pay.

Frequency table   A representation of the frequency of occurrence of two discrete variables.

Full price   The price of a bond including any accrued interest owed to the seller. It is the flat price plus accrued interest.

Fully amortizing loan   A loan or bond with a payment schedule that calls for the complete repayment of principal over the instrument's time to maturity.

Fund investing   In fund investing, the investor invests in assets indirectly by contributing capital to a fund as part of a group of investors. Fund investing is available for all major alternative investment types.

Fund of funds   Funds that hold a portfolio of hedge funds; also called *funds of hedge funds*.

Fundamental analysis   The examination of publicly available information and the formulation of forecasts to estimate the intrinsic value of assets.

Fundamental growth   These strategies use fundamental analysis to identify companies expected to exhibit high growth and capital appreciation.

Fundamental long/short   In this strategy, the hedge fund takes a long position in companies that are trading at inexpensive levels compared to their potential intrinsic value and shorts those that trade in the other direction, with the intention of reversing this trade to obtain alpha.

Fundamental value   These strategies use fundamental analysis to identify undervalued and unloved companies for which there is a possibility that a corporate turnaround, with future revenue and cash flow growth, will result in higher valuations.

Fundamental weighting   An index weighting method in which the weight assigned to each constituent security is based on its underlying company's size. It attempts to address the disadvantages of market-capitalization weighting by using measures that are independent of the constituent security's price.

Fungible   Freely exchangeable, interchangeable, or substitutable with other things of the same type. Money and commodities are the most common examples.

Futures contract   A variation of a forward contract that has essentially the same basic definition but with some additional features, such as a clearinghouse guarantee against credit losses, a daily settlement of gains and losses, and an organized electronic or floor trading facility.

Futures contract basis point value (BPV)   The change in price of a futures contract given a 1 basis point (0.01%) change in yield.

Futures contracts   Forward contracts with standardized sizes, dates, and underlyings that trade on futures exchanges.

Futures margin account   An account held by an exchange clearinghouse for each derivatives counterparty. The funds in such an account are used to ensure that counterparties do not default on their contract obligation.

Futures price   The pre-agreed price at which a futures contract buyer (seller) agrees to pay (receive) for the underlying at the maturity date of the futures contract.

FX swap   The combination of a spot and a forward FX transaction.

G-spread   Yield spread in basis points between a bond's yield-to-maturity and that of an actual or interpolated government bond. It represents the return for bearing risks relative to the government bond.

Game theory   The set of tools decision makers use to incorporate responses by rival decision makers into their strategies.

Gamma   A numerical measure of how sensitive an option's delta (the sensitivity of the derivative's price) is to a change in the value of the underlying.

Gate   A provision that when implemented limits or restricts redemptions for a period of time.

General collateral repo   Rather than involving a specific security, a repo that instead references a specific group of securities as eligible collateral (such as government bonds of a specific maturity).

General collateral repo rate   The interest rate on a general collateral repo.

General obligation (GO) bonds   Unsecured bonds issued by a non-sovereign government which are backed by the taxing authority of the issuer.

General obligation bonds   Also known as GO bonds. Bonds issued by non-sovereign governments for general purposes and repaid from tax cash flows.

General partners (GPs)   Owners of a general partnership or limited partnership with unlimited liability and other attributes as specified in the partnership agreement.

General partnership   A business organizational form owned entirely by general partners.

Geophysical resource endowment   Includes such factors as livable geography and climate as well as access to food and water, which are necessary for sustainable growth. Geophysical resource endowment is highly unequal among countries.

Geopolitics   The study of how geography affects politics and international relations. These relations matter for investments because they contribute to important drivers of investment performance, including economic growth, business performance, market volatility, and transaction costs.

Gilts   Bonds issued by the UK government.

Global depository receipt (GDR)   A depository receipt that is issued outside of the company's home country and outside of the United States.

Global minimum-variance portfolio   The portfolio on the minimum-variance frontier with the smallest variance of return.

Global registered share (GRS)   A common share that is traded on different stock exchanges around the world in different currencies.

Globalization   The process of interaction and integration among people, companies, and governments worldwide. It is marked by the spread of products, information, jobs, and culture across borders.

Gold standard   With respect to a currency, if a currency is on the gold standard a given amount can be converted into a prespecified amount of gold.

Good-on-close   An execution instruction specifying that an order can only be filled at the close of trading. Also called *market-on-close*.

Good-on-open   An execution instruction specifying that an order can only be filled at the opening of trading.

Good-till-cancelled order   An order specifying that it is valid until the entity placing the order has cancelled it (or, commonly, until some specified amount of time such as 60 days has elapsed, whichever comes sooner).

Goodwill   An intangible asset that represents the excess of the purchase price of an acquired company over the value of the net identifiable assets acquired.

Governance tokens   In permissionless networks, governance tokens serve as votes to determine how the particular network is run.

Government debt management   Government policies that relate to the issuance of debt securities, typically handled by a treasurer or finance ministry.

Government equivalent yield   Measures quoted using actual/actual day counts.

Grant date   The day that terms of compensation are communicated by an issuer and accepted by an employee recipient.

Green bonds   Bonds used in green finance whereby the proceeds are earmarked toward environmental-related products.

Greenfield investments   The first stage of development of an infrastructure asset. Greenfield investments involve developing new assets and new infrastructure with the intention either to lease or sell the assets to the government after construction or to hold and operate the assets. Greenfield investors typically invest alongside strategic investors or developers that specialize in developing the underlying assets.

Gross profit margin   The ratio of gross profit to revenues.

Groupthink   The practice of thinking or making decisions as a group in a way that discourages creativity or individual responsibility. For scenario analysis to be useful in portfolio management, teams must work hard to build creative processes, identify scenarios, track these scenarios, and assess the need for action on a regular cadence.

Growth cycle   Refers to fluctuations in economic activity around the long-term potential trend growth level, focusing on how much actual economic activity is below or above trend growth in economic activity.

Growth option   The option to make additional investments in a project at some future time if the financial results are strong. Also called an *expansion option*.

Growth rate cycle   Refers to fluctuations in the growth rate of economic activity.

Haircut   The difference between the market value of the security used as collateral and the value of the loan. Also called *repo margin*.

Halo effect   An emotional bias that extends a favorable evaluation of some characteristics to other characteristics.

Hard commodities   Traded natural resources, such as crude oil and metals, with markets often involving the physical delivery of the underlying upon settlement.

Hard hurdle rate   Hurdle rate where the manager earns fees on annual returns in excess of the hurdle rate.

Hard-bullet covered bonds   Type of security where if payments do not occur according to the original schedule of a covered bond, a bond default is triggered and bond payments are accelerated.

Harmonic mean   A type of weighted mean computed as the reciprocal of the arithmetic average of the reciprocals.

Hedge   The **derivative contract** used in **hedging** an exposure.

Hedge accounting   Accounting standard(s) that allow an issuer to offset a hedging instrument (usually a derivative) against a hedged transaction or balance sheet item to reduce financial statement volatility.

Hedge funds   Private investment vehicles that may invest in public equities or publicly traded fixed-income assets, private capital, and/or real assets, but they are distinguished by their investment *approach* rather than by the investments themselves.

Hedge ratio   The proportion of an underlying that will offset the risk associated with a derivative position.

Hedging   The use of a derivative contract to offset or neutralize existing or anticipated exposure to an **underlying**.

Hegemony   Countries that are regional or even global leaders and use their political or economic influence of others to control resources.

Held-to-maturity   Debt (fixed-income) securities that a company intends to hold to maturity; these are presented at their original cost, updated for any amortisation of discounts or premiums.

Herding   Clustered trading that may or may not be based on information.

Herfindahl-Hirschman Index (HHI)   A measure of market concentration, calculated as the sum of the squares of competitor market shares. Antitrust regulators in some countries consider markets with an HHI between 1,500 and 2,500 moderately concentrated and consider markets with an HHI over 2,500 highly concentrated.

Heteroskedasticity   Non-constant variance across all observations.

Hidden order   An order that is exposed not to the public but only to the brokers or exchanges that receive it.

Hidden revenue business model   Business models that provide services to users at no charge and generate revenues elsewhere.

High yield   Bond issuers and issues rated BB+ (Ba1 on Moody's scale) or lower. Also known as speculative grade and junk.

High-water mark   The highest value, net of fees, that a fund has reached in history. It reflects the highest cumulative return used to calculate an incentive fee.

Hindsight bias   A bias with selective perception and retention aspects in which people may see past events as having been predictable and reasonable to expect.

Holder-of-record date   The date that a shareholder listed on the corporation's books will be deemed to have ownership of the shares for purposes of receiving an upcoming dividend.

Holding period return   The single-period internal rate of return for a real estate property that includes property income and the change in property value over the period.

Home bias   A preference for securities listed on the exchanges of one's home country.

Homogeneity of expectations   The assumption that all investors have the same economic expectations and thus have the same expectations of prices, cash flows, and other investment characteristics.

Homoskedasticity   Constant variance across all observations.

Horizon yield   An investor's total rate of return on a fixed income instrument over their holding period, including reinvested coupon payments. It is an internal rate of return expressed as an annualized rate.

Hostile takeover   When a potential acquirer seeks to acquire a company (the target) against the wishes of the target's board of directors. Typically, a tender offer is used to carry out the hostile takeover, against which a board might use a poison pill in its defense.

Household   A person or a group of people living in the same residence, taken as a basic unit in economic analysis.

Human capital   The present value of an individual's future expected labor income.

Hurdle rate   The rate of return that a project's IRR must exceed for the project to be accepted by the company.

Hypothesis   A proposed explanation or theory that can be tested.

Hypothesis testing   The process of testing of hypotheses about one or more populations using statistical inference.

I-spread   Also known as interpolated spread, it is the yield spread for a bond over the standard swap rate in that currency of the same tenor.

Iceberg order   An order in which the display size is less than the order's full size.

If-converted method   A method for accounting for the effect of convertible securities on earnings per share (EPS) that specifies what EPS would have been if the convertible securities had been converted at the beginning of the period, taking account of the effects of conversion on net income and the weighted average number of shares outstanding.

Illusion of control bias   A bias in which people tend to believe that they can control or influence outcomes when, in fact, they cannot.

Immediate or cancel order   An order that is valid only upon receipt by the broker or exchange. If such an order cannot be filled in part or in whole upon receipt, it cancels immediately. Also called *fill or kill*.

Impact lag   The lag associated with the result of actions affecting the economy with delay.

Implied forward rate   An interest rate or yield over a future period implied by the current term structure of interest rates.

Import license   Specifies the quantity of a good that can be imported into a country.

In-the-money   Describes an option with a positive intrinsic value.

Income tax paid   The actual amount paid for income taxes in the period; not a provision, but the actual cash outflow.

Income tax payable   The income tax owed by the company on the basis of taxable income.

Increasing returns to scale   When a production process leads to increases in output that are proportionately larger than the increase in inputs.

Incurrence test   A financial ratio or other measurement taken prior to an action such as debt issuance, usually on a pro forma basis taking the action into account. Satisfaction of the test (e.g., leverage ratio below a certain value) is linked to covenants between the issuer and investors.

Indenture   A written contract between a lender and borrower that specifies the terms of the loan, such as interest rate, interest payment schedule, or maturity.

Independent   With reference to events, the property that the occurrence of one event does not affect the probability of another event occurring. With reference to two random variables X and Y, they are independent if and only if $P(X,Y) = P(X)P(Y)$.

Independent directors   Members of a corporation's board of directors who do not have an employment or familial relationship with the company, nor do they have a relationship that would impair their independence such as an economic interest in a vendor or competitor of the company.

Independent variable   An explanatory variable in a regression model.

Independently and identically distributed   With respect to random variables, the property of random variables that are independent of each other but follow the identical probability distribution.

Index-linked bonds   A bond whose coupon payments or principal repayment is linked to a specified index.

Indexing   An investment strategy in which an investor constructs a portfolio to mirror the performance of a specified index.

Indicator variable   A variable that takes on only one of two values, 0 or 1, based on a condition. In simple linear regression, the slope is the difference in the dependent variable for the two conditions. Also referred to as a *dummy variable*.

Indifference curve   A curve representing all the combinations of two goods or attributes such that the consumer is entirely indifferent among them.

Indirect taxes   Taxes such as taxes on spending, as opposed to direct taxes.

Inflation premium   An extra return that compensates investors for expected inflation.

Inflation reports   A type of economic publication put out by many central banks.

Inflation-linked bonds   Debt instruments that link the principal and interest to inflation.

Information cascade   The transmission of information from those participants who act first and whose decisions influence the decisions of others.

Information-motivated traders   Traders that trade to profit from information that they believe allows them to predict future prices.

Informationally efficient market   A market in which asset prices reflect new information quickly and rationally.

Infrastructure   A type of real asset that is intended for public use and provides essential services. These assets are typically long-lived fixed assets, such as bridges and toll roads.

Initial coin offering (ICO)   An unregulated process whereby companies raise capital by selling crypto-tokens to investors in exchange for fiat money or another agreed-upon cryptocurrency.

Initial margin   The ratio of the price of collateral to the value of cash exchanged in a repo; a value over 1.0 or 100% indicates overcollateralization.

Initial margin requirement   The margin requirement on the first day of a transaction as well as on any day in which additional margin funds must be deposited.

Initial public offering (IPO)   The first issuance of common shares to the public by a formerly private corporation.

Inside directors   Members of a corporation's board of directors who are not independent. Typically, inside directors are employees or founders (and their family) of the company.

Insolvency   Refers to the condition in which firm value is below the face value of debt used to finance the firm's assets.

Institution   An established organization or practice in a society or culture. An institution can be a formal structure, such as a university, organization, or process backed by law; or it can be informal, such as a custom or behavioral pattern important to society. Institutions can, but need not be, formed by national governments. Examples of institutions include non-governmental organizations, charities, religious customs, family units, the media, political parties, and educational practice.

Intangible assets Assets without a physical form, such as patents and trademarks.

Interbank market The market of loans and deposits between banks for maturities ranging from overnight to one year.

Intercept The estimated value of the dependent variable when the independent variable is zero.

Interest coverage A solvency ratio calculated as EBIT divided by interest payments.

Interest coverage ratio A measure of an issuer's ability to service its debt, typically the ratio of operating income or EBIT to interest expense.

Interest rate A rate of return that reflects the relationship between differently dated cash flows; a discount rate.

Interest rate swap A swap in which the underlying is an interest rate. Can be viewed as a currency swap in which both currencies are the same and can be created as a combination of currency swaps.

Interest-indexed bond A type of index-linked bond for which changes in the index are captured with adjustments to interest payments.

Internal credit enhancements Provisions or methods a borrower initiates to improve their creditworthiness in a structured transaction, such as overcollateralization or excess spread.

Internal rate of return The discount rate that makes net present value equal 0; the discount rate that makes the present value of an investment's costs (outflows) equal to the present value of the investment's benefits (inflows).

Internal rate of return (IRR) The discount rate that makes net present value equal 0; the discount rate that makes the present value of an investment's costs (outflows) equal to the present value of the investment's benefits (inflows).

Internet of things The vast array of physical devices, home appliances, smart buildings, vehicles, and other items that are embedded with electronics, sensors, software, and network connections that enable the objects in the system to interact and share information.

Interquartile range The difference between the third and first quartiles of a dataset.

Intrinsic value The amount gained (per unit) by an option buyer if an option is exercised at any given point in time. May be referred to as the exercise value of the option.

Investment banks Financial intermediaries that provide advice to their mostly corporate clients and help them arrange transactions such as initial and seasoned securities offerings.

Investment grade Bond issuers and issues rated BBB- (Baa3 on Moody's scale).

Investment policy statement A written planning document that describes a client's investment objectives and risk tolerance over a relevant time horizon, along with the constraints that apply to the client's portfolio.

Issue rating A rating which seeks to capture the probability of default or expected loss of the issuer's senior unsecured bonds.

Issuer rating A rating which seeks to capture the credit risk of a specific financial obligation of an issuer which takes such factors as seniority into account.

J-curve effect Represents the initial negative return in the capital commitment phase followed by an acceleration of returns through the capital deployment phase.

Jackknife A resampling method that repeatedly draws samples by taking the original observed data sample and leaving out one observation at a time (without replacement) from the set.

January effect Calendar anomaly that stock market returns in January are significantly higher compared to the rest of the months of the year, with most of the abnormal returns reported during the first five trading days in January. Also called *turn-of-the-year effect*.

Joint probability function A function giving the probability of joint occurrences of values of stated random variables.

Judgmental sampling A procedure of selectively handpicking elements from the population based on a researcher's knowledge and professional judgment.

Junior debt Debt obligation with lower priority of payment than senior debt obligations.

Key rate duration Also known as partial duration, is a measure of a bond's sensitivity to a change in the benchmark yield at a specific maturity.

Keynesians Economists who believe that fiscal policy can have powerful effects on aggregate demand, output, and employment when there is substantial spare capacity in an economy.

Kurtosis The statistical measure that indicates the combined weight of the tails of a distribution relative to the rest of the distribution.

Lagging economic indicators Turning points that take place later than those of the overall economy; they are believed to have value in identifying the economy's past condition.

Law of one price A principle that states that if two investments have the same or equivalent future cash flows regardless of what will happen in the future, then these two investments should have the same current price.

Lead underwriter The lead investment bank in a syndicate of investment banks and broker–dealers involved in a securities underwriting.

Leading economic indicators Turning points that usually precede those of the overall economy; they are believed to have value for predicting the economy's future state, usually near-term.

Legal tender Something that must be accepted when offered in exchange for goods and services.

Lender of last resort An entity willing to lend money when no other entity is ready to do so.

Leptokurtic Describes a distribution that has fatter tails than a normal distribution (also called fat-tailed).

Lessee Tenant or property user that enters a lease with a property owner or lessor.

Lessor Property owner or manager that leases a property to a tenant or property user.

Level of significance The probability of a Type I error in testing a hypothesis.

Leverage A measure for identifying a potentially influential high-leverage point.

Leveraged buyout A transaction whereby the target company management team converts the target to a privately held company by using heavy borrowing to finance the purchase of the target company's outstanding shares.

Leveraged buyout (LBO)   An acquirer (typically an investment fund specializing in LBOs) uses a significant amount of debt to finance the acquisition of a target and then pursues restructuring actions, with the goal of exiting the target with a sale or public listing.

Leveraged buyouts   Buyout equity transactions that utilize a high proportion of debt financing to make a company acquisition.

Leveraged loan   Where private debt investor firms borrow money to make a direct loan to a borrower.

Leveraged loans   Loans made to a borrower or issuer with relatively lower credit quality and/or higher leverage.

Liability-driven investing   An investment industry term that generally encompasses asset allocation that is focused on funding an investor's liabilities in institutional contexts.

Licensing arrangements   Rights to produce a product or have access to intangible assets using someone else's brand name in return for a royalty (often a percentage of revenues).

Lien   A legal right or claim to property by a creditor.

Likelihood   The probability of an observation, given a particular set of conditions.

Limit order   Instructions to a broker or exchange to obtain the best price immediately available when filling an order, but in no event accept a price higher than a specified (limit) price when buying or accept a price lower than a specified (limit) price when selling.

Limit order book   The book or list of limit orders to buy and sell that pertains to a security.

Limited company   A business organizational form owned by shareholders or members with limited liability who elect a board of directors to appoint management. Generally, limited companies have indefinite life and easier transfer of ownership interests than limited partnerships.

Limited liability partnership (LLP)   A business organizational form available in some jurisdictions owned entirely by limited partners with limited liability.

Limited partners (LPs)   Owners of a limited partnership with limited liability and other attributes as specified in the partnership agreement.

Limited partnership   A business organizational form owned by a general partner and limited partners.

Limited partnership agreement (LPA)   A legal document that outlines the rules of the partnership and establishes the framework that ultimately guides the fund's operations throughout its life.

Lin-log model   A functional form for transforming regression model data in which the dependent variable is linear but the independent variable is logarithmic.

Linear derivatives   Firm commitment derivative contracts in which the contract's payoff/profit function is linear with respect to the price of the underlying.

Liquid market   Said of a market in which traders can buy or sell with low total transaction costs when they want to trade.

Liquidity   The extent to which a company is able to meet its short-term obligations using cash flows and those assets that can be readily transformed into cash.

Liquidity premium   An extra return that compensates investors for the risk of loss relative to an investment's fair value if the investment needs to be converted to cash quickly.

Liquidity ratios   Financial ratios measuring the company's ability to meet its short-term obligations to creditors as they come due.

Liquidity risk   A divergence in the cash flow timing of a derivative versus that of an underlying transaction.

Liquidity trap   A condition in which the demand for money becomes infinitely elastic (horizontal demand curve) so that injections of money into the economy will not lower interest rates or affect real activity.

Load fund   A mutual fund in which, in addition to the annual fee, a percentage fee is charged to invest in the fund and/or for redemptions from the fund.

Loan-to-value ratio (LTV)   Ratio of the amount of the mortgage to the property's value. The lower the LTV, the higher the borrower's equity. From the lender's perspective, the higher the borrower's equity, the less likely the borrower is to default.

Loans   Debt instruments agreed to between a borrower and lender, typically a bank.

Lockout or revolving period   For an ABS with a non-amortizing collateral pool, such as credit card debt, is the period in which the cash proceeds from principal repayments are reinvested in additional loans with a principal equal to the principal repaid. During this period, there is no prepayment risk and potential default risk is generally limited. When the lockout period is over, principal repayments are used to pay off the outstanding principal on the ABS. Lockout period and revolving period are interchangeable.

Lockup period   The minimum holding period before investors are allowed to make withdrawals or redeem shares from a fund. Its purpose is to allow the hedge fund manager the required time to implement and potentially realize a strategy's expected results.

Log-lin model   A functional form for transforming regression model data in which the dependent variable is logarithmic but the independent variable is linear.

Log-log model   A functional form for transforming regression model data in which both the dependent and independent variables are in logarithmic form.

Long   A trading position in a **derivative contract** that gains value as the price of the **underlying** moves higher.

Long position   A position in an asset or contract in which one owns the asset or has an exercisable right under the contract.

Long-run average total cost   The curve describing average total cost when no costs are considered fixed.

Loss aversion   The tendency of people to dislike losses more than they like comparable gains.

Loss given default (LGD)   The investor's loss conditional on an issuer event of default.

Loss severity   Portion of a bond's value (including unpaid interest) an investor loses in the event of default.

Loss-aversion bias   A bias in which people tend to strongly prefer avoiding losses as opposed to achieving gains.

Low-cost producer   A firm with lower production costs than its industry competitors.

M²   An appraisal measure that indicates what a portfolio would have returned, assuming the same total risk as the market index.

M² alpha   Difference between the risk-adjusted performance of the portfolio and the performance of the benchmark.

Macaulay duration   The present-value weighted average time to receipt of cash flows for fixed-income instrument, also the holding period needed to balance coupon reinvestment risk and price risk for a one-time instantaneous "parallel" shift in the yield curve once the bond purchase is settled. It is named after Frederick Macaulay, the Canadian economist who introduced the concept in 1938.

Machine learning (ML)   Involves computer-based techniques that seek to extract knowledge from large amounts of data without making any assumptions about the data's underlying probability distribution. The goal of ML algorithms is to automate decision-making processes by generalizing, or "learning," from known examples to determine an underlying structure in the data.

Maintenance capital expenditures   Investments in assets to keep them in operation or increase their efficiency without extending their useful lives.

Maintenance margin   Minimum balance set below the initial margin that each contract buyer and seller must hold in the futures margin account from trade initiation until final settlement at maturity.

Maintenance margin requirement   The margin requirement on any day other than the first day of a transaction.

Management buy-in   A type of leveraged buyout where the current management team is replaced with the acquiring team involved in managing the company.

Management buyout   A type of leveraged buyout where the current management team participates in the acquisition.

Management guidance   Management of public companies may publicly provide targets for earnings, revenues, and other measures (e.g., capital expenditures) for the next quarter, year, or longer term. Guidance can be detailed or rather directional and is often updated throughout the year. Initial guidance for next fiscal year might be provided during the fourth-quarter earnings call and updated for completed quarters, and new information provided at the first-, second-, and third-quarter earnings calls. Also known simply as *guidance*.

Margin call   Request to a derivatives contract counterparty to immediately deposit funds to return the futures margin account balance to the initial margin.

Margin financing   A financing arrangement whereby the prime broker lends shares, bonds, or derivatives and the hedge fund (or investment manager) deposits cash or other collateral into a margin account at the prime broker based on certain fractions of the investment positions.

Margin loan   Money borrowed from a broker to purchase securities.

Marginal propensity to consume   The proportion of an additional unit of disposable income that is consumed or spent; the change in consumption for a small change in income.

Marginal propensity to save   The proportion of an additional unit of disposable income that is saved (not spent).

Mark to market (MTM)   The practice in which a central clearing party assigns profits and losses to counterparties to derivative contracts. In exchange-traded markets, this practice takes place daily and is often referred to as daily settlement.

Market anomaly   Change in the price or return of a security that cannot directly be linked to current relevant information known in the market or to the release of new information into the market.

Market bid–ask spread   The difference between the best bid and the best offer.

Market discount rate   The rate of return required by investors given the risk of the bond investment, also known as the required yield or required rate of return.

Market float   The number of shares that are available to the investing public.

Market makers   **Over-the-counter (OTC) dealers** who typically enter into offsetting bilateral transactions with one another to transfer risk to other parties.

Market model   A regression equation that specifies a linear relationship between the return on a security (or portfolio) and the return on a broad market index.

Market multiple models   Valuation models based on share price multiples or enterprise value multiples.

Market neutral   These strategies use quantitative, fundamental, and technical analysis to identify under- and overvalued equity securities. The hedge fund takes long positions in undervalued securities and short positions in overvalued securities, while seeking to maintain a market-neutral net position.

Market order   Instructions to a broker or exchange to obtain the best price immediately available when filling an order.

Market reference rate   A market-determined interest rate used as the underlying in financial instruments and contracts such as variable-rate debt and interest rate swaps. An example is the Secured Overnight Financing Rate (SOFR), which is an overnight cash borrowing rate collateralized by US Treasuries. Other MRRs include the euro short-term rate (€STR) and the Sterling Overnight Index Average (SONIA).

Market reference rate (MRR)   The interest rate underlying used in interest rate swaps. These rates typically match those of loans or other short-term obligations. Survey-based Libor rates used as reference rates in the past have been replaced by rates based on a daily average of observed market transaction rates. For example, the Secured Overnight Financing Rate (SOFR) is an overnight cash borrowing rate collateralized by US Treasuries. Other MRRs include the euro short-term rate (€STR) and the Sterling Overnight Index Average (SONIA).

Market risk   Risk related to market movements, e.g., unexpected changes in share prices, interest rates, currency exchange rates, and commodity prices.

Market share   A company's or product's revenue expressed as a percentage of its market size.

Market size   Total sales for a good or service, which can be calculated on a global or more regional basis.

Market value   The price at which an asset or security can currently be bought or sold in an open market.

Market-capitalization weighting   An index weighting method in which the weight assigned to each constituent security is determined by dividing its market capitalization by the total market capitalization (sum of the market capitalization) of all securities in the index. Also called *value weighting*.

Market-on-close   An execution instruction specifying that an order can only be filled at the close of trading.

Marketable limit order   A buy limit order in which the limit price is placed above the best offer, or a sell limit order in which the limit price is placed below the best bid. Such orders generally will partially or completely fill right away.

Markowitz efficient frontier   The graph of the set of portfolios offering the maximum expected return for their level of risk (standard deviation of return).

Master limited partnership (MLP)   Has similar features to limited partnerships but is usually a more liquid investment that is often publicly traded.

Master repurchase agreement   A legal document governing all repo trades between two parties.

Match funding   Financing an asset with a source, such as a loan or bond, that is aligned with certain attributes of the asset, such as duration and the respective streams of income and financing costs.

Material (materiality)   Refers to information that is decision-useful for a reasonable investor.

Matrix pricing An estimation process for financial instruments based on the prices of comparable instruments.

Maturity The date of a fixed-income instrument's final payment to investors.

Maturity premium An extra return that compensates investors for the increased sensitivity of the market value of debt to a change in market interest rates as maturity is extended.

Maturity structure of interest rates Also known as the term structure of interest rates, refers to the difference in interest rates or benchmark yields by time-to-maturity.

Mean absolute deviation With reference to a sample, the mean of the absolute values of deviations from the sample mean.

Mean square error (MSE) Calculated as the sum of squares error (SSE) divided by the degrees of freedom, which are the number of observations minus the number of independent variables minus one. Since simple linear regression has just one independent variable, the degrees of freedom calculation is the number of observations minus 2.

Mean square regression (MSR) Calculated as the sum of squares regression (SSR) divided by the number of independent variables in the regression model. In simple linear regression, there is only one independent variable, so MSR equals SSR.

Mean–variance analysis An approach to portfolio analysis using expected means, variances, and covariances of asset returns.

Measure of central tendency A quantitative measure that specifies where data are centered.

Measures of location Quantitative measures that describe the location or distribution of data. They include not only measures of central tendency but also other measures, such as percentiles.

Median The value of the middle item of a set of items that has been sorted into ascending or descending order (i.e., the 50th percentile).

Meme coin A type of altcoin that is often inspired by a joke.

Mental accounting bias An information-processing bias in which people treat one sum of money differently from another equal-sized sum based on which mental account the money is assigned to.

Merger arbitrage Generally, these strategies involve going long (buying) the stock of the company being acquired at a discount to its announced takeover price and going short (selling) the stock of the acquiring company when the merger or acquisition is announced.

Mesokurtic Describes a distribution with kurtosis equal to that of the normal distribution, namely, kurtosis equal to three.

Mezzanine debt Refers to private credit subordinated to senior secured debt but senior to equity in the borrower's capital structure.

Mezzanine-stage financing Mezzanine venture capital that prepares a company to go public as it continues to expand capacity and enhance its growth trajectory. It represents the bridge financing needed to fund a private firm until it can execute an IPO or be sold.

Miner A validator of transactions on the blockchain that locks blocks of transactions into the blockchain and receives compensation for this process in the form of a digital asset.

Minimum efficient scale The smallest output that a firm can produce such that its long-run average total cost is minimized.

Minimum-variance portfolio The portfolio with the minimum variance for each given level of expected return.

Minority shareholder An individual or entity that owns less than a majority of the voting rights in a corporation.

Mode The most frequently occurring value in a distribution.

Modern portfolio theory (MPT) The analysis of rational portfolio choices based on the efficient use of risk.

Modified duration The first derivative of a bond's price with respect to its yield, this statistic is a measure of interest rate risk used to estimate the percentage price change for a given change in yield-to-maturity.

Monetarists Economists who believe that the rate of growth of the money supply is the primary determinant of the rate of inflation.

Monetary policy Actions taken by a nation's central bank to affect aggregate output and prices through changes in bank reserves, reserve requirements, or its target interest rate.

Monetary transmission mechanism The process whereby a central bank's interest rate gets transmitted through the economy and ultimately affects the rate of increase of prices.

Monetary union An economic union in which the members adopt a common currency.

Money convexity A measure that is used to complement modified duration to capture the second-order effect of yield changes on a bond's price, expressed in currency terms.

Money duration A measure of the price change of a fixed-income instrument in currency units from a change in yield-to-maturity. The money duration can be stated per 100 of par value or in terms of the actual position size. In the United States, money duration is commonly called "dollar duration."

Money market The market for short-term debt instruments (one-year maturity or less).

Money market securities Fixed-income securities with original maturities of one year or less.

Money-weighted return The internal rate of return on a portfolio, taking account of all cash flows.

Moneyness Expresses the relationship between an option's value and its exercise price across the full range of possible underlying prices.

Monopolistic competition Highly competitive form of imperfect competition; the competitive characteristic is a notably large number of firms, while the monopoly aspect is the result of product differentiation.

Monopoly In pure monopoly markets, there are no substitutes for the given product or service. There is a single seller, which exercises considerable power over pricing and output decisions.

Monte Carlo simulation A technique that uses the inverse transformation method for converting a randomly generated uniformly distributed number into a simulated value of a random variable of a desired distribution. Each key decision variable in a Monte Carlo simulation requires an assumed statistical distribution; this assumption facilitates incorporating non-normality, fat tails, and tail dependence as well as solving high-dimensionality problems.

Moral principles Beliefs regarding what is good, acceptable, or obligatory behavior and what is bad, unacceptable, or forbidden behavior.

Mortgage loan Agreement to finance real estate by the collateral of a specified property that obliges the borrower to make a predetermined series of payments to the lender.

Mortgage pass-through security Security created when mortgage lenders pool mortgages together and sell securities to investors. The cash flow from the mortgage pool––monthly payments of principal, interest, and prepayments––are "passed through" to the security holders.

Mortgage-backed securities Debt obligations that represent claims to the cash flows from pools of mortgage loans, most commonly on residential property.

Mortgage-backed securities (MBS) Bonds created from the securitization of mortgages.

Multi-factor model A model that explains a variable in terms of the values of a set of factors.

Multi-market indexes Comprised of indexes from different countries, designed to represent multiple security markets.

Multilateral trading facilities See *alternative trading systems.*

Multilateralism The conduct of countries who participate in mutually beneficial trade relationships and extensive rules harmonization. Private firms are fully integrated into global supply chains with multiple trade partners. Examples of multilateral countries include Germany and Singapore.

Multiple of invested capital (MOIC) A simplified calculation that measures the total value of all distributions and residual asset values relative to an initial total investment; also known as a *money multiple.*

Multiple-price auction A debt securities auction in which bidders receive distinct prices based on their bids.

Multiplier models Valuation models based on share price multiples or enterprise value multiples.

Mutual fund A comingled investment pool in which investors in the fund each have a pro-rata claim on the income and value of the fund.

Nash equilibrium When two or more participants in a non-coop-erative game have no incentive to deviate from their respective equilibrium strategies given their opponent's strategies.

Nationalism The promotion of a country's own economic interests to the exclusion or detriment of the interests of other nations. Nationalism is marked by limited economic and financial cooperation. These actors may focus on national production and sales, limited cross-border investment and capital flows, and restricted currency exchange.

Natural language processing (NLP) A field of research within the field of text analytics and at the intersection of computer science, AI, and linguistics that focuses on developing computer programs to analyze and interpret human language.

Natural resources These include commodities (hard and soft), agricultural land (farmland), and timberland.

Negative externalities A cost to a third party because of the production or consumption of a good or service.

Negative pledge clause Limitations on investments, the disposal of assets, or issuance of debt senior to existing obligations. Negative covenants seek to ensure that an issuer maintains the ability to make interest and principal payments.

Net cash An issuer's total debt less cash and marketable securities. When the balance is negative it is referred to as net cash.

Net debt An issuer's total debt less cash and marketable securities. When the balance is positive it is referred to as net debt.

Net investment hedge Refers to a specific **hedge accounting** designation that applies when either a foreign currency bond or a derivative, such as an FX swap or forward, is used to offset the exchange rate risk of the equity of a foreign operation.

Net present value (NPV) The present value of an investment's cash inflows (benefits) minus the present value of its cash outflows (costs).

Net profit margin An indicator of profitability, calculated as net income divided by revenue; indicates how much of each dollar of revenues is left after all costs and expenses. Also called *profit margin* or *return on sales.*

Net tax rate The tax rate net of transfer payments.

Net working capital Working capital excluding short-term items unrelated to business operations, such as cash, marketable securities, and short-term debt.

Network effects A business model that enables users to contribute directly to a product, service, or online content.

Neural networks A type of computer program design based on how the human brain learns and processes information.

Neutral rate of interest The rate of interest that neither spurs on nor slows down the underlying economy.

No-load fund A mutual fund in which there is no fee for investing in the fund or for redeeming fund shares, although there is an annual fee based on a percentage of the fund's net asset value.

Node Each value on a binomial tree from which successive moves or outcomes branch.

Non-agency RMBS MBS backed by residential mortgages that are issued by private entities and not guaranteed by a federal agency or a GSE.

Non-amortizing loans Type of debt where there are no scheduled principal repayments.

Non-cooperative country A country with inconsistent and even arbitrary rules; restricted movement of goods, services, people, and capital across borders; retaliation; and limited technology exchange.

Non-cumulative preference shares Preference shares for which dividends that are not paid in the current or subsequent periods are forfeited permanently (instead of being accrued and paid at a later date).

Non-financial risks Risks that arise from sources other than changes in the external financial markets, such as changes in accounting rules, legal environment, or tax rates.

Non-fungible token (NFT) A unique cryptographic token on the blockchain that cannot be replicated and is used to represent ownership of physical assets, such as artwork, real estate, or other assets.

Non-linear derivatives Derivatives, such as options or other contingent claims, with payoff/profit profiles that are non-linear (asymmetric) with respect to the price of the underlying.

Non-participating preference shares Preference shares that do not entitle shareholders to share in the profits of the company. Instead, shareholders are only entitled to receive a fixed dividend payment and the par value of the shares in the event of liquidation.

Non-probability sampling A sampling plan dependent on factors other than probability considerations, such as a sampler's judgment or the convenience to access data.

Non-recourse loan Loan in which the lender does not have a claim against the borrower and thus can look only to the property to recover the outstanding mortgage balance.

Non-state actors Those that participate in global political, economic, or financial affairs but do not directly control national security or country resources. Examples of non-state actors are non-governmental organizations (NGOs), multinational companies, charities, and even influential individuals, such as business leaders or cultural icons.

Nonparametric test A test that is not concerned with a parameter or that makes minimal assumptions about the population from which a sample comes.

Nonsystematic risk Unique risk that is local or limited to a particular asset or industry that need not affect assets outside of that asset class.

Normal distribution A continuous, symmetric probability distribution that is completely described by its mean and its variance.

Normalized earnings The expected level of mid-cycle earnings for a company in the absence of any unusual or temporary factors that affect profitability (either positively or negatively).

Notching Ratings adjustment methodology where specific issues from the same borrower may be assigned different credit ratings.

Notice period The length of time (typically 30–90 days) in advance that investors may be required to notify a fund of their intent to redeem some or all of their investment. This allows a fund manager to liquidate a position in an orderly fashion without magnifying losses.

Novation process A process thatsubstitutes the initial **swap execution facility(SEF)** contract with identical trades facing the **central counterparty (CCP)**. The CCP serves as **counterparty** for both financial intermediaries, eliminating bilateral **counterparty credit risk** and providing **clearing** and **settlement** services.

Null hypothesis The hypothesis that is tested.

Off-the-run Seasoned government bonds that are often less liquid.

Off-the-run securities Sovereign debt securities outstanding other than on-the-sun securities. Off-the-run securities are less liquid than on-the-run securities.

Offer The price at which a dealer or trader is willing to sell an asset, typically qualified by a maximum quantity (ask size).

Official interest rate An interest rate that a central bank sets and announces publicly; normally the rate at which it is willing to lend money to the commercial banks. Also called *official policy rate* or *policy rate.*

Official policy rate An interest rate that a central bank sets and announces publicly; normally the rate at which it is willing to lend money to the commercial banks.

Oligopoly Market structure with a relatively small number of firms supplying the market.

Omnichannel Refers to a company selling its products or services in multiple channels, such as in store and online.

On-the-run Most recently issued, and liquid, government bonds.

On-the-run securities The most recently issued and liquid sovereign debt securities.

Open interest The number of outstanding contracts.

Open market operations The purchase or sale of bonds by the national central bank to implement monetary policy. The bonds traded are usually sovereign bonds issued by the national government.

Open-end fund A mutual fund that accepts new investment money and issues additional shares at a value equal to the net asset value of the fund at the time of investment.

Operating cycle The length of time between a company's acquisition of goods or raw materials and the collection of cash from sales to customers.

Operating efficiency ratios Ratios that measure how efficiently a company performs day-to-day tasks, such as the collection of receivables and management of inventory.

Operating leases A type of lease which is more akin to the rental of the underlying asset.

Operating leverage The sensitivity of a firm's operating profit to a change in revenues, determined by the composition of fixed and variable operating costs.

Operating profit margin A profitability ratio calculated as operating income (i.e., income before interest and taxes) divided by revenue. Also called *operating margin.*

Operational deposits Bank deposits generated by clearing, custody, and cash management activities.

Operational independence A bank's ability to execute monetary policy and set interest rates in the way it thought would best meet the inflation target.

Operational risk The risk that arises from inadequate or failed people, systems, and internal policies, procedures, and processes, as well as from external events that are beyond the control of the organization but that affect its operations.

Operationally efficient Said of a market, a financial system, or an economy that has relatively low transaction costs.

Opportunistic real estate strategies Include major redevelopment, repurposing of assets, taking on large vacancies, or speculating on significant improvement in market conditions. These may be appealing for investors seeking higher returns and willing to accept additional risks from development, redevelopment, repositioning, and leasing.

Opportunity cost The value that investors forgo by choosing a particular course of action; the value of something in its best alternative use.

Optimal capital structure The capital structure at which the value of the company is maximized.

Option A primary example of a **contingent claim**. A **derivative contract** that provides the buyer the right, but not the obligation, to buy or sell an **underlying**.

Option contract See *option.*

Option premium An amount that is paid upfront from the option buyer to the option seller. Reflects the value of the option buyer's right to exercise in the future.

Option-adjusted price The sum of a bond's flat price and value of an embedded option.

Option-adjusted spread Or OAS for a bond is its Z-spread adjusted for the value of an embedded option.

Option-adjusted yield A yield measure for a bond adjusted for embedded options.

Order A specification of what instrument to trade, how much to trade, and whether to buy or sell.

Order precedence hierarchy With respect to the execution of orders to trade, a set of rules that determines which orders execute before other orders.

Order-driven markets A market (generally an auction market) that uses rules to arrange trades based on the orders that traders submit; in their pure form, such markets do not make use of dealers.

Ordinary shares Equity shares that are subordinate to all other types of equity (e.g., preferred equity). Also called *common stock* or *common shares.*

Organizational form   A legal and tax classification of a business, specific to a jurisdiction, that determines the organization's legal identity, owner–manager relationship, owner liability, taxation, and access to financing.

Out-of-the-money   Describes an option with zero intrinsic value because the option buyer would not rationally exercise the option. An example of such would be the case in which the price of the underlying is less than the option's exercise price for a call option.

Over-the-counter (OTC)   Refers to derivative markets in which **derivative contracts** are created and traded between derivatives end users and **dealers**, or financial intermediaries, such as commercial banks or investment banks.

Overcollateralization   Credit enhancement technique where collateral underlying the transaction exceeds the face value of the issued bonds.

Overconfidence bias   A bias in which people demonstrate unwarranted faith in their own intuitive reasoning, judgments, and/or cognitive abilities.

Overfitting   When a machine learning model learns the input and target dataset too precisely, making the system more likely to discover false relationships or unsubstantiated patterns that will lead to prediction errors.

P-value   The smallest level of significance at which the null hypothesis can be rejected.

Par rate   A yield-to-maturity that makes the present value of a bond's cash flows equal to par.

Par swap rate   The fixed swap rate that equates the present value of all future expected floating cash flows to the present value of fixed cash flows.

Par value   The amount of principal on a bond, also known as face value.

Parallel shift   When all maturities along a yield curve increase or decrease in yield in the same direction by the same magnitude. A parallel shift in the yield curve is implicitly assumed in analytical duration and convexity.

Parameter   A descriptive measure computed from or used to describe a population of data, conventionally represented by Greek letters.

Parametric test   Any test (or procedure) concerned with parameters or whose validity depends on assumptions concerning the population generating the sample.

Pari passu clause   A covenant or contract clause that ensures a debt obligation is treated the same as the borrower's other senior debt instruments and is not subordinated to similar obligations.

Partially amortizing bond   A loan or bond with a payment schedule that calls for the complete repayment of principal over the instrument's time to maturity.

Participating preference shares   Preference shares that entitle shareholders to receive the standard preferred dividend plus the opportunity to receive an additional dividend if the company's profits exceed a pre-specified level.

Pass-through businesses   Businesses that, by virtue of their organizational form and/or other legal and regulatory attributes, do not pay entity-level taxes on income or loss; income or loss is passed through to owners, who pay personal taxes.

Pass-through rate   The coupon rate of a mortgage pass-through security that is received by the investor after administrative charges. It is lower than the weighted average mortgage rate earned on the underlying pool of mortgages because of administrative charges. The pass-through rate that the investor receives is said to be "net interest" or "net coupon."

Passive investment   In the fixed-income context, it is investment that seeks to mimic the prevailing characteristics of the overall investments available in terms of credit quality, type of borrower, maturity, and duration rather than express a specific market view.

Payable date   The day that the company actually mails out (or electronically transfers) a dividend payment.

Payment date   The day that the company actually mails out (or electronically transfers) a dividend payment.

Payment-in-kind   A bond feature whereby coupon payments can be fully or partially paid in the form of additional issuance or added to the principal amount.

Payments system   The system for the transfer of money.

Pearson correlation   A parametric measure of the relationship between two variables.

Pecking order theory   The theory that managers consider how their actions might be interpreted by outsiders and thereby order their preferences for various forms of corporate financing. Forms of financing that are least visible to outsiders (e.g., internally generated funds) are most preferable to managers, and those that are most visible (e.g., equity issuance) are least preferable.

Penetration pricing   A discount pricing approach used when a firm willingly sacrifices margins in order to build scale and market share.

Percentiles   Quantiles that divide a distribution into 100 equal parts that sum to 100.

Perfect competition   A market structure in which the individual firm has virtually no impact on market price, because it is assumed to be a very small seller among a very large number of firms selling essentially identical products.

Performance evaluation   The measurement and assessment of the outcomes of investment management decisions.

Performance fee   Fee paid to the general partner from the limited partner(s) based on realized net profits.

Period costs   Costs (e.g., executives' salaries) that cannot be directly matched with the timing of revenues and which are thus expensed immediately.

Periodicity   Number of periods in a year, used for compound interest. The periodicity of a fixed-income instrument usually matches the frequency of its coupon payments.

Permanent differences   Differences between tax and financial reporting of revenue (expenses) that will not be reversed at some future date. These result in a difference between the company's effective tax rate and statutory tax rate and do not result in a deferred tax item.

Permissioned networks   Networks that are fully open only to select participants on a DLT network.

Permissionless networks   Networks that are fully open to any user on a DLT network.

Perpetual bonds   Bonds with no stated maturity date.

Perpetuity   A perpetual annuity, or a set of never-ending level sequential cash flows, with the first cash flow occurring one period from now.

PESTLE analysis   A framework for analyzing factors that influence an industry's economic outcomes.

Pet projects   A capital investment that is pursued by management but is not economically justifiable by a disinterested party. Motivations for pet projects include self-dealing and vanity.

Physical risks   Economic and financial losses from the increase in the severity and frequency of extreme weather due to climate change—for example, the loss of coastal real estate from a storm.

PIPE (private investment in public equity) A private offering to select investors with fewer disclosures and lower transaction costs that allows the issuer to raise capital more quickly and cost effectively.

Platykurtic Describes a distribution that has relatively less weight in the tails than the normal distribution (also called thin-tailed).

Pledge A legal right or claim to property by a creditor. Also called a lien.

Poison pill Officially known as a shareholder rights plan, a poison pill is a hostile-takeover defense adopted by boards of directors according to rules specified in the corporate charter. There are several types of poison pills. Generally, they allow shareholders, *excluding* the shareholder making the hostile bid and their affiliates, to buy newly issued shares at a discounted price. The share issuance would dilute the bidder's ownership percentage, rendering it impossible for the bidder to attain control.

Policy rate An interest rate that a central bank sets and announces publicly; normally the rate at which it is willing to lend money to the commercial banks.

Portfolio companies The individual companies owned by a private equity firm.

Portfolio investment flows Short-term investments in foreign assets, such as stocks or bonds.

Portfolio planning The process of creating a plan for building a portfolio that is expected to satisfy a client's investment objectives.

Position The quantity of an asset that an entity owns or owes.

Posterior probability An updated probability that reflects or comes after new information.

Power of a test The probability of correctly rejecting the null—that is, rejecting the null hypothesis when it is false.

Pre-funding period Allows the trust to acquire during a certain period of time after the close of the transaction.

Preference shares A type of equity interest which ranks above common shares with respect to the payment of dividends and the distribution of the company's net assets upon liquidation. They have characteristics of both debt and equity securities. Also called *preferred stock*.

Preferred stock See *preference shares*.

Premium In the case of bonds, premium refers to the amount by which a bond is priced above its face (par) value. In the case of an option, the amount paid for the option contract.

Prepayment option May entitle the borrower to prepay all or part of the outstanding mortgage principal prior to maturity. This creates a risk from the lender's or investor's viewpoint because the cash flow amounts and timing cannot be known with certainty.

Prepayment risk The risk that the some or all of a mortgage-backed security's principal is repaid at a different speed than expected, either in the form of contraction risk (or earlier repayment than expected) or extension risk (later repayment).

Present value models Valuation models that estimate the intrinsic value of a security as the present value of the future benefits expected to be received from the security. Also called *discounted cash flow models*.

Pretax margin A profitability ratio calculated as earnings before taxes divided by revenue.

Price discrimination A pricing approach that charges different prices to different customers based on their willingness to pay.

Price index Represents the average prices of a basket of goods and services.

Price limits Establish a band relative to the previous day's settlement price within which all trades must occur.

Price multiple A ratio that compares the share price with some sort of monetary flow or value to allow evaluation of the relative worth of a company's stock.

Price priority The principle that the highest priced buy orders and the lowest priced sell orders execute first.

Price return Measures *only* the price appreciation or percentage change in price of the securities in an index or portfolio.

Price return index An index that reflects *only* the price appreciation or percentage change in price of the constituent securities. Also called *price index*.

Price stability In economics, refers to an inflation rate that is low on average and not subject to wide fluctuation.

Price takers Producers that must accept whatever price the market dictates.

Price value of a basis point (PVBP) An estimate of the change in the full price of a bond given a 1 bp change in its yield-to-maturity. The PVBP is also called the "PV01," standing for the "price value of an 01" or "present value of an 01," where "01" means 1 bp. In the United States, it is commonly called the "DV01" for the "dollar value" of 1 bp.

Price weighting An index weighting method in which the weight assigned to each constituent security is determined by dividing its price by the sum of all the prices of the constituent securities.

Price-setting option The option to adjust prices when demand or supply varies from what is forecast.

Price-to-earnings ratio (P/E) The ratio of share price to earnings per share.

Pricing power A company's ability to set prices and other economic terms with customers without affecting its sales volumes.

Primary bond markets Fixed-income markets comprised of issuers issuing bonds to investors to raise capital, often intermediated by a third-party such as an investment bank.

Primary capital markets (primary markets) The market where securities are first sold and the issuers receive the proceeds.

Primary dealer Financial institution that is authorized to deal in new issues of sovereign bonds and that serves primarily as a trading counterparty of the office responsible for issuing sovereign bonds.

Primary market The market where securities are first sold and the issuers receive the proceeds.

Prime broker A broker that provides services that commonly include custody, administration, lending, short borrowing, and trading.

Prime loans Lending made to borrowers of high credit quality with strong employment and credit histories, a low DTI, substantial equity in the underlying property, and a first lien on the mortgaged property serving as the collateral for the loan.

Principal The amount that an issuer agrees to repay the debtholders on the maturity date.

Principal-agent relationship An arrangement in which one party (the agent) has authority to act for or on behalf of another party (the principal). Such an arrangement imposes a duty on the agent to act in the principal's best interest.

Prior probabilities Probabilities reflecting beliefs prior to the arrival of new information.

Priority of claims Priority of payment, with the most senior or highest ranking debt having the first claim on the cash flows and assets of the issuer.

Private capital Funding provided to companies that is not sourced from the public markets.

Private company A company, typically a limited company, that does not list its equity securities on an exchange.

Private debt Capital extended to companies through a loan or other form of debt.

Private debtholders Investors in an entity's non-securitized debt claims, such as a loan or lease. The most common type of private debtholder is a bank.

Private equity Equity investment capital raised from sources other than public markets and traditional institutions.

Private equity fund A hedge fund that seeks to buy, optimize, and ultimately sell portfolio companies to generate profits. See *venture capital fund*.

Private equity securities Securities that are not listed on public exchanges and have no active secondary market. They are issued primarily to institutional investors via non-public offerings, such as private placements.

Private investment in public equity (PIPE) An investment in the equity of a publicly traded firm that is made at a discount to the market value of the firm's shares.

Private limited company A type of limited company in many jurisdictions with pass-through taxation but restrictions on the number of shareholders or members and on the transfer of ownership interest.

Private placement A sale of debt or equity securities to a small group of investors on an unregulated basis. The terms of the offering are negotiated by the issuer and investors.

Probability of default (POD) The likelihood that an issuer fails to make full and timely payments of principal and interest; typically an annualized measure.

Probability sampling A sampling plan that allows every member of the population to have an equal chance of being selected.

Probability tree diagram A diagram with branches emanating from nodes representing either mutually exclusive chance events or mutually exclusive decisions.

Production flexibility option The option to alter production when demand varies from what is forecast.

Profession An occupational group that has specific education, expert knowledge, and a framework of practice and behavior that underpins community trust, respect, and recognition.

Profit margin An indicator of profitability, calculated as net income divided by revenue; indicates how much of each dollar of revenues is left after all costs and expenses.

Profitability ratios Ratios that measure a company's ability to generate profitable sales from its resources (assets).

Prospectus Legal document in securitization that describes the structure of the transaction, including the priority and amount of payments to be made to the servicer, administrators, and the ABS holders, as well as the credit enhancements used in the securitization.

Protective put A strategy of purchasing an underlying asset and purchasing a put on the same asset.

Proxy contest When a shareholder or group of shareholders campaigns for certain matters they have submitted to a shareholder vote, often a slate of directors who oppose the incumbent board and management. The incumbent board and management simultaneously campaign for their side.

Proxy voting A form of casting a ballot in an election in which a voter authorizes a representative to vote on their behalf according to instructions. In corporate elections, proxy ballots are cast by shareholders that direct a representative, typically the corporate secretary, to enter their votes as instructed.

Public (listed) company A company with its equity securities traded on an exchange.

Public limited companies A type of limited company in many jurisdictions with entity-level taxation but no restrictions on the number of shareholders or transferability of ownership interest; the most suitable organizational form for a company that seeks to go public.

Public–private partnership A long-term contractual relationship between the public and private sectors for the purpose of having the private sector deliver a project or service traditionally provided by the public sector. Infrastructure is increasingly being financed privately through public–private partnerships by local, regional, and national governments.

Public–private partnership (PPP) An agreement between the public sector and the private sector to finance, build, and operate public infrastructure, such as hospitals and toll roads.

Pull on liquidity An action or event that accelerates cash outflows.

Purchase agreement Legal document in a securitization transaction that outlines the representations and warranties that the seller makes about the assets sold.

Pure discount bonds Bonds that do not pay interest during their life. They are issued at a discount to par value and redeemed at par. Also called zero-coupon bonds.

Put An option that gives the holder the right to sell an underlying asset to another party at a fixed price over a specific period of time.

Put option The right to sell an underlying.

Putable bonds Bonds that give the bondholder the right to sell the bond back to the issuer at a predetermined price on specified dates.

Put–call forward parity Describes the no-arbitrage condition in which at $t = 0$ the present value of the price of a long forward commitment plus the price of the long put must equal the price of the long call plus the price of the risk-free asset (with face value of the exercise price of both the call and the put).

Put–call parity Describes the no-arbitrage condition in which at $t = 0$ the price of the long underlying asset plus the price of the long put must equal the price of the long call plus the price of the risk-free asset (with face value of the exercise price of both the call and the put).

Quantile A value at or below which a stated fraction of the data lies. Also referred to as a fractile.

Quantitative easing An expansionary monetary policy based on aggressive open market purchase operations.

Quartiles Quantiles that divide a distribution into four equal parts.

Quick ratio A measure of liquidity that is the ratio of cash, marketable securities, and receivables to current liabilities.

Quintiles Quantiles that divide a distribution into five equal parts.

Quota rents Profits that foreign producers can earn by raising the price of their goods higher than they would without a quota.

Quotas Government policies that restrict the quantity of a good that can be imported into a country, generally for a specified period of time.

Quote-driven market A market in which dealers acting as principals facilitate trading.

Quoted margin Specified spread of a floating rate instrument over a market reference rate or benchmark.

Range The difference between the maximum and minimum values in a dataset.

Rapid amortization provisions Provisions in receivable ABS that may require early principal amortization if specific events occur. Such provisions are referred to as early amortization and are included to safeguard the credit quality of the issue, particularly during the revolving period.

Razor, razorblade pricing A pricing approach that combines a low price on a piece of equipment and high-margin pricing on repeat-purchase consumables.

Real assets Generally, these are tangible physical assets, such as real estate, infrastructure, and natural resources, but they also include such intangibles as patents, intellectual property, and goodwill. Real assets generate current or expected future cash flows and/or are considered a store of value.

Real estate Includes borrowed or ownership capital in buildings or land. Developed land includes commercial and industrial real estate, residential real estate, and infrastructure.

Real option A right, but not an obligation, for management to make a decision with respect to a capital investment that alters future cash flows from the original forecasted scenario.

Real risk-free interest rate The single-period interest rate for a completely risk-free security if no inflation were expected.

Rebalancing In the context of asset allocation, a discipline for adjusting the portfolio to align with the strategic asset allocation.

Rebalancing policy The set of rules that guide the process of restoring a portfolio's asset class weights to those specified in the strategic asset allocation.

Recapitalization Recapitalization via private equity describes the steps a firm takes to increase or introduce leverage to its portfolio company and pay itself a dividend out of the new capital structure.

Recognition lag The lag in government response to an economic problem resulting from the delay in confirming a change in the state of the economy.

Recourse loan Loan in which the lender has a claim against the borrower for the shortfall (deficiency) between the amount of the outstanding mortgage balance and the proceeds received from the sale of the property.

Recovery rate (RR) The percentage of an outstanding debt claim recovered when an issuer defaults

Redemption fee A fee charged to discourage redemptions and to offset the transaction costs for remaining investors in the fund.

Refinancing rate A type of central bank policy rate.

Regionalism In between the two extremes of bilateralism and multilateralism. In regionalism, a group of countries cooperate with one another. Both bilateralism and regionalism can be conducted at the exclusion of other groups. For example, regional blocs may agree to provide trade benefits to one another and increase barriers for those outside of that group.

Registered bonds Bonds for which ownership is recorded by either name or serial number.

Regression analysis Allows us to test hypotheses about the relationship between two variables, by quantifying the strength of the relationship between the two variables, and to use one variable to make predictions about the other variable.

Regression coefficients The collective term for the intercept and slope coefficients in the regression model.

Regret The feeling that an opportunity has been missed; typically, an expression of *hindsight bias*.

Regret-aversion bias An emotional bias in which people tend to avoid making decisions that will result in action out of fear that the decision will turn out poorly.

Relative dispersion The amount of dispersion relative to a reference value or benchmark.

Reopening Issuing bonds by increasing the size of an existing bond issue with a price significantly different from par.

Replication A strategy in which a derivative's cash flow stream may be recreated using a combination of long or short positions in an underlying asset and borrowing or lending cash.

Repo rate The interest rate on a repurchase agreement.

Representativeness bias A belief perseverance bias in which people tend to classify new information based on past experiences and classifications.

Repurchase agreement (Repo) A form of collateralized loan involving the sale of a security with a simultaneous agreement by the seller to buy back the same security from the purchaser at an agreed-on price and future date. The party who sells the security at the inception of the repurchase agreement and buys it back at maturity is borrowing money from the other party, and the security sold and subsequently repurchased represents the collateral.

Repurchase date The date when the party who sold the security at the inception of a repurchase agreement buys back the security from the cash lending counterparty.

Repurchase price The price at which the party who sold the security at the inception of the repurchase agreement buys back the security from the cash lending counterparty.

Required margin Yield spread of a floating rate instrument such that the instrument is priced at par value on a rate reset date.

Required rate of return The rate of return required by investors given the risk of the bond investment, also known as the market discount rate or required yield.

Required yield The rate of return required by investors given the risk of the bond investment, also known as the market discount rate of required rate of return.

Required yield spread The difference in yield-to-maturity between a bond and that of a government benchmark bond with the same or similar time-to-maturity.

Resampling A statistical method that repeatedly draws samples from the original observed data sample for the statistical inference of population parameters.

Reserve currency A currency held by global central banks in significant quantities and widely used to conduct international trade and financial transactions.

Reserve requirement The requirement for banks to hold reserves in proportion to the size of deposits.

Residual The amount of deviation of an observed value of the dependent variable from its estimated value based on the fitted regression line.

Restricted domestic currency A currency with limited convertibility into other currencies due to illiquidity.

Return on assets (ROA)   A profitability ratio calculated as net income divided by average total assets; indicates a company's net profit generated per dollar invested in total assets.

Return on equity (ROE)   A profitability ratio calculated as net income divided by average shareholders' equity.

Return on invested capital (ROIC)   A measure of the profitability of a company relative to the amount of capital invested by the equityholders and debtholders.

Return on sales   An indicator of profitability, calculated as net income divided by revenue; indicates how much of each dollar of revenues is left after all costs and expenses. Also referred to as *net profit margin*.

Return-generating model   A model that can provide an estimate of the expected return of a security given certain parameters and estimates of the values of the independent variables in the model.

Revenue bonds   Bonds issued by non-sovereign governments related to a government sponsored project expected to generate future cash flow as a primary source of repayment.

Reverse repurchase agreement   A repurchase agreement viewed from the perspective of the cash lending counterparty.

Reverse stock split   A reduction in the number of shares outstanding with a corresponding increase in share price, but no change to the company's underlying fundamentals.

Revolving credit agreements   The most reliable form of short-term bank borrowing facilities; they are in effect for multiple years (e.g., three to five years) and can have optional medium-term loan features. Also known as *revolvers*.

Rho   The change in a given derivative instrument for a given small change in the risk-free interest rate, holding everything else constant. Rho measures the sensitivity of the option to the risk-free interest rate.

Ricardian equivalence   An economic theory that implies that it makes no difference whether a government finances a deficit by increasing taxes or issuing debt.

Risk   Exposure to uncertainty. The chance of a loss or adverse outcome as a result of an action, inaction, or external event.

Risk averse   The assumption that an investor will choose the least risky alternative.

Risk aversion   The degree of an investor's inability and unwillingness to take risk.

Risk budgeting   The establishment of objectives for individuals, groups, or divisions of an organization that takes into account the allocation of an acceptable level of risk.

Risk exposure   The state of being exposed or vulnerable to a risk. The extent to which an organization is sensitive to underlying risks.

Risk governance   The top-down process and guidance that directs risk management activities to align with and support the overall enterprise.

Risk management   The process of identifying the level of risk an organization wants, measuring the level of risk the organization currently has, taking actions that bring the actual level of risk to the desired level of risk, and monitoring the new actual level of risk so that it continues to be aligned with the desired level of risk.

Risk management framework   The infrastructure, process, and analytics needed to support effective risk management in an organization.

Risk premium   An extra return expected by investors for bearing some specified risk.

Risk shifting   Actions to change the distribution of risk outcomes.

Risk tolerance   the level of risk an investor is willing and able to bear.

Risk transfer   Actions to pass on a risk to another party, often, but not always, in the form of an insurance policy.

Risk-neutral pricing   A no-arbitrage derivative value established separately from investor views on risk that uses underlying asset volatility and the risk-free rate to calculate the present value of future cash flows.

Risk-neutral probability   The computed probability used in binomial option pricing by which the discounted weighted sum of expected values of the underlying equal the current option price. Specifically, this probability is computed using the risk-free rate and assumed up gross return and down gross return of the underlying.

Rollover risk   The likelihood that a property owner will lose an existing tenant and forgo income until a new one is found.

Safety-first rules   Rules for portfolio selection that focus on the risk that portfolio value or portfolio return will fall below some minimum acceptable level over some time horizon.

Sample correlation coefficient   A standardized measure of how two variables in a sample move together. It is the ratio of the sample covariance to the product of the two variables' standard deviations.

Sample covariance   A measure of how two variables in a sample move together.

Sample excess kurtosis   A sample measure of the degree of a distribution's kurtosis in excess of the normal distribution's kurtosis.

Sample mean   The sum of the sample observations divided by the sample size.

Sample skewness   A sample measure of the degree of asymmetry of a distribution.

Sample standard deviation   The positive square root of the sample variance.

Sample variance   The sum of squared deviations around the mean divided by the degrees of freedom.

Sample-size neglect   A type of representativeness bias in which financial market participants incorrectly assume that small sample sizes are representative of populations (or "real" data).

Sampling distribution   The distribution of all distinct possible values that a statistic can assume when computed from samples of the same size randomly drawn from the same population.

Sampling error   The difference between the observed value of a statistic and the estimate resulting from using subsets of the population.

Sampling plan   The set of rules used to select a sample.

Saving deposits   Bank deposits typically held for non-transactional purposes that often have a stated term.

Scatter plot   A two-dimensional graphical plot of paired observations of values for the independent and dependent variables in a simple linear regression.

Scenario analysis   A variation of the valuation process combining a base case with alternative outcomes, allowing the incorporation of more favorable or adverse scenarios in the valuation process.

Scraping   An automated, large-scale, algorithm-driven approach that retrieves otherwise unstructured data available on websites and creates data in a more structured format.

Seasoned offering   An offering in which an issuer sells additional units of a previously issued security.

Secondary bond markets   Fixed-income markets comprised of investors trading existing bonds amongst themselves.

Secondary market   The market where securities are traded among investors.

Secondary precedence rules   Rules that determine how to rank orders placed at the same time.

Secondary sale   Sale of a private company stake to another private equity firm or group of financial buyers.

Secondary-stage investments   The second stage of development of an infrastructure asset. Secondary-stage investments involve existing infrastructure facilities or fully operational assets that do not require further investment or development over the investment horizon. These assets generate immediate cash flow and returns expected over the investment period.

Sector indexes   Indexes that represent and track different economic sectors—such as consumer goods, energy, finance, health care, and technology—on either a national, regional, or global basis.

Secured   With collateral; secured debt is backed by the cash flows of the issuer and the collateral as a secondary source of repayment.

Secured loans   Loans collateralized by an asset of the borrower.

Security   Evidence of equity or debt interest or in an entity or a related right, such as a derivative. Often standardized to conform to security exchange requirements.

Security characteristic line   A plot of the excess return of a security on the excess return of the market.

Security market index   A portfolio of securities representing a given security market, market segment, or asset class.

Security market line   The graphical representation of the CAPM formula, showing the relationship between expected return and beta.

Security selection   The process of selecting individual securities; typically, security selection has the objective of generating superior risk-adjusted returns relative to a portfolio's benchmark.

Security tokens   Digitizes the ownership rights associated with publicly traded securities.

Segmenting   A process of identifying and grouping customers by decision-useful attributes.

Self-attribution bias   A bias in which people take too much credit for successes (*self-enhancing*) and assign responsibility to others for failures (*self-protecting*).

Self-control bias   A bias in which people fail to act in pursuit of their long-term, overarching goals because of a lack of self-discipline.

Self-investment limits   With respect to investment limitations applying to pension plans, restrictions on the percentage of assets that can be invested in securities issued by the pension plan sponsor.

Sell-side firm   A broker/dealer that sells securities and provides independent investment research and recommendations to their clients (i.e., buy-side firms).

Semi-strong-form efficient market   A market in which security prices reflect all publicly known and available information.

Semiannual bond basis yield   Also known as a semiannual bond equivalent yield, it is an annualized interest rate with a periodicity of two.

Semiannual bond equivalent yield   Also known as a semiannual bond basis yield, it is an annualized interest rate with a periodicity of two.

Senior debt   A debt obligation with higher priority of payment than junior debt obligations.

Senior unsecured debt   The highest-ranked debt in an issuer's capital structure which is a general obligation of the borrower.

Seniority   Priority of payment of various debt obligations.

Sensitivity analysis   A form of analysis used to determine the impact of a change in one or more key variables affecting investment returns or valuation.

Separately managed account (SMA)   An investment portfolio managed exclusively for the benefit of an individual or institution.

Separately managed accounts   Accounts that are managed in accordance with an investor's specific investment preferences and risk tolerance.

Service period   The time between the grant and vesting dates for an employee share-based award, usually measured in years.

Settlement   The closing date at which the counterparties of a derivative contract exchange payment for the underlying as required by the contract.

Settlement price   The price determined by an exchange's clearinghouse in the daily settlement of the mark-to-market process. The price reflects an average of the final futures trades of the day.

Share class   Types of equity securities that have different voting rights—for example, an issuer may issue Class A shares that carry one vote per share and Class B shares that carry ten votes per share.

Share repurchase   A transaction in which a company buys back its own shares. Unlike stock dividends and stock splits, share repurchases use corporate cash.

Shareholder activism   A range of actions by a corporation's shareholders that are intended to result in some change in the corporation, typically a change in the board of directors, management, or business strategy.

Shareholder derivative lawsuit   A legal action by a shareholder on behalf of a company, not the shareholder personally, against a third party. Often, the third party is a director or manager who the shareholder believes has harmed the company.

Shareholder engagement   Shareholder engagement reflects active ownership by investors in which the investor seeks to influence a corporation's decisions on ESG matters, either through dialogue with corporate officers or votes at a shareholder assembly (in the case of equity).

Shareholder theory of corporate governance   Espoused by Milton Friedman in his famous 1970 essay, the shareholder theory holds that the objective of a business is to increase profits and shareholder value.

Shareholders   Hold a direct equity position in a firm, and both individual persons and financial institutions can be shareholders. The term comes from the individual or investment firm literally having a share of the company. It is most commonly used when talking about the rights and responsibilities that come with being an "owner" of a company, such as stewardship, voting, and engagement. This differentiates it from a situation where an individual or an investment firm lends money or invests in a bond (in other words, they are not an equityholder of a company). Because bond investors do not have a share and are not owners of a company, they cannot vote. Nonetheless, expectations around engagement are increasing for those who invest in loans and bonds as well, making the difference between the two terms more subtle.

Shares   Units of ownership interest in a limited company.

Sharpe ratio The average return in excess of the risk-free rate divided by the standard deviation of return; a measure of the average excess return earned per unit of standard deviation of return. Also known as the *reward-to-variability ratio*.

Shelf registration A type of public offering that allows the issuer to file a single, all-encompassing offering circular that covers a series of bond issues.

Short A trading position in a **derivative contract** that gains value as the price of the **underlying** moves lower.

Short biased These strategies use quantitative, technical, and fundamental analysis to short overvalued equity securities with limited or no long-side exposures.

Short position A position in an asset or contract in which one has sold an asset one does not own, or in which a right under a contract can be exercised against oneself.

Short selling A transaction in which borrowed securities are sold with the intention to repurchase them at a lower price at a later date and return them to the lender.

Short-run average total cost The curve describing average total cost when some costs are considered fixed.

Shortfall risk The risk that portfolio value or portfolio return will fall below some minimum acceptable level over some time horizon.

Shutdown point The point at which average revenue is equal to the firm's average variable cost.

Side letter A side agreement created between the GP and specific LPs. These agreements exist *outside* the LPA. These agreements provide additional terms and conditions related to the investment agreement.

Signpost An indicator, market level, data piece, or event that signals a risk is becoming more or less likely. An analyst can think of signposts like a traffic light.

Simple linear regression (SLR) An approach for estimating the linear relationship between a dependent variable and a single independent variable by minimizing the sum of the squared deviations between the fitted line and the observed values.

Simple random sample A subset of a larger population created in such a way that each element of the population has an equal probability of being selected to the subset.

Simple random sampling The procedure of drawing a sample to satisfy the definition of a simple random sample.

Simple yield The sum of the coupon payments plus the straight-line amortized share of the gain or loss divided by the bond's flat price. Simple yields are used mostly to quote JGBs.

Simulation A technique for exploring how a target variable (e.g. portfolio returns) would perform in a hypothetical environment specified by the user, rather than a historical setting.

Simulation trial A complete pass through the steps of a simulation.

Single-price auction A debt securities auction in which all bidders pay the same price.

Sinking fund Provisions that reduce the credit risk of a bond issue by requiring the issuer to retire a portion of the bond's principal outstanding each year.

Situational influences External factors, such as environmental or cultural elements, that shape our behavior.

Skewed Not symmetrical.

Skewness A quantitative measure of skew (lack of symmetry); a synonym of skew. It is computed as the average cubed deviation from the mean standardized by dividing by the standard deviation cubed.

Slope coefficient The change in the estimated value of the dependent variable for a one-unit change in the value of the independent variable.

Small country A country that is a price taker in the world market for a product and cannot influence the world market price.

Smart beta Involves the use of transparent, rules-based strategies as a basis for investment decisions.

Smart contracts Computer programs that are designed to self-execute on the basis of pre-specified terms and conditions agreed to by parties to a contract.

Social infrastructure investments A category of infrastructure investments that are directed toward human activities and include such assets as educational, health care, social housing, and correctional facilities, with the focus on providing, operating, and maintaining the asset infrastructure.

Soft commodities Standardized agricultural products, such as cattle and corn, with markets often involving the physical delivery of the underlying upon settlement.

Soft hurdle rate Hurdle rate where the fee is calculated on the entire return when the hurdle is exceeded. With a soft hurdle, GPs are able to catch up performance fees once the hurdle threshold is exceeded.

Soft power A means of influencing another country's decisions without force or coercion. Soft power can be built over time through actions, such as cultural programs, advertisement, travel grants, and university exchange.

Soft-bullet covered bonds Delay the bond default and payment acceleration of bond cash flows until a new final maturity date, which is usually up to a year after the original maturity date.

Solvency Refers to the condition in which firm value exceeds the face value of debt used to finance the firm's assets.

Solvency ratios Ratios that measure a company's ability to meet its long-term obligations.

Solvency risk The risk that an organization does not survive or succeed because it runs out of cash, even though it might otherwise be solvent.

Sophisticated investors Individuals or entities that are permitted in a jurisdiction to trade unregistered or, generally, less regulated securities, including shares of privately held companies; also called *accredited investors*.

Sovereign immunity A principle limiting the legal recourse of bondholders holding national government debt from forcing the issuer to declare bankruptcy or liquidate assets to settle debt claims.

Spearman rank correlation coefficient A measure of correlation applied to ranked data.

Special dividend A dividend paid by a company that does not pay dividends on a regular schedule, or a dividend that supplements regular cash dividends with an extra payment.

Special purpose acquisition company A "blank check" company that exists solely for the purpose of acquiring an unspecified private company within a predetermined period or return capital to investors.

Special purpose entity (SPE) Also referred to as a special purpose vehicle or SPV, this legal entity is created for a specific economic purpose. In the case of a project SPV, the entity's sole purpose is to facilitate the construction, operation, and financing of an infrastructure asset over its contractual life.

Special purpose vehicle See *special purpose entity*.

Special situations An area of private capital investment which targets return by investing in stressed, distressed, or event-driven opportunities.

Split ratings Complex risks viewed very differently by rating agencies

Sponsored A type of depository receipt in which the foreign company whose shares are held by the depository has a direct involvement in the issuance of the receipts.

Spot curve Yields-to-maturity on a series of default-risk-free zero-coupon bonds.

Spot markets Markets in which specific assets are exchanged at current prices. Spot markets are often referred to as **cash markets**.

Spot prices The current prices prevailing in **spot markets**.

Spot rates Yields-to-maturity on default-risk-free zero-coupon bonds.

Spread The difference in yield-to-maturity between a bond and that of a another bond.

Spread risk Bond price risk arising from changes in the yield spread on credit-risky bonds; reflects changes in the market's assessment and/or pricing of credit migration (or downgrade) risk and market liquidity risk.

Spurious correlation Refers to: 1) correlation between two variables that reflects chance relationships in a particular dataset; 2) correlation induced by a calculation that mixes each of two variables with a third variable; and 3) correlation between two variables arising not from a direct relation between them but from their relation to a third variable.

Stablecoin A cryptocurrency that aims to maintain a stable value relative to a specified asset or to a pool or basket of assets.

Stackelberg model A prominent model of strategic decision making in which firms are assumed to make their decisions sequentially.

Staggered board A structure of board elections in which only part of the board is elected simultaneously—for example, only one-third of the board may be up for election each year, so the board can be replaced over three years, not in one year if all seats were elected annually. This structure fosters greater continuity of board members but is an obstacle for shareholders seeking to effect change.

Stakeholder theory of corporate governance An expansion of the shareholder theory of corporate governance under which the objective of a business is to maximize value for, and balance the interests of, a broad group of stakeholders, including shareholders, employees, society, and the non-human environment.

Stakeholders Any party with an interest, financial or non-financial, in an entity or its actions.

Standard deviation The positive square root of the variance; a measure of dispersion in the same units as the original data.

Standard error of the estimate A measure of the distance between the observed values of the dependent variable and those predicted from the estimated regression. The smaller this value, the better the fit of the model. Also known as the standard error of the regression and the root mean square error.

Standard error of the forecast Used to provide an interval estimate around the estimated regression line. It is necessary because the regression line does not describe the relationship between the dependent and independent variables perfectly.

Standard error of the slope coefficient Calculated for simple linear regression by dividing the standard error of the estimate by the square root of the variation of the independent variable.

Standardization The process of creating protocols for the production, sale, transport, or use of a product or service. Standardization occurs when relevant parties agree to follow these protocols together. It helps support expanded economic and financial activities, such as trade and capital flows that support higher economic growth and standards of living, across borders.

Standards of conduct Behaviors required by a group; established benchmarks that clarify or enhance a group's code of ethics.

Standing limit orders A limit order at a price below market and which therefore is waiting to trade.

State actors Typically national governments, political organizations, or country leaders that exert authority over a country's national security and resources. The South African President, Sultan of Brunei, Malaysia's Parliament, and the British Prime Minister are all examples of state actors.

Statement of cash flows A financial statement that details the movement of cash over a period. The statement is classified into operating, investing, and financing activities.

Static trade-off theory of capital structure A theory pertaining to a company's optimal capital structure; the optimal level of debt is found at the point where additional debt would cause the costs of financial distress to increase by a greater amount than the benefit of the additional tax shield.

Statistically significant A result indicating that the null hypothesis can be rejected; with reference to an estimated regression coefficient, frequently understood to mean a result indicating that the corresponding population regression coefficient is different from zero.

Status quo bias An emotional bias in which people do nothing (i.e., maintain the status quo) instead of making a change.

Statutory voting A common method of voting where each share represents one vote.

Step-up bonds Bonds for which the coupon, be it fixed or floating, increases by specified margins at specified dates.

Stock dividend A type of dividend in which a company distributes additional shares of its common stock to shareholders instead of cash.

Stock exchange An exchange in which equity securities are traded. See *exchanges*.

Stock split An increase in the number of shares outstanding with a consequent decrease in share price, but no change to the company's underlying fundamentals.

Stockholder overhang The downward pressure on the share price of stock as large blocks of shares are being sold on the open market.

Stop order An order in which a trader has specified a stop price condition. Also called *stop-loss order*.

Stop-loss order See *stop order*.

Stranded assets A resource that is no longer economically valuable owing to changes in demand, regulations, or availability of substitutes—for example, a newly discovered oil well that will not be brought into production.

Strategic asset allocation   A long-term strategy that establishes target allocations for various asset classes and aims to optimize the balance between risk and reward by diversifying investments.

Stratified random sampling   A procedure that first divides a population into subpopulations (strata) based on classification criteria and then randomly draws samples from each stratum in sizes proportional to that of each stratum in the population.

Street convention   For yield measures on fixed-income instruments that assume payments are made on scheduled dates and ignore weekends and holidays.

Stress testing   A specific type of scenario analysis that estimates losses in rare and extremely unfavorable combinations of events or scenarios.

Strong-form efficient market   A market in which security prices reflect all public and private information.

Structural budget deficit   Also known as the cyclically adjusted budget deficit. The deficit that would exist if the economy was at full employment (or full potential output).

Structural subordination   Arises in a holding company structure when the debt of operating subsidiaries is serviced by the cash flow and assets of the subsidiaries before funds can be passed to the holding company to service debt at the parent level.

Structured notes   A broad category of securities that incorporate the features of debt instruments and one or more embedded derivatives designed to achieve a particular issuer or investor objective.

Subordinated debt   A class of unsecured debt that ranks below a firm's senior unsecured obligations.

Subordination   A form of internal credit enhancement that relies on creating more than one bond tranche and ordering the claim priorities for ownership or interest in an asset between the tranches. The ordering of the claim priorities is called a senior/subordinated structure, where the tranches of highest seniority are called senior, followed by subordinated or junior tranches. Also called **credit tranching**.

Subprime loans   Lending to borrowers with lower credit quality, high DTI, and/or are loans with higher LTV, and include loans that are secured by second liens otherwise subordinated to other loans.

Sum of squares error (SSE)   A measure of the total deviation between observed and estimated values of the dependent variable. It is calculated by subtracting each estimated value $\hat{Y}_i$ from its corresponding observed value Y_i, squaring each of these differences, and then summing all of these squared differences.

Sum of squares regression (SSR)   A measure of the explained variation in the dependent variable, calculated as the sum of the squared differences between the predicted value of the dependent variable, $\hat{Y}_i$, based on the estimated regression line, and the mean of the dependent variable, $\bar{Y}$.

Sum of squares total (SST)   A measure of the total variation in the dependent variable in a simple linear regression. It is calculated by subtracting the mean of the observed values $\bar{Y}$ from each of the observed values Y_i, squaring each of these differences, and then summing all of these squared differences.

Sunk costs   A cost that has already been incurred.

Supervised learning   A type of machine learning in which the system attempts to learn to model relationships based on labeled training data.

Supervisory board   In some jurisdictions, a corporation's board of directors is formally composed of a supervisory board and a management board. The supervisory board appoints and oversees the management board and often includes representatives of employees and other non-shareholder stakeholders.

Supply chain   The sequence of processes involved in the creation and delivery of a physical product to the end customer, both within and external to a firm, regardless of whether those steps are performed by a single firm.

Supply shock   A typically unexpected disturbance to supply.

Survivorship bias   Relates to the inclusion of only current investment funds in a database. As such, the returns of funds that are no longer available in the marketplace (have been liquidated) are excluded from the database. Also see *backfill bias*.

Swap   A firm commitment involving a periodic exchange of cash flows.

Swap contract   An agreement between two parties to exchange a series of future cash flows.

Swap execution facility (SEF)   A swap trading platform accessed by multiple **dealers**.

Swap rate   The fixed rate to be paid by the fixed-rate payer specified in a swap contract.

Syndicate   A group of lenders, typically made up of banks.

Synthetic protective put   The combination of a synthetic long underlying position (i.e., a long forward and risk-free borrowing) and a purchased put on the underlying.

Systematic risk   The risk of severe damage to the real economy caused by the impairment of (parts of) the financial system.

Systematic sampling   A procedure of selecting every kth member until reaching a sample of the desired size. The sample that results from this procedure should be approximately random.

Systemic risk   Refers to risks supervisory authorities believe are likely to have broad impact across the financial market infrastructure and affect a wide swath of market participants.

Tactical asset allocation   A proactive strategy that adjusts asset class allocations within a portfolio based on short-term market trends, economic conditions, or valuation changes to capitalize on temporary market inefficiencies or opportunities to improve returns or manage risk more effectively.

Target capital structure   Management's desired proportions of debt and equity financing, usually stated on a book value basis or indirectly using a financial leverage metric, such as net or gross debt to EBITDA or credit rating.

Target independent   A bank's ability to determine the definition of inflation that they target, the rate of inflation that they target, and the horizon over which the target is to be achieved.

Target semideviation   A measure of downside risk, calculated as the square root of the average of the squared deviations of observations below the target (also called target downside deviation).

Tariffs   Taxes that a government levies on imported goods.

Tax base   The amount at which an asset or liability is valued for tax purposes.

Tax expense   An aggregate of an entity's income tax payable (or recoverable in the case of a tax benefit) and any changes in deferred tax assets and liabilities. It is essentially the income tax payable or recoverable if these had been determined based on accounting profit rather than taxable income.

Taxable income   The portion of an entity's income that is subject to income taxes under the tax laws of its jurisdiction.

Taxable temporary differences   Temporary differences that result in a taxable amount in a future period when determining the taxable profit as the balance sheet item is recovered or settled.

Technical analysis   A form of security analysis that uses price and volume data, often displayed graphically, in decision making.

Tender offer   A solicitation by a current or prospective shareholder to other shareholders to acquire a substantial percentage, including 100%, of shares at a specified price. This action is usually undertaken by a potential acquirer whose bid was rejected by the issuer's board of directors, prompting the potential acquirer to appeal directly to shareholders.

Tenor   The remaining time to maturity for a bond or derivative contract. Also called term to maturity.

Term repos   Repos with a maturity longer than one day.

Term structure of interest rates   Also known as the maturity structure of interest rates, refers to the difference in interest rates or benchmark yields by time-to-maturity.

Terminal stock value   The expected value of a share at the end of the investment horizon—in effect, the expected selling price. Also called *terminal value*.

Terminal value   The expected value of a share at the end of the investment horizon—in effect, the expected selling price.

Test of the mean of the differences   A statistical test for differences based on paired observations drawn from samples that are dependent on each other.

Text analytics   Involves the use of computer programs to analyze and derive meaning typically from large, unstructured text- or voice-based datasets, such as company filings, written reports, quarterly earnings calls, social media, email, internet postings, and surveys.

Thematic risks   Known risks that evolve and expand over a period of time. Climate change, pattern migration, the rise of populist forces, and the ongoing threat of terrorism fall into this category.

Thin-tailed   Describes a distribution that has relatively less weight in the tails than the normal distribution (also called platykurtic).

Tiered pricing   A pricing approach that charges different prices to different buyers, commonly based on volume purchased.

Timberland investment management organizations   Entities that support institutional investors by managing their investments in timberland by analyzing and acquiring suitable timberland holdings.

Time tranching   Structure of a securitization that allows for the redistribution of "prepayment risk" among bond classes by creating bond classes of different expected maturities.

Time value   The difference between an option's premium and its intrinsic value.

Time value decay   The process by which the time value of an option declines toward zero as the option's expiration date is approached.

Time-weighted rate of return   The compound rate of growth of one unit of currency invested in a portfolio during a stated measurement period; a measure of investment performance that is not sensitive to the timing and amount of withdrawals or additions to the portfolio.

Tokenization   The process of representing ownership rights to physical assets on a blockchain or distributed ledger.

Top-down analysis   An investment selection approach that begins with consideration of macroeconomic conditions and then evaluates markets and industries based upon such conditions.

Total probability rule for expected value   A rule explaining the expected value of a random variable in terms of expected values of the random variable conditional on mutually exclusive and exhaustive scenarios.

Total return   Measures the price appreciation, or percentage change in price of the securities in an index or portfolio, plus any income received over the period.

Total return index   An index that reflects the price appreciation or percentage change in price of the constituent securities plus any income received since inception.

Total working capital   The difference between current assets and current liabilities.

Tracking error   The standard deviation of the differences between a portfolio's returns and its benchmark's returns; a synonym of active risk. Also called *tracking risk*.

Tracking risk   The standard deviation of the differences between a portfolio's returns and its benchmark's returns. Also called *tracking error* and *active risk*.

Trade creation   When regional integration results in the replacement of higher cost domestic production by lower cost imports from other members.

Trade diversion   When regional integration results in lower-cost imports from non-member countries being replaced with higher-cost imports from members.

Trade sale   A portion or division of a private company sold via either direct sale or auction to a strategic buyer interested in increasing the scale and scope of an existing business.

Trade settlement date   The date when the buyer and seller transfer consideration and securities.

Traditional investment markets   Markets for traditional investments, which include all publicly traded debts and equities and shares in pooled investment vehicles that hold publicly traded debts and/or equities.

Tranches   A grouping of securities within an issue with characteristics that vary from other tranches, such as different credit quality and seniority.

Transfer payments   Welfare payments made through the social security system that exist to provide a basic minimum level of income for low-income households.

Transition risks   Economic and financial losses from the transition to a lower-carbon economy in response to climate change—for example, the abandonment of an oil well that is no longer economical.

Treasury Inflation-Protected Securities (TIPS)   US Treasury bonds with a principal that is adjusted for changes in the Consumer Price Index. TIPS are issued in 5-, 10-, and 30-year maturities.

Treynor ratio   A measure of risk-adjusted performance that relates a portfolio's returns in excess of the risk-free rate to a portfolio's beta.

Trimmed mean   A mean computed after excluding a stated small percentage of the lowest and highest observations.

Triparty repo   A repurchase agreement in which the transacting parties agree to use a third-party agent that provides access to a larger collateral pool and multiple counterparties, as well as valuation and safekeeping of assets.

True yield   Measures on fixed-income instruments use actual payment dates, accounting for weekends and holidays. The true yield on an instrument is always lower than the street convention yield.

Turn-of-the-year effect Calendar anomaly that stock market returns in January are significantly higher compared to the rest of the months of the year, with most of the abnormal returns reported during the first five trading days in January.

Two-fund separation theorem The theory that all investors regardless of taste, risk preferences, and initial wealth will hold a combination of two portfolios or funds: a risk-free asset and an optimal portfolio of risky assets.

Two-way table A table of the frequency distribution of observations classified on the basis of two discrete variables. Also known as *Contingency table*.

Two-week repo rate The interest rate on a two-week repurchase agreement; may be used as a policy rate by a central bank.

Type I error The error of rejecting a true null hypothesis; a false positive.

Type II error The error of not rejecting a false null hypothesis; false negative.

Uncommitted lines of credit Sources of bank credit that a bank can refuse to honor. Uncommitted credit lines are made up to a certain principal amount for a pre-determined maximum maturity, charging a market reference rate plus an issuer-specific spread on only the principal outstanding for the period of use.

Underfitted When a machine learning model treats true parameters as if they are noise and is unable to recognize relationships in the training data, making the model more likely to fail to fully discover patterns that underlie the data.

Underlying The asset referred to in a **derivative contract**.

Underwritten offering A type of securities issue mechanism in which the investment bank guarantees the sale of the securities at an offering price that is negotiated with the issuer. Also known as *firm commitment offering*.

Unearned revenue A liability account for money that has been collected for goods or services that have not yet been delivered; payment received in advance of providing a good or service. Also called *deferred revenue* or *deferred income*.

Unimodal A distribution with a single value that is most frequently occurring.

Unit economics The expression of revenues and costs on a per-unit basis.

Unitranche debt A hybrid or blended loan structure combining different tranches of secured and unsecured debt into a single loan with a single, blended interest rate.

Unsecured Without collateral; unsecured debt is backed only by cash flows of the issuer.

Unsponsored A type of depository receipt in which the foreign company whose shares are held by the depository has no involvement in the issuance of the receipts.

Unsupervised learning A type of machine learning in which the system tries to learn the structure of unlabeled data.

Utility tokens Tokens that provide services within a network, such as paying for services and network fees.

Validity instructions Instructions which indicate when the order may be filled.

Value added resellers Businesses that distribute a product and also handle more complex aspects of product installation, customization, service, or support.

Value at risk A money measure of the minimum value of losses expected during a specified time period at a given level of probability.

Value chain The systems and processes in a firm that create value for its customers.

Value proposition The product or service attributes valued by a firm's target customer that lead those customers to prefer that firm's offering.

Value-add real estate strategies Strategies that involve larger-scale redevelopment and repositioning of existing assets and that may allow the investor to earn a higher return compared with core-plus real estate strategies.

Value-based pricing Pricing set primarily by reference to the value of the product or service to customers.

VaR See *value at risk*.

Variance The expected value (the probability-weighted average) of squared deviations from a random variable's expected value.

Variance of a random variable The expected value (the probability-weighted average) of squared deviations from a random variable's expected value.

Variation margin The difference between current margin required and the current collateral price in a repurchase agreement.

Vega The change in a given derivative instrument for a given small change in volatility, holding everything else constant. A sensitivity measure for options that reflects the effect of volatility.

Velocity The pace at which geopolitical risk impacts an investor portfolio.

Venture capital Private equity investment in a startup or early-stage company involving high risk and a high rate of failure.

Venture capital fund A hedge fund that seeks to buy, optimize, and ultimately sell portfolio companies to generate profits. See *private equity fund*.

Venture debt Private debt funding that provides venture capital backing to start-up or early-stage companies that may be generating little or negative cash flow.

Vest To become unconditionally entitled to.

Vesting date The day that an employee becomes unconditionally entitled to compensation.

Vintage year The year in which a private capital fund makes its first investment.

Volatility The standard deviation of the continuously compounded returns on the underlying asset.

Vote by proxy A mechanism that allows a designated party—such as another shareholder, a shareholder representative, or management—to vote on the shareholder's behalf.

Voting rights The power of shareholders to cast votes in corporate elections for directors and other matters submitted to a shareholder vote.

Warrant An attached option that gives its holder the right to buy the underlying stock of the issuing company at a fixed exercise price until the expiration date.

Waterfall structures These represent the distribution order for cash flows and risk to different tranches in a financing structure.

Weak-form efficient market hypothesis The belief that security prices fully reflect all past market data, which refers to all historical price and volume trading information.

Weighted average cost of capital (WACC) The expected cost of debt and equity weighted by the proportion of each used in a company's capital structure.

Weighted average coupon rate (WAC) Rate calculated for a mortgage pass-through security by weighting the mortgage rate of each mortgage in the pool by the percentage of the outstanding mortgage balance relative to the outstanding amount of all the mortgages in the pool.

Weighted average maturity (WAM)   Calculated for a mortgage pass-through security by weighting the remaining number of months to maturity of each mortgage in the pool by the outstanding mortgage balance relative to the outstanding amount of all the mortgages in the pool.

Winsorized mean   A mean computed after assigning a stated percentage of the lowest values equal to one specified low value and a stated percentage of the highest values equal to one specified high value.

Write-off/liquidation   Refers to a transaction that has not gone well, and the investment is likely to lose value. The private equity firm revises the value of its investment downward or liquidates the portfolio company.

Yield curve   A graphical depiction of yields-to-maturity of bonds from the same issuer across maturities.

Yield spread   The difference in yield-to-maturity between a bond and that of a another bond.

Yield-to-call   An internal rate of return on a fixed-income instrument's cash flows assuming cash flows are received on scheduled dates and the bond is called at a certain call price and date.

Yield-to-maturity   The internal rate of return that an investor earns on a bond assuming no default, the bond is held to maturity, and periodic cash flows are reinvested at the yield-to-maturity. Also called yield-to-redemption or redemption yield.

Yield-to-worst   The lowest among a fixed-income instrument's yields-to-call and yield-to-maturity. A commonly cited yield measure for fixed-rate callable bonds.

Z-spread   or zero-volatility spread is a constant yield spread for a bond over a government or swap curve.

Zero-coupon bond   A bond that does not pay a coupon but is priced at a discount and pays its full face value at maturity.

Zero-coupon bonds   Bonds that do not pay interest during their life. They are issued at a discount to par value and redeemed at par. Also called pure discount bond.